I0191789

MARCELLO CERVINI AND ECCLESIASTICAL GOVERNMENT IN TRIDENTINE ITALY

Oil painting of Cervini by an unidentified sixteenth-century Tuscan master; photograph courtesy of Istituto Centrale per il Catalogo e la Documentazione, Rome, Italy: series E, #55616.

Marcello Cervini

AND ECCLESIASTICAL GOVERNMENT IN

Tridentine Italy

WILLIAM V. HUDON

NORTHERN ILLINOIS UNIVERSITY PRESS
DeKalb 1992

Published by the Northern Illinois University Press, DeKalb, Illinois 60115
Manufactured in the United States using acid-free paper
Design by Julia Fauci

Library of Congress Cataloging-in-Publication Data
Hudon, William V., 1956–
Marcello Cervini and ecclesiastical government in Tridentine Italy
/ William V. Hudon.
p. cm.
Revision of author's thesis—University of Chicago.
Includes bibliographical reference and index.
ISBN 0-87580-169-2 (alk. paper)
1. Marcellus II, Pope, 1501–1555. 2. Popes—Biography.
I. Title.
BX1320.H83 1992
282'.092—dc20
[B] 92-1301
CIP

CONTENTS

PREFACE

MARCELLO CERVINI was more than just another Roman curialist in the time of the Counter Reformation. His career spanned a period that many historians consider crucial in the shift of Italian and curialist attitudes toward the Protestant Reformation and its control, but his life spanned more than that one cultural development. He grew up under the influence of the Italian Renaissance and absorbed its humanist educational ideals and methods. He experienced a working environment in the Roman curia that maintained most of the policies associated with the corrupt Renaissance papacy, while its leaders and employees simultaneously struggled with calls for its reform. He participated both in the corrupt legacy of the institution and in the steps, which were halting at best, to effect that reform. He came to lead the curia and the church at large as Pope Marcellus II, in 1555, and gave evidence of an intention and a commitment to undertake real reform, but in a manner quite different from his immediate predecessors and successors in the Roman see.

He stands before us in the late twentieth century, therefore, as a perfect case study, to be asked some significant historical questions. What was, exactly, the practical connection between the Renaissance and Reformation (cultural events that are usually considered separate)? To what extent did individual curial administrators actually accept the ideology that was so supportive of a monarchical government for the church, at the beginning of the development of European absolutism? Was a rejection of Renaissance culture part of that ideology? How could that be, if ecclesiastical leaders were truly individuals who stood as reflections of the fifteenth- and sixteenth-century culture in which they were raised? What position did the Roman Inquisition and individual inquisitors hold in this process? When, exactly, did the incessant calls for religious reform, on the local level, really produce effective results? And who or what was responsible for the results? Was it the ideologists of reform, or individual bishops and administrators? Was it the decrees of the Council of Trent, or those who later implemented the decrees? Is the distinction between *spirituali* and *intransigenti,* which is frequently employed to explain the character of prelates and other ecclesiastical persons in this era, still useful in historical analysis? Full answers to these questions are beyond the scope of this book, but a fresh consideration of the career of Cervini may encourage readers to rethink the standard responses.

Cervini wrote about his life and his work as an ecclesiastical administrator, but not in any systematic manner, not even in a diary. Only his correspondence—the letters he wrote and those he received and saved—exists as testimony of his astounding career and his reaction to the fascinating times in which he lived. The vast majority of that correspondence is contained in the collection known as the *Carte cerviniane*, held in the Florentine State Archive. Seventy volumes cover nearly the entirety of Cervini's life, from a boyhood letter he wrote at the age of ten, reporting to his father on the progress of his studies, to letters he wrote in 1555 just prior to his papal election, addressed to the "Reverendissimi signori" of the Roman Inquisition. The collection includes his personal correspondence, some of it in the form of rough, corrected drafts of letters he sent. It also includes papal documents, booklets of theological opinions copied for him by employees from sources in Rome, biographical sketches of Cervini, and documents generated by relatives, like his nephew Roberto Bellarmino. The collection was sold by the Cervini family in 1771 to the Archduke Leopold of Tuscany, and it was transferred to the archive in 1787. The *Carte cerviniane* serve as the fundamental source for this study, when supplemented by a variety of others. In transcriptions from the collection, I have expanded all abbreviations and have added punctuation and capitalizations where necessary to conform to modern usage. All translations, unless otherwise noted, are my own.

Portions of this work appeared earlier in the form of two articles. Most of Chapter 4 was published in 1988, in the Italian journal *Cristianesimo nella storia*. The article was entitled "Papal, Episcopal and Secular Authority in the Work of Marcello Cervini." Part of Chapter 5 appeared in the *Sixteenth Century Journal* in 1989, under the title "Two Instructions to Preachers from the Tridentine Reformation."

In researching and writing this book I have incurred many debts. I would like to thank the staffs of the Archivio di Stato in Florence, the Archivio Segreto Vaticano and the Biblioteca Apostolica Vaticana in the Vatican, the Biblioteca Palatina in Parma, and the Archivio Vescovile in Reggio Emilia, for their assistance and generosity. I am likewise grateful to the staffs of interlibrary loan departments at the University of Chicago, Fordham University, and Bloomsburg University. Support for the research was provided, in 1991, by the Faculty Professional Development program at Bloomsburg University and the National Endowment for the Humanities.

My largest debts, however, are personal. Giuseppe Alberigo, Giuseppe Billanovich, Elisabeth Gleason, Anthony Grafton, John M. Headley, Massimo Marcocchi, Thomas Mayer, Louis B. Pascoe, and Adriano Prosperi were all kind enough to read portions of this work and to offer helpful criticisms and suggestions. James R. Sperry has supported me in every way possible for a department chair, since my arrival at Bloomsburg in 1989—even to the point of pleading my cause before deans and provosts. Aaron Polonsky provided both professional assistance at the Andruss Library, Bloomsburg University, and personal encouragement through his friendship and humor. Even greater help was provided by Constantin Fasolt, Julius Kirshner, and Bernard McGinn, who guided me through an earlier version of the work—my doctoral dissertation at the University of Chicago. Four scholars in particular went far out of their way to assist me. John W. O'Malley and Frederick J. McGinness both had the patience and kindness to read, correct, and comment on two earlier versions, and they always encouraged me to persevere. Massimo Firpo and Gigliola Fragnito, despite their disagreement with some of the theses presented here, both intervened at crucial points and saved me from innumerable errors. My greatest intellectual debt, however, is to the memory of Eric W. Cochrane. His seminars were inspirational, and they shaped the way I look at the history of early-modern Italy. He was the first to agree that a study of Cervini's career could be important and might contribute to a necessary reconsideration of the history of the church in that period. My doctoral research was conducted under his guidance, but at his death I had barely put fingers to keyboard. My work, I hope, is at least a pale reminder of his contributions and of the theses he argued with such passion and erudition.

I also wish to thank my family. My parents encouraged me to pursue the graduate studies at Chicago that led to this research, and they assisted me with great devotion and at considerable expense. My mother- and father-in-law did the same. But to my wife, Wendy, I owe even more. It was her work in Milan in 1985 that supported my initial research on Cervini, and her constant patient encouragement that enabled me to see this project through to completion. She gave up everything, including her career plans, to follow me in the peregrinations common to modern academics, which in my case required that we endure life in the Bronx for three years. It is to her that I dedicate this book, with thanks, and with all my love.

MARCELLO CERVINI AND ECCLESIASTICAL GOVERNMENT IN TRIDENTINE ITALY

CHAPTER ONE

Cervini in History

From a list of the most prominent figures in the Catholic reform movement at the time of the Council of Trent (1545–1563), it is difficult to identify one individual more significant than Marcello Cervini.[1] He was born in Montefano, near Ancona, on May 6, 1501, and pursued an ecclesiastical career that spanned more than twenty-one years. Ordained a priest in 1535, he served first as a tutor and then as a secretary to Cardinal Alessandro Farnese, the grandson of Pope Paul III (1534–1549), whom he accompanied on legations to the courts of the emperor and of the king of France. While on legation, he became cardinal in 1539, and Paul later bestowed upon him the titular church of Santa Croce. He served as administrator in a number of dioceses, first in that of Nicastro (1539–1540), then in Reggio Emilia (1540–1544), and finally in Gubbio (1544–1555). He helped to oversee the Roman Office of the Inquisition as one of those appointed to the body in the early years of its reinstitution after 1542, and he coordinated activities on behalf of the papacy as the second legate to the Council of Trent during the sessions from 1545 to 1549. The first cardinal to supervise the Vatican library, he was appointed its custodian in 1548, and he himself endowed it with important contributions. He became a confidant of Pope Paul III and a principal supporter of the nascent Society of Jesus: the founder of the society, Ignatius of Loyola, considered him a friend and held him in high esteem. Cervini actively followed and encouraged the progress of Jesuit missionary and educational endeavors.

In 1550 he became cardinal protector of the Servites and later held the same position for both the Augustinian order and the new Jesuit Collegio Germanico in Rome. He corresponded and worked with many of the other important religious figures of the time: Girolamo

Seripando, Reginald Pole, Gian Pietro Carafa, Giovanni Morone, and Gasparo Contarini. He dominated the important, but ultimately unsuccessful, reform commission set up by Pope Julius III in 1550. He was a classical scholar, a mathematician, a translator, and a manuscript collector. On April 9, 1555, after a short conclave, his colleagues in the College of Cardinals elected him pope, Marcellus II, but he died three weeks after the election.[2] Cervini was a multi-faceted, complex man, and a study of his life provides important insights into the equally complex and multi-faceted world of the Tridentine reform, as well as into the way he and that reform have been assessed by historians over the years.

Cervini's high reputation during his life endured after his death in a tradition that rapidly became hagiographical.[3] Antonio Cicarelli and Onofrio Panvinio, the sixteenth-century editor and continuator of Platina's semi-official *History of the Popes,* praised Cervini as a reform-minded man with a "grave and industrious nature." Panvinio particularly commended his desire to see more diligent pastors among the clergy and to purge the papal curia of "obscene and infamous persons."[4] He buttressed his characterization by relating the story of an astrological prediction of Cervini's papacy[5] and by describing the great hopes and expectations that surrounded his election in 1555.[6] Panvinio also related at length the general consternation caused by the pope's untimely demise: Cervini was not given, Panvinio maintained, but only "shown" to the church and the world.

Similarly, Ignatius of Loyola thought Cervini a holy and spiritually minded man who might have initiated a true reform of the church. Ignatius apparently quashed unedifying conversations among the members of his order with the suggestion that they speak instead "about good Pope Marcellus." He held such appreciation of Cervini at least in part because of his fear of another member of the Roman curia, Gian Pietro Carafa. When Ignatius heard that Carafa had succeeded Cervini as Pope Paul IV in 1555, every bone in his body shook, or so said his secretary, Luis da Camera.[7]

Other sixteenth- and seventeenth-century sources, with few exceptions, picked up and passed on the hagiographic thread. Julius Pogianus, who wrote the funeral oration for Marcellus II, praised his industrious nature, explained that he was admired for his learning no less than for his modesty, and cited cardinals like Roberto de'Nobili, Girolamo Seripando, and Reginald Pole, to reinforce his conclusion.[8] Cesare Baronio (1518–1607) similarly praised Cervini's modesty and similarly cited authorities. Seripando (d. 1563), the general of the Augustinians, Baronio related, considered Cervini not a man, but an angel come to earth.[9] Paolo Sarpi (1562–1623) registered the one less-than-glowing assessment and laid the blame for the division of Christendom on the Council of Trent and on Cervini because of his position as legate. He also suggested that Cervini became infatuated with the astrological prediction of his greatness in the church.[10] Sarpi's entire work, including these characterizations, was in turn attacked by Sforza Pallavicino, the Jesuit cardinal who responded to Sarpi with what became the official history of the council. Another seventeenth-century historian, Spinello Benci, praised Cervini in much the same terms as his sixteenth-century colleagues and gave part of the credit to Cervini's mother, Cassandra Benci (he was, after all, Cervini's maternal cousin).[11]

Eighteenth-century historians continued this laudatory assessment, and among them were Ludovico Antonio Muratori, Mauro Sartio, and Giuseppe Piatti. They stressed Cervini's devotion and vigilance concerning the episcopal sees he served as administrator, even to the point of apologizing for his decision to refuse episcopal ordination. Piatti suggested that he did so not because of any lack of commitment, but because of his inability to reside there permanently.[12]

Nineteenth-century authors sustained the tradition, for the most part. Giovan Battista Brilli did so in an oration celebrating the famous native sons of Montepulciano. Gaetano Moroni related an uncorroborated story of two prophetic signs of the impending pontificate, which appeared while Cervini was on his way to Rome for the conclave. However, nineteenth-century analysts did shift the focus of the tradition and created the first modern biographical sketches of Cervini, praising his humanist outlook and intellectual interests. The two greatest historians of the papacy from this age, Leopold von Ranke and Ludwig von Pastor, were part of the group that persisted in the laudatory assessment of Cervini. Ranke indicated that although little could be said about any real results of his administration, Cervini's election did demonstrate the reform spirit that was beginning to prevail. Pastor presented Cervini as a man who, by his "mixture of seriousness and gaiety . . . won the hearts of all" and who "carefully avoided all that was evil." Although some in the curia feared his reform measures because of his personal severity, said Pastor, "the whole world was agreed on his election, and the greatest happiness in April, 1555 belonged to the Catholic reformers."[13]

A large number of twentieth-century historians took over this view. Pio Paschini and Vincenzo Monachino even attributed Cervini's death to his zeal for reform. Giovanni Saccani and Umberto Pesci provided more information about Cervini's work, but they too reinforced the standard view, lauding his administration and lamenting his demise.[14]

Xavier-Marie Le Bachelet emphasized Cervini's friendship with the first Jesuits.[15] Other historians examined his brief papal administration, but from essentially the same perspective, emphasizing his holiness, irreproachable character, and dedication to reform.[16] Stanley Morison made the favorable view shared by all these authors explicitly hagiographical in an article entitled "Marcello Cervini, Pope Marcellus II: Bibliography's Patron Saint."[17]

Much more rooted in the documentation of the period were the views of Hubert Jedin, expressed in his *History of the Council of Trent*.[18] Jedin called Cervini the first pope of the "true Catholic reform." In using this term and applying it to the work done at the council, Jedin attacked a conception of the church in the sixteenth century that still persists, namely that the council was part of a negative Catholic response to the outbreak of Protestantism, and that the effort to renew the established church along the ancient, apostolic model could not have been further from the minds of the conciliar fathers.[19] Jedin argued that two concepts, "Catholic Reform" and "Counter Reformation," must be applied in order to understand the history of the Catholic church in the sixteenth century.[20] Rather than merely reacting to Protestant initiatives, the Catholic church, he maintained, generated a great variety of independent initiatives on the part of many persons of different social categories aimed at spiritual and institutional renovation, the chief product of which was the Council of Trent. These initiatives both pre-dated and post-dated the Lutheran controversy, according to Jedin, and should be referred to as the "Catholic reform." The other concept he considered necessary was that of "Counter Reformation." He described that movement as characterized by efforts to implement the decrees of the council and by the recovery of both individuals and territory that had been lost to the Protestant reformation. Jedin called Cervini the "heart and motor" of the council and suggested that he was, therefore, of crucial importance. Giuseppe Alberigo, one of Jedin's leading Italian disciples, reinforced this characterization and further explored Cervini's role as a pastor in his *I vescovi italiani al Concilio di Trento*, published in 1959. According to Alberigo, Cervini may not have reached the "high point of the post-Tridentine pastors," but he reacted very strenuously against the "tide of immorality" he observed in his diocese.[21]

Other scholars have seen Cervini from a different point of view. Their basic inspiration came from Delio Cantimori, who was interested not in those persons or movements that led to the definition of Tridentine orthodoxy, but rather in those that came to be defined as heterodox. He first presented his theses in *Eretici italiani del Cinquecento*, which is still the authoritative treatment of the subject. According to Cantimori, the Italian heretics developed in an intellectual atmosphere based on a humanistic return to patristic literature, on neoplatonism, and on the mystical and millenarian tradition stemming from Joachim of Fiore. Although exposed to the wide variety of Protestant ideas and literature, Italian heresy largely remained an indigenous phenomenon, fueled by anti-clericalism among the laity and anti-curialism among the clergy.[22]

Cantimori's followers based much of their work on the assumption that there were both orthodox and heterodox reformers who shared basically similar hopes for the reformation of religion and the church. All these reformers have been given a name that was used by many at the time: *spirituali*. The movement or movements of which they were a part are generally referred to as *evangelismo*. And study of these figures has largely been directed toward determining the relative degree of their heterodoxy in accordance with one or another definition of orthodoxy.

In pursuit of that goal, Cantimori's followers divided up the field. Carlo Ginzburg chose the Nicodemites, converts to Protestant reform who outwardly continued to participate in the worship of the Roman Church. Antonio Rotondò chose Italian anti-Trinitarians. Massimo Firpo, who earlier dedicated his work to heretical ex-patriots, has published a five-volume critical edition of the inquisitorial process against Cardinal Giovanni Morone, written in collaboration with Dario Marcatto. He saw Morone as the embodiment of the spiritual approach; but, branded as a heretic, Morone came to be attacked by Gian Pietro Carafa and the other leaders of the Counter Reformation, who based their case upon a rather creative interpretation of the term *evidence*.[23]

Another of Cantimori's followers, Paolo Simoncelli, chose to study a group of "evangelicals" within the Catholic hierarchy who were ultimately unsuccessful in their attempt to encourage a simpler approach to the Christian moral life. Headed by the figure of Gasparo Contarini, this group was exploited by hardline curialists like Carafa (according to Simoncelli) in such enterprises as the doomed Contarini legation to Regensburg. Those same curialists allegedly squashed the group altogether. Simoncelli divided these prelates into two distinct groups, the *spirituali* and the *intransigenti*. Those motivated by a careful reading of the New Testament, who seemed conciliatory toward Protestants, he called *spirituali*. The others he termed "pure traditionalists," who resisted change and who by their emphasis on the need for the Inquisition began the work of the Counter Reformation. He called them the *intransigenti*. Contarini, Pole, and those who, like Morone, later came under the suspicion of the *intransigenti* are in the first group, which also included some female members, notably Giulia Gonzaga and the poet Vittoria Colonna.[24] Cervini, Carafa, and Michele Ghislieri belong to the second.

Many British and American scholars agreed that these categories are suited to an accurate analysis of the field. Dermot Fenlon, in his study of Cardinal Pole, utilized this characterization quite extensively, as did Anne Jacobson Schutte in an examination of the popular publications known as the *Lettere volgare*. Elisabeth Gleason did the same in her useful survey of literature on the topic of Italian evangelism, and in her edition of key primary sources from this period.[25]

In spite of some differences of opinion and frequent avowals that the definition of *spirituali* and *intransigenti* is problematic, all these scholars agree on one essential point: the Counter Reformation, with its reintroduction of the Inquisition and the Council of Trent, wiped out the "spiritual" reform, leaving only "intransigents" to take charge of the church in the future. This historiographical movement has been capped, in a way, by Paolo Simoncelli in a recent article designed to demolish the term *Catholic Reform* as it has been understood through the work of Jedin, Alberigo, and others. Simoncelli insists that the concept was fabricated by these historians in the post–World War II context of political and cultural fear of Protestant propaganda, as part of an aggressive, militant Catholic historiography that purposefully ignored and even distorted the work of other historians, like Pio Paschini, who were beginning to identify the real nature of the Catholic church in the sixteenth century. That reality was, according to Simoncelli, a broad program of repression—both of religious dissent and of curial abuses—through control of the history of the church and of the church hierarchy, accomplished by the work of the Roman Inquisition. He maintains that this reality was firmly set in place by 1555, with the accession of Marcellus II and Paul IV to the papal throne. His view dovetails with the standard interpretation of late sixteenth-century Italy as a society dominated by religious, cultural, and political repression, combined with economic decline and depression that perdured until, roughly speaking, the Risorgimento.[26]

This, then, is the state of affairs. From straightforward hagiography, scholars have moved to far subtler representations of the period. As far as Cervini is concerned, the most remarkable consequence seems to be that, at present, he has lost virtually all the halo he was once endowed with and has been ranged firmly in the camp of Catholic reaction and repression. Restoration of the halo is neither deserved nor necessary, but the increased sophistication of contemporary historical analysis has led to new and equally sophisticated questions.

To begin, it is important to note that the *spirituali* and *intransigenti* had a great deal in common, a fact recognized by many of the very historians who see this as the essential distinction. Both groups participated in church government at the very highest levels. Most of them, in fact the vast majority of them, shared the same kind of humanistic education and participated in the humanistic culture of Italy in general and of Rome in particular. All of them were reformers, who desired, at least in theory, to eliminate curial and clerical abuses commonly associated with the late medieval and Renaissance papacy: simony, absenteeism, pluralism, reservation of ecclesiastical monies for relatives, and provisions of benefices to unworthy and unqualified candidates both at the parish and at the curial levels. It has been maintained that the split between the *spirituali* and the *intransigenti* only occurred in the 1530s and the early 1540s as doctrinal differences between Catholics and Protestants became drawn more clearly and as the hope for reconciliation faded. According to these historians, the two groups then involved themselves in a ferocious war over the politics and ideology of church reform, over the instruments to be used in the process, and over the ultimate goals of reform. In this battle over the most important theological and disciplinary issues facing the church, the *spirituali* chose the way of accommodation and reconciliation; the *intransigenti* chose the way of confrontation and domination. The latter, therefore, are the ones who are commonly held responsible for the war. They are said to have insisted on the creation of a church that was hierarchically controlled and repressively rigid. The struggle thus was fought in only one direction: the *intransigenti* battled viciously against the *spirituali*. The *spirituali* were wholly on the defensive.

Twentieth-century attitudes toward the Catholic church, however, appear to inform these definitions and interpretations. The historians whose views have just been outlined assume that the post-Tridentine church was monolithic and fundamentally clerical and authoritarian, and that this situation went unchanged for some four hundred years. They believe that the "spiritual" approach to Catholicism passed away in the sixteenth century, never to be revived until (roughly speaking) Vatican Council II. When asked to explain its demise, these historians find their answer in the identification of a group that suppressed those with a "spiritual" approach to Catholicism, eliminated the possibility of an accord with Protestants, and muscled through the papal agenda at the Council of Trent—in a word, the *intransigenti*.

Such a view appears to rest on a rather questionable and quite likely anachronistic basis, namely, the very distinction between *intransigenti* and *spirituali* itself. Barbara McClung Hallman attacked Jedin's concept of Catholic reform as a spontaneous, genuine, widespread, and locally effective movement within the sixteenth-century church. Many scholars have considered the famous 1537 *Consilium de emendanda ecclesia*, with its attack upon the curial system and the abuses in ecclesiastical finance and its simultaneous recommendation of the pastoral model for all those with the care of souls, as a kind of manifesto of this movement and as incontrovertible evidence that such a movement did indeed exist. Hallman, however, presented a devastating counter-argument. She demonstrated that on an economic level such a movement never existed. She explained that in regard to benefices and other ecclesiastical monies, reformers and non-reformers alike acted along identical lines throughout the first half of the sixteenth century. Reform, she suggested, might have been an idealistic goal of certain cardinals, but from 1492 to 1563 it never really touched such practical and highly revealing matters as their maintenance of a dignified lifestyle and the enrichment of their relatives.[27]

The thesis forces us either to deny truly reformatory qualities to the *spirituali* or to redefine the notion of reform—although it might be difficult to invent a notion of reform that accommodates luxury and patronage—and thus to allow reformatory qualities to the *intransigenti*. In either case, the argument reduces the difference between *spirituali* and *intransigenti*. All of these prelates treated the monetary aspect of their ecclesiastical life as a business, renting and "farming" benefices. Even *spirituali* like Federigo Fregoso and Gasparo Contarini, Hallman proved, were pluralists throughout their careers.

The correspondence of another member of the *spirituali*, Marcantonio Flaminio, presents an additional problem. Massimo Firpo, in reviewing a recent edition of that correspondence, pointed out the different views held over the years by this man who was one of those to revise the *Beneficio di Cristo*, attributed to Benedetto da Mantova. For Flaminio was not only connected with the Oratory of Divine Love in Genoa and a friend of such notable *spirituali* as Gian Matteo Giberti, Contarini, and Fregoso, but he was also treated "like a son" by none other than Gian Pietro Carafa himself. Firpo noted all this and even pointed out that Flaminio rejected the "false religious zeal" he believed to be characteristic of both sides of sixteenth-century religious controversy after the 1540s. But Firpo then went on to insist that the terms *evangelismo* and *spirituale* should simply be defined with greater precision and more closely related to the hardening of positions in the 1540s in order to accommodate such facts.[28]

The recent, powerfully argued, and controversial article of Simoncelli raises still further questions. A considerable body of historical literature contradicts his argument quite directly. Paul Grendler, for example, insisted that although some oppression of Italian intellectual life occurred in this period, ecclesiastical leaders did not force the Counter Reformation down the throats of the rest of the members of that society. Another student of Italian religious life in this period, Arnaldo D'Addario, objected to characterizations of the Counter Reformation not unlike Simoncelli's. Even Paschini published works that tend to uphold Jedin's conceptions of the papacy in the period. There are also views of the Inquisition at variance with that of Simoncelli, among others one recently presented by Edward Peters in a major work.[29] New, contrasting views of the general situation in Italy during this period exist as well, which focus upon the peace, prosperity, and cultural efflorescence in that society, a point largely ignored by historians in the nineteenth and twentieth centuries.[30] The important question raised by all this debate is whether the basic distinction between *spirituali* and *intransigenti* itself, however much refined and elaborated, does not serve to obscure rather than to illuminate sixteenth-century Italian church history.

Recently a few brave scholars have posed just this question. Prosperi argued that the unification of Italy in the nineteenth century and the essential character of that movement led to a description of the Inquisition three centuries earlier that asserted a strong, even inherent, connection between the Italian intellectuals who became the focus of its attack and the rest of Protestant, liberal Europe. He also expressed hope that additional archival research will enable historians to finally abandon characterizations of the institution as "evil" or "mild," which stand as obstacles prohibiting a correct understanding of the period. Schutte surveyed developments in Italian religious historiography at large since the ground-breaking work of Cantimori and argued that other ways of dividing up the field and its chronology are at least possible. Gigliola Fragnito went even farther and insisted that hope for reconciliation between Catholics and Protestants did not end with the traditionally cited events of 1541 and 1542, and that *evangelismo* did not suddenly expire over the course of those two years, either. Silvana Seidel-Menchi insisted that between 1535 and 1555, inquisitors frequently maintained an attitude of dialogue and even solidarity with those they investigated, not one of repression or coercion. They became systematically repressive only during the pontificate of Paul IV, she suggested, and she argued that rethinking of the standard periodization of Italian religious history is necessary.[31]

Careful consideration and analysis of the career of Marcello Cervini will constitute a major contribution to that very basic question. Cervini maintained close contact with most of those categorized as either *spirituali* or *intransigenti*, and he is especially interesting as a man right on the supposed borderline between the two groups. Indeed, it seems virtually impossible to account for his life and thoughts while sustaining both the coherence of the *spirituali* and their irreconcilability with a Counter Reformation. Cervini's abundant correspondence establishes beyond a shadow of a doubt his importance both to *evangelismo* and to the Counter Reformation. This material, generated as it was by an insider in the growing curial bureaucracy, establishes Cervini's importance for the evaluation of the character of both ecclesiastical and specifically papal government in the first half of the sixteenth century.[32] His correspondence reveals, although not completely, minute details of his public and occasionally of his private life. It reveals a man equally undeserving of the halo of hagiography and of the negative assessment implied in the term *intransigente*.

Portions of this large corpus have been selected, edited, and published in collections centering on particular friends of Cervini or elements in their common work, but the bulk of his correspondence is still unpublished and remains in the Archivio di Stato in Florence.[33] The evidence contained in the seventy volumes there collected does not support the earlier assessments of Cervini. The long-standing hagiographical tradition ignores the opinions he held, the nature of the work he did for others, and the actions he took on his own authority, all of which are abundantly documented in his correspondence. Similarly, the characterization of Cervini as an intransigent participant in a conflict against men of spiritual attitudes is not borne out. It conflicts with his friendship and close collaboration with people on both sides of that presumed division; his genuine piety; and his concern, proven through action, for the reform of church practice on many levels. Such friendship, piety, and concern are fundamental elements in most descriptions of the *spirituali* and call into question both that term and its correlative opposite, *intransigente*, which is most often applied to Cervini.

Instead of seeing Cervini as a saint, or inserting him into a preestablished framework with contemporary ideological implications, we should try to understand him by referring to the work that he did. Cervini was an administrator on two levels: the curial and the episcopal. On the curial level he served the papacy as a bureaucrat or factotum. In this function, he appears as a hard-headed pragmatist, who obediently carried out the instructions of others, rather than as a speculative thinker, who innovatively formulated programs of reform. He was preeminently trustworthy, a loyal and hard-working man who believed above all in the efficient exercise of legitimate authority. He was valued by those he worked with and worked for because he could get things done.

As an episcopal administrator, on the other hand, he proceeded in a more independent fashion. He sought above all to act, to begin to carry out a program for the reform of the church that he had conceptualized in confrontation with the problems he observed over the course of his career, both as a legate and as a confidant of Pope Paul III. In this office he possessed the authority to reform on his own initiative and make changes as he saw fit. He acted often, in fact wherever possible, and in a predictably pragmatic and efficient manner. His actions in his function as an episcopal administrator are comprehensible only in light of the humanistic preparation he received, and the concept of authority and ecclesiology he adopted as a curial administrator.

To say it in another way, Cervini did not demand a return to a papal-directed reform throughout the entire clerical population in order to foster the creation of a repressively rigid, monolithic church engaged in total war against any who disagreed or stood in its way. Rather, pursuing a search for the most authentic model for the church that was inspired by humanistic attention to the past, by his experience in curial administration, by his belief in the possibilities of a fully reformed papacy, and by his awareness of how serious the problems confronting the church really were and how badly they needed a swift practical resolution, he chose to work for reform under the leadership of the papacy. In his mind, it was the model most in harmony with the Apostolic church and the teaching of the Fathers, and he became convinced that it would be the most practicable and expeditious solution. He certainly disagreed with his colleagues at times. But he would have been baffled by the epithet *intransigente*, and he would have been astonished had he been told he did not belong to those concerned with spiritual reform.

A preliminary note is also necessary on some of the terms that have been applied to Cervini over the years. The first of these terms is *humanist*. There can be no doubt that he was affected by the culture of humanism in sixteenth-century Italy, and he encountered this culture through a humanist education. His teachers seem to have focused on the practical benefit of humanist education—to prepare him for a managerial career, either on his father's land in Tuscany or in the church. Humanism as Cervini put it into practice is best defined in much the same way: he used it as a tool to recover the most ancient model of the church. Cervini believed that this search would provide not only an authentic but also an effective, practical model for the reforms he believed were necessary in the sixteenth-century church.

Hence, Cervini's humanism is comprehensible only in relation to another term, *reformation*. Perhaps in no other age was the desire for the reform of ecclesiastical practices in the Christian religion more pervasively felt. This was due to spontaneous Catholic efforts both to achieve reform in religious orders and on the diocesan level, as well as to respond to the traditionally understood Protestant challenge. But Cervini and the group of his acquaintances and collaborators were significant as humanist reformers. They sought to apply humanist academic methodology to issues of reform. Unquestionably, they believed that the application of existing church law would go a long way in achieving general reform, but the model they chose as a normative ideal to be instituted in the sixteenth century was one discovered through humanistic methods. Through the study of and the attempt to fully understand the most ancient sources of Christianity, they adopted the model of the Apostolic church, which they believed ought in turn to be adapted to address the contemporary problems of the church in the sixteenth century. A careful reading of Scripture, patristic authors, and the decrees of ancient councils, they believed, would result in the proper understanding of the church as well as the proper understanding of the role of the bishop and all those who exercised authority in the church.

By their approach to the questions of reform, then, Cervini and these humanist reformers are to be differentiated from other reformers of the same period. Although, one might argue, Scripture constitutes a segment of the law of the church, the scriptural and patristic emphasis of these humanists differentiated them from reformers who insisted the situation only required adherence to already-established church laws to arrive at the reform of the church. They are differentiated also from "conciliarist" reformers, such as the Spanish and Neapolitan imperial party among the Tridentine Fathers, who sought a major shift in the understanding of the derivation of ecclesiastical authority as a necessary prerequisite for the initiation of real reform. And they are to be differentiated from Protestant reformers, who believed that a radically new doctrinal synthesis as well as a shift from hierarchical authority centered in the pope was necessary to resolve the problems of the sixteenth-century church.

This understanding of the humanist reformer, one concerned with a close reading of Scripture and desirous of applying it to issues of reform in the contemporary setting, has curiously enough been identified as one of the key points in understanding the *spirituali* as a group. Historians credit Gasparo Contarini, Reginald Pole, Jacopo Sadoleto, Giovanni Morone, and others with this sort of outlook and seem to view them as prototypical of the Vatican II reformers (who broke through Roman Catholic stagnation often traced to unbroken adherence to the decrees of the Council of Trent). The group, however, has to be enlarged. For it must be admitted that the Catholic prelates who were committed to such a reading of Scripture as an important source in reforming the sixteenth-century church included individuals who were convinced that the leadership on reform programs had to come from the pope and then be extended through the bishops. Cervini, a case in point, adhered to such a reading of Scripture and to the principle of papally implemented reform, not out of any ideological differences with his friends and collaborators, but because he believed that, in order to be genuine as well as effective, reform had to be carried out in this manner. He and his colleagues consistently asserted that it was possible to attain the model at issue without abandoning contemporary ecclesiastical institutions—provided, however, they were properly understood and renewed. The humanists were aware of contemporary clerical practices, and they were critical of them, but they also insisted that real reform of the hierarchy was possible and that the hierarchy was still the best vehicle to carry any reform to the church at large.

Cervini and his colleagues proposed and developed a method that is significant also because their method was the one finally adopted in carrying out the reform of the sixteenth-century church and in institutionalizing the decrees of Trent. It was they who began to elaborate the patristic bases of doctrinal decrees. It was they who pointed to the disciples of Christ and the Pauline epistles in the search for models of the episcopal office. It was they who through experimentation in their own dioceses attempted to put such models into practice.

These managerial churchmen must be studied in order to assess the connections between humanism and reformation. Further, as has been recently pointed out, it is precisely this sort of activity on the part of individuals who can be considered humanists and reformers that may make it possible in the future to question whether religious convictions are an adequate basis for division between the Renaissance and the Reformation as historical periods.[34] Here at least, it seems, Cervini and his associates may have constituted a bridge between the two periods, sharing the objectives of Renaissance humanists and on that basis implementing practical and positive solutions for problems in the church.

Cervini was above all a pragmatist devoted to one thing: returning the sixteenth-century church to the apostolic model he accepted as an ideal. In order to achieve this end he recommended practical reform of the papal curia, real pastoral leadership at all levels of the church hierarchy, doctrinal clarity and unity, renewal of monastic religious life, and renewal of the diocesan religious life of the faithful. In this effort he took whatever actions he was permitted in the office he held. As a confidant of Paul III he utilized his position of influence to recommend curial reforms. As legate he urged and implemented a program designed to solidify the papal position and suggested the allocation of rewards and punishments as a practical way to facilitate success. He consistently carried out diocesan reform in the areas under his jurisdiction through his correspondence and through his vicars. As a member of the Roman Inquisition, he willingly employed methods of investigation and punishment in order to foster doctrinal unity and clarity, but in a way different from some of the more infamous members of the body. While recommending changes in the papacy and curia he believed urgent, if the incumbent pope chose not to follow his recommendations, he supported the papacy as it was until he himself attained the office and then attempted to apply practical reforms to the ecclesiastical institutions he considered in greatest need.

Cervini embodied, therefore, the consistent goal of Catholic ecclesiastical reformers between the fifteenth and sixteenth centuries. The overall goal was the recovery of the apostolic ideal for the church within the context of the ecclesiastical institutions already in place—papacy, council, curia, and episcopacy. Despite whatever secondary goals the church and especially the papacy were pursuing simultaneously, such as peace, the recovery of territory, or adherence to dogma, this overall goal was consistent.[35] It is a mistake to overemphasize the importance of 1542 as a turning point in the means and methodology used to attain this goal, and Cervini and his associates constitute the proof. These individuals were churchmen who lived and worked together on both sides of this presumed dividing line, consistently seeking that overall goal, and always within an ecclesiastical context. Cervini stands among the clearest examples of such churchmen, because he embodied that goal on a personal level. He tried to bring it about on a small scale in his own diocese and in his recommendations to Paul III and Julius III, and then on a large scale during his few days as pope. If all this is true, the Tridentine Reformation can be seen as a one-piece phenomenon, with roots in medieval reform movements, as continuous through the experimentations of the Italian episcopacy, and as reaching its culmination in the implementation of the decrees of the Council of Trent.[36] In addition, we can abandon the terms *spirituali* and *intransigenti* for what they are: terms hopelessly loaded with positive and negative connotations that conceal an improper secondary agenda. Further, it will be simpler to explain the questionable and even violent actions of some of those who succeeded Cervini in the papacy, like Gian Pietro Carafa: their abuse of inquisitorial processes was motivated far more by personal *vendette* than by anything approaching a coherent policy of religious repression that began with the death of Contarini, the flight of Bernardino Ochino, and the reinstitution of the Roman Inquisition.[37]

This study aims through the use of archival sources to describe, more thoroughly than studies presently available, the career of Cervini and his attitude toward reform on the curial and diocesan levels, as well as his attitude toward the exercise of authority in church government. It will present a complex individual who cannot be forced into one of the camps among sixteenth-century prelates identified by modern historiography. It will also demonstrate Cervini's close connection and collaboration with other contemporary Catholic reformers. Perhaps the study will contribute to a more nuanced understanding of the term *Tridentine Reformation* in the sixteenth century.

CHAPTER TWO

Preparation as Humanist and Curialist

THE CERVINI FAMILY

The Cervini family resided in the town of Montepulciano as early as the thirteenth century, according to Vittorio Spreti, a historian of the noble families of Italy. Allegedly the family came originally from France, an assumption Spreti may have made because in 1230 the head of the family was named Pierre, but certainly by the fifteenth century they were well established among the noble families of Tuscany. Ricciardo Cervini, later the father of Marcello, was born in Montepulciano on February 4, 1454, the firstborn son of Antonio Cervini and his second wife, the Florentine Elizabetta Machiavelli.[1]

Ricciardo grew up in Florence, raised by Elizabetta after the death of his father. Here, as a student of humanistic subjects, he attended the Academy of Lorenzo de' Medici, and first made the acquaintance of Alessandro Farnese, later Pope Paul III.[2] Ricciardo later traveled to Siena to continue his education. This move might have been due in part to the legal battle over the division of the estate left by his father, as Marco Palma points out. Nevertheless, while in Siena he won the friendship of the wealthy Spannocchi family, to whom he sent his own son for a similar education some thirty-five years later. Ricciardo served as administrator of the Spannocchi patrimony after the death of Ambrogio and also looked after the education of Ambrogio's sons Antonio and Giulio. The Spannocchi had a high profile due to their prominence in banking circles, and especially due to their loans on behalf of the papacy.[3] Owing to the family's patronage and protection, Ricciardo not only became enrolled in the Sienese nobility in 1493 but, after the completion of his legal studies in Siena, successfully purchased the office of *scrittore* in the apostolic Penitentiary in Rome—the Spannocchi generously lent him the money to do so in 1485.

Ricciardo married Cassandra di Domenico Benci of Montepulciano sometime before 1500. She was a member of one of the prominent ancient families of the town. She and Ricciardo had five children, three of whom survived: a daughter Pera, then Marcello, and finally another daughter, Camilla. Ricciardo would have been made a cardinal under Pope Alexander VI (1492–1503) if not for this marital status, or so maintained his son by his second marriage, Alessandro Cervini.[4] Nevertheless, Ricciardo did obtain the important office of governor of the treasury in the March of Ancona under the same papal administration.

As governor of the treasury, an office he was granted toward the end of the fifteenth century, he enjoyed the lucrative position of tax collector for the papacy. Over the nine years in which he held the position, he made a great deal of money and earned the envy of some in the region. A number of these who aspired to his position hatched a plot to ambush him, and he narrowly escaped the attack.[5]

Marcello was born during this administration, in Montefano, near Macerata and Loreto in the Marches, at a little after noon on May 6, 1501. His father recorded the time of the birth, following the common practice in Tuscany. Alessandro Cervini's sketch of the life of his half-brother is filled with humanistic allusions, beginning with his relation of this event. He indicated that Ricciardo was, at that moment, in the presence of an astrologer, and the two were measuring the height of the sun. Virgo was in ascendance, Alessandro recounted, and the configuration of the other heavenly bodies was such that the two of them judged "this child would be great in the church of God." Ricciardo allegedly confirmed all of this through mathematical calculations and other means. Alessandro explained the great joy at the *natività* of the child, but that later the baby suddenly stopped taking milk and all feared for his life. Only God, Alessandro said, preserved Marcello to the age at which he could take solid food.[6] The family returned to Montepulciano not long after the birth and baptism of Marcello, which was administered by Antonio Ugolini Sinibaldi (+1515), the bishop of Osimo from 1498 until his death. Thus Marcello had, in a manner of speaking, a double *patria*, as Alessandro explained—"one by culture, where he was born . . . in Montefano . . . and the other Montepulciano . . . a city noble and rich." Alessandro quite likely borrowed this allusion to the concept of a double *patria* from Cicero's *De legibus*.[7]

There in Montepulciano Marcello grew up, and there also his mother died, on September 17, 1509, after a long illness. Among those following hagiographical and humanist topoi by praising Cassandra, her piety, and her influence on Marcello were both Spinello Benci and Onofrio Panvinio, as well as Alessandro Cervini who, even though he never met her, called her a "most diligent and industrious governess of the family." Her loving qualities, he maintained, permit her to be compared favorably with the "most celebrated women" of the ancient world.[8]

Ricciardo's second wife was named Leonora, a descendant of the Cassiaconti family of Siena, and she bore seven children with him.[9] Their two sons were named Alessandro and Romolo, and the five daughters Celia, Elizabetta, Giulia, Cintia, and Silvia. Alessandro (who in 1542 was *gonfalone* "standard-bearer" in Montepulciano as well as Marcello's biographer somewhat later) and his sister Cintia both married into the Bellarmino family. The Bellarminos were also among the first families of Montepulciano, although somewhat less well-to-do than the Cervinis.

The descendants of both families subsequently gained considerable ecclesiastical prominence. Cintia Cervini (1526–1575), who had a reputation for piety and austerity, gave birth in 1542 to Roberto Bellarmino (+1621), the Jesuit theologian, cardinal, and saint. Giulia entered the religious life in the order of Saint Clare, and Romolo attempted to pattern his career after that of his older half-brother Marcello.[10] Marcello oversaw his education, entrusting Romolo to his friends Bernardino Maffei and Paolo Manuzio, later suggesting that he study law in Padua. Such a study would, of course, make Romolo employable not just in ecclesiastical circles, but also in the growing secular administration of Tuscany. Marcello also ceded to Romolo the titles of the abbacies of Capella a Napoli, Saint'Emiliano in Gubbio, and Cuneo in Valdelsa, in addition to playing an instrumental role in Romolo's acquisition of the office of master of the registry of apostolic letters in 1548 under Pope Paul III (1534–1549). Romolo, it is said, did not have the talent of his half-brother in academic pursuits, but Marcello did utilize him as an intermediary in his work with the Venetian printing house headed by Aldo and Paolo Manuzio while Romolo pursued studies at Padua.[11] Romolo died suddenly in 1551, before his ecclesiastical career, enriched through the actions of his half-brother, really commenced. Such was not the case with Marcello, or with the several other members of the family who later received appointments in the hierarchy of the church. Marcello's namesake served successively as bishop of Sovanna (1645–1652) and of Montepulciano (1652–1663). Antonio Cervini succeeded him in Montepulciano and served there until his death in 1707. The family also produced two archbishops: Tomasso Cervini, archbishop of Nicomedia (1721–1734) and titular archbishop of Jerusalem (1734–1751); and Alessandro Cervini, archbishop of Siena (1747–1771).

MARCELLO'S EDUCATION

Not long after the birth of Marcello, Ricciardo and his family returned to Montepulciano and to the large farm they owned, Castiglione d'Orcia. At the farm, on the northern slope of Monte Amiata not far from Montepulciano, Ricciardo occupied himself with his two main academic interests, astronomy and chronology, and also with the administration of the patrimony and the cultivation of the land, at which he was particularly adept. In addition, he saw to Marcello's early education.[12]

Marcello's education began at the age of eight, and it was a broad education that included many subjects. He learned grammar—"the first letters," as Alessandro explained—under his father, who employed the writings of Julius Caesar, as they are "most necessary to men that have to operate in the world." Ricciardo also taught him the more "mechanical arts," including architecture, ironmaking, baking, and the assembly of books, but for two different reasons. These subjects constituted not only a diversion from other studies, as Alessandro said, but also served "to give him every perfection."[13] In addition, Ricciardo instructed him in the rudiments of agriculture. As the proprietor of large amounts of land in the vicinity, Ricciardo enjoyed considerable success in his cultivations and passed this skill to his son, as became evident later. Ricciardo also devoted a significant amount of time to the instruction of Marcello in mathematics and *astrologia naturale*.

Ricciardo concentrated a great deal of his own time on natural astrology, or the study of the laws of the movement of heavenly bodies, which during the Renaissance began to be called astronomy. This interest also he passed to his son. Natural astrology was differentiated from (but, in the sixteenth century, still connected with) *astrologia giudiziaria,* the prediction of natural and human events that allegedly result from the laws of planetary movement.[14] Ricciardo utilized this knowledge in an effort to reform the calendar, a work he began when Pope Leo X (1513–1521) made it known that, like his predecessor Julius II (1503–1513), he wanted to promote progress on the project. In fact, Leo requested academies and learned persons to look into the matter and presented this request, even setting up a commission of his own to coordinate the effort, during the tenth session of the Fifth Lateran Council in 1515.[15] Several works were produced as a direct result of

Leo's interest. Ricciardo dedicated his work to Leo X, and later to his successor Clement VII (1523–1534). Since Ricciardo did much of his work on this project at the time of Marcello's early education, Marcello had occasion to learn a great deal about astronomy. Indeed, familiarity with this area of study proved to be both important and profitable to him later in Rome. After he completed his early education under his father, Marcello did not travel to Rome but to Siena, the third place that made a claim to him as its native son.

Ricciardo had good reason to send his son to Siena. He had a long-standing relationship with many of the members of the Sienese ruling and social elite, especially with Pandolfo Petrucci. He could also send with Marcello a letter of introduction and recommendation addressed to Cardinal Giovanni Piccolomini. In addition, the Spannocchi family had offered sometime before to take the young Cervini into their home and to help him continue his education. Thus, the second home of Ricciardo rapidly became the same for Marcello.[16] In his letter of February 26, 1520, Marcello told of his arrival, of the nice room that had been given to him in the Spannocchi household, and of his visit to Monsignor Piccolomini. In Siena, Marcello undertook studies that centered on the Greek and Latin classics (in which he distinguished himself) and that also included mathematics, dialectics, philosophy, and astronomy. "In studies of humanistic subjects, he was most truly excellent," his brother Alessandro eulogistically explained, while he could express himself with elegance both in prose and in verse. And in the "understanding of ancient things," Alessandro further maintained, he was second to none.[17]

Alessandro most certainly overdrew the portrait, but the diligence of Marcello in study is apparent in the letters he wrote to his father during his years in Siena. Cervini spent a good deal of time in Siena, at least through the spring of 1522. During this period he wrote with great frequency to his father on the progress of his studies. He reported with the greatest regularity on the subjects of astronomy, mathematics, and Greek. At times, he seemed to complain about the abstract nature of some of his studies. His work on Euclid, for example, always seemed to tire him—apparently he had difficulty imagining the solid forms necessary for the study.[18] He undertook lessons in Greek on a daily basis from a teacher identified only as Magister Ugo, and in this subject particularly he became quite expert. In April 1520, he related that he was already working on the declension of nouns and adjectives, and that on the first of May he would begin hearing lectures in Greek. He also began collecting books at this time, especially ones in Greek. This became one of his life-long passions. He sent frequently to Venice for these books, and though relatives, especially his cousin Giovanni Battista Cervini, at times provided the funds for the purchases, Marcello did not hesitate to ask his father for money to cover such expenses.[19]

Marcello and his father both suffered from delicate constitutions, and this also is apparent in the letters from Siena. Marcello battled migraine and an "ill-disposed stomach" in particular, and he described his difficulties in detail, indicating that only serious illness could take him completely away from his studies. Indeed, when he felt better, he typically vowed to pursue his studies more fervently.[20] Ricciardo suffered problems a good deal more severe. He experienced urinary disorders apparently linked to the prostate, and Marcello spoke on his father's behalf with doctors in Siena. They prescribed baths and herbal concoctions in May and June 1520, and these resulted in some improvement. Marcello relayed their instructions and prescriptions in his correspondence. Marcello also showed considerable impatience with his father when he was slow to reply and describe his condition.[21] This trait he demonstrated throughout his life, whenever his subordinates, and occasionally even his superiors, were slow to reply to his letters. In this precise instance, he displayed concerns that were quite reasonable in light of the later medical history of the family. Although his father lived a long life, Marcello and a number of his brothers and sisters died at relatively young ages. At any rate, Marcello both rejoiced when his father periodically regained his health and exhorted him to patience and faith in facing this chronic illness.[22]

As Marcello followed his father's educational plan, he showed early evidence of administrative and agricultural abilities. At times during 1521 and 1523, Marcello administered the family concerns in Montepulciano in his father's absence. Not surprisingly, among the primary concerns Marcello related to his father in letters from this period were the family vineyards that produced the well-known Montepulciano wines, and the accounts of their creditors.[23] Though Marcello proved himself more than capable in such matters, both at this time, then later in 1525, and again after the death of his father in 1534, Ricciardo did not envision for his son a career in Tuscany at the service of the family, but one in Rome at the service of the church.

In all probability, Ricciardo allowed the astrological prediction of Marcello's greatness in the church to lead him to take the unusual step of deputing a son for an ecclesiastical career at a time when there were no other male heirs in the family.[24] On the other hand, a number of historians have suggested, even recently, that Marcello felt he was called by God to his work on behalf of the church. Although historically this is difficult to demonstrate, reference is typically made to a letter written to Marcello on May 5, 1520, by Ambrogio Catarino (c. 1484–1553), a native of Montepulciano and a Dominican prominent in controversial circles at this time. In the letter, Catarino suggested that Marcello consider life in a religious order. It has been argued that this was the first sign of a religious orientation in the young man.[25] Catarino in this letter certainly exhorted Marcello to the religious life and to the avoidance of pride in his studies, but it is hardly such a first sign. Marcello at least suggested a religious attitude much earlier in his letters to his father. One might draw that conclusion simply by glancing at his correspondence from this period, as most of the sheets he topped with the sign of the cross, but that was in fact a common practice designed to drive away evil spirits. A better indication comes from the letters themselves, which are replete with pious wishes for the mercy or grace of God either for himself or for Ricciardo, although this too constituted fairly common practice in the genre from this period. The evidence that Marcello felt any sort of vocation to work in the church is circumstantial, at best. He did not follow Catarino's suggestion to follow the way of perfection in a religious order, even if he sensed a call, and Ricciardo's plan for his son's career would probably have been the strongest influence in setting him on the path of secular clerical orders.

At any rate, Ricciardo sent Marcello to Rome in 1524, not long after the election of Pope Clement VII, recommending him to Cardinal Alessandro Farnese, who later served in the papacy as Paul III. Ricciardo sent him there to continue his education and also to put himself and the rest of the Cervini family at the service of the new pope.[26] He made this offer at a most opportune time; just the time, in fact, of the prediction made to Clement of a famine followed by a great flood, a prediction based upon a major planetary conjunction. Astrological predictions of such events became something of an obsession in Rome during the decade between 1520 and 1530.[27] No less than 56 authors wrote 133 pamphlets making such forecasts, which some have used to argue that a collective anxiety and hysteria was typical prior to the Sack of Rome in 1527.[28] The prediction in question threatened a deluge only "slightly smaller than that of the time of Noah" and had, in fact, been confirmed by astrologers. The pope allegedly prepared himself "to flee to Tivoli or another high place." Marcello presented to Clement his father's repudiation of that prediction, demonstrating, in a sense, the connection that existed between natural and judicial astrology in the sixteenth century. He pointed out the error in the calculation of the astrologers who had predicted the flood.[29] In fact, no flood came in 1524, or at least not on the scale predicted by some, although there were heavy rains during a good portion of that year. At any rate, suitably impressed,

Clement asked Marcello to work with his father on the still-incomplete correction of the calendar, and to return to Rome with the results of their calculations. Marcello did so and subsequently came to live in Rome, making the acquaintance of the literati of the curia.[30]

MARCELLO'S FRIENDS

Marcello fostered friendships at this time that were critical to his future career, for they provided an impetus to his academic pursuits. During this period, he demonstrated "rare learning" in verse and prose, in Greek, Latin, and Italian. The friendships also served to establish him solidly among those with increasing influence in the papal curia. According to his half-brother Alessandro, he made the acquaintance of the humanists Benedetto Lampridio, Antonio Tebaldeo, Carlo Gualteruzzi, and Pietro Bembo, in addition to Angelo Colocci, who considered Marcello his best friend.[31]

Bembo (1470–1547), who became a cardinal about a year before Cervini and was ordained a priest in 1539, made his real mark as a poet. He also served from 1530 until his death as the official historiographer and librarian of the Republic of Venice. One of the more recent evaluators of his career maintains that Bembo viewed membership in the College of Cardinals very pragmatically: although ultimately uninterested in any particular brand of religious reform, he found the cardinalate in a church at the forefront of humanistic culture to be "well worth a Mass." Indeed, with the money he gained through the accumulation of benefices, he spent his life happily in literary leisure. Bembo held Cervini in considerable esteem allegedly because of his learning, prudence, and good judgment, but just as likely because of favors he had done Bembo in the past.[32] Gualteruzzi (1500–1577) served as a kind of intermediary in the friendship between Bembo and Cervini and due to the influence of both became, briefly, secretary of the Council of Trent.[33]

Colocci (1474–1549), who similarly was enriched through papal favors and offices, depended upon Cervini and others for translations and interpretations of Greek sources to augment his considerable antiquarian interests. He owned an important collection of statues and other antiquities, in addition to a well-known library stocked with scriptural texts, the Latin and Greek Fathers, and the works of modern authors like Enea Silvio Piccolomini and Pietro Balbi. Cervini picked over this collection after Colocci's death, apparently under orders from Paul III, with a view to increasing the holdings of the burgeoning Vatican library. Colocci also named Cervini as executor of his will. But although Cervini's ecclesiastical career thus commenced auspiciously, it was interrupted briefly with the outbreak of plague in Rome during 1525 and 1526.[34]

Ricciardo ordered his son to return to Montepulciano in 1525, and Marcello promptly obeyed. He maintained unwavering reverence for his father, and he was reputed to have asked the permission of his father in all things. But he expressed this perhaps most strongly in such prompt obedience. He employed the conventional closing "Your obedient son" in ending each of his letters to his father.[35] And his actions suggest that those words were more than lip service.

Marcello remained in Montepulciano from the outbreak of the plague until the end of the war after the Sack of Rome in 1527. During this time he carried out the duties of *economo* or administrator for his father on the farm. He "oversaw the vines, olives, and trees of diverse sorts," promoting and cultivating them, his half-brother Alessandro related, and "with his prudence" Marcello "amplified the patrimony."[36] At this time he also maintained his interest in study, translating into Italian Cicero's *De amicitia*.[37] But devotion to his family duties came first. Marcello demonstrated this devotion again after his return to Rome. When his father lay gravely ill in Montepulciano in 1534, Marcello came home again, but his duties were somewhat different. Ricciardo died on April 2, 1534, leaving a considerable amount of money, and Marcello settled the estate. At that time he arranged marriages for three of his sisters, including Cintia, as well as Giulia's entry into religious life. According to his father's wishes, Marcello himself received a substantial yearly income, and, entrusting the estate to his half-brothers Alessandro and Romolo, he returned again to Rome, where his father's good friend Alessandro Farnese had just been elected to the pontificate.[38]

Pope Paul III, acquainted with the Cervini family from his childhood, was apparently impressed with Marcello after his first stay in Rome in 1524. This may well have been due, at least in part, to Paul's interest in astrology, which echoed that of his predecessor Clement VII. Paul opened his curia to a number of seers and astrologers, among them Luca Gaurico (+1558), and spurred others to praise him for restoring astrology as an academic discipline.[39] Paul must have been impressed with Cervini's ability to explain the error in the flood prediction of 1524. In addition, the new Farnese pope had, while still a cardinal, already favored Marcello by taking him into his household for a year, from 1531 to 1532. This time, as pope, he not only took him in but immediately offered him a job. Paul had promoted his two young grandsons Alessandro Farnese and Guido Ascanio Sforza to the cardinalate in 1534, and he put Cervini in charge of the education of Alessandro. In this office, Cervini replaced the famous educator from

Udine, Romolo Amaseo (1489–1552), who returned to tutor Alessandro when Cervini was too busy with other duties in 1544.[40] Paul appointed Cervini, under whom Alessandro demonstrated the "ability to learn," at least to some degree because of the reputation for virtue already associated with Cervini. Paul apparently intended him to serve, too, as a companion to the young Farnese, in accord with the Renaissance ideal that education should mold not only the intellect but the character as well. The pope allegedly wanted Alessandro "spending his time in honorable work . . . and surrounded by men of virtue."[41] Others in the young cardinal's household at this time were Sebastiano Delio (+1544), who later served as bishop of Bitonto, and Bernardino Maffei (1514–1553), who became a lifelong friend of Cervini.[42]

It was among all these that "Marcello began to show evidence of his prudence," according to Alessandro Cervini.[43] Although such prudence may be difficult to demonstrate, two other things are certainly true: first, these events constituted the beginning of a long close friendship between Cervini and the Farnese family, and second, as a result of this work for and friendship with the family, Cervini enjoyed rapid promotion in the ecclesiastical hierarchy during the early years of Paul's pontificate.

Cervini maintained a close association with the Farnese family for the rest of his life, and the mutual esteem that characterized this relationship is evident in his correspondence. Cervini received warm congratulations from members of the family upon his various ecclesiastical promotions, as was typical of such relationships in sixteenth-century Italy. Ottavio Farnese, another of the grandsons of Paul III who later became the duke of Parma after the assassination of his father Pierluigi in 1549, addressed his congratulations in conventional terms in a letter to Cervini dated January 4, 1540. In the letter he referred to Cervini's "singular merits" and of his own "infinite happiness" over the news.[44] A more interesting twist on the congratulatory letter was provided by Alessandro's father. He argued that the opposition of significant individuals to Cervini's elevation constituted proof of the level of esteem in which he was held by the pope.[45] Pierluigi did not name the members of this opposition, and the suggestion that such opposition existed contradicts most other sources, which indicate that the promotions of Cervini met with virtually unanimous approval.

At any rate, Cervini similarly enjoyed the concern of various Farnese family members for his own safety and health when he accompanied Alessandro on legations in northern Europe. Alessandro's mother inquired into the health of both of them in January 1540 and wished them success in their legation as well. The genuine nature of their mutual esteem and concern is demonstrated in the continuation of such correspondence long after the death of Paul III and the end of the legations undertaken together by Alessandro and Cervini.[46] Not only did the concern of Alessandro's parents Pierluigi and Gerolama for the health of Cervini continue, but they frequently asked for his advice and especially for his influence in the papal court, both to affect the appointments they considered crucial and to assuage curial opposition to the activities of the family later during the pontificate of Julius III.

One of the more noteworthy examples of this request for influence was the plea of Ottavio Farnese addressed to Cervini in 1552. He begged the prelate's aid in convincing the pope of his continued loyalty. At one point, Gerolama even sent him a gift—a boar from their estate in Parma, which she hoped he would enjoy at his table at Christmas. In addition, Cervini continued to write frequently to them, consoling Pierluigi on the death of his sister in 1545, for example. He did whatever he could for them on a practical level, providing accommodations for a family friend on one occasion at a monastery he held *in commendam* in southern Italy. "You know, your excellency," Cervini wrote to Gerolama in agreeing to this request, "that I wish to dispose of all my possessions as if they were your own." He informed her that he had instructed his people in Naples to accommodate the woman in question whenever she expressed the need.[47]

Cervini also received lucrative promotions in the curia of Paul III as a result of this relationship. While serving as tutor to Alessandro, he became one of the proto-notaries of the court, and (at least according to Ranuccio Farnese in a story retold by Spinello Benci) Paul "did nothing of importance without first consulting Marcello."[48] If this was indeed true, Paul did not have far to go in seeking such consultation, as Cervini lived in "a room within a few steps of that of Paul III," and the two held meetings "for a certain period of time" every morning.[49] His rapid rise to prominence within the curia was later demonstrated also by his work as secretary and companion to the papal secretary of state Alessandro Farnese in 1538, and by his own appointment to the cardinalate in 1539.

Still, his influence at this stage had limits, although these were ignored by authors like Benci. If Paul III actually did do nothing of importance without consulting him first, it is difficult to understand why Cervini did not become part of the curial group formed in 1536 that framed the famous *Consilium de emendanda ecclesia*.[50] After all, Cervini possessed the sort of humanistic education and reputation for virtue that seems equated with that group made up of men almost universally held to be prominent humanists and prominent reformers.[51] For all practical purposes Gasparo Contarini, the Venetian noble who came to Rome in 1535 upon his appointment as cardinal, formed the group himself. Not only was the group made up primarily of his close friends, but Contarini himself wrote to each one ahead of time to prepare them for the invitations to be issued by the pope. Contarini also induced the pope to add the names of Archbishop Girolamo Aleandro and the Dominican Master of the Sacred Palace, Tommaso Badia, to the list that already included cardinals Gian Pietro Carafa, Jacopo Sadoleto, and Reginald Pole, Archbishop Federigo Fregoso, Bishop Gian Matteo Giberti, and Abbot Gregorio Cortese.[52] Possible reasons for the failure to include Cervini in that group are many. Although he had in common with them his education, closeness to the pope, and reputation for virtue, Cervini was considerably younger than most of them and at this time not yet an especially close friend of Contarini. He had attained in 1536 neither the public stature nor the theological expertise of the other members, and, busy with the tutelage of Alessandro Farnese, Cervini soon departed on legation as his companion.

However, the document that this committee issued was filled with ideas Cervini later echoed in his correspondence. Although the precise authorship of the *Consilium* is an open question, many historians hold the primary authors to be the unlikely partners Gasparo Contarini and Gian Pietro Carafa, the joint heads of the commission.[53] This partnership was unlikely at least in light of the contemporary assessment of these men as adversaries. If there is one man who is considered typical of the *spirituali* it is Contarini, and similarly Carafa is the prototypical *intransigente*. No matter who the principal authors of this committee-generated document might have been, the document itself stressed several things: hope in the current pope for effective reform, the need to set bishops in firm control of preaching and of the religious orders in their dioceses, and concern for clerical education. In addition, it identified papal responsibility for the current ills of the church and quite logically concluded that reform should begin, therefore, in the papal curia itself. Cervini expressed all these concerns in his later correspondence, without exception, and frequently in nearly identical language. And while these men Cervini, Contarini, Carafa, and the others might have disagreed on the particular expression of uncertain sixteenth-century theological issues like justification and original sin, they were friends, they cooperated with one another, and they held common concerns. These facts form a major stumbling block in the acceptance of the terms *spirituali* and *intransigenti* as referring to coherent parties at this time.

Nevertheless, the signatories of the document, notably Gian Pietro Carafa, Gasparo Contarini, and Reginald Pole, as well as the curialists earlier mentioned whom Cervini had met in 1524, constituted the group of friends he cultivated during the mid–1530s.[54] Already well practiced in philosophy as well as in the study and writing of both Latin and Greek, these friends encouraged Cervini in his studies. One of them, Angelo Colocci, apparently gave impetus to Cervini's continued critical studies of classical authors, though Colocci's own work employed a more poetic expression than that of Cervini.

It has been suggested that Cervini always considered his first love to be study and the collection of books, a love that he pursued both personally and on behalf of the institutional church in the form of the papal library. He found this work interrupted many times by the larger demands of the church and papacy. The first major interruption took place in 1539.

FIRST LEGATIONS

When the papal grandson and secretary of state, Cardinal Alessandro Farnese, began to undertake diplomatic legations in 1539, his tutor-turned-secretary accompanied him. A considerable amount of the correspondence from this legation survives in the *Carte cerviniane* in the form of draft copies created by Cervini for the legate, as well as draft copies for letters Cervini sent later as legate himself. As other authors have recently pointed out, it is crucial to utilize such sources in order to attain a clearer, more realistic, and more human picture of the papacy and the curia in this period.[55]

Farnese and Cervini commenced these legations in 1539 and visited Emperor Charles V in Spain and in Flanders, as well as King Francis I in France. Farnese held the title of *vicecancellario,* a position to which he had been appointed on August 13, 1535, after the death of Ippolito de' Medici. Cervini held the title *nunzio apostolico* and drafted the diplomatic correspondence that went out over Farnese's signature. The two were sent primarily to insure that a ten-year truce between Francis I and Charles V, negotiated in the previous year, was not broken. This was an essential prerequisite for the holding of a council, as had been clearly demonstrated between 1535 and 1538.[56] Peace between the two was obviously necessary to guarantee the participation of prelates from both realms at a council, since safe conduct to the chosen site had to be insured.

The monarchical designs of the two rulers, however, played an essential part in the development of their policies, and the two heads of state helped create an enormously complicated situation. Francis believed that a council would serve primarily as a step in the emperor's plan to subjugate Protestant opposition and, hence, as a step toward his ultimate goal of universal monarchy. Francis therefore emphatically opposed the notion of a council held within the emperor's sphere of influence. He also held negotiations of his own, aimed at reconciliation with French Protestants, to strengthen his connection with the Protestant princes of Germany and to further undermine the emperor's plan. Francis had another reason to take this attitude—a council dominated by the emperor, he reasoned, would be likely to issue a condemnation of his ally the king of England, which he wished to avoid. Francis desired simultaneously to remain in the good graces of the pope and to demonstrate his sincere Catholicism. He attempted, therefore, to pursue a complex policy, one complicated further by the warnings issued through the theologians of the University of Paris. They urged him to avoid connecting himself with the uncompromising positions taken by German Protestants.[57]

The emperor, on the other hand, believed that any conciliar assembly that did not meet the desires of the Protestants, that is, a "free Christian council in German lands" would condemn Protestants in absentia, thereby provoking a war of religion. He feared the prospect of such an upheaval, desiring instead a relatively harmonious empire, an essential asset for what he believed was an impending conflict with France. So he pursued his religious policy, which was parallel to some very political considerations.[58] Simultaneously, Charles V harbored the hope of a reunion or understanding between Protestants and Catholics on doctrinal issues, and this too had an effect on the Farnese legation. If, for whatever reason, Paul III was unwilling or unable to convene a council, a negotiated reunion in Germany would still produce Charles's desired effect: a united empire. Charles pursued this plan for an imperial diet from 1539 to 1541. The legation of Farnese, as well as that of Giovanni Morone and other papal diplomats, sought to stop this policy of reunion. They believed the policy would probably mean the apostasy of the entire German nation.

A reflection of many of these concerns can be seen in the instructions given to Farnese for this legation and in his correspondence. The pope instructed his grandson to understand that peace, and if possible friendship, should be the goal of the mission. He told Farnese to exhort the monarchs to leave aside their personal goals to attain this end, which would permit the celebration of a council. He considered this crucial to the church in the context of the loss of England and the rebellion of Germany and Switzerland. He instructed Farnese to insist that the provision of a remedy for this situation was largely in the hands of the monarchs.[59] Farnese then began his mission, first visiting Francis and then Charles. He successfully defused the possibility of war between the monarchs from 1539 until the spring of 1540, when he was recalled to Rome. Cervini stayed on to continue the negotiations, serving as legate from May until October 1540. His special assignment was to report to the curia the intentions and activities of the emperor, who decided that spring to hold an assembly at Speyer to deal himself with the religious problems of Germany.[60]

Cervini took up his new duties with the title of *legate,* but only after promotion to the College of Cardinals. Cervini, formerly just a secretary to the legate, needed to command the respect of those he visited as legate in his own right, and the pope apparently judged the promotion necessary to attain this end. There was something ironic in the reasoning, since Farnese became legate in 1539 at the age of nineteen, and it may well be that the secretary had been doing the real work all along.

At any rate, after his appointment to the college on December 19, 1539, Cervini received a flood of congratulatory letters from his new colleagues. Gasparo Contarini wrote on December 27 that this promotion was a great "new turn to our old friendship," adding that all the cardinals were in agreement and that Cervini's appointment brought much happiness. Contarini praised Cervini's integrity and virtue and indicated his conviction that Cervini would prove through action the validity of the strong public recommendation he had given to Cervini's candidacy. "I am most certain," Contarini said, "that your reverence will answer even more greatly with work than I demonstrated with words."[61] Reginald Pole similarly praised Cervini's virtue and gave thanks "for the blessing to the church and to the Apostolic See that your promotion represents."[62] Some of these congratulatory letters indicated that Cervini had earned and deserved the exaltation, notably that of Cardinal Cristoforo Jacobatio, the bishop of Cassano, who had been appointed to the college just three years earlier.[63] Many of the letters also referred to the influence of Alessandro Farnese and his father, Pierluigi Farnese, the duke of Parma and Piacenza, in securing Cervini's appointment.[64] Bartolomeo Guidiccione (+1549), who received his appointment to the cardinalate on the same day, gave thanks to God for the *beneficio* He bestowed on both of them, but he gave at least part of the credit to "the hot intercession" of Cardinal Farnese.[65] In a joint letter, Cardinal Ubertus de Gambara (+1548), the bishop of Tortona, and Cardinal Ascanio Parisano (+1549), the bishop of Rimini, confirmed the importance of lobbying by the Farnese. It was "the favor and help of Monsignor (Farnese) our common patron and the duke his father," they maintained, that "caused His Holiness to add you together with us in the sacred college."[66]

Cervini took seriously the added responsibilities he faced, but he expressed obvious elation over this promotion, and his gratitude to the entire Farnese family was deep. He complained that a large weight had been added to his weak shoulders while he simultaneously asked Pole to always "admonish my imperfections." Similarly, he told Contarini of his intention to do all the good that his new position of power would permit him, while requesting that Contarini also watch over his activities and inform him of any errors he might make.[67]

Cervini expressed his elation at the appointment in his letter of January 8, 1540, to Guido Ascanio Sforza, the other grandson of Paul III, who first informed Cervini of the consistory in which he was made cardinal. After thanking Sforza for the news of this honor and his congratulations, he signed the letter "Most humbly yours, the Cardinal of Nicastro."[68] The "C" of "Cardinale" is enormous, by far the largest single letter on the page. The importance of the Farnese family in this promotion was not lost, however, in Cervini's jubilation: the seal and coat of arms he adopted as a cardinal included prominently the Farnese fleur-de-lis.

While on legation immediately after his appointment as cardinal, Cervini sent letters that demonstrate further his enrapture with the ambassadorial post and the honors that went along with it, even though he was still traveling with Farnese. These letters are rich in detail and constitute a kind of travelog, in addition to describing the business he undertook. Cervini in many cases described even the time of day they traveled and the routes they took. He recounted their entry into Paris at the end of December 1539 in a letter of January 7, 1540. From the suburbs of the city they received a warm welcome, being greeted in turn by representatives of Cardinal Jean du Bellay, who served as bishop of Paris from 1532 until 1551; a number of other French prelates; four presidents of the Parisian Parlement; and four representatives of the university.[69] In that series of meetings it is likely that Cervini gained a sense of the complicated relationship between the bishop, the faculty of the university, and the Parlement, in the context of the attempted reformation of the faculty of theology of Paris some years earlier, which the bishop had supported. It is also more than likely that during this trip he made the acquaintance of Johann Sleidan, the secretary of Jean du Bellay and one of the early controversialist historians of the Protestant reformation.[70]

Beyond this, Cervini also gained from these individuals a clear sense of popular French devotional life. The cardinal and others took him on a tour of the cathedral church, during which they met a large contingent of the religious of the diocese. Cervini found himself "impressed with the piety of the people" who took holy water at the entrance to the church and who were praying privately during the chapter's recitation of the Psalms.[71]

He and Farnese finally gained an audience with the king on January 1 in the cathedral, and the days that followed were packed with meetings with such personages as the queen of France, the king and queen of Navarre, ladies of the royal court, and others from the household of Charles de Guise, the cardinal of Lorraine. A banquet at which they were all fêted featured a meal presented on tableware of gold and silver—such riches, Cervini explained, that it was not possible to imagine any greater.[72]

The occasion for this feast was the journey of Charles V to the Netherlands: he had been invited to pass through France by Francis I, who held a number of banquets, hunting parties, and jousts for him along the way. The hiatus in their dynastic struggle that made all this possible has been described by one recent author as a truce, effective primarily due to exhaustion rather than to any diplomatic efforts, especially on the part of the pope or his legates. Still, the two monarchs avoided hostilities until the summer of 1542, when Francis once again declared war. During the time he spent at the imperial court in Brussels, Cervini kept in close contact with the nuncio to France Filiberto Ferrerio, which enabled him to respond to occasional challenges with appropriate diplomatic measures. When, for example, Francis I demanded an assurance that the defensive league concluded between Charles V and the other Catholic princes in Germany really was defensive, Cervini's information enabled Ferrerio to give that assurance.[73] But despite the constant badgering Cervini was instructed to give the monarchs and their representatives—namely, to leave aside consideration of their own good and to work together for the improvement of the church—no real progress was made toward the second goal of the legation, which was to procure a general council.

Cervini frequently offered his services to further the plans of the Farnese pontificate during these legations. He issued this offer in letters to the two cardinal grandsons, as well as in letters addressed to the pope himself. "Order me," Cervini said, "and see how I desire and seek to serve you and to travel, paying back my persistent debt." Paul took frequent advantage of the offer. As a result, Cervini became employed in widely varying activities, even while occupied with more important diplomatic assignments. He delivered, for example, a cardinal's biretta to Antonius de Sanguine, the new cardinal of Orleans, during this busy legation to the imperial court, which took him to the cities of Amiens and Ghent as well.[74]

It was the intention of the emperor to settle the religious problems associated with Luther independently of any general council, and this became the cause of other negotiations that occupied Cervini's days in 1540. The correspondence generated around these negotiations illuminates the character of the legate. In the spring and summer of 1540, the emperor sought to convene an imperial diet. He planned to attend in person and, in conjunction with it, to hold a religious colloquy designed to find the grounds for compromise between German Protestants and Catholics. The compromise would be elaborated and confirmed by the diet. In his diplomatic work, Cervini depended upon two sources of information in order to provide the pope with a complete assessment of the emperor's plan. One source was his own series of discussions with the emperor, which he related in letters to Alessandro Farnese in Rome. The other source was Giovanni Morone, the bishop of Modena. Morone served at that time as nuncio to Charles's brother Ferdinand, king of the Romans (1503–1564), who was also intimately involved in the emperor's plan. Morone enjoyed the confidence of Ferdinand and was therefore an especially good source of information.

The development of this plan began in December 1539 and January 1540. Morone related to Cervini the substance of a Lutheran legation to Ferdinand that took place at that time. He explained the fear of the Lutheran representatives of an attempt by the emperor, under the pretext of reestablishing Catholicism, to subjugate the German princes, and he explained the religious demands they had actually presented.[75] They sought assurance that they would be left alone regarding three items, he related: their desire "not to obey the Apostolic See or to recognize the pope as head of the church," their desire for communion "under both species," and their desire for the right of priests to marry. Morone suggested that Cervini convince the emperor to seek the permission of the pope for the latter two items, ostensibly to eliminate the possibility that the emperor would usurp papal power and grant these demands on his own, in the name of reformation, as the king of England had done. More likely, Morone believed, such a request to the pope would fall upon deaf ears and further undermine the colloquy. Morone also suggested that the reason for all these demands was German despair over the possibility of a real council ever convening. They stood firm in their belief that the pope was not seriously interested in reform.[76] Cervini himself echoed precisely these same sentiments to the pope on other occasions.

As the plan for the imperial colloquy and diet became solidified, Paul III and his advisors consented to it but out of essentially political considerations. Charles V had granted the claims of the Farnese family to the lordship of Camerino, and the pope gave in to the demand for a colloquy and diet partly in return for this concession. The pope also apparently believed that it would be counter-productive to attempt to hold a council with Germany in such a state of upheaval and that, if the emperor's diet were held without papal representation, the Protestant side would appear to have secured a victory. He delegated Morone to attend the meetings, but with carefully circumscribed instructions. Morone himself believed the discussions to be useless, but he was told to insist that only the pope could approve the means for a settlement.[77] After some delay, the colloquy opened in Hagenau on June 12, 1540.

In the meantime, the pope and cardinals in consistory elected Gasparo Contarini as legate to Germany. They made this appointment in a consistory held on May 21, 1540. Despite Contarini's personal misgivings about accepting the assignment (elaborated in a letter to Cervini), they judged that his reputation as a reformer and his theological expertise were the qualifications needed for this mission.[78] They must have believed as well that Contarini's prominence and reputation would indicate the seriousness with which they considered the Protestant demands.

After the appointment was made but before the arrival of the new legate, Morone continued to raise, in letters to Cervini, the issue of effective ecclesiastical reform in Germany. Morone hoped that Cervini himself would come to Hagenau to meet with Ferdinand and assist in the colloquy. But even if this were not possible, Morone argued, perhaps it might be expedient for Cervini to urge the emperor to declare to the princes in writing his will to maintain the Catholicism of the German territories. These princes would in turn be able to encourage the disheartened bishops, Morone argued, in what seems a reference to their despair for effective reform suggested in his earlier letter.[79] The colloquy effected no real work until transferred to Worms, but there Morone expressed irritation at the Protestant omission of any reference to the Holy See in the opening statement. He became even less optimistic for the prospects of settlement after a meeting with the Protestant theologians Philip Melanchthon, Wolfgang Capito, and Johann Sturm—he found them adverse to the idea of reunion, and the meeting was again postponed.

The colloquy finally began on April 7, 1541, at Regensburg, the site chosen by the emperor for the diet designed to implement the solution created by the colloquy. Charles hoped for an establishment of peace between Protestant and Catholic estates in Germany, and thus for a religious settlement that would permit a greater political good—the confirmation of his own authority. The diet was, in fact, an utter failure in reestablishing relative religious or political stability, as the religious discussion broke down over issues of authoritative interpretation of Scripture and Contarini's insistence upon maintaining the concept of transubstantiation against Protestant objections.[80] Cervini's attitude over the course of these negotiations is in itself interesting, apart from the outcome of the colloquy.

Cervini maintained in this episode that Morone's concern over clerical and curial reform was important. He held this view even though he did not approve in every instance of the work being done by Morone, or of Contarini's appointment without significant qualification. He staked out a position that reflected both his determination to defend the prerogatives of the Farnese pontificate and his own conception of correct ecclesiastical reform. In doing so, he effectively distinguished between the definition of orthodox belief and the correction of clerical and curial abuses. They were, in his view, completely separate issues.

He wrote letters to Alessandro Farnese on August 8 and 10, 1540, that help demonstrate the point. After a backhanded swipe at Morone for not keeping him or Farnese particularly well informed of the status of negotiations at the colloquy currently meeting at Hagenau, he indicated that the emperor himself had asked his advice on the appropriateness of a colloquy and diet.[81] Cervini took this opportunity to explain his position to Farnese. He indicated to Charles that he ought to "consider well the danger posed by both the diet and the colloquy" to religious issues, but Cervini attempted in the process to avoid giving his complete opinion until he had received instructions from Rome. Pressed to speak immediately, Cervini went ahead. "I said," he reported, "that if we discuss religious issues in any way other than as our predecessors did, we could not hope for a good outcome." If the emperor intended through his appeal for the diet to suggest the convocation of a meeting where religious differences could be discussed, Cervini maintained, then a diet would not be improper. But if the emperor intended the diet to make determinations on religious questions independently of the Holy See, Cervini argued, then he could not possibly support it.[82]

This is not to suggest that Cervini especially distrusted the emperor. Quite to the contrary, Cervini insisted that Charles was knowledgeable on religious matters, was exceedingly Catholic, and sought only to avoid the "accelerated ruin" of Germany. Nevertheless, Cervini feared the colloquy that Paul III decided to support, and he expressed this view clearly in a letter to Farnese. "It seems to me," he said, "that we have to insure by every possible means that we do not lose our way in this colloquy."[83] He feared that in the confusion of the discussion, the essence of important issues would be lost, and, although many historians insist Cervini handpicked Gasparo Contarini as his successor in the legation to the emperor, he also harbored serious misgivings over Contarini's ability to handle such a situation. It would be an oversimplification to say he did not trust Contarini, but it would similarly be wrong to accept at face value Cervini's characterization of the legate as "wonderfully chosen." Cervini told Farnese he believed other prelates should be sent with Contarini. He had in mind prelates who possessed the sensitivity to precise theological and legal issues, as well as to the needs and concerns of the Roman curia, which he believed the Venetian lacked.[84]

This was mild criticism compared to that of others in the curia—one of these in a letter written soon after the appointment called Contarini "a brother in the flesh of Lucifer."[85] Cervini's criticism may have been in part a response to the choice of Contarini over Girolamo Aleandro (1480–1542), a cardinal who over the previous few years had been involved in the study of reform problems affecting the curia, and who was not chosen for the post for a variety of reasons. Not the least of these reasons were his ill health and his considerable role in promulgating the excommunication of Luther. One of those Cervini had in mind to accompany Contarini was Gregorio Cortese (1483?–1548), an influential Benedictine and reformer who was among the signatories of the *Consilium de emendanda ecclesia*. It is likely that another was Tommaso Badia (1483–1547), the Dominican Master of the Sacred Palace (or official theologian at the papal court) under Clement VII, who was also a signatory to the *Consilium*.[86] To all these factors influencing Cervini's assessment of the situation and his recommendation regarding what ought to be done, another should be added: he criticized the same abuses that concerned the German bishops and that were promised some hearing at the colloquy by the mere presence of Contarini. Cervini voiced this concern in his August letter to Farnese. He indicated his agreement that before the diet took place, the curia would be well advised to undertake a serious self-reformation. "The truth is," he said, "that in every other thing we are better able to defend ourselves than in our abuses."[87]

This legation and the correspondence it generated demonstrate the early development by Cervini of an interesting approach to the religious upheaval of the sixteenth century. Although at all times prior to the death of Paul III he sought to give loyal service to the policies set by the pope and his grandson, he had to balance this effort with what seems a fairly powerful personal desire to see a different, two-pronged policy pursued. He suggested that the papacy move quickly to elaborate a doctrinal but apolitical solution to the Lutheran controversy. Simultaneously, he suggested, quick action should be taken to reform on a disciplinary level the practices of the members of the curia, as they were under direct papal jurisdiction. He pursued the essential elements of this policy by recommending the plan to the Farnese family not only at this point in 1540 but also throughout his tenure as legate to the Council of Trent. (See my discussion of this in Chapters 3 and 4.) In addition, he took actions that suggested he would follow the plan directly and even more comprehensively when he attained the papal throne in 1555.

Throughout the entire period of these diplomatic duties, Cervini was especially concerned with the pope's assessment of his performance as legate. The concern is perhaps not too surprising because this legation was the first important diplomatic assignment given him in which he was directly responsible for the outcome. "I am pleased," he wrote, "that His Holiness remains satisfied with my service . . . and that it can be seen through the letters that I have not lost a chance to work for the fullness of peace, keeping before my eyes the faith and the good of Christianity."[88] Such concerns are echoed repeatedly, almost to the point of obsession, in his later letters from the conciliar period, when he seemed again especially concerned to carry out to the letter the instructions of Paul III.

Cervini's humanistic interests and research were not entirely absent from the correspondence from this legation. In August 1540 he wrote to Maffei about books and antiquities he found in Holland. Among them were "two marble inscriptions, one from the time of Severus, the other from the time of Pertinax." He considered acquiring these, as well as some books.[89] Such interest, common among scholars and *antiquarii* in this period, was significant for the development of humanist historiography, although the two disciplines of history and antiquarian studies had, even then, important differences. Cervini shared this interest, and even on legation he was continually in search of books on all subjects, especially those associated with humanism.[90] It was this set of literary, antiquarian, and humanistic concerns that occupied him during the next few years in Rome.

HUMANISTIC ACTIVITIES IN ROME: 1540–1545

Cervini arrived back in Rome in October 1540. Some two years earlier, Paul III had placed Agostino Steuco of Gubbio (1497–1548) in charge of the Vatican library, but recent study of the library indicates that by this time Cervini was actively involved in a variety of related enterprises.[91] Though Steuco was highly regarded for his learning, especially in Greek and Hebrew, it was Cervini who, from the end of

1540 onward, provided funds and encouragement for the publication of manuscripts held in the Vatican.[92] He was praised for his desire that Greek manuscripts of Holy Scripture be published first, to be followed by those of philosophy, rhetoric, and poetry. A font was even cut for these publications under Cervini's orders, but it turned out to be too expensive to use.[93] Scholars enjoying Cervini's patronage undertook much of the work.

Delayed yet again in the summer of 1541 by a trip with the pope to a meeting at Lucca with Charles V, Cervini began the publication projects in the fall of that year. At this time, his interests grew to include the publication of Latin works as well. In 1542, Francesco Priscianese printed the Cervini-sponsored edition of the letters of Pope Nicholas I, and the letters and decretals of Pope Innocent III.[94] Cervini thus began by sponsoring publication of the views of two of the most famous and effective spokesmen for the papal plenitude of power, not of scriptural texts. Cervini might well have believed a need existed for such publications, especially in the context of Protestant demands he directly experienced during his legations in northern Europe.

Through the printing house of Antonio Blado in Rome, Cervini sponsored an edition of a Greek commentary on the Gospels, by Theophilus, the archbishop of Bulgaria. Many other works followed during the years prior to Cervini's appointment as legate to the Council of Trent, in 1545. Among them were the *Assertio septem sacramentorum*, Henry VIII's treatise against Luther; the letters of Cicero; Theodoret of Cyrus's ten sermons on Providence; an Italian translation of Suetonius; and an edition of Plato with the commentary of Marsilio Ficino. He also contracted with Blado to undertake the publication of the commentary of Eustathius on Homer. It was this kind of work that led Polidorus to credit Cervini and his initiatives with the foundation of the Vatican press, while his reputation as a bibliophile and collector led to the enrichment of the library long before he became its formal protector.[95]

Cervini did not quit his humanistic and literary activities upon his appointment as legate to Trent. On the contrary, his early months there before the council opened afforded him a great deal of time, during which he worked on Greek manuscripts associates provided him from Venice. Primary among these were the works of John Chrysostom, which were later edited and published by a humanist colleague of Cervini, Genziano Herveto (1499–1584).[96] Cervini became famous for his interest in the Fathers of the church and owned an enormous collection of both the Greek and Latin Fathers.[97] Another of his collaborators in these literary projects was Luigi Lippomano (1500–1559), later the bishop of Verona, who worked for many years on a collection of the lives of the saints. Attempting to replace standard accounts of the saints with ones formulated according to humanistic historical criticism, he and Cervini did ground-breaking work. This kind of historical and literary criticism is usually not identified with them but with the later sessions of the Council of Trent.[98] Lippomano sought, as he said, "good and trusted authors," to provide the church "all that is sincere and authentic in the lives of the saints." Lippomano's collection eventually filled an eight-volume edition published in Venice and Rome, and a condensed version was published in 1564 under another title in Louvain.[99]

Cervini's primary collaborator in these works, especially during the conciliar period, was Guglielmo Sirleto (1514–1585). A classical and patristic scholar in his own right, he became custodian of the Vatican library in 1554.[100] Although it is not certain when Cervini met Sirleto, it is not surprising they became collaborators, given Cervini's interests and literary projects and Sirleto's expertise in Greek. During his period as legate at Trent, Cervini used Sirleto to track down historical information and also for translations and editorial work.[101] In his own travels, Sirleto sought out manuscripts for Cervini. The two carried on a substantial correspondence, primarily on textual, literary, and library concerns.[102] In their letters between 1546 and 1548, they discussed, among other things, the condition of the library and its holdings during the tenure of Steuco, who died suddenly on March 15, 1548. Steuco inadequately cared for the library according to one historian, and Cervini made the same assessment in his letters to Sirleto. "I pray that God may inspire His Holiness to make a good choice," he wrote in 1548, "and that the library will come to a better order than it has had in the past." Romolo Amaseo (1489–1552), Cervini's predecessor as tutor to the papal grandsons Sforza and Farnese, was considered for the post but did not receive it. Instead, later that year Paul III named the first cardinal to direct the Vatican library: Marcello Cervini. Since Cervini was in Trent at the time of the appointment, his associate Bernardino Maffei exercised the office. Cervini formally held the post until his death, as Paul's appointment was reconfirmed by Pope Julius III in 1550, and Cervini appointed no successor during his short reign as pope.[103] Cervini took this duty seriously and expressed his conviction of the importance of maintaining and improving the collection both in his words and his deeds. He procured, among other things, 143 Greek manuscripts for the library during his tenure, the last purchase being made on April 4, 1555, the same day the conclave that elected him pope opened. At the end of his life, Cervini described the library as "the greatest asset that the Apostolic See possesses, because in it the faith is protected from heresy."[104]

Thus Marcello, the obedient son of Ricciardo, entered the ecclesiastical hierarchy and remained an obedient son—of the Farnese family. Through his rapid promotion and the variety of works he was asked to undertake, he received a thorough education in the operations of the Roman curia and its relationship with ecclesiastical and political leaders in other countries. He learned to be a loyal and dependable curial functionary. But he became much more than just a functionary, because of his personal qualities, hard work, broad-ranging interests, and especially because of his candid advice and practical recommendations. This education and those qualities were tested severely during his years at the Council of Trent.

CHAPTER THREE

At the Council of Trent

THE OPENING OF THE COUNCIL

Despite Paul III's announced desire upon his election to hold the council that his predecessor Clement VII had avoided, prelates, princes, and people of the church had little reason to believe it would ever come to pass. Paul convened and postponed a council no less than five times in the first six years of his pontificate.[1] The failure of the Diet of Regensburg in 1541 to make any steps toward reunion with Protestants and the warnings—even by Gasparo Contarini—that the hated heresy would soon spread over the Alps spurred papal action, but there was also a very real threat of a war that would render the convocation of a council impossible.[2] Political considerations led to both the suggestion and the abandonment of cities such as Mantua, Ferrara, Modena, and Cambrai as possible sites for the council. Giovanni Morone gained agreement on the city of Trent, but the proposed convocation there on All Saint's Day (November 1) 1542 never occurred because of the declaration, by Francis I, of war against the emperor, on July 10 of that same year. Legates had been sent, but after six months the number of prelates who had come to the council was still small. Eventually, two of the legates were recalled, and a commission of cardinals was set up to study the problem. Among them was Cervini.[3] In the same month that Francis declared war, Paul III suspended the council in a secret consistory.

Only the emperor's threat to settle the ecclesiastical disputes of Germany at an imperial diet and the Treaty of Crépy of September 18,

1544, reopened the door for a council. Due to the threat, the pope feared a partisan solution from the diet, which he judged would be dangerous to both church unity and his own authority. The treaty ended the war between the emperor and the king of France, and in a secret clause Francis I abandoned his opposition to a council and stated that he would agree to the convocation at Trent, Cambrai, or Metz, on a date to be determined by the emperor.[4] The papal curia again issued a bull of convocation, setting the date and location as March 15, 1545, at Trent. This time Cervini, Giovan Maria de' Ciocchi del Monte, and Reginald Pole were selected to serve as legates and to preside at the council. Along with the appointment made on February 22, 1545, each of them received a monthly stipend of five hundred scudi, designed to cover all their personal expenses.[5] Monte received the status of first legate or president of the assembly. When he failed to attend sessions due to episodes of gout or other illness, Cervini presided in his place.

The bull of convocation, entitled *Laetare Jerusalem*, was read in the consistories of November 19 and 22, 1544. In the bull, Paul III expressed his joy that the long process of arriving at peace and of calling the council was finally over. He stated the objectives of the conciliar assembly in conventional terms that suited the resumption of so venerable a tradition as the meeting of a general council: the elimination of religious discord, the reform of the Christian people, and the liberation of Christians in territories held by the Turks.[6]

In organizing the congregation, Paul III acted according to the principle, well established especially after the Council of Basel (1431–1447), of retaining full control over the proceedings. Like Julius II, who at the Fifth Lateran Council (1512–1517) sought to control the assembly and prevent rebuke for his delay in convening it, Paul wished the council to be carried out completely under his authority.[7] This action reflects Paul's character as it has typically been understood: he brought men with serious moral purpose and outstanding educational credentials into the College of Cardinals and was not entirely opposed to holding a council, but he was intent on maintaining the authority of his office, like any good Renaissance prince.[8] In his case, that authority happened to be religious as well as political. Paul took several actions to ensure that his program for doctrinal and disciplinary reform was sustained on the occasion of the convocation of the meeting at Trent. He made the personal attendance of bishops obligatory and forbade the employment of procurators, with the exception of German prelates.[9] He parted from the fifteenth-century tradition of voting by nation and instituted an individual vote.[10] Under this voting system, he expected and relied upon both the loyalty and the numerical superiority of the Italian bishops.

The real key both to that loyalty and to Paul's general control of the assembly at Trent was the position and the powers he granted the legates. Paul gave Monte, Cervini, and Pole wide-ranging powers as papal legates to the council. While presiding over the assembly, they had the exclusive right of proposal in the council. This meant that throughout the proceedings they held full control of the agenda for the meeting. In addition, though the three were empowered to preside together, the principle that Cervini or Pole could replace Monte as president if he became ill was extended even further by the pope on March 8, 1545. On that day he issued a brief that gave full power over the assembly to each of the legates personally. A separate, secret bull gave the legates the power to transfer the council if necessary, and even to dissolve it. They further possessed the right to wield ecclesiastical censures if any of the conciliar prelates chose to question such powers.[11] Although the bull of convocation stated three objectives for the council, only two of them could actually be carried out by the assembly: the settlement of doctrinal controversies and the disciplinary reform of the church. Crusades against the Turks would come later. Through his legates, Paul indicated that during the deliberations of the council, doctrinal settlement was always to take chronological precedence over disciplinary reform. Widespread dissatisfaction, led by the emperor's opposite listing of conciliar priorities, later forced a compromise on the issue of order in treating the two topics under these two headings. The legates nevertheless always retained exclusive control over the council's agenda.

The simultaneous plan for the emperor to spearhead a military campaign against the Schmalkaldic League led to another postponement of the assembly. In the course of developing this plan, the emperor forged an offensive alliance with the pope, and when the alliance became known German reaction delayed the opening once again.[12] Cervini was irritated by this last postponement. He opposed the offensive alliance in principle and, in addition, had spent long months as legate promoting peace so that a council might be held. He reacted strongly, and he related some of his reaction in the legates' common letter, which he drafted, to Alessandro Farnese. Having gone through the trouble of making arrangements for the council and waiting for the order to open it, they faced a dilemma: open the council against the wishes of secular rulers with the threat of war overhanging (which would make it impossible for many to come, undermining the ecumenical character of the meeting) or wait, with heresy growing, and still further delay effective action against ecclesiastical abuses.[13] Cervini intimated his own disappointment, not only over the delay but over the very idea of an offensive military alliance, in a personal letter to Farnese. "We have not used the year of peace well," he said, "and when we wish to hold a council, we cannot. The Pope can give better aid against infidels and heretics with an open council than without."[14]

With the arrival of prelates from Spain and France as well as from Italy, during the summer of 1545, the council took on at least a pretense, if not the fact, of universality or ecumenicity. An assurance that the council would open on December 13 even arrived in Trent on November 7, but that was still not enough to dissuade the fears of those convinced the opening would again be postponed. A German bishop even wrote to Cervini that the packing of his bags for Trent was the occasion for laughter and derision from his family and friends.[15] Only on December 11 did the legates receive the formal order for the opening of the council. Monte celebrated the Mass of the Holy Spirit on December 13, and it was determined that the first working session would be held on January 7, 1546. The discussions that took place immediately after the opening proved that Paul's concerns with establishing firm control of the assembly had been well advised from the papal point of view. Although discussions touched procedural, doctrinal, and disciplinary concerns, it could easily be maintained that power, control, and authority were the real issues at stake.

The heritage of conciliarism, especially from the councils of Constance and Basel, insured the continuation of the power struggle between the pope and the council fathers over procedures.[16] Paul III and those closest to him in 1545 feared a repetition of the confusion and contention for authority between council members and the papacy that characterized the meetings at Constance (1414–1418) and Basel (1431–1435). In addition to the possibility that the council fathers might attempt to seize independent control of the proceedings, Paul was not a young man and was in questionable health. His death could provoke a crisis over ecclesiastical authority unmatched since the Great Western Schism. Cervini himself, just after the opening of the Tridentine assembly, informed the papal court of the existence of attitudes similar to those held at Constance and Basel. There was fear on the part of many of a repetition of the events, he said, "at Pisa and Constance, which confirmed dogma but left the reformation to Alexander V and Martin, and nothing else was done."[17] He mentioned the dragon of conciliarism, which both he and the pope feared, for a particular reason: to spur Paul to undertake the serious reform of the Roman curia that might alleviate pressure on the papacy. Indeed, the powers Paul gave to the legates demonstrate that he intended to ensure no repetition of any of those events. He even issued another bull as a kind of insurance policy. *Ad prudentes patris familias officium* stated that the College of Cardinals held the exclusive right to elect a successor in the event of his death, and that the conclave must be held in Rome or another city under papal control, even if he were to die while physically present at the council.[18]

Disputes and disagreements concerning doctrinal matters discussed at the early sessions could often be reduced to a sort of jousting for power and authority. The so-called imperial party attempted frequently to delay discussion of certain dogmatic points, arguing that clerical and especially episcopal residence should be discussed first. Their intention, in Cervini's opinion, was to force by this means the reform of the Roman curia, which they believed the pope had no serious desire to undertake. At the discussion on the list of canonical scriptures, the question of certain traditions and their weight relative to Scripture was raised. Some argued against placing the two on the same level, not unlike Luther's approach to the question.[19] In the discussions on biblical study and preaching, to cite another example, the question was quickly raised of the episcopal right to supervise preachers who were members of religious orders. Similarly, in regard to disciplinary issues, questions of authority were implicit. Perhaps taking as a model Sigismund, the king of the Romans who pressed for the convocation of the Council of Constance, Charles V asserted throughout this period that he would personally attend to religious disciplinary reform in Germany in the absence of a council. He certainly doubted Paul III's determination to treat such problems, and at the same time he asserted his own competence in religious matters.

The prelates who attended the opening sessions of the council reflected these disputes directly. They can, for all practical purposes, be divided into two groups: the Spanish and Neapolitan imperial party and the mostly Italian papal or curial party. The French, one might argue, constituted a third group, but at this time their numbers were small—just six prelates and three ambassadors—and, although technically independent, they opposed the imperial group more often than they opposed the papal group.

The imperial party included, among others, Cardinal Francesco Mendoza y Bobadilla (+1567), Bishop Pedro Pacheco of Jaen (+1560), Bishop Francisco de Navarra of Badajos (+1563), and the bishops of Astorga, Huesca, and Lerida, who all came from Spain and had long careers in the ecclesiastical hierarchy.[20] Their associates from Naples included Bishop Giovanni da Fonseca of Castellammare (+1559), Bishop Coriolano Martiranno of San Marco (1503–1557), and Bishop Enrico Loffredi of Capaccio (1507–1547).[21] Loyalty to the emperor's program at the council could be expected from these prelates, and in addition there were a few German procurators in attendance, as well as a representative from Charles V's native land, Bishop Roberto de Croy of Cambrai (+1556). Yet another imperial loyalist was Cardinal Cristoforo Madruzzo (1512–1567) of Trent, the host of the assembly.[22] Madruzzo faced the unenviable task of providing hospitality to a group of prelates who did not relish the idea of residing in the foothills of the Alps, especially during the winter.[23] Over all of these was the emperor's *orator* or ambassador, Don Diego Hurtado de Mendoza. Among the prelates, the strongest leaders were Madruzzo and Pacheco. During the opening sessions this group concentrated on the problems of reform, and from the outset they urged that the assembly assert its autonomy from the pope. They demonstrated this most clearly in their ultimately unfulfilled desire that the title of the council be changed to include the words *universalem ecclesiam representans*. It has been suggested that, like the Spanish bishops at the Council of Vienne (1311–1312), they sought an increase in episcopal power achieved at the expense of the power of the Roman curia.[24] Whether or not one agrees with the tone of that assessment, it is certainly true that they desired to see discussions on reform commence immediately with the opening of the council, to see those discussions touch all levels of the church hierarchy and include the topics of benefices, clerical residence, and the *cura animarum*. In regard to this last issue especially, they received the sympathy and cooperation of the small Portuguese group that desired reform in the same areas and distrusted the curial party.

The papal or curial party was not a national group, strictly speaking, as its members identified themselves according to the city or region in Italy from which they came, and because it included prelates such as Olef Magno, the bishop of Upsala who, though originally from Scandinavia, had for years been a curial dependent. Moreover, while all Italian bishops were in theory ordered to attend the council in 1545, in practice, after the formal opening, Italian prelates were then "chosen" to attend based on the criterion of who would be most faithful to the program of the Holy See.[25] Yet their cooperation was anything but guaranteed. An example of their sometimes independent (if not incoherent) attitude, which often bothered the legates and the pope, can be found in Tommaso Campeggio (1481/83?–1564). A doctor in both civil and canon law who had a long curial career, Campeggio became bishop of Feltre in 1520. One of the few Italians trusted and esteemed by the Dutch pope Adrian VI (1522–1523), he seemed, at least through his dedication to his diocese and closeness to Gian Pietro Carafa, enamored of rigorous ecclesiastical reform. But he concerned himself with providing a reform that would not overturn curial traditions and practices (perhaps an implicit contradiction) and even addressed to Paul III in 1537 a memo on the topic of how such a reform might be applied to the Datary. Nonetheless, he was considered to be of pro-imperial tendencies, and Julius III (1550–1555) found little that pleased him in Campeggio's later service as legate to the council.[26]

A considerable number of such problems existed during the first period of the Council of Trent (1545–1547), and the papal grandsons Alessandro Farnese and Guido Ascanio Sforza (Cardinal Santa Fiora, the head of the *camera apostolica*) used public reproach and correction to attempt to force non-conformist Italian prelates back into line with the rest of the papal majority. The standard authority on the activities of Italian prelates during this period of the council argued that, although this might constitute an example of intolerance, it is incorrect to assert that the freedom of the council was thereby compromised.[27] Cervini attempted other forms of manipulation in this context, which might argue for another conclusion, and these will be described later (see end of this chapter).

This curial group pursued the goal, notwithstanding such differences, of insuring that papal authority be upheld. They desired, especially in regard to reform topics, that no new regulations be established, but rather that existing law be applied rigorously. Their support for the translation of the council to Bologna in 1547 is a case in point: without the change in location, according to the legates and their supporters, a sufficient number of curial loyalists could not be retained to control the assembly. With such violently contrasting aims and programs, difficulties and disagreements at the council were in abundance. And other situations added to the tension. Paul III ordered four members of the new Society of Jesus to be sent to the assembly as theological experts; three of them did in fact attend. The presence of this Spanish group raised eyebrows, especially among the Italian prelates. This was due in part to the accusation of heterodoxy faced by Ignatius and his followers while at Alcalà and Paris. As one of the papal legates, Cervini worked hard to defuse such disagreements and to insure that business ran smoothly. He deftly handled the problem with the Jesuits. Long impressed by their learning and piety, Cervini asked one of them, Diego Lainez (+1565), to serve as his confessor. The confidence demonstrated by that request was reinforced by the Jesuit display of erudition and theological expertise at the assembly, and a number of other Italian prelates followed the example of Cervini in appointing Jesuit confessors.[28]

CERVINI'S DUTIES AS LEGATE

Cervini undertook a wide variety of responsibilities in his role as legate. He personally oversaw the appropriation of papal funds for the council, the drafting of correspondence with Roman authorities, and the publication of conciliar decrees, as well as more mundane but very delicate problems such as organizing the seating arrangement in the assembly. In regard to monetary provisions, Cervini counted upon the assistance of Antonio Manelli, the *depositario*, who lived in Cervini's household and apparently kept track of disbursements there as well. Not only did Cervini, through Manelli, pay the subsidies necessary to enable poorer prelates to attend the assembly, but he also retained soldiers to insure protection and safety for the congregation at large. The need for such monies became desperate at times, and Cervini took it upon himself to make such situations clearly understood in Rome. He wrote to Bernardino Maffei, for example, in 1548, when payment for the soldiers in Bologna was long overdue, and begged him to speak with the reverend *padrone,* Alessandro Farnese, and to exhort him "to deeds and not just words" so that they might be paid without delay. Cervini feared violent consequences if such provision was not made.[29] Most of the requests for monies to be contributed to poorer prelates for living expenses appear in correspondence addressed by the Cardinals Legate to Guido Ascanio Sforza or to other curial figures, but the vast majority of these letters Cervini wrote himself, and rough drafts of the letters can be found in the *Carte cerviniane*. "We do not wish to continually bother you," Cervini wrote in October 1546, "but do not be late in sending the money for the subsidy of the poor prelates." He clearly suggested that prompt payment of the stipend was the only way to maintain the presence of Italian prelates who were anxious to find an excuse to go home. Cervini paid out an average of twenty-five scudi per month to each of the prelates, out of the funds provided by Rome. Compared with the six scudi per day paid by the emperor to insure the participation of those who would loyally support his policies, Cervini wielded considerably less leverage. In the first period of the council the number of subsidized prelates never exceeded fifteen, while a few received extraordinary subventions to purchase such necessities as winter clothing. Although these monies were crucial to the prelates who received them, the sum was certainly not enough to suggest that votes were thereby purchased for the papal program. The payments might have insured the presence of those already loyal to curial policy, but they never were used in an attempt to bribe a member of the opposition into conformity with the legates and their plan. There simply was not enough money involved to purchase votes.[30]

Cervini faced a different but still serious problem regarding the order of seating. On May 16, 1545, Cervini wrote on behalf of the other legates and advised Rome that "we expect a dispute" over the order of seating in the council, especially on the part of some German bishops, who were also princes. At issue was the honor accorded individual bishops in the order in which the prelates were seated. It affected the Germans most directly because of their status as prince-bishops. They expected such status to grant them priority in the order and were concerned as well about the places accorded their vassals. After the first working session of the council, Cervini reported to Maffei the solution of the problem and the seating arrangement used, but the problem came up again just five days later, when an order for seating the ambassadors in attendance was required.[31] Cervini did not work alone on this problem, either, as a three-member commission oversaw the adjudication of the dispute. Bishop Filiberto Ferrerio of Ivrea (+1549), Bishop Giovanni Tommaso Sanfelice of Cava (1494–1585), and Bishop Tommaso Campeggio of Feltre comprised the commission, and they did so at least in part because of their position as the three senior active bishops in attendance.[32] As part of the solution worked out, cardinals took the first place. Bishops followed, seated in order according to the date of their promotion. The ambassadors in attendance on behalf of princes and kings took a place between the cardinals and bishops. In order to underline the distinction between voting members of the assembly and those without such right, the diplomatic representatives remained standing during the solemn sessions in which votes were taken on the approval of individual decrees.[33]

The conciliar fathers brought up a seemingly infinite variety of complaints over the physical environment of Trent and the work that was demanded of them. These complaints, rather than creating a major problem for Cervini, instead provided him with something he needed. The complaints focused around poverty, Trent's high prices, and the terrible cold they expected in the coming winter. Not only the legates, who had been complaining about such things since their own arrival, but also all the prelates gathered in August 1545 agreed it was inconceivable that sessions could be held in the frigid church during the winter and that the inconveniences of holding a council in Germany (not the least of which was the slow exchange of mail) were simply too great. They considered the lack of popular support, which they defined as "the obstinacy of Lutherans" and the "neglect and coldness of the Catholics" in Trent, yet another part of the intolerable situation.

These complaints became a set of reasons Cervini transmitted to the pope, which might serve as ammunition in convincing the emperor to agree to a transferal of the council even before it opened. The pope hoped that the assembly might be held within the territory he controlled personally, thus enabling him to count realistically on the presence of larger numbers of Italian prelates through which he might control the proceedings. (Paul did gain such a transferal in the spring of 1547.) Cervini provided this information to the pope through Ludovico Beccadelli (1501–1572), the legates' emissary, who traveled to Rome to report on the arrival of prelates for the conciliar assembly. Prelates continued to make these complaints throughout Cervini's tenure, and in this complaining at least one of the legates provided leadership. Monte, the president of the council, held Trent responsible for everything from the toothaches and headcolds he suffered to his melancholic moods.[34]

Such tasks, however, also help to point out Cervini's primary duty: to serve as a mediator between the conciliar fathers and the Roman curia, while consistently upholding the papal program. In this job, he said, "poor Marcello is terribly harassed and broken down," as those who hoped it possible to "speak in the council regarding the authority of the Apostolic See are battling strenuously" with the legates.[35] He made these comments in January 1546, but opposition to the papal program as carried out by the legates was expressed on still other issues even before the formal opening of the council.

CERVINI AS MEDIATOR

In the summer of 1545 Cervini faced the challenge of pacifying prelates in their complaints over the physical environment of Trent, but once the time of formal inauguration became imminent, the problems shifted focus. Shortly before the first session, the Spanish imperial faction made a suggestion. They argued that the council's title should be changed to include the words *universalem ecclesiam representans*. The legates first asked for advice and instructions on this issue in a letter to Alessandro Farnese written on January 5 and 6, 1546. They hardly needed to wait for a response, as they knew the curia would want to exclude those words, because of the possibility they would be understood as the Spanish faction intended: granting the council independent, autonomous power, separate from the papacy. Cervini argued that such a formulation was not necessary, as Antonio Massarelli (+1566), the secretary of the council and later bishop of Telese, recorded in his diary. During the assembly of January 8, Cervini indicated that the phrase had been used infrequently in the past (in fact just fifteen times) and only in order to act against a pope when there was doubt about the existence of a legitimate papacy. He cited the examples of John XIII (965–972),

Benedict XIII (antipope, 1394–1423), and Gregory XII (1406–1415) and added, "in such cases the 'universal' church was truly in the council" because technically there was no pope. No such doubt existed in 1545, so he attempted to find a middle ground between the two demands, urging that the words *oecumenica et universalis* be added instead. Paul III in all his letters and briefs regarding the council had used the same words, Cervini argued, adding, "the reverend legates can thus hardly call it otherwise."[36]

With this action Cervini merited only a rebuke from the pope, who seemed fond of neither formulation. Paul became upset not so much over the implicit expression of opposition to papal authority embodied in the request to change the title, as by the legates' slowness in reporting the situation. Cervini bore the brunt of this stern criticism, addressed to him by Alessandro Farnese. Cervini above all, Farnese said, should know the mind of the pope and his desire to be advised fully on all the proceedings, no matter how small. He was pleased to learn specifically who opposed the papal program at Trent, but he preferred to receive his first notice about new controversies at the assembly from the correspondence of Cervini, not from some other source while on his evening walk in the piazza.[37]

The controversy continued through the winter and into the spring of 1546. Monte protested in February that "undoubtedly the pope alone" had convened this congregation, but he apparently convinced few of the other prelates. Cervini brought forth a barrage of evidence in the general congregation of April 1, 1546, attempting to prove that the formulation had not been used by ancient councils and other sources of authoritative teaching. He cited everything, from the Gospel according to Matthew to Gregory the Great and Gelasius, to the decrees of church councils from Carthage to Pisa and Constance. At the end of this exercise, which was a display of what Cervini considered humanist methodology in practice, he suggested that the standard formulation *ecumenical and general council* be used, as it had been in the past, and it was, in fact, the one finally employed.[38]

A dispute also arose in the opening sessions over the right of abbots to vote in the assembly. In all likelihood, the real issue was the power of bishops to reform monasteries and even to restrict the jurisdiction of abbots in their own dioceses. Again, Cervini reinforced the reasoning of the pope. He argued that the rights of abbots be maintained, at least in the conciliar congregation, and he used language that put the abbots on an equal footing with bishops. "They have the privilege to use both the mitre and crozier," he said, and "the pope called abbots (to this congregation) . . . you are not able to exclude them."[39]

In both these disputes, the same prelates opposed the papal program. They were Diego de Alaba of Astorga, Francisco de Navarra of Badajoz, Enrico Loffredi of Capaccio, and Braccio Martelli (1501–1559), the bishop of Fiesole.[40] Cervini sought to refute their arguments and to embarrass them, and he obviously viewed them with no small degree of contempt. He seemed to enjoy, as he related in a letter to Maffei, "scrambling (their) understanding vigorously," while "speaking clearly of the authority of His Holiness." At one point, early in the sessions of the council, he even called them collectively the *repugnanti*.[41]

It was an impossible assignment, even a contradiction perhaps, for Cervini or anyone else to mediate fully between the pope and these opposition prelates while simultaneously upholding the outlines of the papal program. Once Cervini received the rebuke of the pope over the issue of the title of the congregation, he focused his efforts on pleasing the pope and other curial authorities rather than the opposition prelates at Trent. But in choosing, to coordinate the passage of the papal program in the council, someone who would not appear unfair or overtly heavy-handed, Paul III could not have been more shrewd. Many have attested to Cervini's simple and sincere piety, to his inclination toward a broad-ranging reform evident from his earliest days in Rome, and to his untiring patience in listening to theologians and prelates at the council.[42] Cervini created through such qualities a foundation upon which he could be trusted by the vast majority of prelates at the council. He demonstrated sincerity, hard work, and above all learning, in the arguments he presented in defense of the papal agenda. He was consistent, and his colleagues knew what to expect from him.

The pope's trust, on the other hand, must have been based upon Cervini's relentless support and loyalty, demonstrated throughout his ecclesiastical career. Perhaps Paul had a right to expect such loyalty because of his personal sponsorship and promotion of the legate, but Cervini himself frequently mentioned his debt to Paul and to Alessandro, as well as his desire to repay it through hard work and loyal service. When Alessandro and others questioned his actions, Cervini replied in disbelief that anyone could think he pursued anything other than to carry out the papal program and to defend papal prerogatives with intense vigor, and in the most efficient and persuasive manner possible. "From the beginning of this council until today," he said in response to Alessandro's criticism in January 1546, "not only have we always maintained the authority of His Holiness without diminution, but also sought to elucidate it more and more."[43] For Cervini, this was more than a matter of simply doing his job or repaying a debt. Despite his disagreement at times with the steps (or lack thereof) that Paul took in pursuing his program, Cervini genuinely believed in the validity of papal prerogatives and the practicability of employing them in the work of reforming the church.

HUMANISM AND PRAGMATISM AT THE COUNCIL

Cervini believed that he understood the papal goals for the council as stated in the bull of convocation and reinforced by continual repetition in the correspondence from Rome, and he consistently recommended pragmatic methods to carry them out. The bull indicated that the two main tasks of the council were to be the resolution of doctrinal controversies and the reform of clerical morals and discipline. Cervini well understood that, for Paul, the "resolution of doctrinal controversies" referred not to a reconciliation between Protestant and Catholic doctrinal differences—the pope believed that to be impossible even before the failure of the colloquy at Regensburg—but rather to a clarification of Catholic doctrine and its presentation in a unified form, rather than according to the divergent opinions of competing Catholic theological schools. He also understood that the disciplinary reform of the church, an overhaul demanded from many quarters over a very long period of time, would require several different things. Among these were a reform of the Roman curia as well as of the monastic mendicant orders, remedies for clerical ignorance and moral laxity, and a redefinition of the lines of ecclesiastical authority. Like the majority of his colleagues in the Italian episcopacy, Cervini did not believe a council was the proper forum for the latter problem, but he did believe that a council could solve the former dogmatic problem. He employed his considerable administrative skills to accomplish that goal, continually stressing the need for efficiency and for a humanistic search to identify the proper solutions.

In this search, Cervini insisted above all on access to ancient and original texts and on imitation of ancient councils. His response, seen above, to the demand for a change in the title of the conciliar assembly constitutes a clear example of that attitude. Another example can be found in the first decree issued by the prelates in Trent. After the long delay in convening the council and getting down to business, Cervini believed it was important to accomplish something in the general congregation of February 4, 1546. In the very first general congregation (December 13, 1545) the prelates merely agreed to the date of the succeeding session to be held after the Christmas holidays. In the second (January 7, 1546) they issued an exhortation to the people of Trent and to all in attendance at the council to conduct themselves moderately, piously, and with attention to prayer. These were hardly substantive decrees. To begin the consideration of real issues, Cervini apparently considered it important to address something on which the prelates could come to quick agreement. With discussions incomplete on the other issues currently on the agenda, the legates did not want the session to pass without a vote on some matter. They chose to issue a profession of common faith at least in part over this concern to issue a decree with some substance. In addition, Cervini maintained, such an action would constitute proper imitation of earlier councils. This decree, he wrote to Maffei on February 5, 1546, "was made first in order to imitate the ancient councils, and then in order not to allow this session to pass without a vote on something." In the common letter of the legates to Farnese describing the same day, he repeated the concern over imitation of earlier councils.[44]

Later that month, the council became embroiled in debate over the list of canonical scriptures and which books of the Bible belonged on that list. Cervini again employed the pursuit of sources and imitation of earlier councils to solve a difficult problem. Cervini and his colleague Reginald Pole would have liked to have seen each book of the Bible examined and voted upon singly, but they were persuaded to follow the lead of Monte and gain acceptance of the list issued by the Council of Ferrara-Florence (1438–1439). A group of the prelates, led by Diego de Alaba and Giacomo Nacchianti, the bishop of Chioggia, denied the validity of this document.[45] They argued that the list was completed after the departure of the Greeks and Armenians from the assembly at Florence (thus questioning its ecumenical character) and that it also failed to include the clause "Sacro approbante concilio" (with the approval of the sacred council). Without this clause, the document would fail to conform to the conventions followed in drafting conciliar decrees and, hence, its authenticity would be suspect. The legates considered agreement on a list of canonical scriptures crucial, because heresy had frequently in the past been based on the misinterpretation of Scripture and because the Lutheran position in 1545 called into question the authoritative status of at least one book in the canon, the Epistle of St. James. Cervini wrote to Farnese and to Maffei, asking that the original bull or a certified copy be found and sent to Trent in order to settle the dispute. Maffei secured and sent the original, which arrived at Trent on March 28. Cervini found that the text included the disputed clause and irrefutably proved the bull's validity. This attempt to convince his adversaries had an unforeseen and negative consequence: the original document was lost, apparently in transit, after this episode at Trent.[46]

On this occasion as well as others, Cervini and his colleague Monte consistently urged the conciliar fathers in the theological discussions to argue not according to their own opinion, but according to concepts held by the ancient church.[47] Clearly, Cervini searched the most ancient texts for one purpose only: in order to authenticate desired religious teachings and practices by the precedent of the ancient apostolic church, which he considered normative. That was the method of a humanist. In this work, Cervini employed other scholars as well. One such research adviser was Bernardino Maffei. Cervini asked him in November 1545 for a copy of Pius II's commentary on the Council of Basel.[48] He utilized this in the speech he made to argue against the change in the title of the Council of Trent urged by the opposition prelates. Guglielmo Sirleto, one of the most important Greek scholars in the ecclesiastical hierarchy at this time, was another. He first came under the patronage of Cervini when he was needed as an assistant in the literary and publication projects of the prelate before the convocation of the council. Sirleto also worked closely for Cervini during his years as legate, looking up historical information and theological opinions in Roman libraries and sending the results of the research to Cervini, who employed the information in the theological discussions he chaired. Sirleto provided data on a variety of issues, from analysis of versions of the Old Testament that may have been used by the apostles to views on the sacraments held by Fathers of the church for the writings of Saint Irenaeus on the authority of Peter.

Sirleto, who became cardinal in 1565, even carried out Cervini's directions for the administration of the Vatican library during his years as legate at Trent. Later still he composed his *Annotationes in Novum Testamentum [contra Erasmus]*, at the request of Cervini.[49] The correspondence between these two while Sirleto was engaged in the project suggests that Cervini assigned him the task out of conviction that Sirleto was the only individual qualified to undertake the project. There can be no doubt that Cervini viewed the work as necessary, but there is little evidence in the letters to indicate that Cervini in any way directed the effort, and virtually no mention at all of Erasmus by name. The two may have worked out a strategy for the project together in person, not in written form, but there is likewise no evidence in Cervini's letters of any such strategy. Where there is discussion of the work in his correspondence, Cervini praises Sirleto's progress and leaves issues of content to his personal discretion.[50] But, after all, Sirleto was the better Greek scholar of the two, and Cervini knew it. It is interesting and puzzling to find few references and no extended treatment of Erasmus in Cervini's papers. The attitude Cervini held toward the great humanist remains, therefore, obscure.

Cervini served in the same consultative capacity for other Roman curial figures. He attempted to provide information, for example, to Gregorio Cortese, who was attempting to locate the most authentic copy of the canons of the eighth general council of the church, also known as the Fourth Council of Constantinople (869–870). In April 1545, Cortese inquired if Cervini knew of the location of a copy of the documents in Rome, or if he might have a copy with him in Trent. Cervini responded that he did not possess a copy, and he also used the occasion to write a letter to Agostino Steuco, urging more careful administration of the papal library.[51] Cervini did secure a copy on July 23 from the emperor's ambassador to Trent, Don Diego de Mendoza, who had arranged that some Greek books and manuscripts, acquired from the library of San Marco, be brought from Venice. Angelo Massarelli, a member of Cervini's household and the secretary of the council, related the gift of Mendoza in his diary, as well as Mendoza's gift of a life of Pope Urban V (1362–1370) and documents from a number of other Greek synods.[52] Cervini instructed Massarelli to make careful copies of the material and for good reason, since there were no copies in Rome. In addition, Cervini probably found interest in both the life of Urban V and the synod at Constantinople: Urban attempted in his administration at Avignon to restrain the same monetary abuses Cervini disdained in the Roman church of his own time, and the synod treated issues like lay interference in episcopal elections, the problems associated with ending schism, and the affirmation of Roman primacy, all of which were crucial issues in the sixteenth century. But the copy of the synod documents was soon no longer needed, as Mendoza, apparently overjoyed at the visit of Cervini to his sickbed a few days later, gave the legate the original recovered from Venice. Cervini forwarded the document to his friend Cortese later that fall.[53]

In the conciliar discussions regarding Bible study, Cervini also expressed his concern for humanistic learning and methodology. He urged a direct return to scriptural and patristic sources in clerical education, for two reasons. First, he found contemporary theological study unappealing: theologians tended to study the sacred writings through the use of commentaries rather than the original texts. As a result, their understanding of Scripture was at best indirect, and they focused instead on theological controversies, which were of no practical consequence or real instructional value, at least for a popular audience. Second, he found that this adversely affected pastoral care: preachers trained in such a system could not avoid the speculative problems and philosophical language of the schools. But a return to direct study of the sources, he suggested, might permit explanation of doctrine in biblical and patristic terminology, more easily understood by an unlearned audience.[54] Cervini expressed these ideas in a meeting at Trent on March 1, 1546, the first day the issue of biblical reform was discussed. The enthusiastic response for these ideas led to a decision by the legates to establish a commission to investigate more fully the problems with scriptural study and to suggest particular remedies. Later that spring, Domingo Soto (+1560), a Dominican theologian and one of the outstanding proponents of scholastic theology at the council, shot down this enthusiasm, arguing that scholasticism provided a stronger weapon against heresy, and the impetus for a more humanistic approach to clerical education was abandoned.

Cervini found in doctrinal disputes at Trent another opportunity to apply his desire for the recovery and understanding of sources. Although he did not believe that reunion based on a compromise with Protestants was possible or desirable, Cervini insisted that, during the debates on the sacraments and other issues, Protestant criticisms be understood. With the help of his theological advisers Girolamo Seripando and the Jesuit Diego Lainez (+1565), he examined Luther's *Babylonian Captivity*, Melanchthon's *Loci Communes*, and other Protestant texts. Seripando also made a series of excerpts from heretical books, which constituted, for all practical purposes, a list of their errors, and the list was examined by the conciliar theologians.[55] After preliminary versions of the decree on justification found their way to German printing houses and were reproduced along with Protestant counter-arguments, Cervini anxiously sought access to those criticisms. He procured copies of the Protestant-annotated edition of the Catholic exposition of justification as well as new editions of texts written by Luther himself. Cervini obtained the texts through an agent in Venice.[56]

Cervini believed that reference to ancient authorities and ancient practice in the church was important in the modification and correction of sixteenth-century religious practices. He demonstrated this in a series of letters exchanged with Seripando in the summer of 1547, while he was still busy as legate to the now-translated Council of Trent at Bologna. Cervini and Seripando had first worked together some years earlier (1543–1545), when Cervini served as a judge in a jurisdictional dispute over the administration of an Augustinian monastery in Venice influenced by the Council of Ten, which Seripando sought to reform as part of his work as general of the order. Cervini apparently was able to convince two members of the opposition to change their minds, and Seripando emerged as the victor in the dispute.[57] In 1547, the two worked together again, as Cervini attempted to complete the preparatory background work necessary for the upcoming discussion of conciliar theologians on the topic of indulgences, a set of concerns that were settled by the council only in 1563, long after Cervini's death. In one letter he asked Seripando to look into the topic, particularly when he was in Rome, "where the use of these indulgences is more common than in other places."[58] Cervini concerned himself particularly with indulgences granted in the stational churches of Rome. There was a cycle of stational visits by the bishops of Rome that may have begun as early as the third century. This cycle was primarily penitential in nature and was most often held during Lent and Advent. The pope and parish clergy from Rome commonly processed to one of the stational churches, where an elaborate liturgy would then be held, and an indulgence was associated with participation in the event. In the early sixteenth century, the processions were not common, and they did not become fashionable until the latter part of the century, during the pontificate of Sixtus V (1585–1590).

Cervini asked Seripando to seek out the most ancient sources relative to these indulgences, either in printed and manuscript sources or in the marble inscriptions at the individual churches themselves.[59] In another letter to Seripando from this period, Cervini expressed his own assessment of another topic relevant to the problem of indulgences and, in general, to the consideration of contemporary religious practices. After he had received a letter from Seripando dated July 19, 1547, Cervini wrote that, in his opinion, the problems associated with indulgences did not stem from their origin or from their use, but rather from the fact that the severity of penances imposed by confessors had changed over time. As a result, he maintained, indulgences were now superfluous. Canonical penance in the (ancient) church, he argued, "justly took into account two things: divine justice and ecclesiastical discipline, and these together made the penance long and severe, and prohibited the penitent from communion during the time of penance, with the exception of the moment of death." The church, "not wishing so many to go without communion for so long," he said, "decided to separate the two aspects, diminishing that part that is due to the church." Indulgences were used, he argued, to lighten harsh penances that in sixteenth-century practice were no longer employed. Perhaps, he suggested, the part due to divine justice ought to be treated as it was in the ancient church and according to apostolic practice—it "ought to be imposed by the confessor, either tacitly or outright, as something that was owed by the penitent, either in this world or in the next."[60] That way, Cervini apparently believed, indulgences would be more meaningful and more correctly understood.

In contrast, Cervini displayed a concern for and insistence upon efficiency, designed not so much for the purpose of arriving at a truth that all could accept, but for arriving at an orderly and rapid conclusion to the council. Truth "that all could accept" he seemed to have considered a contradiction in terms, and, under the circumstances that existed between 1545 and 1547, he judged Paul's plan the best and acted accordingly. First, in order to get the papal program adopted, Cervini needed prelates. He needed a representative body that, at least by its numbers if not by its international character, would help give the decrees authority. No one, with the possible exception of the legate Monte, could have been more sensitive to this problem than Cervini. The two of them arrived together in Trent on March 13, 1545, and spent nine months waiting for (among other things) the arrival of a sufficient number of prelates to warrant the opening of the council. When Monte and Cervini first arrived, there was only one other prelate there to meet them, in addition to Cardinal Marduzzo, the host. The representative of the emperor, Diego Mendoza, arrived next. Other prelates appeared very slowly, and even the Italians really began to arrive only in May 1545. The presence of foreign prelates was needed to make the assembly appear more truly representative. For that reason, the legates wrote on more than one occasion to the pope, urging not only that he order the attendance of all bishops but that he suspend or even remove from their benefices those prelates that chose not to comply. When the legates finally proclaimed the opening of the council on December 13, of the twenty-nine cardinals, archbishops, and bishops in attendance, sixteen were Italian, and thirteen were from other countries.[61] Of the five generals of religious orders present, four were Italian. These numbers failed to lend the international tone to the assembly that the legates had in mind, but it was a beginning.

Cervini personally received most of the letters written to inform the legates that certain prelates (for reasons of age, ill health, or the performance of other duties) would either be late in arriving or would not come at all. He continued to receive such notifications throughout the spring and summer of 1546.[62] In addition, the subsidies paid to poorer prelates prior to the opening of the council had to be continued throughout Cervini's tenure as legate, to insure their participation. Cervini described in October 1546 what he considered to be the three keys to the success of the papal program at the council, and he identified among them the necessity to "retain here those who wish to leave." He recommended an increase in their subsidy, "not twenty-five scudi per month," as he said, "but fifty or one hundred scudi according to the rank of persons," since they were threatening to depart from Trent. He seemed to suggest that if the pope were not willing to make this increase now, that he might later need to provide much more money as an incentive to return.[63]

Once the prelates were at Trent and participating in the discussions, Cervini sought cooperation. He critically assessed the help or hindrance provided by individual prelates toward the accomplishment of the papal agenda and meted out praise or blame, even rewards or punishments, based on that assessment. The praise or blame he usually reported to the Roman curia in his correspondence. In cases where forceful correction was necessary, in addition to notifying Rome, he delivered verbal criticism to the offender in person. The rewards or punishments Cervini issued were monetary and usually separate from the subsidies paid to those who could not support themselves at Trent. The rewards appear, for all practical purposes, to constitute bribery.

Cervini held nothing back when describing prelates who opposed the legates. Cervini almost continuously faced the opposition of the bishops of Fiesole, Capaccio, and others, who apparently took it upon themselves to insure that the legates' ability to direct and control the assembly was something less than complete. But Cervini became most concerned with them when they sought, as he said, "to enlist the Cardinal of Trent" Madruzzo, the host prelate of the assembly, to lend authority to their activities against the papal program. Apparently he believed Madruzzo's influence would sway other prelates. In describing these men to Alessandro Farnese, Cervini called Capaccio the "most malicious" of the group, and Fiesole "foppish." He also placed the bishop of Chioggia, Giacomo Nacchianti, in this group and identified the basis of his opposition as pride and ambition. After he issued a warning to Cardinal Madruzzo of Trent, Cervini hoped that he would "return to the right path" and not be influenced by the group. When Madruzzo received Cervini's warning, and then letters from Alessandro Farnese encouraging his cooperation, Madruzzo apologized and even asked the pardon of the legates for the discussions that had not gone smoothly during the early sessions, promising to make it up to them in forthcoming meetings.[64] The disputes over the title of the assembly and the voting rights of abbots were the episodes to which Madruzzo referred, as he and those who sought to use his influence were at the heart of each.

Cervini extended criticism to other prelates, like Hermann von Wied, who took actions contrary to the religious policy of the papacy. Wied, who served as archbishop of Cologne from 1515 until 1547, sponsored discussions between the theologians Johann Gropper (1503–1559) and Martin Bucer (1491–1551) in an attempt to formulate a plan for the reformation of his see. As a result of the discussions, Gropper produced a Catholic reform program that enjoyed favorable curial reaction, but Wied decided not to implement it and instead adopted a plan formulated by Bucer.[65] This "Cologne Reformation" came under attack from both Catholics and Protestants, and Wied persisted in his refusal to abandon the Protestant innovations allegedly found in the plan by Gropper and others. Cervini wrote a terse comment on the situation, addressed to the pope through his secretary Bernardino Maffei. "It is best not to tolerate any longer the insolence of the Archbishop of Cologne," Cervini explained, "because the Holy See is lowered thereby." The pope apparently took the advice of Cervini in this matter, since he issued a bull of excommunication against the prelate just twelve days after Cervini sent his opinion.[66]

In contrast, Cervini supported those prelates who aided the papal program. Among them were Tommaso Caselli (1511–1571), the Dominican bishop of Bertinoro; Giovanni Michele Saraceno (1498–1568), the archbishop of Matera; and Pietro Bertano (1501–1558), the Dominican bishop of Fano.[67] Cervini praised these men, and frequently contrasted them with the *repugnanti*. Caselli, Cervini said, "from the beginning has always conducted himself well, and among other things, he is the remedy for the bishop of Fiesole."[68] Cervini praised Saraceno and Caselli in the same letter, which he wrote on behalf of all the legates, and recommended that the two be rewarded for their service. For Saraceno, he said, a dispute over a pension he had to pay but could not afford ought to be settled in his favor by the pope. He urged that the settlement be quick and final, so that this cloud would no longer hang over the prelate. He argued in terms Alessandro, as one of the largest accumulators of benefices in the sixteenth century, could understand—Saraceno was a man of a certain quality and needed to maintain a lifestyle that reflected it, and this was a large part of the reason he could not afford to pay the pension.[69] For Caselli, Cervini recommended a transfer to the vacant diocese of Umbriatico. Cervini urged this transfer as a reward, but he added that Caselli desired it because it was closer to his hometown. This consideration, Cervini indicated, was more important to Caselli than the fact that the benefice was worth fully one hundred ducats more than Bertinoro. Cervini and the other legates believed that such encouragement would expedite the council in the long run, and he urged Alessandro to recommend the action as vigorously as he would for a brother.[70]

In a personal letter to Farnese and in another document referring to the same matters, Cervini indicated emphatic approval of both the recommendations and the real consideration behind them: to encourage adherence to the papal program. Speaking of Caselli and Saraceno, he argued, "Both of them merit these and greater rewards." Later, he recommended the granting of an additional benefice to Saraceno in a further attempt to alleviate the pension problem. A vacant abbey should be given to him, Cervini argued, not only because of his assistance "from the first day" in favor of the papal program at the council, "but also to serve as an example, so that it will be seen that those who . . . pay their debt of reverence to His Holiness and the Apostolic See are remembered for their service and receive some remuneration."[71]

The legates made another recommendation in 1546. They suggested in a letter to Farnese that the priorate of San Severino be given to the conciliar secretary, Angelo Massarelli. He happened to be a relative and compatriot of the holder of the benefice, whose health was rapidly deteriorating. They argued that Massarelli had served the council diligently and merited some gratitude. They urged Farnese to persuade the pope to reserve the apparently soon-to-be-available benefice for the secretary. Cervini undoubtedly pushed Massarelli's cause in this matter, for when he did in fact receive the appointment in 1548 Massarelli addressed his thanks to Cervini. The bestowal of previous benefices, he explained, was something he never sought actively, but this one, "which has been added to my honor and that of my family . . . has changed me." He had learned through a relative in Rome, he added, the value of the benefice.[72] Without question, Cervini believed that actions such as these would expedite the council and, in addition, help to achieve the desired results. To cite another example, Cervini recommended Girolamo Seripando for an archepiscopal see because of his work in the difficult project of drafting the Tridentine decree on justification. When Seripando finally did gain such a see (that of Salerno in 1553), Cervini expressed satisfaction. As he said in another context, "in the end, rewards and punishments are what help one govern the world well."[73]

Cervini participated in the issuance of penalties or punishments at Trent much less frequently, but they too did occur. The infamous Saturday afternoon discussion on July 17, 1546, which ended in fisticuffs, resulted in one example. A dispute took place between the Franciscan bishop of Mylopotamos and Chironissa, Dennis de Zannettini (+1566), also known as Grechetto, and Giovanni Tommaso Sanfelice, a Neapolitan and the bishop of Cava. Zannettini appeared at Trent due to the urging of Cervini, for whom he had worked earlier procuring Greek manuscripts.[74] Sanfelice held the post of papal commissary at Trent and worked closely with Madruzzo, overseeing accommodations, provisions, and postal service for the prelates. He also helped to keep those in attendance apprised of events in Germany. The problem between the two began when Sanfelice actively employed Lutheran terminology such as *servile will* and *sola fide* during the early debates on the problem of justification. Zannettini, who was infamous as one historian said, for finding "heretics in every corner," opposed Sanfelice and responded during the debates by characterizing Sanfelice and other prelates like Contarini, Pole, and Morone as "crypto-Lutherans."[75]

At the end of the Saturday congregation, as some of the prelates were leaving, Zannettini muttered that Sanfelice's opinion on the two states of justification was held out of either arrogance or ignorance. Sanfelice overheard, and when he questioned Zannettini on his comment, the latter repeated it loudly enough for all to hear. Sanfelice responded to the public affront by striking Zannettini and pulling at his beard.[76] The congregation reconvened later that evening and recommended that Sanfelice be incarcerated, even though he was apparently guilty of a personal injury punishable by excommunication. The prelates adopted this lenient position at least in part because of Sanfelice's service to the council as commissary, and to Zannettini's clear provocation. The legates ordered Sanfelice to be placed in a cell in the Franciscan convent of San Bernardino and recommended that his share of the papal subsidies be distributed among the other prelates. They later advised Rome that no restitution of the subsidy to Sanfelice was necessary or desirable upon his release. Sanfelice left Trent at the end of August that same year to reside in his diocese. It is interesting to note that even this event spurred controversy over the question of papal authority relative to the council. The legates maintained that Sanfelice should seek absolution from the pope, while the imperial party insisted that the issues should be settled by the council. The council did finally adjudicate the issue when Zannettini himself argued on Sanfelice's behalf.[77]

In addition to these concerns over personnel, Cervini insisted from the very beginning on efficiency and a pragmatic approach when it came to procedural issues. During January and February 1546, he and the other legates discussed the order in which to take up the topics of dogma and reform. They suggested, on the recommendation of Tommaso Campeggio, that the two be considered simultaneously. They made this proposal to create a compromise between the papal and imperial positions on the order of proceeding. The pope desired dogmatic questions discussed and settled first, while the emperor wished reform topics to take precedence. Each reflected his own particular conception of what constituted the most important business for the council to undertake, and naturally a parallel confrontation developed among the assembled prelates at Trent: the legates and their supporters favoring the papal position, Madruzzo and his supporters favoring the imperial position. Campeggio suggested the formulation of a dual agenda as a compromise between the two stands, but the reasons in favor of the plan that Cervini ventured were of a different nature. While looking at dogmatic issues, Cervini said, "by attending at the same time also to the reformation, the council will be able to finish more quickly."[78] In his proposal, Campeggio envisioned that it would be carried out by dividing the assembled prelates into three groups, each presided over by one of the legates. Each group would then take up one of the three stated concerns of the council, enumerated in the bull of convocation: dogma, reform, and peace. Cervini viewed the division of the prelates as an efficient solution, and indeed, by balancing in each group the supporters and opponents of the papal program, it was hoped the groups could be managed effectively. The three groups could digest, he said, the matters in question before they were raised in the general congregation. This prior analysis, he believed, would simplify and expedite later discussions. The legates set up the divisions. Cervini headed the dogma group, made up primarily of theologians; Monte headed the reform group, made up primarily of canon lawyers; and Pole headed the peace group.[79]

The triple division was short-lived. This was due in no small part to papal dissatisfaction with the plan and to the difficulty the legates had in managing it. Farnese communicated the pope's displeasure with the arrangement in a letter dated February 7, 1546, but he said that since the commissions had already been established, it would be difficult to abolish them without the appearance that the order had come directly from Rome. Nevertheless, the division was abolished in the spring of 1546, and the council came to be divided into two commissions instead: one for dogma headed by Cervini, and one for reform headed by Monte. This arrangement reflected the real work of the council and also certain practical considerations, as Pole departed from Trent for reasons ostensibly related to health in late June 1546. In reality his departure might also have been linked to his dissatisfaction over the tone and content of the decree on justification. This rendered the tripartite division impossible. Even though he departed, Cervini and Monte still sought Pole's advice and service on questions faced by the council.[80]

In one of the more humorous passages from the correspondence of Cervini, Maffei reported the reflections of those in Rome on the division of the assembly. The two of you, he said, "have acquired the names of Martha and Mary." He added a joke on clerical celibacy and reform, stating, "it is expected from your reverence that priests will be able to take wives in order to do a double penance for their sins."[81]

Cervini easily brought together his role as chairman of the dogmatic commission with his concern over the efficient and expeditious implementation of the papal program. He understood and agreed with Paul III's desire. They sought first to settle the dogmatic issues through decrees that clarified the Catholic faith and that pulled it out of the muddle and bickering that characterized late medieval theology. Only then should the disciplinary reform of the church be undertaken. In addition, on the basis of his actions at Trent in this first period and on the basis of the conception of ecclesiastical authority he elaborated in his letters, it appears that Cervini believed the settlement of dogmatic issues was the only work that properly belonged to the council. (For that conception of authority, see Chapter 4 below.) With great energy and hard work he proposed to create solutions for a long list of complicated dogmatic issues. These included the formulation of a list of canonical scriptures and the elaboration of a unified position on several questions: original sin, justification, and the relative importance of Scripture and tradition in theological study. Cervini focused the work of his commission upon these issues throughout the first two active years of the council, 1546 and 1547.

Cervini planned the work of the council during these years, partly out of an interest in the theological problems to be ironed out in the decrees and in the methods employed to do so. Yet his ideas did not always meet with the approval of the rest of the assembly. He and Seripando agreed, for example, that the Vulgate edition of the Bible represented a correct explanation of the faith but that at particular points it needed correction through recourse to the most ancient texts in the original languages. They urged, therefore, a limited correction, to be followed by approval of the text as a standard.[82] This idea was somewhat discounted in the decree on Holy Scripture, however, which approved the Vulgate edition as it was, indicating that the text should be printed "in the most correct manner possible," but without suggesting any systematic emendation.

During the discussions and negotiations over the decree on justification in the same period, Cervini gave evidence of two other attitudes—first his conviction that on key doctrinal issues the Protestant position was wrong and second his conviction that any formulation other than that approved by curialists in Rome ought to be abandoned. Cervini apparently liked the treatise on justification written by Seripando in July 1546, and why not, since the theologian conspicuously avoided dependence upon scholastic terminology that Cervini disdained.[83] When Seripando orally delivered the substance of the treatise, he received a favorable reaction from the assembly (in part because of his considerable rhetorical skills), and Cervini ordered Seripando to draw up the first draft of a decree. Seripando did not receive a favorable response to this effort, however, either from the assembly in Trent or from the curia in Rome. Cervini ordered him to prepare a new draft, which Seripando submitted on August 11. Although Seripando provided a drastically different proposal, over the next few months it was dropped by Cervini, who had a final version prepared, not by a theologian in the dogmatic commission, but by Monte and another prelate in the reform commission, Cornelio Musso (1511–1574), the bishop of Bitonto.[84] Cervini did this without informing Seripando, who was extremely disappointed with the final wording of the decree, and who believed that it reflected fear of Lutheran errors rather than providing a convincing argument for another, more correct position. Cervini had turned his back on a man whom he consulted on every other important theological issue, and whom he once described as "a man sent from heaven to support . . . our work."[85] Seripando, with good reason, probably considered the move an insult. Cervini turned his back for no other apparent reason than that the Roman curia was dissatisfied with Seripando's draft.

Cervini also attempted during this period to get preparatory work done for the decrees to be written later on the sacraments. He maintained that lengthy discussion of these topics would be unnecessary due to broad Catholic consensus on sacramental issues. He did, however, represent real zeal on the correct understanding of the Eucharist, both in his words and in his actions. He corrected theologians in the dogmatic commission especially on errors relating to this sacrament, and he even distributed communion personally in an attempt to reinforce his points.[86]

While Cervini undertook this sort of work in the dogmatic commission, he simultaneously called, more and more frequently, for direct papal intervention in the area of disciplinary reform. Hubert Jedin argued that all of this activity and, in fact, Cervini's entire emphasis on dogmatic questions as well were designed with one purpose in mind: to give the pope time to initiate curial reforms and thereby avoid the possibility that the council would do so itself.[87] Cervini clearly provided the time, but the pope just as clearly failed to take the urgency of reform seriously. Cervini pleaded with the pope incessantly to begin reforms in the papal curia, and the letters issuing these pleas demonstrate Jedin's point. But the letters also demonstrate that Cervini believed reform on all levels of ecclesiastical government, not just the curial, ought to be undertaken immediately by the pope himself.

HIS RECOMMENDATIONS ON REFORM

Cervini wrote recommendations to the papal curia on the conduct of Catholic efforts to reform ecclesiastical practices while he was at the council. Over the months he gradually issued stronger and stronger appeals, but his primary concerns were always practicability, expedience, and safety. Even before the council opened, he recommended in April 1545 that the pope furnish a carefully and "sweetly" worded brief, exhorting the German bishops to accept the episcopal consecration they had avoided and to look after the pastoral duties with which they were entrusted. He urged Paul III "not therefore to wait until the last minute," but to seek a solution more rapidly in order to please God. No particularly outstanding piety is suggested in this statement, for he pursued another, practical goal in this recommendation: to initiate papal-ordered reform efforts before the imperial diet took action on its own.[88] Cervini later wrote that papal reform of the curia and of the Datary would "shorten the council by several months," and still later that, without such work, the Apostolic See would lose the obedience of many. This reform, Cervini said, "I wish that His Holiness would make himself and not leave . . . to the discretion of the council." He urged the pope to "take the more secure and more honorable position" and undertake the reforming task himself, believing that in this way the pope would "better resist both the disordered desires of the princes and the malice of some bishops."[89]

The recommendations Cervini made are significant for a number of reasons. First, he argued in favor of the same sort of action urged by other writers in this period. He stood, therefore, in continuity with the ideas circulating at the Fifth Lateran Council, as well as with those elaborated in the *Consilium de emendanda ecclesia*.[90] Lest one focus too much on the similarities, it is important to note that the idealistic tone of the earlier authors of reform programs like Giles of Viterbo and Cajetan is absent in Cervini's recommendations. His were formed within a number of different contexts. First, Cervini developed his ideas within the diplomatic context of papal administration. The second context was a social one: the needs of local episcopal administrators in their attempt to improve devotional life in the diocese. The third context was humanistic in origin: the desire to bring the sixteenth-century church into line with a simpler, more apostolic (and therefore more valid) mode of government.

Cervini's recommendations were also significant because they were taken seriously by Paul III and reflected in his later actions. Paul issued a reform bull on December 31, 1546, which aimed at the office of the Datary, and he made another decision on February 18, 1547, which forbade the accumulation of multiple bishoprics by cardinals. Although dispensations continued to be given frequently from these regulations, they laid a certain groundwork for the decisions of the later sessions of the council undertaken by Pius IV (1559–1565), which themselves were in part due to the arm-twisting of Emperor Ferdinand I.[91] Perhaps most important, Cervini clearly stated in his recommendations an important and interesting conception of how power and authority should operate in the church.

CHAPTER FOUR

Sixteenth-Century Ecclesiastical Authority

Marcello Cervini was by no means a theological expert. Similarly, he did not undergo formal training in canon law. All prelates who advanced to the level of ecclesiastical government attained by Cervini certainly had a familiarity with and practical experience in handling theological and legal issues, but only some of them received training that would qualify them as specialists. So it is not surprising that Cervini left no lengthy theological statements or opinions, no treatises on questions pertaining to canon law, and no especially thorough or original comments upon problems discussed at the conciliar sessions he attended. It is not surprising that he relied upon Seripando and the Jesuits Alonso Salmerón (1515–1585) and Diego Lainez (1512–1565) for theological advice at Trent, and that he personally preferred to work behind the scenes and debates at the assembly.[1] Nor is it surprising that his conception of how authority in the church is derived and exercised can best be seen by observing his activities as an ecclesiastical legate and administrator.

Just as Cervini followed a pragmatic and efficient course in his duties as legate to the Council of Trent, so he presented a practical and pragmatic attitude toward authority and power in the church. He gave evidence of this attitude before, during, and after his period as legate at Trent and consistently attempted to create realistic, workable results by urging popes to make better use of their power and by exercising power himself as an administrator. He urged the adoption of what he considered to be the most efficient means of arriving at church reform, whether it be through the elaboration of papal authority, in settling issues at the council, in applying episcopal authority in a diocese, or in treating the relationship between ecclesiastical and secular authority. He placed great emphasis in his correspondence on the efficient exercise of legitimately delegated authority at the two essential levels of ecclesiastical power: the level of the papacy and the level of the episcopacy. He placed emphasis on the exercise of authority at a level that belonged particularly to the church of his time in Italy: the level of the vicar or visitor in an individual diocese or monastery. Those from whom jurisdiction emanates, Cervini maintained, have the authority to change, revoke, or moderate it, and to reform those to whom such jurisdiction has been granted. This authority according to Cervini stemmed, naturally and in all cases, from the Apostolic See. Indeed, Cervini, like many of his contemporaries, was concerned with the prestige of the papacy and was unable to conceive of a general reform of the church that did not proceed from the papal office as its center.[2]

PAPAL AUTHORITY

Cervini consistently upheld papal authority as a general concept in addition to recommending its practical application in specific areas. At times, he privately acknowledged his belief that the papacy had slipped from its position of moral authority in the ancient church, the model he adopted as an ideal. He suggested that this authority was held in the past due to the holiness of the institution and that a degeneration from holiness to sinfulness was the cause of deterioration in papal moral leadership. He indicated this on several occasions to Alessandro Farnese, in rather guarded language. He chose his words carefully for good reason, since Alessandro was the grandson of Cervini's patron and employer—the incumbent in that see. In 1540 he urged Alessandro to persuade his grandfather to commence a serious reform of the curia to improve their bargaining position with Charles V. "It is true," Cervini said, "that in every other thing we are better able to defend ourselves than in our abuses." On another occasion he wrote that the reputation of the Apostolic See "is not as it was in ancient times, because of our sins."[3] There was nothing especially new about this line of reasoning, for in the recent past both Pope Adrian VI and the authors of the *Consilium de emendanda ecclesia* had made the same point.[4]

But Cervini always held firmly to the belief that the papacy was an institution set up by God himself, and that it held supreme authority over the entire church. He stated it clearly in 1541, in a long instruction he drafted on behalf of Alessandro Farnese. It was to be sent to Gasparo Contarini, currently on legation to the Diet of Regensburg. Cervini outlined a reproof as much as an instruction, which accurately reflects his own view as well as that of the Farnese family. "The whole authority was given by God to Saint Peter," he said, "first in the words 'I give you the keys of the kingdom of heaven' after the Passion, and then at the time of the Ascension . . . 'feed my sheep.' " Avoid, Cervini told him, words that suggest that after establishing "the hierarchy of the church and placing in it bishops, archbishops, patriarchs and primates, God then constituted the Roman pontiff to serve the unity of the whole." For these words, Cervini added, "serve those who say the pontiff is useful to conserve the church but was not ordained specifically by God, and [those] who wish all bishops considered equal to him."[5]

Contemporary prelates, notably Reginald Pole, made the same argument for essentially the same reasons. Pole explained the derivation of papal authority from the identical scriptural passages in his text *De concilio liber* and expressed the hope that such an understanding might lead Protestants to accept Roman primacy.[6] Cervini restated the argument in a more personal letter addressed to Bernardino Maffei, not long after the assembly at Trent had been convened. Now that the council is open, he said, "it is time with all diligence to hold this body united and obedient to the pope." Using a mystical body analogy, Cervini added that the pope "is head of the assembly," and can "affect in the members love and charity." By demonstrating that he intends to keep account of the actions of those at the council, the pope can insure "that no questioning is possible of whose authority is greater."[7]

In the instructions to Contarini, Cervini also insisted that no aspect of papal authority be given up in the course of confrontation and disputation with Protestants. Earlier he wrote to Contarini and expressed his hope that a settlement on dogmatic issues could be arranged, but papal authority, he believed, was non-negotiable. "Do not," Cervini wrote, "under the desire for concord consent to some determination that is not completely Catholic," instead, "remit all to the Apostolic See." "The authority of the pope," Cervini asserted, "has to be upheld by the Protestants too," and concord on all the other disputed points would be in vain if disagreement remained on that more important issue.[8] This attitude was also common among churchmen of Cervini's time, even among those like Gregorio Cortese, who were credited with a "conciliatory" approach toward Protestants.[9] The true road, Cervini maintained, was the course mapped out by God, and directions for it came through the Apostolic See. He made this point again clearly in relaying money from Rome to Contarini while he was on legation to Regensburg in 1541. The money, Cervini explained, was designed to be distributed among German princes participating in the League of

Nürnberg. This Catholic league, created in 1538, planned to counter the Protestant League of Schmalkalden, and the papal funds were to be used, apparently, in the development of a military power that could reduce the other league to Catholic obedience, by force if necessary. The League of Nürnberg was ineffective, although it lasted for eleven years. The pope was also more than willing to spend the same money, Cervini explained, to reach a solution without violence. He hastened to add that the pope had no intention to bribe Protestants into agreement. A bribe would have the effect of reinforcing their "damnable opinions," he believed, and would simply lead to "greater errors." A penalty, not a reward, should be the result of deviation from Catholic doctrine, he suggested.[10]

Cervini believed that Protestants' dogmatic innovation excluded them from Catholicism, as did their position relative to ecclesiastical authority. During his legation to Trent, Cervini wrote to Maffei, "Do not be afraid of the imperial prelates' assertion that they can make an accord with the Lutherans . . . they [the Lutherans] are accustomed to doing that which is better for themselves . . . for the true cause of the discord," he added, would not "easily allow a compromise." But Cervini did believe in treating these issues with the hope that eventually Protestants would be enlightened by God, return to their senses, and return to Catholicism. He told Contarini at Regensburg to keep his "eyes open," in case God might grant the grace necessary for them to return to the "true road." He later linked this hope with the opening of a general council to discuss the disputed doctrines. By means of the council, the Catholics would keep the door open for the return of Protestants to the church. The heretics, he suggested to Alessandro Farnese, would be less irritated by the actions of a council than by the correction of the pope alone.[11]

In an instruction to preachers in the diocese of Gubbio, Cervini used the controversial terminology of the *plenitude of powers* to reinforce his explanation of the concept of papal authority. The document is undated but can be assigned to the years 1544–1555, the period in which Cervini oversaw the diocese as an episcopal administrator.[12] In regard to indulgences, he told his readers to teach that there is an inexhaustible treasury of merits found in Christ and in the saints. He added that it was the right of the pope to dispense this treasury by virtue of the papal plenitude of powers.[13] By linking these two concepts in his discussion of indulgences, Cervini followed in a long line of discussion stretching from Gregory the Great (590–604), whose prototypical "absolution" meant an intercessory prayer for the remission of sins to be pronounced by a holder of the apostolic power of the keys. Extension of the use of indulgences was theoretically justified in a full sense only in the thirteenth century. At that time, Hugh of St. Cher (1200–1263), reflecting the earlier insistence of Huguccio (+1210) that jurisdiction must be held over recipients of indulgences, elaborated the doctrine of the "treasury," arguing that every sin has been punished in the sufferings of Christ and the martyrs, and that the church holds the keys to this treasury. Thomas Aquinas (1225–1274) reserved the application of indulgences to the pope alone, since he heads the church to which the treasury allegedly belongs. The crucial statement on indulgences, which Luther rejected in 1518, was the bull *Unigenitus* (1343), of Clement VI (1342–1352).[14] Even after Cervini's death, papal control over this application was reaffirmed by Trent. The council indicated that bishops must report to the Roman See on indulgences granted in their churches. The pontiff would decide if these were to be continued, so that indulgences would be granted "holily" and "without corruption" in the future.[15]

Similarly, *plenitudo potestatis*, the concept through which application of the treasury was justified by Cervini and many others, was fully elaborated only in the late twelfth and early thirteenth centuries by Huguccio and Innocent III (1198–1216), especially at the Fourth Lateran Council (1215).[16] After the conciliar period, Eugenius IV (1431–1447) and his successors Nicholas V (1447–1455), Pius II (1458–1464), and Paul II (1464–1471) gradually reasserted this definition of papal primacy.[17] They accomplished this not only through Pius II's famous bull *Execrabilis* (1460), which declared that decisions made by a pope could not be appealed to a future council, but also through the efforts of canonists in the papal court like Lorenzo Aretino (fl. 1440), Rodrigo Sánchez de Arévalo (1404–1470), and Juan de Torquemada (1388–1468). In two tracts written in the late 1460s, Arévalo for instance argued that *plenitudo potestatis* meant that the pope's power was equal to that of Peter and that all reform must come through papal initiative. Torquemada also presented the papacy as the sole source of ecclesiastical authority and the church as fundamentally hierarchical in nature.[18]

Cervini used the term *plenitudo potestatis* in a manner consistent with such theories, as well as with its use by other Roman curialists in the sixteenth century. Both those curialists who would be termed controversialists and those who might be called humanists accepted the notion of papal *plenitudo potestatis* and a rigidly vertical understanding of the derivation of church offices, but for different reasons. The controversialists upheld it because they viewed Luther's doctrinal challenge as an implicit attack on papal primacy. Cervini must have been familiar with such arguments from Cajetan's (Tommaso de Vio's) 1511 and 1521 tracts on papal primacy, entitled *Tractatus de comparatione auctoritatis papae et concilii* and *De divina institutione pontificatus romani pontificis.*[19] Cervini, like Cajetan, focused considerable attention upon the texts "Tu es Petrus" and "Pasce oves meas" in his discussion of papal power. He was undoubtedly familiar with the ideas of Ambrogio Catarino as well. He may also have known other controversial texts, such as the 1518 work of Silvester Prierias, *In praesumtuosas Martini Lutheri conclusiones de potestate papae dialogus,* and the 1521 work of Cristoforo Marcello, *De authoritate summi pontificis et his quae ad illam pertinent adversus impia Martini Lutheri dogmata.*[20]

Roman humanists, on the other hand, were probably imbued with a better historical sense of Peter's actions and certainly were confronted on a continual basis with constant reminders of his life and work in that city. But they could also find support for their views on papal authority in patristic studies. For example, Chrysostom, with whom Cervini was more than a little familiar, sustained Petrine primacy in a manner that suggested *plenitudo potestatis.* He did so in his elaboration on Matthew 16:19 and John 21:16–17, the two biblical texts Cervini cited in his letter to Contarini. Cervini employed the text from the Gospel of John in his preaching instruction. In these uses of the notion of papal primacy, however, he failed to cite any other authorities, beyond a vague reference to the fact that all the doctors of the church agree on this point. Even Contarini used similar suggestions in his own written reaction to Melanchthon's 1530 edition of the Augsburg Confession, entitled *Confutatio articulorum seu quaestionum Lutheranorum.* In that text, he focused no doubt upon honesty of life, humility, and imitation of Christ as the essence of pontifical and episcopal power. He did not explicitly use the terminology *plenitudo potestatis,* but argued that innumerable citations from sacred letters and the Fathers uphold the primacy of the pope, suggested universal leadership, and stated that in practical terms the unity of the church required that primacy.[21]

Cervini represented, therefore, continuity with both the controversialist and the humanist line of curial reflection on the meaning of *plenitudo potestatis,* but he did not seem to agree with the extension of the term to the papal exercise of secular authority. Under Julius II, for instance, the concept was employed to urge the pope to attain, or even to attempt to surpass, the model of Roman imperial greatness. This is a crucial distinction, because it suggests that Cervini did not affirm papal authority with the intention of fully supporting the growth of a form of papal monarchy that became the prototype for later European absolutism. On at least one occasion, Cervini took direct exception to such activity. He indicated in a letter to Alessandro Farnese his belief that war "is not the art for priests" and elsewhere suggested that spiritual and temporal power are two separate things that should remain separate.[22]

Cervini therefore disagreed with certain applications of the concept and also seemed to limit his explicit use of the term to his 1541 instruction to Contarini and his recommendations to the preachers in Gubbio. But still he was, for his time, what Jedin called him, the "decisive defender" of the notion that the papacy was the only source of legitimate authority in the church.[23] He considered *plenitudo potestatis* as a given, unquestionable element in the proper structure of the church. Unless he accepted this, there would be little reason for him to recommend the concept to preachers in his diocese, for their defense of papal employment of the "treasury of merits" in the form of indulgences. Many of his colleagues disagreed vigorously with him, notably the Spanish and Neapolitan imperial party at the council.

In addition to upholding a general theory of the papal plenitude of powers, Cervini developed his views on *plenitudo potestatis* and applied them to the issues of curial reform, the general council, and ecclesiastical benefices. It was most urgent, Cervini believed, for the pope to initiate reform of the papal curia and the College of Cardinals, especially once the Council of Trent had opened. He called for this work incessantly in his letters to Maffei and Farnese. He wrote an especially large group of letters in late December 1545 and in January 1546. In them he expressed his belief that this part of the general reform of the church should be carried out through direct papal action in the form of a bull. Papal action was the most proper method, he maintained, and was also the safest method. It was proper, he said, in fact "it is true and holy that the reformation begin in the house of God, that is, the church and sacristy."[24]

He considered it the safest method for another reason. Cervini expected that if direct papal action were delayed and the council fathers gathered at Trent were permitted to undertake general reforms, they would commence their work with the Roman curia. Two things, Cervini believed, would occur with the opening of such a discussion of reform topics. First, the Roman abuse of assigning multiple benefices to cardinals without requiring residence in any individual church would be questioned. Shortly thereafter, the parallel demand of secular rulers for the presence of certain prelates at their own courts, which also rendered residence impossible, would be examined. He expressed this in a letter to Farnese in December 1545 and said, "I hope to see His Holiness make the reform of the Roman curia himself, and not leave this part to the discretion of the council." And indeed, he correctly foresaw the danger. As early as May 28, 1546, when the legates proposed in the general congregation to discuss not reform but the creation of the first substantial dogmatic decree on original sin, the bishops of the imperial party immediately objected and said that episcopal residence ought to be discussed first.[25]

In practical terms, the creation of the institution of the papacy by Christ, Cervini maintained, proved that the pope stood above any council in authority. Once again, Cervini demonstrated this attitude in a variety of texts. In his cautions to Contarini on the legation to the emperor and the imperial Diet at Regensburg in 1541, Cervini first warned him of the errors contained in the emperor's proposals for a compromise. His proposals on the subjects of the church council and on papal primacy were simply incorrect, according to Cervini. They do not assert, he told Contarini, that the convocation of a council "pertains solely to the Roman pontiff" as does the "approbation of its decrees." Citing the instructions of Christ to Peter to "Feed my sheep," Cervini then reminded Contarini that "all the doctors of the church, both Latin and Greek, . . . and many councils have also upheld this jurisdiction of the Roman pontiff over the universal church."[26] Thus he consistently placed his comments about church councils in the context of papal control. It was the pope, he said, who should seek out the "tribulations afflicting Christianity," and use the celebration of the council to pacify the divine wrath. Writing for Monte as well as himself in a letter to Farnese, Cervini expressed this attitude even more bluntly. "Our requests all come down to this," he said, "that His Holiness remain the absolute master of the council." In all this, Cervini bore a remarkable resemblance to other significant figures in the sixteenth-century Catholic church. Pietro Querini (c. 1479–1514), a monk in the strict Camaldolese order, wrote during 1512 in support of the idea that the pope was superior to any council, and that one could be convened only by papal authority. Gasparo Contarini argued similarly in a text entitled *De potestate pontificis quod divinitus sit tradita* in 1533.[27]

Cervini upheld papal supremacy also in the difficult problem of papal control over church benefices. Here again, Cervini urged swift, efficient action. On more than one occasion, Cervini was informed of abuses concerning benefices by other bishops. The Florentine Cardinal Niccolò Gaddi (+1552), for example, wrote to Cervini twice in the spring of 1541, apparently seeking advice after visiting his own diocese. "I have found many abuses," he said, "and among others, I have found two priests here that were ordained in Avignon." He added simply, "they cannot read." He also said, "I have come up against many scandals and falsities on the assignment of benefices," and later added, "the two things most scandalous from my point of view are this ignorance and the conferral of benefices on unfit persons." He indicated that he was fearful of the long-range consequences of such a situation.[28] Cervini reacted negatively to this kind of information. He believed that such behavior angered the Catholic faithful and that the pope should personally see to its elimination, suggesting new legislation reversing that under which abuses flourished. The current way of life of priests, he wrote to Maffei, "which people no longer wish to tolerate," and the improper granting of benefices must be changed, and changed by the pope. He also firmly believed that such maladministration constituted a danger to papal authority. If the pope does not do it, Cervini said, the council will take it up, and that would be to fall from the frying pan into the fire.[29]

A few months later, he wrote again to Maffei and fully explained his opinion on the question of benefices and other papal privileges. He stated at the outset that reformation in this area could be done "either by the pope or in the council." But, he said, "the revocation or moderation of graces and dispensations already made by the Holy See permitting the plurality of cathedral churches and minor benefices as well as non-residence . . . properly belongs to the Apostolic See, from which these things emanate," and in such matters the pope "cannot nor ought to be judged by anyone other than God."[30] In support of this last point, Cervini cited the spurious Council of Sinuessa, supposedly held during the reign of Pope Marcellinus (296–304). "The council," he said, "would not be able to lay a hand on such areas" if the pope acted on his own, and such action would abbreviate the length of the assembly. He stressed that it was the pope's decision to act or to leave these matters to the council. Clerics and their benefices, Cervini argued, were directly under the authority of the pope, and therefore it was not necessary to allow a conciliar contribution to the adjudication of problems connected with these persons or their salaries. Furthermore, he maintained, it was not even desirable to do so. If the pope chose to leave such matters to the council, he should indicate to the legates how he wanted them to proceed in the discussions. He further warned that if this method were followed, "a brief will also be necessary to maintain the authority of the Holy See," since the pope would derogate his legitimate power in such an action.[31] Cervini made his opinion clear: the pope had complete control and authority in this area, and he ought to use it rather than surrender it to anyone.

In other letters, Cervini further suggested that the papal plenitude of power should be exercised in dogmatic, as well as clerical, reform. He maintained this position not in order to increase papal power by any means possible, but rather because he believed the exercise of such control would result in the swift resolution of the controversies facing the church, once the initial step of reforming the papacy was undertaken. At one point, Cervini proposed a suspension of the council and the simultaneous convocation at Rome of a reform assembly. He described this plan in a series of letters written throughout the autumn of 1546. It must be distinguished both from the early plan for the translation of the council in the summer of 1546, which was opposed by the emperor, and from the March 1547 plan to translate the council from Trent to Bologna. The latter was eventually carried out, despite the objections of the emperor and his supporters.[32]

Cervini wrote to Maffei in 1546 and indicated that the act of convening a reform assembly simultaneously with the suspension of the council would anticipate and defuse the criticism of the emperor. The emperor, he reasoned, might judge that such a suspension indicated lack of interest in reform on the part of the papacy. He made a practical recommendation. "Suspend it [the council], and call together all those prelates who are here," he said, "to make a good and general reformation . . . without loss of time." He repeated the recommendation on the same day in one of his relatively few personal letters to the pope, underlining his conviction of the importance of this plan. "Your Holiness will be considered most prudent . . . and a good dialectician," he said, "to turn the argument of the imperial prelates against them and call them . . . to your presence to make the model of a general reformation as they demand and desire." Any loss of time, he added, "is good neither for your age nor for the needs of the world."[33]

Such papal-directed reform synods had been held in Rome before, and Cervini believed such meetings might constitute part of the machinery necessary to return the papacy to a publicly recognized position of genuine, effective, and morally justified leadership, with the support of an international body of bishops. This public recognition based on realistic clerical and curial reform might also, Cervini suggested, support papal leadership on dogmatic controversies. At the time these letters were written, the imperial party opposed the publication of the decree on justification, and Cervini's suggestion seems at least in part designed to expedite a solution of the two main questions for which the council was convened. But he adamantly maintained that genuine, papal-directed curial and clerical reform was the necessary first step, for without a firm resolution to undertake this, not to mention systematic implementation of the resolution, calling the prelates to Rome could be dangerous.[34]

On this occasion, Cervini seemed to indicate that a genuinely reformed papacy, working against contemporary abuses on the curial and episcopal level, would be able to fully control both the reform of degenerate clerical practices and the much-needed doctrinal clarifications. This is the reason he so frequently exhorted Paul III to begin the process of reform in the curia. He harbored no illusions: he viewed the contemporary papacy as a corrupt institution. As long as the papacy continued to drag its feet on problems of reform, while it simultaneously faced doctrinal upheaval, Cervini believed it was legitimate to begin with both papal and conciliar-sponsored efforts. The pope, since he held jurisdiction over the clergy, should initiate curial and clerical reform, while the council's role should be limited to matters of faith. Such a distinction was made by a prominent canonist, Marco Mantova Benavides (1489–1582), in his *Dialogo de concilio*, published in 1541. Cervini might well have had that text read to him during this legation.[35] The position was certainly one way of countering the conciliar challenge expressed by the imperial party. But Cervini never gave up his ideal of a reformed hierarchy exerting leadership in all ecclesiastical affairs: that was the best way to bring the sixteenth-century church most rapidly into correspondence with the apostolic church, and it was the way he sought to follow during his own brief papacy. His attitude might be called more pragmatic than most, but Cervini was not alone among his contemporaries in suggesting that the proper form of ecclesiastical authority emanated from a reformed papacy, which took its pastoral duties seriously. Nor was he alone in hoping that the focus of that authority should be the imitation of the church in the apostolic age. His friends and colleagues Reginald Pole and Gasparo Contarini maintained similar positions in their sixteenth-century texts on papal power.[36]

EPISCOPAL AUTHORITY

For the episcopacy, Cervini also insisted upon a similarly efficacious exercise of the authority delegated to bishops. He seemed to be speaking only of the jurisdictional authority delegated to bishops, avoiding the question of whether episcopal authority is established by divine law. He believed bishops ought to look after, and reform if necessary, individuals and practices under their jurisdiction, but always in relation to Roman leadership. Bishops were to undertake the duties entrusted to them; but when difficult problems arose, appeal to a cardinal or directly to the pope was Cervini's preferred method of recourse.

He demonstrated this viewpoint in his correspondence with the bishop of Foligno, Isidoro Chiari (1495–1555). Chiari held the see of Foligno from 1547 until his death and was a member of the Benedictine congregation of Santa Giustina of Padua. The congregation was formally established in 1421 and came to be called the Cassinese congregation after the abbey of Montecassino joined in 1502. The group became famous for its humanistic approach to the study of Scripture and Greek patristic writings. Cervini first encountered Chiari at Trent where he served, along with Luciano degli Ottoni and Crisostomo Calvini, as one of the theological experts sent by the congregation. They became suspect of heresy by many at Trent, especially prelates like Domingo de Soto, who was head of the council's commission on heretical writings, and others, such as the infamous Zannettini. Chiari enjoyed a brief popularity at the council, mainly because of his assertion that the doctrine of justification had been muddled by scholastic theologians. He presented the congregation's central position on restoration as the true pattern of salvation, which was ultimately rejected by the council, and was an admirer, though not an uncritical one, of Erasmus. Despite the suspicion of heresy, Cervini maintained a sympathetic attitude toward the Cassinese congregation in general and toward Chiari in particular. Chiari received frequent advice and encouragement from Cervini in his episcopal work in Foligno.[37] He became known as an exemplary bishop, at least in part because of the fifteen-volume corpus of sermons he preached there. In his work, Chiari had found "disorder" among his clergy.

One of the four synods Chiari held there during his tenure took place in December 1550. He reported on the meeting to Cervini, and especially upon his attempt to incorporate some of Cervini's recommendations, specifically those involving the recitation of the divine office among the clerics in the diocese. Chiari remembered, he said, Cervini's advice that he "would not be able to beg for everything all at once." He apparently took the advice: instead of beseeching his clerics, Chiari simply issued orders. Facing rebellion of the canons over his order that they sing matins in choir, Chiari saw the confrontation prolonged by an appeal of one of them to the Roman Rota. Cervini assured him that the issue would be resolved by removing it from the tribunal and handing it over to a cardinal, who would decide quickly, "without quarrel or long delay."[38]

Did Cervini give this advice and provide this assistance simply out of empathy for Chiari and out of his own disdain for the Roman Rota? Either would be possible since Cervini faced similar problems with the Rota in his own pastoral work, specifically over an appointment to the *prepositura* in Gubbio in 1545 and 1546. In this instance he certainly did not suggest that the cardinalate held any kind of superiority over the bishop, except a kind of practical superiority—a cardinal could see to the resolution of a case like this more quickly, as a disinterested third party. Cervini knew that the decision of the cardinal would be more likely to support the bishop than a decision from the Rota. Perhaps he hoped, therefore, that the strength of the cardinal's decision would reinforce Chiari's authority. It does appear, at least, that he believed expedience to be among the primary considerations in such disputes. Appeals to the Rota were, after all, a particularly tedious problem for bishops attempting to exercise their authority in the diocese. Still, Cervini did not fully define in written form his attitude toward episcopal authority. The reason for this might be easier to understand than the lack of definition itself. Cervini possessed this authority. In analyzing all levels of ecclesiastical authority he maintained that action should be taken and changes should be made, and hence most of the evidence Cervini gave for his attitude toward the position of the bishop and his authority came in the form of example.

Any confusion over the precise duties and powers of a bishop was, in the sixteenth century, compounded by the practice of non-residence. The true cornerstone of the reformation, wrote the legates to the Council of Trent in May 1546, was episcopal residence. They believed, like many others at the council, that it was the fundamental issue and that, without agreement on it, reform in any other area (be it preaching, clerical morality, or administration of the sacraments) could not be adequately undertaken. Absence of prelates from their dioceses was most frequently lamented when required for service in the Roman curia or in secular courts, but even attendance at the council often required such absences.[39] Sixteenth-century prelates employed essentially two solutions to this problem, known as the vicar and the visitor. These also had an important place in Cervini's view of ecclesiastical authority.

In practice, Cervini used a great number of vicars to look after his pastoral duties, because of his absence from the dioceses he oversaw as episcopal administrator while serving the pope both in the Roman curia and on his numerous legations. Cervini even refused episcopal consecration on the grounds that, due to his position as legate, he was unable to live up to his responsibilities and to exercise his full powers.[40] He also applied to these vicars his ecclesiological ideal of the efficient exercise of legitimately delegated authority. He expected and demanded productive action from them, and he corrected them sharply when such action was not forthcoming.

Cervini, on various occasions, employed the bishop of Bergamo Vittore Soranzo (1500–1558), another prelate suspected of holding heretical views, in such a vicarial position.[41] Soranzo originally became connected with the see in 1544, by serving as coadjutor in the diocese for the bishop Pietro Bembo. Soranzo owed not only this office but also an earlier curial appointment, and probably his acquaintance with Reginald Pole and Vittoria Colonna, to his friendship with Bembo. Soranzo twice came under suspicion of heresy, in part because of his connection with Pole's Viterbo group and his association with Giovanni Morone.

In 1544 as coadjutor at Bergamo, he undertook the issuance of diocesan constitutions to satisfy the need for correction of clerical behavior. In those orders he sought to eliminate concubinage and the carrying of weapons, to insure the residence of parish priests, to improve the administration of sacraments, and to thwart the distribution of heretical literature. At the death of Bembo, he became bishop, and he held the see when apparently libelous rumors began to circulate in 1548 suggesting he was less than vigilant concerning heresy in Bergamo. Heresy spread there especially through the circulation of Protestant literature. The infamous inquisitor Michele Ghislieri, later Pope Pius V (1566–1572), was sent to investigate, at the urging of Cervini.[42] Hence, when Cervini wrote to Soranzo in 1549 informing him of irregularities in the monastic life practiced at the Servite monastery known as the Paradiso in Bergamo, Soranzo was already under suspicion, and Cervini would have known of his connection with Pole and the others at Viterbo.

Despite all this, Cervini employed him to visit the monastery and correct the religious there, in Cervini's name as protector of the Servites. Cervini apparently became disappointed with the slow pace at which Soranzo accomplished this work. "You chose through your goodness," he wrote, "to undertake this work. So use the authority I gave you, without waiting each time for my new orders."[43] Cervini implied in this letter that he did not mean Soranzo was to stop writing to him, but he wanted action taken, and he wanted to avoid delays. When he wrote this direction, Cervini gave considerable latitude, in the context of a monastic visitation, to someone of questionable orthodoxy. Soranzo came under suspicion again in 1550, confessed to owning Protestant materials, and was not allowed to return to the diocese. He received a sort of rehabilitation, carried out through the work of another close friend and colleague of Cervini Ludovico Beccadelli, and was permitted to return to Bergamo in 1554. Soranzo obviously posed no threat in the eyes of Cervini, who participated in the proceedings of the Roman Inquisition throughout this period. With the election to the papacy in 1555 of Gian Pietro Carafa, a very different character from Cervini, Soranzo's problems were renewed, and he suffered deposition from the bishopric in 1558.

ECCLESIASTICAL AND SECULAR AUTHORITY

On the relationship between ecclesiastical and secular authority, Cervini held an ambivalent attitude. He consistently upheld the primacy of ecclesiastical authority over religious issues and religious persons, while insisting that imperial authority be discounted in these matters. He was not, however, adverse to making use of secular authority if it might contribute to the end he had in mind.

Before the assembly at Trent formally opened, papal ambassadors found the emperor willing to defer to the decisions of the future council, despite his interest in the immediate practical reform of the church and his threat to undertake this in Germany through a diet if a council were not convened. Fabio Mignanelli, nuncio to Ferdinand king of the Romans and bishop of Lucerne from 1540 to 1553, wrote from Worms in 1545 that Charles V would support the proposal that religious issues be remitted to the impending Council of Trent. Charles's cooperation waned during the spring and summer of 1545, however, until he eventually indicated his desire that only reform—not dogma—be discussed at the council, in order to avoid irritating the Lutherans. He made this desire known to Alessandro Farnese through his personal secretary, Juan de Andalot, and Farnese in turn forwarded the information to the legates.[44] The emperor increasingly refused cooperation in the conciliar proceedings over the first two years of the assembly, primarily through the prelates who represented his positions, and the problem came to a head in 1547 when an issue arose in which Cervini sought to exclude entirely the influence of secular authority. That issue was the translation of the council from Trent to Bologna.

The ostensible reasons for the transfer of the council were two. First, the war of the Schmalkaldic League presented a real threat to the security of Trent and the prelates gathered there. Second, the outbreak of plague in Trent during the spring of 1547 generated even more than the usual complaints over the physical environment, especially after the bishop of Capaccio, Enrico Loffredi, died in early March. When the possibility of a translation first came up in the summer of 1546, Cervini focused upon these concerns when arguing in favor of the plan. It was a reasonable policy, he maintained, in that one of the primary reasons the pope had originally convened the council in Trent, the safety and security of that location, had been undercut by the threat of war. Cervini obviously considered the belligerent attitude Charles V maintained toward the league as the primary reason for this turn of events, blaming him directly. "The Emperor," he said, "has rendered this place insecure." When Madruzzo, the cardinal of Trent and one of the strongest supporters of the imperial position at the council, returned from a trip to Rome and told the legates he believed the pope was committed to keeping the assembly in Trent, Cervini answered him curtly. "I showed that it was not possible to believe," he wrote to Maffei, "that His

Holiness would not transfer it to another place, because the reasons have ceased for which he placed it here."[45] When Loffredi died, the legates had much more support for the translation, as a majority of the prelates considered the move to Bologna a good plan. But these were not the real reasons why Cervini favored the translation.

Cervini wished to exclude imperial interference with the council because it threatened papal authority. He believed that ecclesiastical authority was completely separate from and superior to the imperial in matters of religion, and he maintained this as a consistent policy throughout his career. In 1541, for example, Cervini warned Contarini to insist in negotiations with the emperor that he stay out of doctrinal and reform matters that were better left to ecclesiastical authorities. He suggested unilateral action, indicating that he considered papal authority superior to all secular authorities (not just the emperor) when treating religious matters. He urged that "conscious of his authority," the pope ought to "follow the example of his holy predecessors, . . . and suspend" the council, "without consultation of the princes."[46] When the pope did not follow this recommendation, Cervini supported translation as an acceptable, but not ideal, alternative. Such an action, in his view, would help defuse the challenge to papal authority but not solve the problem of reform.

When the translation to Bologna was finalized in 1547, Cervini clearly explained in a letter to Maffei the reason behind his support for the move. The translation, which had gained legitimacy through the outbreak of plague, was an act of God and "not a human work," he maintained, but it "was necessary, if we did not wish to remain in the hands of the Spanish, and place His Holiness and the Apostolic See under their control for the present and in the future."[47] Undoubtedly, when referring to the "Spanish," Cervini also expressed his disdain of the entire imperial party, which had delayed the conclusion of the decree on justification, over which he had personally expended so much energy.

Cervini believed in this exclusion of imperial authority from religious matters and applied it fearlessly in his own life. He incurred the hatred of the emperor as a result of his legation to the council, and because of the translation. Charles V considered him a francophile and later opposed Cervini's papal election. During the controversy over the suspension or translation of the council, Aurelio Cattaneo (1515–c.1564), the secretary of Madruzzo, came to visit Cervini. Cattaneo served Madruzzo for many years on diplomatic missions at Rome and at the imperial court.[48] Cattaneo had recently visited the court, and he told Cervini that the emperor believed he was attempting to dissolve the council. He further insinuated that Cervini intended to bribe those who chose not to leave Trent and that he was doing all this under direct orders from the pope. Cattaneo related the emperor's double demand that Cervini cease such activities and be punished for them. He further indicated that if the pope did not see fit to take such action, the emperor would punish Cervini himself. Cervini should no longer consider himself safe in any place, Cattaneo implied.

Cervini responded with stiff defiance to this threat, and he related the story of the meeting in a letter to Paul III. He explained to Cattaneo that he and the other legates urged suspension, not dissolution of the council, and that those two things were very different. "But nonetheless, . . . if I have erred," Cervini said, "only Your Holiness is able and ought to punish me, and His Majesty by right has no authority over me." If he wishes to use force, "since I am just a poor priest," Cervini said, "then I will be helpless." But the emperor will die too, he added, "and we all have to give account for our actions before the same judge." Cervini again pledged his loyalty to the pope, saying, "Neither this nor any other thing will keep me from faithfully executing my office as long as I live."[49] Cervini's later actions indicate that he supported the emperor's desire for wide-ranging reform of clerical behavior, not Roman attempts to make such reform impossible. Beyond this, the emperor may have been quite correct in suggesting that many prelates would look upon suspension as the practical end of the council, given the long difficulties in convening it. But Cervini did not lose this chance to explain his disdain for the emperor's threat and attempt to control him. The incident may have made Cervini all the more determined to eliminate outside interference with papal control of the council.

Cervini took certain other positions that indicate how firmly he rejected the notion of secular influence over ecclesiastical affairs—his criticism of Madruzzo is a good example. Cervini found fault with Madruzzo for buckling under the pressure of the emperor and assisting his battle against ecclesiastical authority. He believed that as a result the cardinal of Trent could not be trusted. "All the waters of the sea," Cervini once said, "cannot wash away the suspicions we have of him."[50]

Still, there were times Cervini needed the power and influence of secular authority. He never denied that, on the practical level, such authorities were needed for the implementation of decrees the council would issue. Among the primary concerns the pope should have in mind, he said, first should be the "conservation of the church and the health of the people," and second, "the Christian princes, because they are princes and because they are needed for the implementation of decrees."[51] He hastened to add that the church and the people should come first, especially in the present situation where the princes were uncooperative, but he still excluded the princes from any influence other than this executive function. In maintaining this position, Cervini reflected an approach that was quite typical for the sixteenth century. Protestant churches, too, needed and courted the assistance of secular authorities.[52]

Cervini also provided evidence to suggest that he accepted a certain amount of collaboration between ecclesiastical and secular on the local and diocesan level. The priors and standard-bearers of Montepulciano, for example, wrote to Cervini in 1541 to request help. They hoped to procure his assistance in establishing a *studium* in the Augustinian house of friars in their town. They appealed to him as their "singular benefactor" and said that such a school "would be of use to the diocesan clergy also, and contribute to both the general extirpation of ignorance and the progress of the reformation."[53] Ludovico Beccadelli, one of Cervini's closest coworkers, reported another situation that required cooperation with local secular leaders. Beccadelli engaged in a struggle to restrain a man from repeated visits to a convent of sisters. The motivation for his visits was apparently other than spiritual in nature, and the situation had caused a great scandal. It seems Beccadelli found himself unable to convince the man on his own and therefore went to the governor of the province, who did stop the activity.[54]

Cervini thus maintained a multi-sided view of the relationship between secular and ecclesiastical authority. It is perhaps best described as relative, and a position that depended upon his assessment of the usefulness of collaboration in particular cases. When, as in the case of the conciliar debates, he believed the positions of secular rulers might complicate the resolution of problems, he demanded a strict separation, contending that a princely or imperial power had no right to meddle in church affairs. When, on the other hand, ecclesiastical powers and penalties were insufficient to gain the results he desired, Cervini believed in collaborative activity. All of this may help explain why Cervini's views on these topics were significantly, but in no way fully, developed. He maintained the approach of a pragmatist rather than an ideologue. He concerned himself more with the application and consequences of authority than with elaborating its theoretical justification.

CONSEQUENCES

Cervini held that once power and authority were delegated, whether by God to the pope, by God and the pope to a bishop, or by a bishop to a vicar, it became an obligation to exercise them. He believed that those holding authority should likewise be judged, at least in part, according to the efficiency, productivity, and effectiveness of the stewardship they exercised, as well as the propriety of that stewardship. The pope himself, as supreme pastor, would have to answer for his leadership of the church at large, and one important part of his duty was to handle problems with speed and decisiveness. In addition, when making recommendations to Paul III on the conduct of ecclesiastical reform, Cervini employed another, more traditional rationale. He frequently appealed to the pontiff, urging him to take actions to ensure his future salvation and simultaneously bring honor and glory to his family, the Farnese. Such statements might have been merely conventional admonishments designed to spur the pope into action, except that Cervini applied precisely the same reasoning in his exhortations to bishops. Even in congratulating his friend Bernardino Maffei on his promotion to the see of Massa, Cervini warned him: "Consider well," he said, "that with the honor to which you have been raised goes the burden to render account of all those you have under your care."[55] Cervini probably derived this idea from what he considered more ancient and more genuine models of pastoral duty from the New Testament. He used language virtually identical to the description of church leaders and the account required of them in Hebrews 13:17 and in James 3:1—those who teach will be judged with greater strictness than others.[56] Such a view is consonant with the position held by the reform group in the fifteenth and early sixteenth century that urged a renewal of the episcopal office. Recent historical assessments of this position have tended to bypass the figure of Cervini and concentrate instead upon persons like Gasparo Contarini and Gian Matteo Giberti. Contarini encouraged such renewal in his *De officio viri boni ac probi episcopi*, addressed to Pietro Lippomano, the bishop-elect of Bergamo in 1517. Giberti encouraged the same by example in his diocese of Verona.[57] Many historians correctly consider these ideas an important current feeding into the Council of Trent, which were adopted by such prelates as Carlo Borromeo and then had impact throughout the next several generations of Catholic churchmen. Cervini was clearly one of those encouraging the recovery of that ideal.

For Cervini, however, the main consequence of this view of authority in the church was frustration. He believed the long-established hierarchical and authoritarian order in the church had to be maintained, but he also believed it had to be reformed. Faced with a lack of cooperation and even hostility at the council, as well as with reports of pastoral problems in a variety of dioceses (including his own), he asked many times for direct action by the pope. When instructions and advice on conciliar matters arrived late from the Roman curia, sometimes even too late to be useful in the congregations, Cervini began to express that frustration. "We are trying," he said, "to salvage the honor of the Apostolic See and the Roman court in the face of a council convened for the reformation of the world, and it is greatly dissatisfied with that same court."[58] These difficulties were compounded by several other factors. The correspondence traveled with varying degrees of rapidity between Rome and Trent, while rumors (and consequent misunderstandings about the legates and their activities and about the opinions of curial administrators) frequently moved more quickly than diplomatic parcels.

Cervini appeared more frustrated by the lack of papal action. Paul III moved with a consummate lethargy, which was even described by his secretary Maffei on certain occasions as procrastination. This was never more apparent than when Cervini asked Paul to initiate curial reforms. Nearly a year passed between Cervini's first suggestions on the topic and his receipt of a letter saying that Paul was in agreement and "would undertake the reformation" himself without waiting for the council to act. In 1547, after the council had been transferred to Bologna, Cervini again expressed his frustration, saying if the reform "is done well and according to the world's expectations and desires, no one will consider where the good was done or by whom, just whether it was done or not." He also pledged his own efforts, so that "no one will be able to say this time was lost to the Christian republic because nothing was done."[59]

Cervini began to make good on this pledge after relief from his conciliar duties in 1549. First he did so by attending directly to the pastoral needs of his diocese of Gubbio. He did so later in his few days as pope, by attempting to initiate the reform activities he so often urged Paul III to undertake. Both these actions were logically demanded by his view of ecclesiastical and secular authority. For Cervini, who was neither a trained theologian nor a canon lawyer, this view constituted a kind of practical or working ecclesiology. It was not fully elaborated in technical theological terms, but it was in operation behind every recommendation he made and behind every action he took in promoting church reform. Formed by a humanistic and very practical education, Cervini carefully considered the problems facing the sixteenth-century church.[60] He sought to solve those problems through a method developed as a result of his education; and in implementing solutions, he argued, practicality and productivity were important considerations. If each person within the ecclesiastical hierarchy, pope, bishop, and priest, attended in a practical and efficient manner to the pastoral duties implied in the office they held, the problems of the church could be solved in short order. He insisted that the established hierarchy must spearhead those efforts, not in order to squash opponents of that hierarchy but because, in his opinion, the hierarchy had the right to carry out the process. Even more important, according to Cervini, the hierarchy had the power and the duty to carry it out. He also came to believe, through practical experience at the council, that the hierarchy could accomplish this more quickly and efficiently than any other method he could conceive.

Cervini was not alone in this conviction. In addition to the prelates cited earlier, Giovanni Morone, for example, wrote a letter to Cervini while on legation in Vienna in which he expressed similar concerns. He argued, just like Cervini, that the German prelates despaired of effective papal action for ecclesiastical reform, but Morone suggested that someone find a way to convince the emperor to seek the changes he desired through the pope. Any other method, Morone maintained, would be usurping power. Frustration with lethargic popes, cardinals, and bishops and commitment to the model of reform articulated in such documents as the *Consilium de emendanda ecclesia* helped produce this sort of attitude toward ecclesiastical power and its exercise in prelates like Cervini. The attitude was refined at the later sessions of the Council of Trent and then passed on to a new generation of churchmen, prelates like Carlo Borromeo. For him, affirmation of episcopal authority went hand in hand with what one author called a "quest for holiness . . . articulated with pastoral commitment."[61] But similarity between Cervini and these others should not be surprising, as they constituted the group of his immediate colleagues and successors in the sixteenth-century Catholic episcopacy.

CHAPTER FIVE

Episcopal and Inquisitorial Activity to 1550

Marcello Cervini administered a succession of dioceses during his ecclesiastical career. He gained appointment to the see of Nicastro in Calabria on August 17, 1539, while serving as *protonotario apostolico* and vice-chancellor to Alessandro Farnese, the papal secretary of state. Pope Paul III transferred him to the see of Reggio Emilia, a town about sixty kilometers northwest of Bologna, on September 24, 1540. The death, in August 1540, of the incumbent in that see, Hugo di Rangone, precipitated the appointment. On November 29, 1544, Cervini was transferred again, this time to the diocese of Gubbio, about thirty kilometers northeast of Perugia, in the province of Umbria. In that see he succeeded the famous Venetian humanist Pietro Bembo (1470–1547), who in 1544 was himself transferred to the more lucrative see of Bergamo.[1] Cervini retained the governance of Gubbio until his papal election on April 9, 1555. It is important to note that, while appointed to these sees, Cervini served in each case as administrator rather than as bishop. He did not receive episcopal consecration until his accession to the papacy demanded it. He maintained this position as administrator intentionally and actually refused consecration. He was not in a position to provide responsible or effective leadership in the diocese. He lacked the ability to exercise both the power of jurisdiction and the power of order implied in the consecration, let alone the ability to fulfill the residence requirement. He argued this was because throughout this series of appointments he was employed on lengthy legations both in and outside Italy.[2] Other considerations probably motivated his decision to accept these benefices when he knew residence would be impossible. The benefices represented substantial income, and status as the administrator of such a see was required for appointment to the office of papal nuncio.

Varying amounts of information are available on Cervini's work in each of these dioceses. Virtually nothing has been published on his short tenure in Nicastro, and no wonder—by his own admission, Cervini never set foot in the diocese. In 1540 he expressed remorse over this in a letter to Maffei and indicated a desire to renounce the benefice. He argued from the same point of view in a letter written seven years later to Alessandro Farnese requesting leave to reside in and look after the needs of Gubbio. He did not want to neglect that diocese as he had Nicastro and Reggio. He also sought relief from the rather intense pressures he had experienced that year at the council. More is known of his pastoral care during the three and a half years he oversaw Reggio Emilia. In that see he employed a vicar general, Ludovico Beccadelli (1501–1572), who was a long-time friend and collaborator.[3] Cervini also appointed a special *commissario* in Reggio, Antonio Lorenzini, a lawyer from his hometown of Montepulciano. Lorenzini served as head of Cervini's household in Trent and held the same post in Rome following Cervini's papal election. Lorenzini also undertook a general pastoral visitation of Reggio on behalf of Cervini between February 7 and May 26, 1543. Cervini visited Reggio himself during Lorenzini's review, on April 4, 1543. His administration in Gubbio is best known of all. There Cervini maintained a much higher profile and intervened in a fascinating dispute with the cathedral chapter. He also addressed an instruction to the preachers in Gubbio regarding proper topics and approaches to be employed in popular sermons.[4]

Cervini's tenure as administrator in Nicastro was very different from his service to Reggio Emilia or Gubbio. He held responsibility for Nicastro over one short year. He administered Reggio for four years, and Gubbio for ten. Nicastro is located near the southernmost point in Italy. It was bestowed upon Cervini while he participated in a papal legation with Alessandro Farnese in some of the northernmost points in all Europe, and he gained transferal to another see before he even returned. So there is no reason to believe residence in Nicastro was even remotely expected of him. It appears more likely that the diocese was granted him solely for the purpose of the income it provided, and as a reward from Paul III for his service. Ludwig von Pastor insisted that Cervini administered Nicastro "with zeal and vigilance," but this is grossly misleading, as there are very few references to the diocese in the letters of Cervini from that period. The paucity of references indicates that Cervini held something less than urgent concern for the diocese.

Cervini drafted all the legatine correspondence sent to the curia, and the one time he referred to himself as "Monsignor di Nicastro" was not to inquire into the situation in the diocese itself, but rather to complain that his biretta had not arrived from Rome.[5]

Although at one point Cervini did express feelings of guilt over his inability to attend to Nicastro personally, the correspondence during his administration of Reggio and Gubbio is strikingly different. Cervini repeatedly appealed for papal and vicarial action and even begged for freedom from other duties in order to reside and to take direct action for the improvement of those dioceses. He suggested in his correspondence that he came to consider Reggio (perhaps because of the visitation of the diocese he ordered) the place where he first exercised the responsibilities of a bishop. He wrote a letter on March 29, 1548, to Alessandro Farnese, and in his rough copy the phrase "Reggio, having been administrator of the church" is crossed out, and written above is the correction "having been bishop of Reggio."[6]

Thus, with the exception of Nicastro, Cervini was devoted to the needs and problems of the diocese to which he had been assigned, although his career transported him to the highest levels of ecclesiastical administration. He displayed an attitude not unlike that of Gian Matteo Giberti, and other Spanish and Italian prelates from this period, who took their episcopal duties seriously. In so doing, however, he distinguished himself from far more of his contemporaries, including Alessandro Farnese, who became notorious for his collection of bishoprics (and who remained so until that practice was outlawed in 1547, when he became the outstanding accumulator of lesser benefices, a practice that was the "reformed" means for cardinals to maintain vast wealth). Those who employed excuses and papal dispensations from residence requirements far outnumbered those who did not. The problem was also not restricted to the prelates of Italy. A view of the church as "property" was common among French bishops, for example, who apparently felt no need to disguise the attitude.[7]

EPISCOPAL RESIDENCE AS OBLIGATION

Cervini—through his humanistic outlook, his experiences in Rome and on legation, and his conception of the proper exercise of ecclesiastical authority—came to accept the long-neglected obligation of episcopal residence as just that: an obligation. A knowledge of Greek patristic sources and of church history enabled him consistently to seek ancient concepts and practices to solve the problems of the contemporary church. He did so in seeking advice and in asserting his own opinion on a variety of issues, including indulgences, papal authority, and doctrinal questions at the council. He encouraged the adoption of New Testament ideals in exhortations to other bishops. He gained many opportunities, through his long career in Rome and his wide-ranging travels in Europe, to become familiar with the doctrinal and disciplinary problems facing the church at large. And he received regular correspondence from those trying to solve such problems on the practical level. Repair and maintenance of churches and baptistries, the provision of qualified and morally acceptable candidates in local church offices, the instruction of the clergy and laymen in Catholic doctrine, the control of heretical books, and the appointment of preachers for the important Lenten and Advent sermon series are just a few examples from that host of challenges Cervini and other episcopal administrators faced. He frequently expressed his desire for the ecclesiastical hierarchy to encourage effective action and to create real improvement in these areas. But he believed that the only way to accomplish this in individual dioceses was for those entrusted with the care of such territories to accept the ideal of episcopal residence as an obligation.

This ideal, transmitted from the church of the age of the Fathers, for centuries was exemplified more in the breach than in the practice, but it was revived in Gasparo Contarini's *De officio viri boni ac probi episcopi*.[8] As a student in Padua from 1501 and 1509, Contarini observed Pietro Barozzi, bishop of that city from 1487 to 1507. Contarini used Barozzi as the example of a model bishop in *De officio*. He addressed the study to a friend, Pietro Lippomano, upon his appointment to the see of Bergamo in 1517. In Book 1 of the treatise, Contarini sought to explain the "human" and "divine" qualities necessary in a bishop, while he devoted Book 2 to a set of practical recommendations. Contarini urged Lippomano to imitate Barozzi, above all his practice of residence in the diocese. And he highlighted the importance of residence by treating it, not in Book 2 as a recommendation, but in Book 1 as a necessary prerequisite for the proper fulfillment of Gospel precepts relating to the office of bishop.

Contarini insisted that it was "the calamity of our times" that so few bishops lived in the cities entrusted to their care. Many, he said, believing they had done their duty, appointed a vicar, continued to receive the revenues of the diocese, joined the household of a Roman curialist, and did not even seek information about the faithful living in the territory. "Is this imitation of the disciples of Christ?" he asked. "The good bishop," he continued, will not "hand over the care of his flock to another." He made, however, an exception for non-residence due to the legitimate needs of the papacy. "[The good bishop] will be away from the sheepfold for the shortest time possible," he said, "unless for some reason the pope calls him to serve in some office."[9] He thus distinguished between those bishops actually required to perform some service for the pope and those who left their sees and came to Rome in the hope of securing some appointment. Contarini also suggested that Lippomano seek to conform himself to the New Testament ideal for the outward bearing of a bishop. He specifically cited the description of a temperate, peaceable, hospitable, and modest church elder found in the first letter to Timothy (3:1–6), and the similar account in the letter to Titus (1:7–9). He used these to reinforce his recommendation that Lippomano sustain a high level of honesty and integrity in office.

Contarini made practical suggestions in Book 2, which he circumscribed in considerable detail. For a bishop's prayer, he insisted upon the celebration, or at least the hearing, of mass on a daily basis. He likewise commended faithful recitation of the divine office. In overseeing the diocese, he urged careful attention to punishment of superstitious practices among the faithful, and a vigilant concern for the health of members of the episcopal household. He also suggested that Lippomano grant audiences to anyone seeking his help or counsel. After lamenting the contemporary situation in which wicked and ignorant men served in the priesthood, he urged the bishop to give great attention to the selection of clerical candidates. "There will be little work for the bishop to do in directing the clergy if he has not made errors in the choice of his clerics," Contarini said. He also stated that a good bishop ought not to transfer his duty of preaching to others but, instead, ought to look upon the charge as an honor, not merely as a duty to be fulfilled. The current neglect of an ancient custom of the church fathers to preach at least on feast days ought to be reversed, he said, "for the honor of instructing the people pertains especially to the bishop." If not before all the people, he added, the bishop should preach, "with the clergy present . . . and by this means the sermon will be carried to all." Attention to education and encouragement of the pursuit of Christian wisdom in reading and study were proper for the bishop, he argued, while the contemporary pomp and luxury in episcopal palaces should, in his opinion, be eschewed.[10]

Contarini reinforced these points in additional writings, and other prelates maintained the same position. Contarini exhorted the German bishops gathered at the Diet of Regensburg in 1541 to attend carefully to their pastoral duties, and to view residence as the best means to that end. He underlined the necessity of attending to the education of the young, to the provision of good preachers, to the consideration of the needs of the poor, and to the physical and spiritual care of the members of their own episcopal households.[11]

Contarini wrote still other texts that reinforced the basic tone of the *De officio*, like his *De usu potestatis clavium*, directed to Pope Paul III, and his *Oratio ad deputatos de reformanda ecclesia habita*.[12] Both of these he wrote in the spring of 1537, and the point he made in each was that the spiritual power of all appointed prelates should be understood in a pastoral manner. Never, he argued, should monetary collections be sought (much less demanded, as they often were) in return for dispensations and other spiritual favors. These should be given gratis, he maintained, arguing that sale of such favors was just another form of simony.

Some churchmen in this period extended Contarini's suggestions and argued that adherence to the plan might help extinguish heresy. Gregorio Cortese, a mutual friend of Contarini and Cervini, used an argument reminiscent of the *De officio* in a letter of 1540. He wrote to Contarini, praising a controversial work written by the bishop of Cologne. He described it as one of exceptional sincerity, modesty, and piety. He also asserted his hope that with such expansion of learning, correct doctrine, and pious instruction, Christians might dodge the weapons of the heretics.[13] A further example is the writings of Genziano Herveto, another associate of Cervini. Herveto. He wrote a memorandum in 1563 to the Jesuit theologian Salmerón at Trent, expressing his opinion on the matter of episcopal residence. He presented a view reminiscent of the *Consilium* document Contarini probably helped draft, insisting that repair of this form of ecclesiastical discipline would constitute the remedy, not just for the abuses characteristic of the Roman curia, but also for heresy. Like Contarini in the *De officio*, he stressed some of the spiritual aspects of the episcopal office and likened the relationship between the bishop and the diocese to that between husband and wife.[14]

Cervini similarly had knowledge of the *De officio* and employed Contarini's recommendations. Although he never specifically cited it, Cervini owned two manuscript copies of the text.[15] In addition, his close friends and collaborators were familiar with the text. Galeazzo Florimonte (1478–1567) referred to it approvingly in a letter to Cosimo Gheri, and Luigi Lippomano, a frequent correspondent with Cervini, did the same in his letters. Luigi acted as coadjutor for his brother Pietro in Bergamo from 1538 until 1544, and he often referred to concepts from the *De officio* in his letters to Cervini. On one occasion he said, "the good bishop will desire to serve God in the vocation of preaching," and on another, "I wish to preach in my church on all the feast days of the year."[16]

Cervini himself encouraged Luigi when the prelate later succeeded Pietro in the diocese of Verona, in 1548. That diocese had earlier been made famous by another bishop who took the duty of residence seriously, Gian Matteo Giberti.[17] Contarini's ideal was later accepted and incorporated into the decrees of Trent and was then further reinforced by the activity of a number of prominent post-Tridentine bishops. Carlo Borromeo proved to be the most famous of these, and, as a recent study of his career pointed out, he was not the initiator of a revived Catholic episcopacy but rather the heir or interpreter of the tradition of episcopal activity based on the writings of Contarini and the actions of persons like Giberti, the Lippomano brothers, Cervini, and others.[18]

Cervini became convinced that the acceptance of this model constituted the only practical way to effect the reforms he said, "all the world desires." He gave evidence of both this conviction and his essential nature as a practical, rather than a theoretical, person throughout his career. He met a poor man in his diocese of Gubbio, for example, who had contracted a consanguinous marriage out of ignorance. He put into concrete practice Contarini's theory on the need to administer such dispensations freely, when he urged the dispensation be given without any form of payment and gained the necessary action from the Roman curia.[19]

Beyond these obvious successes, Cervini's conviction seems to have caused him great frustration. As a reward—apparently for his prudence and good judgment in ecclesiastical concerns, as well as for his loyalty and hard work—Paul III granted him the status of cardinal and a succession of episcopal benefices.[20] Along with the status and revenues, Cervini gained administrative power. He personally possessed the authority to create reform and to change abusive practices in one place only—the diocese. Yet Paul demanded extensive work from him on behalf of the Roman curia, which physically removed him from that place. Cervini considered himself thwarted, even plagued, by outside circumstances, which reduced his effectiveness in his diocese because he had to carry out action through third parties. Languid exchange of correspondence and sluggish bureaucrats in Rome contributed to his frustration, but above all Cervini felt isolated and hampered by the great distances from his diocese demanded by papal legations, particularly the one to Trent.

Cervini frequently asked to be relieved of his duties as legate. He knew that such relief was necessary for him to attend adequately to his pastoral obligations, and he hoped it might also improve his chronic ill health. He longed to be released from "this prison" of Trent, he said, in order to "retire in the church that His Holiness wished me to have under my care." He obviously felt considerable remorse over his inability to attend to his obligations in the sees previously entrusted to him. He made virtually an identical argument nearly a year later in a letter to Alessandro Farnese, again pleading for permission to make the journey. A troubled conscience, he explained, was the result of his inability to reside and attend to the needs of the inhabitants of Nicastro and Reggio. "The one [diocese] I never saw, and at the other I have spent only one night," he said. He even suggested that due to his lack of residence he had received the revenue associated with the benefice in a sinful manner and hoped to make restitution. Above all, he did not want to see the situation repeated in his administration of Gubbio.[21]

Cervini made similar requests in rapid succession, more incessantly for this than for anything he had ever requested or recommended before, even more than his repeated calls for papal action in disciplinary reform. He made strenuous efforts to fulfill what he and others had come to look upon as an obligation. There are examples of similar requests, notably from Carlo Borromeo and others, like Giovanni Francesco Bonomi (+1587), who became involved in long legations much later, in the cause of the implementation of the Tridentine decrees.[22] Only incessant pleading enabled Borromeo to escape curial duties in the Rome of his uncle Pius IV (1559–1565), while his friend and schoolmate Bonomi sought to attend to pastoral duties in the diocese of Vercelli while being employed as nuncio in Switzerland and later at the imperial court in Cologne. In Cervini's case, such incessant pleas were at least partly motivated by his lengthy and at times very difficult legations, especially at Trent. These requests must be read as sincere and serious, first because of the long period of time over which they were spread, and second because of the position of the persons to whom he addressed them. He wrote at least fifteen between February 27, 1546, and June 25, 1547, and sent them primarily to the papal secretary, Maffei, but also to the pope's grandson.[23] Cervini maintained a close relationship with both prelates, and both were naturally in a position to influence the one man who could relieve him of his conciliar duties. In addition, Cervini addressed a number of the requests directly to Paul III. He provided further proof of the sincerity of his requests when he did receive an extended leave from conciliar duties. This occurred a short time after the transferal of the council to Bologna, and he sought to return to his diocese immediately.

VICARS AND VISITATIONS

In the meantime, Cervini attempted to put the ideal into practice through correspondence with his vicar. This technique was common. Understanding that non-residence was canonically permissible only if a bishop provided a worthy substitute in the form of a vicar, sixteenth-century prelates committed to the improvement of religious practice and devotion sought to go one step further. They appointed vicars and then attempted to supervise and direct their activities through frequent exchanges of correspondence. Some historians even maintain that this practice was so widespread it "heralded the age of bureaucracy." Among the vicars Cervini employed were rather obscure prelates like Lorenzini; another who worked for him in Reggio late in 1542, Scipione Bianchini; and one who worked for him in Gubbio, Carlo Vannetti.[24]

Far better known are two other of his vicars, Galeazzo Florimonte and Ludovico Beccadelli. Florimonte was born in Sessa Aurunca, a town about fifty kilometers northwest of Naples, and served in his own right as bishop of Aquino from 1543 until 1552, when he became bishop of his home diocese. He held that see until his death at the age of eighty-nine. He lived in the household of Giberti between 1532 and 1537 and thus was intimately familiar with the sort of episcopal administration that became the ideal in sixteenth-century Italy. Among his patrons was also Gasparo Contarini. Florimonte demonstrated his own adaptation of the new episcopal ideal in a letter he wrote in 1537, exhorting another holder of an ecclesiastical benefice Galasso Ariosto to prayer and, above all, to residence. He even suggested that administration through the means of a vicar, if done without legitimate need, constituted simony.[25]

Beccadelli was born in Bologna in 1501, and he also had extensive contact with Contarini, beginning in 1536. He accompanied Contarini on trips to Nice (1538) and to the Diet of Regensburg (1541). He later became vicar general for Cervini in Reggio. He served in this capacity from the spring of 1542 until he agreed in the spring of 1544 to serve as secretary for the newly appointed legate to Bologna, Giovanni Morone.

Beccadelli too became committed to the episcopal ideal expressed in the writings of Contarini, and he proved it in his own life. In March 1554 he wrote a letter to Cervini asking for relief from his legation to Venice (1550–1554) so that he could attend to his obligations in the bishopric of Ravello, a small diocese in the kingdom of Naples that he held from 1549 until he became archbishop of Ragusa in 1555. He had earlier wished to resign the benefice altogether due to his inability to reside. "I have been bishop for five years already," he complained to Cervini, and, having been unable to care for his "flock" while being aware of his "obligations with God," he asked for Cervini's guidance and help in gaining papal permission to quit the legation.[26]

But putting the ideal into practice for Cervini frequently meant much more than the mere provision and direction of vicars like Florimonte and Beccadelli. He struggled to overcome numerous obstacles in carrying out the specific obligations implied in his episcopal administration, one of which was to assure the appointment of trustworthy dependents who might carry out the pastoral functions the administrator could not attend to himself. In this regard, Cervini encountered tremendous difficulties, and one of these arose in 1545 while Cervini was in Trent awaiting the arrival of the other bishops for the opening of the council. A certain Galasso de Beni sought to take possession of the office of *preposito*—head of the cathedral chapter—and of the benefice that went with it, in Gubbio. Apparently under Cervini's direction, the cathedral chapter had already elected another candidate to the post. Cervini and his associate in Rome, Ludovico Beccadelli, described the controversy in a series of letters in late 1545 and early 1546.

There is little in these letters specifically regarding the legal points Galasso employed in his case. Apparently the former *preposito* was notoriously absent from his responsibilities and then died. Galasso, however, had made a claim to the office based upon the absence of the incumbent before his death. Cervini and the cathedral chapter went ahead and elected a new *preposito,* unaware of Galasso's claim. He on his own part had renewed his earlier demand, still unaware that the incumbent had died. The situation was further complicated in Rome by a delay in issuing the official copy of the indult dispensing Cervini from his obligation of residence in Gubbio. He had recently been transferred to the diocese, and such an indult would have empowered him to exercise his administrative rights, like that of electing a new *preposito,* while still at Trent. Galasso thereupon appealed to the Roman Rota, an action which then suspended the exercise of the disputed office.[27] Situations like this involving cathedral chapters were common, especially when a bishop or administrator became convinced of the validity of his own position and launched a determined campaign to impose it. Similar opposition by the cathedral chapter existed during the administration of Ascanio Parisanio as legate in Perugia, during the administration in Brescia of Domenico Bollani (1559–1579), during Giberti's tenure in Verona, and during that of Girolamo Seripando in Salerno.[28] Seripando's biographer indicated that the problem irritated all "reforming bishops," who found themselves constricted by labyrinthine legal processes in disputation with diocesan clergy, prior to the reinforcement of episcopal power at the council.[29]

Galasso based his appeal on the assertion that the election of his rival was uncanonical. His real reason lay in his hope for support from two persons: the bishop of Todi, Federico de' Cesi (1500–1565), who had recently been made a cardinal, and Tommaso Tano, Galasso's friend and an *auditore* of the Rota. Cervini understood the real reason, and his version of the case was different. Galasso, he said, was trying to "intrude by force into that office," and he was seeking to accomplish this by dragging out the procedure before the Rota. His appeal was illegal, Cervini said. Rather than seeking a judgment according to the law, he sought "to weave and plot" so that the case would become so complicated, it would be adjudicated in his favor. This impression was confirmed by Ludovico Beccadelli, who spoke with Galasso in Rome. According to Beccadelli, "it is not enough for him to create a mess in Rome, but he also intends to block the election by appeal to the duke of Urbino, saying that the territory is being disturbed."[30] Galasso demonstrated some shrewdness in this move. After 1384, the town of Gubbio became part of the possessions of the dukes of Urbino. The duke at the time of this particular controversy was Guidobaldo II, who served from 1538 until his death in 1574. Guidobaldo was concerned with the extirpation of heresy from the territory, and he corresponded with Cervini regarding this problem. He also had important connections with the Farnese family, which Galasso hoped to exploit. Guidobaldo later solidified those connections when in 1547 he took Vittoria Farnese, granddaughter of Paul III, as his second wife.[31]

Cervini outlined the controversy to Paul III in considerable detail and indicated that Beccadelli, then secretary to the Council of Trent, possessed additional information should he require it.[32] Cervini asked Paul to assist in a just resolution of the case, either by means of a brief or by a two-sided order, instructing the Rota to expedite the case and Galasso to desist in his efforts to delay it any further. Cervini also tried to head off any attempted influence by Galasso's patron, Cardinal de' Cesi. Cesi, Cervini pointed out, was not "well informed of [Galasso's] insolence and disrespect." He pleaded with the pope to free him "from this mental torture" and his church "from this great danger in which it finds itself."[33]

Cesi, in time, defended the actions of Galasso before Beccadelli in Rome. He insisted that Cervini had been misinformed, but he did so cautiously. Cesi "was most certain," Beccadelli related, "that your Reverence is good and fair minded but . . . the bad information has placed not only Galasso, but also him [Cesi] in your bad graces." Cesi wanted the situation cleared up as rapidly as possible, ostensibly because he judged it to be a mere misunderstanding but also because he expected to meet Cervini soon at Trent and wanted to remain on good terms with him. If it were indeed merely a misunderstanding, then a solution would not be hard to find. Cesi seemed concerned with the effect this controversy might have upon his relationship with Cervini. He even suggested a hope that, whatever solution were gained, above all it should enable Cervini to feel as if he had won. "I wish," Cesi concluded, "that even if Galasso is right, that he remain in obedience to his Reverence [Cervini]."[34]

In his correspondence regarding the adjudication of this case, Cervini displayed attitudes consistent with his understanding of ecclesiastical authority. He believed that as bishop he was best informed about the case, and that he best knew the needs of his diocese. He also believed that any conflict over the proper exercise of his authority ought to be settled by the superior who had granted that authority in the first place—the pope. He therefore rejected Cesi's plea categorically and insisted that Cesi's information was incorrect. Although he did not say so, he knew well that Cesi was acting according to a solidly established tradition: that of making appointments in accordance, not with merit, but with kinship or some other form of special interest. The tradition was so well established, in fact, that the old view, which implies that the cardinalate as an institution was comprehensively "reformed" during the later years of the administration of Paul III, has been decisively disproved.[35]

Cervini exposed his distaste for this tradition and criterion again several years later. Upon his election to the papacy, he gave strict orders for all his relatives to stay at home.[36] Cervini also believed that secular authorities should not intervene in questions concerning appointment to ecclesiastical office. So he made no reference whatsoever to the threat Galasso made to appeal to the duke, even though he had been informed of it by Beccadelli. Virtue alone, he believed, was the only proper vehicle by which one should gain ecclesiastical office, not "through force and underhanded means," as Galasso had done.[37]

The final outcome of the case is not described in these letters, but, under pressure from Cesi, Galasso agreed to the arbitration of an outside judge, separate from the Rota. Cervini empowered Beccadelli to agree on his behalf to the naming of any judge, as long as the person was beyond suspicion of favoritism.[38] In this action, many historians would argue, Cervini was merely participating in the shift in early modern Italian ecclesiastical organization from an oligarchical model, symbolized in election of the *preposito* by the chapter, to a more monarchical form, marked by increased episcopal control over all diocesan benefices. Cervini undoubtedly participated in that gradual shift, but it is simplistic to assert that a desire to effect that change in Gubbio was either foremost in his mind or the sole motivation for his actions in this controversy. There is nothing especially monarchical, after all, about turning such a dispute over to an impartial judge. Cervini clearly desired the reinforcement of his own authority in the matter, but he just as clearly maintained a strong concern about the qualifications, especially the moral qualifications, of the contending candidates. Despite all the battling, the problem was still unresolved in late December 1546.

A related episcopal obligation was to ensure that the clerics who served in the diocese executed their functions properly. Cervini faced a major obstacle in the clerics of his diocese of Reggio. They apparently allowed vast amounts of church property to fall into disrepair and, in addition, conducted themselves in a less-than-edifying manner. Detained at the papal court, Cervini handed over the actual work of reforming them to Antonio Lorenzini. He sent Lorenzini to the diocese in 1543 and intended that the lawyer would inquire into the qualifications and typical behavior of the clerics, so that diocesan statutes designed to improve the situation could be issued later. Lorenzini made a systematic review, and it is evident in Lorenzini's diary and in the memoranda of the visitation that Cervini felt there was much work to do.[39]

Clerics in Reggio in 1543 practiced concubinage on a fairly widespread basis. Lorenzini reported thirty-one instances of the practice, involving thirty-four clerics, somewhat less than 10 percent of the 432 clerics visited. He identified five of these individuals specifically as priests and indicated that all of them held benefices that required the "care of souls." Lorenzini seemed to be especially distressed when such activity was "infamous," that is, when it created a public scandal because of the presence of offspring, or because it had an obvious effect upon the professional performance of the cleric.[40]

Clerical ignorance and improper behavior proved to be an even greater problem. Although he said that many could read Latin, Lorenzini found few to be worthy of the description *sufficiens*.[41] In addition, he found that their outward bearing left much to be desired. "Many clerics and ecclesiastical persons," it was reported, "not only commit blasphemy," but also "carry weapons and by doing so place their souls in great danger and [place] shame on all clerics." Through Lorenzini and a commissary who continued to monitor the situation in 1544, Cervini gave specific descriptions of the sort of change he expected among these dependents. No longer were they to dare "blaspheme the name of God or of the saints," or to carry arms, except for a spear, "the shaft of which is not to exceed three arms length, and the point [not to exceed] the length of the palm of the hand."[42] He laid down a set of fines to be imposed if the clerics did not observe these new regulations. He demanded that they were to give an account of themselves, presumably before the *commissario,* in the following year.

Cervini then issued diocesan statutes based upon this visitation, which were confirmed by Paul III with a bull in 1543. Cervini stated his pastoral intent at the outset. He recognized his need to promote in Reggio both good morals among the clergy and improved devotion among the people. He began, therefore, with paragraphs regularizing the prayer of diocesan clergy, and he instituted fines for those who failed to comply. A considerable number of the early paragraphs also reinforced the bishop's power to license and control clerics in the diocese. The vast majority of the rules, however, treated different aspects of clerical behavior or work, with little mention of the problem of popular devotion stated at the beginning.[43] He issued injunctions against clerical entry into taverns, their cohabitation with concubines, their blasphemy, and their gambling. Other paragraphs focused on their pastoral work, giving detailed directions concerning the administration of the sacraments.

The document underlines two important points. First, by focusing on the clergy, Cervini demonstrated his conviction that improvement of their work and behavior would have the effect of promoting proper devotion in the people. Second, he insisted that all diocesan clergy be subject to the direct control of the bishop. He did this explicitly, and for two reasons. It was, to begin with, in harmony with his understanding of the derivation of ecclesiastical authority. In addition, he believed that other forms of governance (especially through the cathedral chapter) had proven themselves ineffective—otherwise the long list of offenses he stood against would hardly be necessary.

In later years, Cervini advised others who attempted to resolve similar issues. They all, not coincidentally, employed the same means as he did: the visitation. In the summer of 1548, Luigi Lippomano struggled to improve the clergy of the diocese of Verona, in which he was employed as coadjutor. He wrote frequently to Cervini for advice and assistance. In the visitation Lippomano, like Cervini, inquired closely into the daily life and reputation of the clerics in his diocese. But he congratulated himself in the course of a letter for possessing the cleverness to devise a means to extract the truth more readily. He released a list of the topics into which he would inquire eight days ahead of the visit. This apparently led the clerics to cooperate more fully in the investigation.[44] As a result, Lippomano seemed to consider them in even worse condition than the clergy described by Lorenzini in the visit to Reggio. He hoped to effect so much change that Cervini would be proud of his work, should the legate ever pass through Verona. He even requested the intervention of Cervini in order to gain the necessary authority to settle problems he thought he could solve on his own. He sought, for example, the power to absolve not just members of the laity but also secular and regular clerics who had read heretical books and were repentant, effectively circumventing inquisitorial proceedings. In other cases he realized that he was up against far more considerable odds, and he sought advice. The previous overseer of the diocese had placed "a dirty gang of ignorant men in the priesthood," he explained in one letter.[45] In another he lamented the fact that notorious sodomites were among the clergy there and might have enough support within the diocese to block his attempts to eradicate the evil by depriving those clerics of their income. Control over this income, he explained, could not be exercised by the bishop alone, but only with the collaboration of the cathedral chapter. If he were to proceed by actual trial for such crimes, much harsher action would be required. He suggested that it might be necessary to employ the torture of the *strappado* in these cases, or even executions; but he hastened to add that this would dishonor the clergy of the entire diocese, that it would constitute a great burden to the city, and that it would distress him "to no small degree."[46] He asked for the advice of Cervini in this matter and indicated that he hoped the pope himself would ultimately step in to provide a resolution.

Another who wrote to Cervini regarding problems similar to those confronted in the Reggio visitation was Sebastiano Lecavela, bishop of Naxos. In 1548, in a place called Santarini, he confronted not only clerical ignorance but concurrent arrogance. A priest in the territory, whom Lecavela described as ignorant and morally degenerate, because of his public concubinage and gambling, petitioned the Holy See for the office of vicar in the diocese. Lecavela himself had received charge of the diocese under questionable circumstances, since it was given him as a source of income in return for service to the local duke, and because the money was available due to the long-standing absence of the real bishop.[47] Lecavela also sat in attendance at the council, and his own absence from the land further complicated the situation. The ignorant priest in question may have pursued the post of vicar as much to provide real leadership for the diocese as to gain any income the position might provide.

Galeazzo Florimonte related similar pastoral problems in his diocese of Aquino in 1548. He reacted in dismay to the serious lack of basic knowledge in Latin that was widespread among clerical officeholders. He even designed examinations to test the clerics. He encountered two young priests who had been ordained despite what Florimonte considered their complete ignorance of Latin grammar. What was probably worse, from his perspective, was that the clerics argued they had no need of such learning. Apparently they and seventy-eight others had paid for their ordinations, as well as for dispensations from the basic learning required of priests. Florimonte said it was no wonder that the vineyard of Christ was less than well tended. A third cleric proved incapable, under the examination of Florimonte, to distinguish between cases and declensions or between persons and voices—basic points of Latin grammar. He had been ordained in another diocese and had procured a dimissory letter from the curia in Rome before coming to Aquino.[48] Florimonte ended the letter with a plea to Cervini for advice on how he might provide a remedy for situations like these.

The records of his visitation and his later correspondence with other prelates on pastoral issues therefore demonstrate that Cervini served as a model as well as an adviser, who backed his suggestions with practical experience and with an authoritative position in the curia. Cervini followed a process that had been used earlier in other dioceses and that was also used by prelates many years later. The techniques were employed by Giberti in Verona, by Bollani in Brescia, and by Borromeo in Milan, but they were not utilized exclusively in Italy. Recent research suggests that identical procedures found application in France and Germany as well.[49]

By way of contrast and comparison, the diary of the visitation ordered by Cervini presented quite a positive view of the laity in the diocese. They lamented the non-residence of the secular clergy, their concubinage, and their ignorance. The members of the laity, not the clergy, were apparently the zealous Christians in this territory. Indeed, their own Eucharistic and Marian devotions led them to form in Reggio the Confraternity of the Body of Christ and the societies of Mary and Saint Sebastian. They even undertook the construction of a new church. Again, such attitudes, activities, and devotions were not confined to Italy in this period. Members of the laity in France held a similar view of their secular clergy and gave strong support to confraternities and sodalities that paralleled institutions in Italy. The repair and rebuilding of churches in Germany in the late sixteenth century, in the opinion of one of the foremost scholars of the Reformation, constituted an opportunity for townspeople and burghers to express their piety and independence from the diocesan clergy.[50]

PREACHING

A problem related to the clergy that Cervini sought to ameliorate involved preaching.[51] Members of religious orders, or the regular clergy, participated much more extensively in the instruction of the laity through sermons in Italian dioceses than did secular clerics. Preachers who fell into doctrinal "errors" in the sixteenth century represented a threat to the dissemination of orthodox beliefs, so bishops and administrators sought to correct and punish such clerics. A further complication arose when many of them, as members of specific religious orders, claimed exemption from episcopal control and correction, based upon rights and immunities granted by previous popes at the initial institution of the orders. The question was, Who constituted the "ordinary" superior of a religious preacher—the superior in the order, or the bishop of the diocese in which the person lived and worked? A papal bull published as late as 1534 reinforced the notion that superiors were the real "ordinaries" when regular clergy were accused of heresy in their preaching. The document stated that Franciscans under suspicion should not be judged by local inquisitions, but rather that such cases should be referred to the superior.[52]

Cervini discussed this problem in an exchange of letters in 1546 with Girolamo Seripando, who faced such problems regularly as general of the Augustinian order, and with Alessandro Farnese. Apparently Cervini had requested the opinion of Seripando on the topic, since in the spring of 1546 the problem was under discussion at Trent. In strong words, Seripando told Cervini that the flocks of preachers belonging to religious orders ought to remain under the control of the pope, not the individual bishop. They ought to be in the hands of the Apostolic See, he argued, because they were instituted by that see. In addition, it is the only way, Seripando said, that "all will be better united in one doctrine." He added a heavy criticism of the bishops aiming to reverse the procedure, who, in his opinion, simultaneously ignored their own responsibilities. "When bishops do not fulfill their duty to preach," he said, "they cannot rightly demand to be the judges of preachers."[53]

Cervini related his own assessment of the problem in a letter to Farnese. While he agreed that these regular preachers should remain under the control of the papacy on the basis of the derivation of ecclesiastical authority, he certainly believed that it was the duty of bishops to oversee and direct diocesan clergy, especially over the content of their sermons. He demonstrated this in his actions as well as in his words. But he was still more than sensitive to the desire of individual bishops to hold a regular preacher accountable. He also argued in favor of Seripando's basic point in a letter of the three legates to Farnese. All preaching issues, he maintained, were problems related to the neglect of the duty of episcopal residence. One of the fundamental responsibilities of the bishop is to preach, but that is a moot point if the duty to reside is not fulfilled first.[54]

Seripando undoubtedly gained appreciation for the episcopal point of view through the exchange with Cervini. He then helped create a compromise between these competing authorities of bishop and religious superior at the debates at Trent later that spring. He suggested a policy that was incorporated into the reform decree of the fifth session (June 17, 1546) of the council. It stipulated that regulars must receive the permission of the local bishop to preach, if the church in which the sermon was to be given fell under the bishop's jurisdiction. In their own churches, religious orders possessed virtually complete freedom, as preachers there were to be examined regarding doctrine by their superiors in the order.[55]

Cervini obviously took the direct responsibility of the individual local bishop very seriously, since he wrote a set of instructions to preachers in the diocese of Gubbio. In this document, Cervini showed his concern over the impact of heretical doctrine and what preachers might do to remedy the situation, a concern he shared with many of his contemporaries. He addressed his set of instructions to a preacher at Pergola, a town some thirty kilometers northeast of Gubbio itself.[56] Although the instructions are undated, they undoubtedly were prepared at some point during his administration of the diocese. Given his admonition to concentrate on the concepts of free will, original sin, and justification as defined at Trent, it is clear they were prepared and sent sometime after the sixth session of the council (January 19, 1547), when work on those topics was completed.

One might argue, on even stronger related evidence, that they were written late in the fall of 1549. At that time, Carlo Vannetti was acting as vicar for Cervini in Gubbio, and a problem arose over a report of questionable preaching on the part of a certain friar, Bartolomeo of Pergola, who had delivered the Lenten series in Pergola the previous spring. Bartolomeo had come under suspicion before, for allegedly preaching false doctrine in a series of sermons delivered at the request of Giovanni Morone in Modena in 1544, but he had received a full absolution and an attestation of orthodoxy from Inquisitor General Michele Ghislieri.[57] Vannetti reported to Cervini on October 24, 1549, that he had spoken with another friar in the territory regarding Bartolomeo. The friar, a certain Don Paulo, assured him that he had discerned no defect in the preacher, but rather that he was always properly submissive and respectful toward the Roman church. Vannetti went on to say there were problems of heresy in Pergola. In particular, the opinion was circulating that masses and offices said for the dead were unnecessary and that, as a result, such prayers constituted a kind of false devotion leading to the neglect of charity. Precisely this argument was addressed by Cervini in his preaching instructions. In an attempt to provide a solution, Vannetti recommended to Cervini that since "this evil was caused by some preachers who in the past have preached licentiously . . . [who] were for the most part unlearned," then, "nothing would be more expedient than to make provision for good preachers."[58] Overseeing the appointment of Lenten preachers (a procedure Cervini frequently sought to follow) and the issuance of a set of instructions for preachers would be two crucial ways to make the kind of provision Vannetti suggested. Regardless of whether Cervini wrote the text in direct response to the problems Vannetti related, these instructions reflect Cervini's understanding of the problem of heresy as well as his long-standing concern for the improvement of clerical education and conduct.

Cervini began his instructions with some general remarks. First, he asserted, preachers should, in accord with apostolic doctrine, preserve the foundation of the faith. That foundation (which should always be considered first, he stated) is simply the person of Jesus Christ. He added the task of understanding and preserving that faith as related in its most ancient sources: the Scriptures, the tradition of the church from the Apostles, and the councils as confirmed by the sacred doctors of the church.[59] He instructed his readers to cut through heresy and any stray doctrines carried into the Church of Christ. He suggested other changes as well. His readers were to be concerned first with making the spread of heresy impossible, but they were also to beware of the desire to show off their learning, as this might lead them into the sort of "innane questions" and "windy disputations" that ought to be avoided. Those suspected of heresy should be contradicted without entering into disputations, he maintained, by the assertion of Catholic truth, that is, what the church has declared through its councils and long-standing tradition. He insisted that his readers be clear and comprehensible in their preaching, without hedging or equivocating.

Cervini then shifted his attention, as he said, "to the particulars." Maintaining his point that the simple articles of faith should be emphasized, he argued that the lack of full understanding of such articles made the work of heretics easier. It was through the elaboration of simple elements in the faith that heretics typically attempted to introduce their own ideas. He began his description of the crucial and basic elements of the faith, not surprisingly, with the unity of the church. Teach the unity of the church, Cervini said, which is one under its supreme head, Christ. It was Christ, he said, who instituted the church on earth through his words, "Feed my sheep," which were addressed to Peter and to all his successors. Peter and Paul consecrated that Roman church with their blood, maintained Cervini, and Peter's successors the vicars of Christ have presided over it. Through this church and through these Petrine successors, he argued, all receive and hold the confession of faith.

Cervini continued by presenting guidance on how to handle the most controversial problems of the age: original sin, justification, and free will. These were complex problems, he maintained, since, in addition to the obviously bad extremes of Manichaeanism and Lutheranism into which one could fall, there was also the danger of Pelagianism. Without discussing any of the concepts in detail, he urged that, on these topics, those under his jurisdiction should "preach and follow the doctrines declared in the Council of Trent." He had good reason to make this suggestion. It squared perfectly with his earlier point that the decrees of councils constitute one of the primary sources for a correct understanding of the faith. In addition, the decrees issued to that point in Trent had attempted to avoid the contentious disputes of scholastic theology, just as he recommended in his opening remarks of his instructions. Beyond this, the decrees had been hammered out after careful consideration of Lutheran positions on the pertinent issues, which Cervini instructed his readers to correct in public. And moreover, Cervini personally guided to completion the most heavily debated and controversial of those decrees, that on justification.

Cervini also urged his readers to concentrate on simple explication of basic doctrine on a number of other topics. He stressed the importance of virtue made explicit in charity, arguing that faith lacking this outreaching quality was useless, and he exhorted the preachers themselves to seek greater perfection in poverty, chastity, and obedience. On predestination, he said, center on the simple words of Paul in the first letter to Timothy, which state that God desires the salvation of all, through Christ Jesus, the one mediator between God and man. Concerning the sacraments, his readers were to teach that Christ was really present in the Eucharist, and that mass was to be understood as an efficacious sacrifice. On penance, he instructed them to exhort their listeners always to contrition, confession, and satisfaction for their sins. Further, he insisted they maintain the existence of purgatory in accordance with Scripture and the church fathers; that the treasury of merits is rightly dispensed by the pope through indulgences, by virtue of his plenitude of power; and that the teaching of the church on the proper veneration of the saints as expressed in the tradition of the church and in the councils should be affirmed in his readers' sermons.

Cervini concluded his remarks by ordering that this set of instructions be delivered to all the preachers in the area, both secular and regular. He told them firmly to use these suggestions, arguing that the doctrines that remain strong are those "which are not hidden from the Christian people, but are preached and made public." He instructed his readers never to be silent, or "to pass over those things that are necessary for the salvation of souls." He had become convinced that encouragement of such activity was necessary in his own diocese, and reports from other territories confirmed his opinion. Tommaso Stella, the bishop of Lavello, wrote to him in 1548 and indicated that preachers were the cause of the expansion of heresy. He recommended much firmer action than the writing of instructions for preachers, as he saw little chance of improving the situation without prohibiting many from exercising the office.[60] In March and April 1548, Cervini received information from the vice-legate of Romagna regarding preachers who attempted to explain such things as proper procedure in excommunication, the nature of hell, purgatory and limbo, and the process of absolution. Under Cervini's recommendation, the priests in question were instructed to steer away from those topics and focus on basic doctrine, and, according to the vice-legate, they did.[61]

In the text of his instructions to preachers, Cervini displayed attitudes that were much in line with his collaborators and contemporaries in the sixteenth-century episcopacy. There are striking similarities between this text and one written about ten years earlier for the identical purpose by Gasparo Contarini, which indicates the wide common ground shared by Cervini and Contarini on pastoral and doctrinal instruction.[62] They both maintained that preachers should stick to the basic, fundamental elements of faith and preach simply and clearly without ambiguity or ostentation. They both stated that the heart of the message to be preached was Jesus Christ, and they both sought to educate clergy on correct doctrine and on their role in spreading it. They also both focused upon the importance of proper preaching when explaining the sacraments.

There are, to be sure, important differences between the two texts. One might argue, for example, that Contarini's insistence that certain theological topics were to be preached in sermons before more educated audiences but to be avoided in sermons before more "common" people indicates that he, like others in the period, might have believed in a division between religion for the few and religion for the majority. Any argument made on the basis of this point in the text of Contarini should be tempered with a number of facts. First, the notion of adaptation to the audience was common in preaching texts. Second, the point squared with concepts derived from classical rhetoric, specifically Cicero's injunction that eloquent speakers make their orations *apte*. Third, the Council of Trent itself made the same admonition to bishops—they should explain the sacraments to the faithful, but always in accordance with their listeners' mental ability.[63]

Cervini cautioned his preachers to be simple and clear in their explanations, but the suggestion of a real distinction between a religion for the common people and a religion for the highly educated seems absent from his view. He insisted instead that preachers should not hide any doctrines and should present them all, in their Tridentine form, as clearly as possible. Contarini, it seems, held a less-democratic view of the theological capacity of a typical diocesan audience. Cervini provided a more pragmatic, solution-oriented approach than Contarini, and since he wrote later Cervini referred to doctrines that had been elaborated at Trent. Contarini's text might reflect the theological uncertainty that existed in the Catholic world at the time he wrote, as well as the bitter disputes among theologians of differing schools to which he was apparently so sensitive (not to mention his concern for the possible chaos among the laity that heretical preaching might cause). But the two had far more in common, including a concern for control of the "shrewd satans" who preached the "Lutheran disease," as Contarini put it.[64]

Reginald Pole and others held similar attitudes and recommended similar policies. Pole maintained a strategy for the control of heresy that involved two basic points: the simple explanation of the Gospel without recourse to scholastic language, and submission to the doctrines of the church. He even buttressed his conception of authority in the church in just the same manner as Cervini, with the promises of Christ to Peter, and hoped Protestants might be persuaded to accept Roman primacy.[65] Such similarities make it difficult to agree that prelates like Pole and Contarini are to be credited with a conciliatory attitude toward sixteenth-century heretics. That seems to be as much an oversimplification as the assertion that identical remarks from the lips and pen of Cervini could have been purely a "cover" for the desire to extend and expand papal supremacy.

Other Italian prelates who maintained the same position can also be cited. In his visitations of the diocese of Verona in 1530 and 1541, Gian Matteo Giberti encouraged his clergy to inculcate the fundamentals of faith through preaching in a way that avoided disputatious language and focused on useful things. He also wrote a manual for preachers, in 1540, entitled *Per li padri predicatori*. Gregorio Cortese expressed similar pastoral concerns. His most recent biographer argued that he was especially solicitous of proper religious guidance for uneducated persons, in a way that distinguished him from Contarini, but he also urged that a preacher ought to adapt material according to the capacity of his listeners. The same attitude found an echo in Carlo Bascapè, who served as bishop of Novara between 1593 and 1615. He warned his clergy to avoid complex doctrinal problems in preaching before the people.[66]

There is another fascinating sidelight to Cervini's instruction to preachers—the appearance of the text in two very different contexts. Cervini used it again in his work as head of the reform commission under Julius III, and the text was incorporated, in its entirety, in the bull drafted by that committee. In addition, Giovanni Morone (or someone working on his behalf) had Cervini's text copied and attributed to Morone while preparing a collection of documents to be used in his defense against the charge of heresy. A note attached to the text from a Milanese scribe in 1559 attests to the authenticity of the document and indicates that Morone sent it to his own vicar in the diocese of Novara in 1554. Firpo and Marcatto, the modern editors of the documents of Morone's trial, incorrectly surmised that the text was generated by Morone or one of his associates, in accord with the information given in the attestation of authenticity.[67] But correction of the attribution fails to answer other questions regarding the connection between Morone and Cervini that are raised by this text. Apparently, Morone sought to use the document disingenuously in order to prove his innocence and to suggest that he undertook serious pastoral efforts for the control of heresy; but why did he do this, and how did he (or one of his associates) secure a copy of the text? Such a blatant plagiarism should have been caught by anyone familiar with the reform document generated by Julius's commission. It may be that Cervini sent a copy of the text to Morone upon request in 1554. He certainly provided such assistance to other prelates throughout his career. But according to most assessments Cervini was a shrewd assessor of his colleagues, and it would be strange if he could not see through the request to Morone's real intention, if he shared, or even knew very much about, the suspicions surrounding Morone's orthodoxy harbored by Gian Pietro Carafa and other prelates. And he clearly knew plenty about those suspicions.

Although direct communication between Cervini and Morone regarding this text and these pastoral issues cannot be proved, Cervini provided advice on the appointment of preachers for his own vicars and for other prelates. Beccadelli wrote from Reggio in 1542, asking him "to make provision for a Lenten preacher, without delay." Later, Beccadelli reported that a certain Brother Andrea, a Franciscan, had been retained and was preaching "to the satisfaction of the city." Similarly Pietro Galliano, the bishop of Pistoia, thanked Cervini in 1549 for the recommendation of a certain Father Ercole of Mantova. "He not only preached catholically," Galliano said, "but where it was necessary he attacked the modern heresies, reproved vices and gained much fruit."[68]

The episcopal duty of visitation and correction of monasteries was another that Cervini wished to attend to himself, but again legations forced him to rely on others. In December 1540 he requested that this kind of work be undertaken by Diego Lainez, who later served as a theologian at the council and as the second superior general of the Society of Jesus. At the urging of Cervini, he preached to the nuns of Santo Thoma in Reggio Emilia. He aimed to improve their personal devotion to religious life and to their monastic rule. "I can only thank you for going to Reggio," Cervini wrote soon after. "Your preaching has borne good fruit," he said, because "they have changed their ways and are dedicated to hold on to that good life that pertains to their profession and to true religious life." Cervini even asked for the prayers of Lainez, "that they will persevere . . . until I am able personally to exhort them."[69] Lainez, he suggested, had performed the duty he hoped eventually to assume himself.

Cervini used Jesuit priests in additional monastic visitations, and to carry out other pastoral functions. He became familiar with Ignatius of Loyola and his companions from their first days in Rome.[70] This close association and friendship encouraged Ignatius to grant Cervini's requests for Jesuit monastic visitors. Antonio de Araoz (1516–1573) carried out a visitation of an abbey in Naples under Cervini's control in the same year as Lainez's visitation of Santo Thoma, and Paschase Broët (1500–1562) in Reggio made a visit to a community of religious women known as Santa Clara for five months in 1544.[71] The close association also encouraged swift approval of Cervini's request that Broët be sent to Montepulciano at a time when the new order was short of manpower. He sent the Jesuit there to get to know the Cervini family, and Broët became the spiritual director of a number of them. In fact, Cervini's half-brother Alessandro and his wife, Girolama, as well as two of Alessandro's sisters followed the Jesuit *Spiritual Exercises* under Broët's direction.[72] Cervini also employed Jesuits to propagate increased devotion to and reception of the sacraments and encouraged their foundation of colleges promoting a humanistic curriculum. He even encouraged the opening of a Jesuit college in Montepulciano, which was founded in 1557 but was very short-lived.[73]

In addition to the Jesuits, Cervini enlisted assistance for monastic visitations from other clerics. One of them was Ludovico Beccadelli, who was appointed to visit an Augustinian monastery in Venice in 1544, after Cervini began to oversee the adjudication of a dispute concerning the community. Three monks there, who went by the names of Peter

Aurelius Sanutus, Nicholas of Venice, and Mark of Padua, instigated opposition to the reform program of Girolamo Seripando, general of the order. They apparently accused Seripando of misbehavior of his own, and they hoped for support in their opposition from the Venetian Council of Ten. Beccadelli conducted the visitation after the three refused to journey to Rome when summoned. He succeeded, it seems, in convincing them of their error, and two of the three retracted their charges against Seripando. Cervini, who served as judge in the case, treated at least these two leniently.[74]

THE ROMAN INQUISITION

Another obligation of those in episcopal office in the mid-sixteenth century was to preserve orthodoxy. The obligation was not just related to, but was even implied in, most of the other categories of pastoral activity noted above. Yet, Italian bishops in the period increasingly undertook this duty in cooperation with local inquisitors and commissioners sent under the authority of the Roman Inquisition. The history of the Inquisition, or more properly of the various inquisitions in their local Spanish and Roman forms, has never lacked investigators. The goal has been to find an unbiased, objective description of those institutions, which will enlarge understanding of each of the inquisitions themselves, and of the essential nature of the Catholic church whenever and wherever those institutions existed. Still, historians seem distant from that goal.[75]

The character of the Roman Inquisition in the early years of its reinstitution after 1542 remains a matter for debate. Traditionally, historians have asserted that Paul III intended the revived Roman Inquisition, which began to function through the bull *Licet ab initio* (July 4, 1542), to operate in a moderate fashion. There is considerable evidence to support this view. Apparently Gian Pietro Carafa convinced the pope to re-create the organization, but Paul actively solicited the advice of others regarding the policies any such tribunal should follow, and among those were some with "spiritual" credentials, like Gregorio Cortese. When the bull of reinstitution was published, Paul placed Carafa and another prelate also famous for intransigent orthodoxy, Juan Alvarez de Toledo, at the head of the tribunal. But, according to Girolamo Seripando, he also placed persons there who might balance and moderate the group, in harmony with both his intention and his essential nature. Among those were Pier Paolo Parisio, Bartolomeo Guidiccione, Dionisio Laurerio, and Tommaso Badia, and certain other prelates were appointed later, like Cortese.[76] Some historians also point to the action of Paul III in revoking powers given to Carafa for the reform of curial offices, and they indicate that this too was part of Paul's attempt to reduce the authority and moderate the policies of Carafa. Scholars arguing from a different point of view indicate that the very use of terms like *moderate* (or *immoderate,* for that matter) imply improper historical judgments and insist that the essential plan driving the institution aimed at internal control of the church and its hierarchy.[77] There is considerable evidence to support this view, including the initiatives begun against the cardinals Giovanni Morone and Reginald Pole, and the attempt to insure the orthodoxy of lower-level clergy in diocesan and parish settings. The best evidence for this view is the history of the tribunal later in the sixteenth century, under Paul IV and Pius V. At any rate, the institution was not static, and a complete description will not be possible as long as the records of the Roman Inquisition are inaccessible.

Analysis of the work of Cervini on this front will therefore not provide a real solution to the debate, but his work is still of crucial importance. Like few of his colleagues, he confronted both sides of the contemporary Italian struggle to preserve orthodoxy, and he developed a wide variety of approaches when engaged in the myriad issues raised in that struggle. He undertook to solve problems of orthodoxy and heterodoxy in his work on a local level as an episcopal administrator, and at the same time he participated in efforts on a much broader level as a member of the directorship of the Roman Inquisition. He did not, in any sense, develop a perfectly uniform or consistent policy in treating heretics. Using the term *lutherani,* the sixteenth-century Italian code word for all Protestant groups, Cervini, in his letters, frequently condemned their "perverse obstinacy" and especially their pursuit of "innovations, not traditions."[78] He also argued that the use of force was among the principal options to be considered in dealing with heresy.[79] As a member of the board of directors of the Roman Inquisition, Cervini worked to create and implement policies and procedures aimed at destroying that obstinacy, and apparently with little reluctance to resort to force if necessary. In administrative practice in the territories under his jurisdiction, however, his policy varied widely.

As an episcopal administrator, Cervini judged that effective response to the problem of heresy was crucial in his office. His handling of this issue indicates he considered it an essentially pastoral function. He became concerned, for instance, with the impact of the text attributed to Benedetto da Mantova, *Il beneficio di Cristo.* He certainly knew of the criticisms leveled against the book, and he read the polemical tract produced to outline its errors, the *Compendio d'errori e inganni luterani* published by Ambrogio Catarino in 1544. Cervini wrote in that same year to Ludovico Beccadelli, who served as his vicar in Reggio, to learn whether or not *Il beneficio* was widely known in the territory, and to ask what effect it was having. Beccadelli had read the text three years earlier, apparently soon after it was completed and before it first appeared in an anonymous edition printed in Venice in 1543. "I have neither seen nor read it," Cervini reported to Beccadelli on January 10, 1544, but he indicated he was inclined to insist that it not be circulated or read in Reggio because it was considered heretical by the inquisitor Tommaso da Vicenza.[80]

Nine days later Cervini wrote to say that he had finally read the text, and that he found "many good things and many bad things" in it but still believed it should be banned in the diocese. He also explained his reasons. Cervini believed the book confused rather than clarified essential points of the Catholic faith, specifically justification. He argued that the author failed to distinguish between the means and the end of justification and failed also to distinguish among the various stages of grace: how it is received, how it progresses, and how one ought to persevere in it. He criticized the lack of attention in the book to the "other obligations" given to Christians besides the obligation of faith, and what he considered its predestinarian character. The author of such a doctrine, he argued, "would send to heaven, clothed and shoed, those in mortal sin." He told Beccadelli in no uncertain terms that he did not want the people of Reggio taught any such thing, but rather that "all should hope" in the justice of God, convinced that he would "not send anyone to hell" who does not merit it, but instead would "give his reward to every good work . . . done in faith and with charity." He also correctly identified the author as a "black monk," or member of the Cassinese congregation of the Benedictine order, a congregation with which he later became familiar at Trent.[81]

Beccadelli answered the letters ten days later. He sensed the force with which Cervini held his conviction about *Il beneficio*, but he too had read the book, and he expressed his own opinion anyway. The author had personally sent a copy to him, he explained, and he insisted that if it did contain errors, he would abandon his earlier positive assessment of the work. Thus he suggested that the criticisms of neither Catarino nor Cervini had satisfied him. He also attempted to answer Cervini's concern about its distribution in Reggio. He said that it was not currently being sold there and that few had any interest in reading it. He argued that prohibition and public burning of the book would be counter-productive, since people are by nature more curious about prohibited things.[82]

His argument had an effect he probably never expected—Cervini agreed with him. Always the pragmatist, he considered Beccadelli's point prudent and told him to handle whatever related problems might later arise on a case-by-case basis. If the book "should be found in the hands of anyone," he should make the prohibition "carefully," Cervini said, clarifying the "dubious, subtle and overly confusing things," so that it will not cause others to fall into error.[83] Cervini demonstrated that his primary concern was to eliminate pastoral problems and find a manner in which the members of the diocese could be taught clear Catholic doctrine. Beccadelli knew the real situation in Reggio, and Cervini acted upon his advice.

Concern that heretical literature might have a detrimental effect in Italy resulted in some contact, at approximately this time, between Cervini and Vittoria Colonna (1490–1547). She was one of the most prominent women of sixteenth-century Italy, the daughter of Fabrizio and Agnese Colonna, and granddaughter of Federico da Montefeltro, the duke of Urbino. At the age of seven she became engaged to Ferrante d'Avalos, the marquis of Pescara, and they were married in 1509. After his death in battle in 1525, she intended to enter a convent, but this move was blocked by her brother Ascanio. In Naples in 1530, she had contact with a group brought together around the religious teaching and preaching of Juan de Valdés, and she also was attracted to the teachings of the Capuchin branch of the Franciscan order. She corresponded with a number of other important figures, both clerics and laymen, during her adult life—Gasparo Contarini, Michelangelo, Reginald Pole, Charles V, Pietro Bembo, Carlo Gualteruzzi, and Baldassare Castiglione, to name a few.

Colonna became concerned, in 1542, over correspondence that had reached her from the ex-Capuchin Bernardino Ochino, whom she had originally met in Rome in 1534. She found his personal qualities and the religious ideals of his order attractive, and she even defended the order in a letter addressed to Gasparo Contarini in 1536. In 1542, after his infamous flight in the face of an imminent inquisitorial trial, Ochino sent her a letter from Bologna and with it a small book of his sermons. She wrote about the book to Cervini in December 1542. The little book in question was printed in Geneva in October 1542, and in her letter Colonna expressed fear that the publication of the work might result in the further diffusion of the ideas of the now-discredited Ochino. A historian recently reviewing the relationship between Colonna and Cervini considered it less than cordial. Although they possessed a common interest in poetry and in contemporary art, and they collected many of the same books and manuscripts, their real interests diverged.

They were also, apparently, critical of one another. Toward the end of the life of Paul III, Colonna expressed her preference for the accession of a cardinal other than Cervini to the papal office. Cervini may indeed have disapproved of her contacts with prelates like Bembo, Giberti, and Pole, but there is little in the way of correspondence or other evidence to support this. When Colonna informed Cervini of the publication of Ochino's sermons, it might have been out of a desire to minimize the association between herself and the former Franciscan. If indeed an effort at self-protection, it was not well timed, since Cervini had not yet been appointed to the Roman tribunal. Just as likely, she may have been expressing the same concern over proliferation of Protestant, heretical literature that characterized Cervini, Contarini, and numerous other persons during the Tridentine reformation.[84]

Cervini also faced problems related to orthodoxy in his administration of Gubbio. Pressure was even exerted upon him by the secular ruler of the territory to find a solution to the problem of heretical preaching. Guidobaldo della Rovere, the duke of Urbino, wrote to Cervini in the fall of 1549 to express his concern. He indicated his desire to "extirpate Lutheran impiety completely" in the duchy. He asked Cervini "to instruct" his vicar to procure information about "persons who have this stain" by means of the regular clergy "or other spies." He also expressed his own commitment to assist in the elimination of heresy whenever possible. The duke had probably heard the rumors circulating about heresy in Pergola.[85]

The procedure Cervini followed in this particular instance is important because of the difficulty of extracting the "truth" of the case. It is also important because, once again, he took the advice of his correspondent. After a brief visit to the diocese, Cervini sent his vicar Carlo Vannetti to inquire into the report of Bartolomeo's heretical preaching in Pergola. Vannetti reported the results of his investigation in two letters dated October 1549. Under Cervini's orders, he assured those giving information that they would be protected with secrecy. They would be spies of a sort, just as the duke had suggested. Vannetti then procured information from Don Paulo, another monk in Pergola, who had previously denounced Bartolomeo before Cervini in Rome. This time, he changed his story and argued instead the innocence of Bartolomeo. When he did, Vannetti took pains to check the evidence independently.[86]

Cervini considered everything carefully and then suggested in a letter to Vannetti that the testimony of Don Paulo was probably not very reliable. Cervini may have wondered why someone wishing to change a denunciation previously given would ask for a guarantee of secrecy.

Vannetti later reported that he had run into Don Paulo on another occasion, and that as a result of the meeting he agreed with Cervini's assessment. His air, Vannetti reported, "had the same presumption." But Vannetti did not stop there. "I went to ask of his status in Pergola among the religious," he related, and even "coming to his own monastery . . . I found in effect a united consensus that the aforesaid Don Paulo is a ruined man and . . . that he has one of the saddest and most pernicious tongues there is in Pergola."[87] The local vicar was mystified at the reversal of information but was also quite convinced of the error of Bartolomeo. Others in the diocese, such as the prior of the local Augustinian monastery, also urged Cervini to take action to ensure orthodox preaching. And thus the case, in all likelihood, generated the pastoral response embodied in Cervini's set of instructions to preachers.

Beyond addressing problems in areas under his personal control, Cervini frequently served as consultor on inquisitorial problems, as a result of his status as member of the directorship of the tribunal. The precise date of his appointment to this post remains unknown. He certainly did not become a member in 1542, as his name does not appear among the six appointed by *Licet ab initio*. Pastor surmised that he might have begun to serve as early as 1545, upon the death of another inquisitor, but the first certain indication comes from 1546, when he was listed among the four members of the tribunal, along with Toledo, Sfondrato, and Carafa. Thereafter, Cervini apparently served on the board irregularly. He was not among the six appointed by Julius III when reconfirming the institution, but he was listed among the seven members in February 1551 and seemed to remain in the position until his papal election in 1555. The other six appointed in 1551 were Rodolpho Pio da Carpi, Juan Alvarez de Toledo, Marcello Crescenzi, Girolamo Verallo, Reginald Pole, and the omnipresent Gian Pietro Carafa.[88]

Cervini became a point of reference for inquisitors and for bishops and administrators facing inquisitorial problems. Luigi Lippomano wrote to Cervini from Bologna in 1547, outlining a case in Venice that required his attention. A certain member of the conventual Franciscans, whom Lippomano described as "the greatest Lutheran in the world," was held for a long time in a Venetian prison and had allegedly taught some other prisoners that they ought not to confess or receive communion at the point of death. He explained that the man had been handed over to secular authorities since he had shown no repentance. He also warned Cervini that the man had defenders at the secular court. Lippomano believed that, as a result of their position, the friar would receive lenient treatment. He asked Cervini to suggest that the pope "hotly intercede" with the Venetian ambassador in Rome, so that these defenders might be reproved for their lack of zeal.[89]

Lippomano then lamented what he considered generally lackadaisical treatment of those suspected of heresy and exclaimed, "Why . . . is there not placed a more severe inquisition against these sad Lutherans . . . [to] castigate them in accordance with their faults?" He had heard the inquisitions of Spain and Portugal were severe and effective, and he suggested their example should be followed, in order to bring under control a problem that, he said, "begins with the Our Father and ends in the arcibus." Language like this, found nowhere in Cervini's own letters, was common for Lippomano. His response to the identification of heresy was always more extreme than Cervini's. When he found examples of it in his diocese of Verona, he wrote no brief instruction to preachers but commissioned two clerics to write a summary of the faith. He hoped all those in the diocese would read it, but when the two clerics were finished, he spent twenty months revising and expanding it himself. When the final product was printed, it ran to more than a thousand pages. The comments of Lippomano in the 1547 case are all the more shocking (or perhaps comical) in light of the end of his letter. He begged Cervini's pardon, lest in his writing he appeared overly zealous.[90]

As a member of the directorship of the Roman tribunal, Cervini also participated in the case against Giacomo Nacchianti, the bishop of Chioggia. Nacchianti came under scrutiny because of his comments in debate at Trent in 1547, where he allegedly demonstrated sympathy for Lutheran teachings, and due to an allegation that in his own diocese he praised preaching that utilized terminology reminiscent of "salvation by faith alone." He was tried for these reasons in 1548 and 1549. Normally, a case like this would have been referred to a local inquisitor, but instead testimony was taken in Rome from a Chioggian schoolteacher, and the Roman tribunal, almost certainly following Cervini's suggestion, sent Angelo Massarelli from Bologna (where he was serving as secretary of the transferred council) to Chioggia to investigate. Massarelli indicated that, from what he could learn, the accusations were correct, but friends of Nacchianti protested to the tribunal in Rome that Massarelli had conducted his investigation improperly. They charged that Massarelli sought depositions only from the enemies of Nacchianti, notably Tommaso Stella. Cervini did not take this protest lightly, despite his own receipt of information questioning Nacchianti's character and even though he always referred to Massarelli as a well-trusted secretary.[91] He ordered Massarelli to send copies of the interviews conducted. Massarelli did so, insisting that his investigation had been proper and fair, and indeed he had interviewed persons favorable to the bishop. Nacchianti was held in the monastery of San Francesco in Bologna in February 1549, and Cervini received the commission to make a final resolution in the case. He ordered still further investigation, instructing Massarelli to interrogate Nacchianti again. The bishop then indicated that he had lied in earlier testimony. Cervini threatened him with trial in Rome if he refused to tell the full truth, and in April Nacchianti fled. Massarelli felt vindicated by the flight, but somehow Nacchianti was absolved. He attended all the later sessions of Trent and became famous for his pastoral work in Chioggia, a see he held until his death in 1569. In this case, Cervini ordered a systematic investigation, and when the procedures came under question, even when conducted by a man he trusted well, he insisted upon additional queries and a personal review of the question. He certainly did not act without consideration of both sides in the dispute.

There is an interesting sidelight to this story. While on the trip to Chioggia in late December 1548, Massarelli happened to meet Benedetto da Mantova, who was himself under investigation. Benedetto requested the intervention of Massarelli with the president of the Cassinese congregation, who was conducting the inquiry. Massarelli himself had no real influence with such a person, so it seems likely that Benedetto hoped the secretary would pass his request on to Cervini. The modern editor of Benedetto's work indicated that this request for the protection of Cervini is not surprising, despite his status on the Roman tribunal, since the Benedictines had long possessed the power to conduct their own investigations concerning the orthodoxy of their members. The request is not surprising for other reasons as well: Benedetto probably knew of Cervini's originally favorable reaction, at Trent, to the members of the congregation and their ideas, of Cervini's interest in sources like John Chrysostom that inspired the theology of the congregation, and perhaps even of Cervini's work with Isidoro Chiari, another member of the congregation.[92] If he had any knowledge of Cervini's general approach on inquiries regarding orthodoxy, or of his policy in Reggio regarding *Il beneficio*, he could certainly have expected Cervini to insist the investigation be thorough and even-handed.

As a member of the Roman tribunal, Cervini became closely involved in the direction of inquisitorial work in the city of Bologna in the late 1540s. In that work he confronted a number of interesting situations, some better known than others. Angelo Massarelli and a number of other persons related one complicated case in a series of letters between August 1548 and September 1549. The Contessa of a small town about thirty-five kilometers southeast of Bologna, Bagno, contacted Massarelli and asked him to recommend to Cervini a certain friar, Pellegrino Fantaguzzo of Cesena. The friar had become suspected of heresy as a result of his Lenten preaching in 1546, with which the Contessa was familiar. He became suspect again, after the series he delivered two years later. She considered the new accusations a mere rehashing of the old and hoped Cervini would intercede. She believed the preacher to be innocent and suggested the problem be referred to another local prelate, who might be able to settle the matter in consultation with the local Franciscan minister. Massarelli urged her to write her own recommendation, which he included with his letter, and asked Cervini to advise him on a response to the woman. Before forwarding his decision, another letter concerned with the case was sent to Cervini, from Giovan Antonio Delphino, the local father minister in Bologna. Delphino indicated that he had kept the friar imprisoned for some months, ever since he became aware of the second series of accusations. The friar later escaped and, according to Delphino, had sought refuge at the house of the Contessa. Delphino also related his more general concern about the spread of heresy in the "castles of Romagna," where he said in the past one foreign priest spread heresies that "Luther never spoke or ever wrote." He suggested that this new situation might have the same outcome.[93]

Cervini told Massarelli he was reticent to suggest any solution. The problem should be left to the man's immediate superiors, he argued, the ministers in his own monastery and in the general administration of the order. Those prelates, he added, could have the praise if they were able to find an adequate solution, and the blame and responsibility "to render account to God and to men" if they should fall short. He refused to become involved if the situation did not somehow touch him directly. If Fantaguzzo wished to be cleared of the charges made against him before the Roman curia and before Cervini himself, he added, then the friar would have to appear personally in Rome, where he promised to "hear him patiently." The general of the Franciscan order later prohibited Fantaguzzo from preaching altogether, and Delphino presented the injunction to him personally. Delphino related this news to Cervini with a certain amount of satisfaction at having tracked down the slippery friar.[94]

Apparently Fantaguzzo made his way into the pulpit again and faced renewed accusations in 1549. This time the legate Giovan Maria del Monte appealed to Cervini through a letter written by Massarelli. Monte considered him a person of "good blood" and urged Cervini to seek reliable information in the case, but he insisted that he too did not want to become involved and would be perfectly satisfied with the solution when Cervini was convinced justice had been done. In fact, Monte frequently complained that the demands of his position as legate to the council precluded his spending much time on inquisitorial matters.[95]

Cervini also handled a case involving a bookseller indicted on a variety of charges. A certain Francesco, bookseller in Bologna, was charged with holding "bad opinions," with "selling prohibited books," and with "fleeing incarceration" after escape from detainment on the two previous counts. Monte received an offer from the man to make satisfaction by means of a fine and by whatever imprisonment was deemed appropriate by the inquisitors. He then instructed Massarelli to write to Cervini and ask for advice. Cervini ordered a lenient sentence. Massarelli explained about three months later that Francesco had satisfied the sentence and had been reconciled. For "fleeing prison" the bookseller paid an unspecified fine and underwent a gradual release—he spent some days in the headquarters of the inquisitor, some days under house arrest, a few with freedom to move about the city but under orders not to go into his shop, and then was given full release. After confessing to the charge of "selling prohibited books," he was required to provide the names of his conspirators, but those were kept secret and no proceedings were taken against them. Francesco also confessed to holding "bad opinions," but these Cervini apparently considered of no real importance. For that crime the bookseller received absolution and was given an unspecified "spiritual" penance. He also received a warning to see to it he did not slip again. If it ever happened, he was told, one of Cervini's informants in Bologna, Giovan Battista Scotti, would be there to catch him.[96]

Cervini encountered others in the city who wished to declare themselves penitent. He employed two Jesuits Paschase Broët and Alfonso Salmerón for other pastoral work in Bologna in 1548, and he gave them authority to absolve heretics if they judged it to be appropriate. As Broët indicated in his report to their superior, Ignatius of Loyola, they were granted the power by Cervini to absolve persons without recourse to inquisitorial processes, if "those heretics or Lutherans . . . wish to return to the obedience of the Holy Church."[97]

In another case, Monte informed him of a group of heretics who had confessed their errors and were ready to do the penance required. After consultation with the other members of the tribunal, Cervini decided the clerics in question should make an abjuration in Bologna and then travel to Rome to receive and perform their penance. Monte shot back a quick, but lengthy, response. He criticized the decision for the unreasonable cost involved in the trip, both for the repentent heretics and for himself, since he would have to send a guard. He suggested that the entire procedure be handled in one place or the other.[98]

Cervini also received appeals concerning inquisitorial sentences already handed down. One such appeal came in 1548 from Antonio Maria Thita, who explained how he had been suspended from preaching, from the hearing of confessions, and from even speaking about Scripture, in addition to being exiled and imprisoned. He made the appeal after serving five months of a prison sentence of unspecified length. He maintained that he was innocent from the beginning but asked Cervini for a pardon and a diminution of the sentence.[99] Although interesting, it is impossible to know the real significance of the letter, in the absence of a pardon granted or denied. That Thita made the request suggests he held some reasonable expectation that the appeal to Cervini might be taken seriously.

Angelo Massarelli, the conciliar secretary, kept Cervini advised of the situation involving Giovanni Ferro, another who faced inquisitorial action. A large bail was arranged for him, which allowed his release from prison but also guaranteed his presence in Bologna should inquisitors feel the need to contact or question him any further. Part of the bond was posted by a member of his family, although one of his brothers refused to participate. Massarelli explained to Cervini that a delay in communication regarding the terms and arrangements demanded for the bond had some unforeseen and unpleasant, but not unuseful, consequences. Because the conditions of the bond were not known in time, Ferro was held in prison for two days until the information arrived. "As they say who know him better than me," Massarelli related, "he was rather humiliated." Then the secretary let slip a telling line. "It is sometimes necessary," he said, "to use the whip when enticements do not work."[100]

So Cervini maintained a policy toward inquisitorial work in this period that clearly varied according to individual circumstances. He certainly supported the use of force in theory but, in practice, often sought to mitigate such procedures. He even advocated absolution, at times, and full circumvention of inquisitorial procedures, and he placed the power to carry this out in persons unconnected with the tribunal. Such a policy was not dissimilar from that of Giovanni Morone, who at times expressed satisfaction when force was employed and at other times suggested absolution, as his colleague had done.[101] For Cervini, though, return to the doctrines defined by the church and acceptance of the duty of obedience to its hierarchical authority was undoubtedly the deciding factor. The information that is available seems to indicate that Cervini's approach could certainly be characterized as thorough, and perhaps even as cautious or balanced.

Cervini's pastoral work prior to 1550 was primarily carried out via correspondence, the only mode that was open to him. His only opportunities to visit his diocese in person during this time were his one-night visit to Reggio, mentioned above, and a brief stay in Gubbio during September and early October 1549. Nonetheless, his work was recognized and even served as a model for other bishops. The diocesan statutes he ordered as a result of Lorenzini's visit in 1543 became the model for one of his successors at Reggio, G. B. Grossi (bishop 1549–1569), who issued his own *Costituzione sulla vita ed onestà del clero*. Isidoro Chiari, the bishop of Foligno, also knew Cervini's statutes. Cervini received a letter from him in 1550, after Isidoro held a synod in his own diocese. Isidoro used these statutes, he explained, "to enhance not only the episcopal office, but also divine worship and the [spiritual] health of the clergy."[102] In this, Cervini resembled Gian Matteo Giberti, who had earlier become a model for Italian bishops seeking renewal and improvement of devotion in their dioceses. The work of Cervini, like that of Giberti, was to move from abstract programs of reform to concrete action. Later, after Cervini made his brief visit to Gubbio, his work was even recognized by a man not particularly noted for serious interest in ecclesiastical reform, Giovan Maria del Monte, who was soon to be Pope Julius III. "I can see your intent to hold a little synod and to make a good little reformation," he said in a letter in 1549, one that will "serve as an example, or should I say a common model for the other bishops." He added, "May God make all your actions prosper."[103]

Despite this recognition, Cervini faced others who were not as sympathetic to his desire to reside in and care for his diocese, and so, for him, the frustration continued. After years of entreaty, Cervini finally gained permission from the Farnese family to visit his diocese. But on September 30, when Cervini had been in Gubbio barely twelve or fifteen days, Pope Paul III and his grandson Alessandro demanded his return to Rome. "Presupposing that your Reverence already in large part has satisfied the desire to attend to the things of your church," Alessandro wrote, "to our Lord [the pope] it seems that your Reverence should return to Rome without delay, by the 8th or 9th of next month."[104] There is something ironic in the suggestion that the purpose of a visit to a diocese the bishop had never seen could be satisfied in two weeks, coming from a man who was an enormous accumulator of benefices. Cervini could not have missed that irony. Nevertheless, he obeyed and returned on October 9. But whether his efforts were appreciated at the time or not, they establish him among those who sought the improvement of diocesan life before this was fully mandated by the Council of Trent.

CHAPTER SIX

Episcopal and Inquisitorial Activity after 1550

THE EFFECT OF JULIUS III

The ecclesiastical life and work of Marcello Cervini changed dramatically after 1550. When the papacy came into the hands of Giovan Maria del Monte early that year, Cervini finally began to escape the frustration associated with his earlier pastoral work. He had believed, or at least had thought loyalty demanded he believe, that Paul III had the piety, strength of character, and determination to undertake a genuine and effective reform of the entire church. For that reason, Cervini had resigned himself to working in the background, continually urging Paul to swifter action, but with patience, waiting for the pope to act. He had even made a trip to Rome from the conciliar assembly at Trent with the hope that his presence and urging might have some effect in spurring Paul to carry out the work he considered crucial, regardless of whether the council ever concluded its business. Cervini did not, however, hold a similar conviction of the personal qualities and determination of Monte when he ascended the papal throne, after a long conclave, on February 8, 1550.[1] Cervini found his opinion confirmed by the early decisions of the new pope, and he then gradually separated himself from the Roman curia in the years between 1550 and his own papal election in 1555.

Among those decisions was Julius's first appointment to the status of cardinal—it went, in perfect unreformed style, to his seventeen-year-old adopted nephew, Innocenzio del Monte (1532–1577). Innocenzio, the illegitimate son of a poor woman in Piacenza, received the assistance of

Monte when the legate took the boy and his entire family into his household. The future pope allegedly saw promise in the young man and turned him over to a tutor. Julius made the boy cardinal over the unanimous opposition of the other members of the college, whose impression of him turned out to be accurate: although legitimated by papal bull in 1552, Innocenzio failed to live up to the confidence Julius placed in him, became infamous later for a double homicide, and even served time in Castel' Sant'Angelo.[2] Although he had seen worse in the policies of Paul III, notably the promotion of three grandsons to the cardinalate and the donation of a considerable chunk of the papal temporal state to his son Pier Luigi, such actions by the new pope left Cervini disappointed. Since he owed nothing to Monte in comparison with the Farnese family, who had sponsored his career, Cervini left no doubt regarding his disagreement. Through "infrequent and late attendance in the consistory" (according to one of his biographers) "and with his stern silence," he demonstrated his dissatisfaction, although he did not have the courage or the "disposition to censure [Julius] publicly." As a result, Cervini did not feel compelled to remain in Rome, and he sought as quickly as possible to attend, actively and personally, to the problems of reform that fell under his own jurisdiction. Disgust for the curia had driven other prelates from Rome in the past, notably Gian Matteo Giberti, who also turned his efforts to pastoral work.[3]

Illness prevented Cervini from attending the election and coronation of Julius III, and another bout in May 1550 allegedly caused his departure from Rome. Massarelli reported in his diary that on May 7, 1550, Cervini suffered from an "extraordinary fever" and that he received the Eucharist on May 13, fearing for his life. After a near-miraculous cure he left Rome, Massarelli said, to take his "native air" in Montepulciano to aid in his recovery. One of Cervini's biographers, however, suggested that this excuse, and the one like it toward the end of the pontificate of Julius III, was not completely genuine. It was really his disappointment over the decisions of Julius that led Cervini to leave Rome "under the cover" of the need for convalescence at home.[4] Whether Cervini's need for the air of Montepulciano was real or not, Julius III considered the request reasonable, as he apparently raised no objections to Cervini's departure on May 22. After about two months, Cervini left Montepulciano, but not to return to Rome—by August 2 he had arrived in Gubbio.

Thereafter, Cervini divided his time between Rome and Gubbio. He spent most of the summer and part of the fall in Gubbio during each of the next four years, for periods between four and five months. The longest was his trip in 1551, which ran from early July until early

December. The shortest was in 1550, from about August 2 until October 25. In 1554 he remained in Gubbio for a relatively short time, from late May until mid-October, perhaps because of the failing health of Julius III and the expectation of an imminent conclave.[5] The length of these periods in Gubbio makes it difficult to pass off the sojourns as merely convenient escapes from the heat of the Roman summers. Cervini's pastoral focus and his repeated expressions of interest in attending to his diocese also make it difficult to sustain this interpretation. During those periods Cervini finally found the time necessary to give real, personal attention to Gubbio, while serving as cardinal protector of the Augustinian and Servite orders and in various other capacities via correspondence.

The title of "cardinal protector" is most commonly understood to refer to a cardinal who, at the request of the individual order, is assigned by the pope (usually through actual appointment by the papal secretary of state) as a counselor, helper, and advocate in regard to issues involving the order and its members that come to the attention of the pope and curia.[6] This office was instituted in the thirteenth century, when Cardinal Ugolino received appointment as pastor of the Franciscan movement by Pope Honorius III (1216–1227). Gregory XI (1370–1378) more carefully circumscribed the duties of the office in 1373, to include presiding over general chapters, appointing procurators, dividing provinces, and confirming the acts of general chapters. Innocent XII (1691–1700) gave the institution a final form in the papal constitution *Christi fidelium,* on February 16, 1694.

In exercising this office, Cervini undertook specific actions aimed at the general improvement of the orders under his protectorship.[7] His correspondence indicates that there was much to be done. He saw the post as requiring a person committed to the encouragement of religious life. He received the charge to work in this capacity for the Augustinian order in early 1550, after the death of the previous protector, Niccolò Ridolfi, on January 31. Seripando, the general of the order, was delighted at the appointment. He had admired Cervini since their days at Trent, despite their disagreements, and he referred to the prelate as "our good anchor, who appears to have been sent by heaven to support us in our work." Cervini obviously took his duties seriously and acted immediately, urging Seripando to reform the monastery in Montepulciano during his convalescence there that spring. He also worked hard to ensure that the order would receive good governance. He approved completely of the reform efforts undertaken by Seripando and wished to guarantee they would continue, when the general suffered a partially paralyzing stroke in 1550. Cervini urged him to remain in charge as long as possible, then he helped steer the general chapter toward the election of Cristoforo Patavino (+1569), the man Seripando considered best qualified to replace him as general.[8]

Cervini faced an example of extreme moral decay involving the Augustinians in 1550. It revolved around their monastery in Macerata, a town about fifty kilometers south of Ancona. He received a letter from Bernardo Buongiovanni, the bishop of Camerino, who as vice-legate of the Marches was engaged in a visitation of the town. In a prison there he found a number of Augustinian friars from the monastery of Santa Maria della Fonte. "In collaboration with another monastery of the same order," he said, they "violated a cloister of nuns in such a way that not only that place, but the whole province was filled with a bad spirit against the order." They had been in prison for some time, but, he added, the prior general desired their imprisonment to be permanent, to pacify the people. He requested the advice of Cervini since he was protector of the order. "Just so that you can see how ugly this case is," he explained, "I enclose a copy of the letter that the aforesaid friars sent to the nuns."[9] There followed a letter explaining the reactions of both the people and the Augustinian prior general. In the letter, the abbot of the monastery and seven others from the house recalled their visit to the "venerable sisters," where they had enjoyed access to the entire complex, including the cells of individual nuns.[10] The document bore the signatures of all eight.

Cervini sent another prelate, Paolo Mancini, to visit the Augustinian monastery in Montepulciano. He encountered a very different situation there, involving financial irregularities. The monastery had endured a long history of "scandalous times," he explained, when the income of the institution was abused by those entrusted with its care. "Grave shortages of bread, oil and wood" resulted, and so Mancini, under Cervini's direction, "placed at the service of the . . . convent a good and honored family," who would insure that the brothers were well treated. The new caretakers were also entrusted with the duty to thwart those who "would steal the goods of Saint Augustine." This sort of practical advice by Cervini was neither unique nor limited to problems of individual convents. Cervini concerned himself with the public image of the order and had practical recommendations for enhancing that too. He wrote to Cristoforo Patavino, the general of the Augustinians, in 1551. "Go to Trent," he told him, "with four or six of the most learned theologians [in the order] . . . and choose those that are . . . of exemplary life, so they will compare favorably with honor and edification, to the members of the . . . other religious orders present." And "consider well," he added, "the importance of the choice of these theologians."[11]

With respect to the Servites, Cervini similarly guided and oversaw action in a variety of cases. Vittore Soranzo (1500–1558), in his capacity as bishop of Bergamo, visited two Servite cloisters located in the territory and reported what he found to Cervini. He related that both the male and female institutions were in a "most scandalous" condition, and that the situation was long-standing. Few years had passed, he explained, in which there was not some noteworthy problem, the latest concerning one of the Servite friars from the monastery of San Gottardo—he had impregnated a sister from the cloister known as Il Paradiso. He indicated he would write to the superior general, Agostino Bonucci, and request immediate transfer of the woman to another convent. He then told Cervini that he believed such a response, although necessary in Bergamo due to improper governance on the part of local superiors, had limited usefulness. The problems he encountered were so severe he feared even provision for the transferal of the guilty parties and for their replacement with other friars and sisters would still be inadequate "to disinfect" those monasteries. Cervini appointed Soranzo visitor of those Servite institutions under his own authority and continued to direct him on these matters in 1550. In light of additional information, Soranzo related his determination to undertake a still more vigorous visitation of the two religious houses. The information came from persons whom he trusted, but who also had requested anonymity. He told Cervini that he was ashamed just to think about the charges related to him, much less to write them down. But he did record one case, explaining how one of the friars was surprised in the act of fornication—and not in his cell but in the church connected to the monastery.[12]

All of this is surprising, in light of Soranzo's own career. Born to a Venetian noble family and a student at Padua, Soranzo initially gained prominence through his friendships with persons like Pietro Bembo, and with Reginald Pole and the rest of the famous group that congregated with him in Viterbo. The group included the Marchesa of Pescara, Vittoria Colonna. Soranzo spent part of a year in 1541 cultivating his friendships in Viterbo, but it was through Bembo that he received the greatest help—an education and also the curial office he held during the administration of Clement VII. He also received from Bembo an appointment to the position of coadjutor in the diocese of Bergamo, in June 1544. Over the next few years he concerned himself in Bergamo with correction of clerical activity, and in 1544 he undertook to issue diocesan constitutions addressing the problems of concubinage, the residence of parish priests, the administration of the sacraments, and the control of heretical literature. The constitutions, which also recommended the pursuit of jubilee indulgences from the papacy for diocesan visitations, went through eight editions. He also made the visitation himself, which one historian indicated was the most complete undertaken before the Council of Trent and which compared favorably with those of Carlo Borromeo. Soranzo became bishop of Bergamo in his own right after the death of Bembo in 1547.[13]

Thereafter, Soranzo encountered difficulties with which Cervini was familiar. In 1548 he was attacked by a public notice accusing him of connection with a monastery that the civil authorities (who were themselves vigilant in the pursuit of heresy) considered infected. He also faced the charge of personal possession of heretical literature. Ghislieri was sent to look into the matter, but no action was taken against Soranzo at the time. Cervini most certainly would have known the details of the investigation, since he was the one who suggested that Ghislieri be sent, and in all likelihood he also knew of the connection between Soranzo and the Viterbo group, since Cervini, Soranzo, and Pole were all together for a time at Trent in 1546.

Despite knowledge of his background and of these questions, Cervini utilized Soranzo in a delicate matter concerning the Servites. He apparently judged Soranzo's other pastoral work to be a more accurate indication of the prelate's character than the suspicions surrounding his orthodoxy. Cervini may also have attempted through the appointment to provide Soranzo with an opportunity to improve his reputation and clear his name. Concern over the separation of ecclesiastical and secular authority may have been another motive for Cervini's charge to Soranzo. His acting to subvert secular participation in the visitation of monasteries and convents would be consistent with his limiting the involvement of secular authorities in ecclesiastical matters. The *Consiglio comunale* in Bergamo had, since the late fifteenth century, appointed lay deputies to assist in canonical visitations of these institutions, to guarantee greater vigilance.[14]

Cervini guided another visitor, Girolamo Sauli (+1559), to a Servite monastery in Bologna. Sauli served as the vice-legate to that city, and also as archbishop of Genoa between 1550 and 1559. Although neither he nor Cervini identified the precise issue in their correspondence, Cervini evidently directed Sauli's investigation of a charge that monks there were less than rigorous in their observance of the rule. Sauli received a commission to visit the convent and was encouraged to contact Cervini for advice, since he was protector of the order. Sauli reported that this convent was "very lax." In fact, a split between observant and conventual Servites persisted in this period until 1570. At any rate, the issue was serious enough to warrant severe punishments. Cervini insisted that Sauli "use all diligence to get to the source of the ulcer, so that it will not reappear with time." He also ordered the transferal of some more observant friars to the Bolognese convent. Twenty-eight of the friars received censures: from one was removed the faculty to say mass, from others the faculty to hear confessions, while others were required to pay unspecified fines. Still others were punished with a diet of bread and water or were banished altogether.[15]

Cervini received information, in 1551, concerning a certain Venetian Servite whose orthodoxy had been questioned. The friar, identified as Father Giovanni Jacomo Milo, gained an assignment from his superior to preach the Lenten series in 1549 in the nearby town of Senigállia. The local bishop, Urbano Vigerio (+1570), later wrote to Cervini in defense of the preacher. He indicated that he had been present in the diocese for the entire period and had, in fact, personally attended the sermons. "I never heard anything [from him] that was not truly Catholic," he said. The people enjoyed the sermons too, and Vigerio felt so satisfied with the friar that he hoped the Servite chapter would agree to send him more often, so that he might preach before audiences in other portions of the diocese. Jealousy rather than fact, he surmised, was most likely the inspiration for the rumor of heresy. "If there is nothing more against him from a clearly trustworthy person," he added, "be persuaded that this is a brotherly persecution."[16]

In this manner, Cervini acquired plenty of information about the problems of religious life and discipline, and he stood ready to take action to alleviate those problems. He helped gain approbation of new Augustinian constitutions in 1551. The constitutions had been proposed by Seripando, and they enhanced the administrative power of the general. Cervini used his influence to persuade Julius III to accept the new rules, which were to be applied to all provinces and congregations of the order, even those that had not yet been touched by Seripando's considerable reform efforts. He succeeded in this despite disagreement over the constitutions within the order itself.[17]

He also attempted to directly influence the governmental procedures of the Servite order through a general chapter in the spring of 1554. The meeting was held in Verona. Cervini instructed his good friend and collaborator Luigi Lippomano, who was then bishop of that diocese, to watch over the proceedings. Lippomano's letters indicate the extent to which Cervini hoped to control the assembly and its work. He sent a set of constitutions to the assembly that he wished to see adopted.

Some, Lippomano indicated, were approved simply and expeditiously, while others underwent revision before approval. Among other things, Cervini desired to change the procedure for electing the general of the order. He wanted it undertaken through a secret ballot, and this proposal carried by a wide majority. He received complete information from Lippomano, including the number of votes received by each candidate for the office. Lippomano also urged him to forward other suggestions for reform of the administration of property and of general governance in the order.

All this action was easily reconcilable with Cervini's views on the derivation of ecclesiastical authority. His efforts in procuring the acceptance of the new Augustinian constitutions brought all members of the order under closer control of the general. This superior, in Cervini's view, should both hold and exercise leadership in the organization, and for good reason. After all, it was the general who, in the person of Seripando, had done all the significant reform work for the order in recent years. But the actions Cervini took did not always point in the direction of papal control over religious orders through the cardinal protectors and generals. He supported, for example, quick implementation of Cristoforo Patavino's 1555 instruction for Augustinian preachers. First among its provisions was to insist that preachers secure permission to preach from the local bishop.[18]

During this later period of administration, as throughout his career, Cervini also served as consultor for bishops and administrators seeking advice on pastoral problems. Many appeals for advice and assistance were addressed to Cervini because of his "discretion" and his "zeal" for the improvement of religious life. Those who knew him best asked for his influence and intercession with authorities in Rome because they knew he could also get things done.

That confidence was well founded and is proved in a situation faced by Luigi Lippomano in Verona. He wrote a series of letters to Cervini describing his predicament, beginning in 1548, and the problem was resolved to Lippomano's satisfaction only in 1550. Lippomano received appointment to a legation in Germany in 1548 and, as a result, had to abandon his post of coadjutor at the assistance of his brother Pietro, bishop of Verona. He was concerned to ensure adequate administration and care of the diocese in his absence. To complicate matters, Pietro died soon after Luigi's departure.[19] Lippomano had heard, he said, of the "great discourse . . . [that] the licentiate [Alfonso] Salmerón of the company of Ignatius" had with the people of Verona and the good work he was doing. This pleased him, but he had also heard of Ignatius's desire to send Salmerón to Germany to open a college. Arguing that

Salmerón, who could speak no German, could do little for the effort in Germany that could not be done by someone else, Lippomano sought the help of Cervini. "I beg your Reverence to help me in this negotiation," he said, "do not interrupt this good work already done . . . [but] leave him there until my return when I can make some other provision." He counted on the persuasive ability of Cervini, and on his concurrence with the argument. "I am certain," he insisted, "that with one word of yours to Ignatius, nothing else would be necessary."[20] As it turned out, Lippomano was not entirely correct. Although Cervini could not prevent Salmerón's mission to Germany with Peter Canisius (1521–1597), Salmerón did return to Verona in the fall of 1550, and Lippomano thanked Cervini for his assistance in the matter.[21] As bishop, he also might have wished to add an "I told you so" to this letter to Cervini. During his absence he received information that, as he said, a little "bad Lutheran grass" had sprung up in Verona, and this spurred him to generate his 1553 summary of the faith for his people.[22]

During this period, Cervini continued to work closely with members of the new Society of Jesus. He received regular reports on Jesuit missionary work, especially that of Francis Xavier in the Far East. Cervini also encouraged Jesuit educational endeavors and requested, in 1552, that a college be set up in Montepulciano. It was established in 1557, after Cervini's death, but did not last long. In addition, a Jesuit college was established in Gubbio in the early 1550s, as a direct result of Cervini's interest.[23] Cervini offered his aid in establishing the Jesuit *Collegio Romano*, which opened in February 1551 and later became known as the Gregorian University. He also assisted in the program to develop the so-called German College or *Germanicum* in Rome. This house was founded by Ignatius just eighteen months after the Roman College and was designed as a place where promising students from Germany might live and prepare for advanced studies in theology at the Roman College. This was part of the Jesuit founder's larger plan to establish a number of these colleges for various "nations," according to the model he had seen during his own days as a student at the University of Paris. He intended that the graduates of these colleges would eventually return to their native countries and staff colleges for the preparation of better-educated clerics.[24] Cervini became one of the cardinal protectors of the *Germanicum* in 1554, while his intercession on behalf of the Roman College in the same year resulted in a substantial papal subsidy. In recognition of these efforts, Cervini received many letters of gratitude from Ignatius. The Jesuit general encouraged Diego Lainez, who later succeeded him in that office, to seek the assistance of Cervini in the future.[25]

Cervini also retained his position as a member of the Roman Inquisition in this later period of pastoral activity. He continued to work on the tribunal and participated in its judgments. He continued to advise others as they sought recommendations regarding inquisitorial problems. The Roman Inquisition between 1550 and 1555, however, was distinctly different from what it was between 1542 and 1550. Cervini's own participation was also different. The tribunal in this period reflected the interests, personality, and work habits of Julius III, who had reconfirmed its existence after he ascended the papal throne. Like his predecessor Paul III, Julius opposed severe action against clerics accused of heresy who were willing to abjure their errors privately. In cases like this, a private absolution and penance would be given, and a bull outlining this policy was published under the pope's order in April 1550. But, unlike his predecessor and in apparent contradiction with his own published policy, he was not determined to restrain the control over the tribunal entrusted to Gian Pietro Carafa. Carafa was not interested in privacy or in mitigation concerning inquisitorial proceedings. When Julius came to his papal administration, the existence of the 1547 Tridentine decree and canons on justification made the definition of heresy clearer, and this provided Carafa with the tool he needed to pursue clerics he suspected of heresy with the vigor he considered necessary. Julius himself was a victim of Carafa's hot-headed manipulation. The pope was apparently able to secure the mitigated, limited trials he desired only when he agreed to Carafa's demand that no cleric under indictment be permitted any future ecclesiastical promotion.[26]

According to the available documentation, Cervini himself participated in the Roman Inquisition between 1550 and 1555 differently from the way he had earlier. Little of his work had to do with persons under his own episcopal administration; more of his work had to do with members of the Servite order he oversaw as cardinal protector. Longer and more frequent visits to his diocese meant that Cervini absented himself from a good deal of the work of the tribunal. On the other hand, he remained informed on several cases through a couple of remarkable letters addressed to him by the commissioner general, Michele Ghislieri. Surprisingly enough, Cervini also became the target of an anonymous denunciation that questioned his own vigilance against heresy.

A record exists of Cervini's judgment in one inquisitorial proceeding from 1551. He acted as judge in the case of Annibale Montarenti, a doctor in *utroque iure* from Bologna. It seems he pronounced a new, mitigated sentence, probably based upon appeal by Montarenti. The attorney proved himself worthy, Cervini said, to receive the alteration "in part [of] the penalty imposed upon him." In the new sentence Cervini required him to pay a fine to the rectors of the poor society of Bologna within a year and to ensure that proof of the payment be forwarded to the Holy Office. Cervini also restored his degree and public faculties as doctor of laws but, specifically, did not restore his former ecclesiastical benefice. Further, he ordered that the man recite the seven penitential psalms every sixth day and give an unspecified amount of alms, those suggested to the penitent by the Holy Spirit, as a result of the recitations. Cervini insisted that Montarenti confess and receive communion three times a year, and that he present himself before the local inquisitors with even greater frequency—three times a month. His exile in Genoa could be commuted to allow him to remain living within the confines of Bologna, at the discretion of the inquisitors in Genoa. Cervini indicated there were two reasons for the change to this milder sentence, which focused on prayer and good works. The first was to lead the man, through this clemency, to seek the clemency of God, and the second was to satisfy God's desire that his ministers "seek the salvation" of all heretics.[27]

The anonymous denunciation made against a layman in Gubbio called into question Cervini's episcopal administration. The denunciation was addressed to Ghislieri as the chief inquisitor and was written in the same year, 1551. The real target of the accusation was Pietro Pamphilo, who appeared in the eyes of the author of the denunciation as a "public and notorious Lutheran" who operated under cover of "the spirit." Pamphilo had allegedly performed a variety of actions that had earned him this title. According to the document, he had argued in public that charity, confession, and good works were useless, he had dishonored the saints and the famous Madonna of Loreto, and he had criticized the authority of the papacy. The author also accused Pamphilo of assisting other heretics in the territory, among them Bartolomeo of Pergola and Nicolo da Mondavio. He added an implicit criticism of Cervini, reminding Ghislieri that "the most reverend cardinal of Santa Croce" knew all these heretics well and that, incidentally, these "also live without purgation of such errors." Cervini would receive the same information in a separate letter, according to the author, and apparently Ghislieri also shared the denunciation with him.[28]

Although Cervini tended at times to support mitigation and the commutation of sentences, he certainly did not do so in all cases, even when he received information from a trusted associate urging leniency. He received such a plea in 1552 from Ludovico Beccadelli, whose opinion Cervini obviously took seriously. Beccadelli wrote simultaneously to a number of cardinals to recommend lenient treatment of

Giovan Francesco Verdura, the bishop of Chironissa since 1549, who was accused of supporting the teachings of Juan de Valdés. Verdura faced trial and then imprisonment in Rome in 1558 and was one of those released in the popular uprising celebrating the death of Paul IV in 1559. The appeal to Cervini does not survive, but it is reasonable to assume it was similar in tone to the ones Beccadelli wrote on October 8, 1552, to Innocenzio del Monte, to the cardinal who oversaw Verdura's homeland, Giovanni Andrea Mercurio, and to Fabio Mignanelli. In those letters, Beccadelli cautiously recommended Verdura. He indicated that his sources confirmed he was a "good prelate," and he urged that testimony be carefully scrutinized in order to treat both Verdura and his diocese fairly. Cervini responded to Beccadelli's plea in October 1552 and quite vehemently defended actions taken by the inquisitors to hold heretics in prison. Persons who suggested that prisoners were held without good reason in Rome were incorrect, Cervini argued. Incarceration was not used against those who were willing to confess, but only when it was necessary, he insisted, "to convince obstinate ones." No one was held "for a single day," he added, "who [was] not worthy to remain there all his life."[29] Cervini spoke in this instance in harsher terms than he had ever done during his earlier work on the tribunal. In this language he may have begun to reflect some of the hardening of opinions usually associated with the Catholic hierarchy (and the Roman Inquisition) in the period after 1542. But Cervini may just as easily have been reacting hotly to a suggestion by a trusted colleague that the inquisitorial actions in which he was participating were somehow improper.

Cervini also became involved, between 1552 and 1554, in additional heresy proceedings taken against members of the two orders he served as protector—the Augustinians and the Servites. In these cases he apparently sensed no conflict of interest. Assisting the overall improvement of the orders and exercising vigilance on heresy within them constituted, for Cervini, two sides of the same coin. In December 1552 he received an anonymous denunciation against five Servites. The author of the document characterized them as "thieving" and "dishonest" and leveled against them the accusation of heresy. The author encouraged Cervini to ensure that these characters, in future, could not gain positions of authority in general chapters of the order. The denunciator indicated they were not to be trusted on another level, recommending that under all circumstances they be forbidden entrance to female monasteries.[30]

Michele Ghislieri also wrote from Rome in 1554 to inform Cervini that depositions had been received against an Augustinian named Andrea de Volterra regarding his preaching in Udine, a city about one hundred kilometers northeast of Venice. According to Ghislieri, Andrea, a native of Volterra (a town about forty-five kilometers northwest of Siena), preached that good works done out of charity were "dirty" and not helpful in the pursuit of eternal life.[31] He also faced the accusation that he erred in preaching on Saint Peter. Ghislieri ordered him imprisoned and seized his writings, among them a letter that insinuated he knew he was in need of correction on elements of the faith. The inquisitor forwarded, in the same letter, a list of sixteen Servites who had similarly spread Lutheran doctrines in their preaching.[32]

Cervini answered the letter a few days later from Gubbio. He indicated that Andrea's heresy was all the worse since the preacher had abjured similar opinions in 1545. The larger of the two problems related, for Cervini, was the frequency with which questionable preaching seemed to surface within the Servite order. Although he was their protector and was therefore interested in nurturing their development in the church, Cervini suggested a comprehensive investigation. "I would desire," he said, to examine each one of those named "with great diligence . . . to see if it is possible once and for all to drive the plague from that organization." Since he was absent from Rome, Cervini was not in a position to participate himself, and apparently he had no burning desire to rush back and play any sort of direct role. Nevertheless, he received a copy of the sentence that was later handed down against eleven of them. Their punishment varied from "perpetual banishment" to an unspecified "castigation and punishment," while one was "condemned" and ordered to present himself to Cervini within thirty days. One was removed from the office of teaching, and another was deprived of his degree of bachelor for three years.[33]

Ghislieri also kept Cervini informed of other procedures that he missed because of his determination to reside at Gubbio. He forwarded copies of two depositions as well as information on several other cases in 1553. He described the result of torture applied to a certain priest, Mattheo di Aversa, who remained firm despite subjection to the strappado, but who later (probably under the threat of a repetition of the torture) confessed to all the errors on the sacraments and the nature of Christ of which he had been accused.[34] In this case, as in the previous one, Cervini remained informed but apparently had no direct participation.

At the very least, this lack of participation underlines the importance he attributed to his personal residence and direct administration in his diocese. As a member of the tribunal, he could have remained in Rome and participated if he had wished, particularly if he had considered that work more important, interesting, or enjoyable than the work he did in

Gubbio. He may have had his fill of inquisitorial investigations and procedures during the time he did spend in Rome each year. He may have tired of the attitude of those more vigorous than he in the pursuit of heresy. His own letters do not indicate the delight at the discovery and identification of heresy that can be seen in the correspondence of some of his colleagues. In addition, certain members of the tribunal were at the time targeting one of Cervini's long-standing associates, Ludovico Beccadelli, for his lack of rigor against heresy as nuncio to Venice.[35]

Further evidence that Cervini may have actively sought to separate himself from certain members and certain activities of the tribunal comes from a letter of Girolamo Vida (+1566), the bishop of Alba. In 1553 he wrote to inform Cervini of some disquieting rumors circulating in Rome. He had learned, through a friend in the city, that certain persons had influenced the tribunal against the memory of Marc Antonio Flaminio, one of the authors of *Il beneficio*.[36] Those persons apparently were convinced that Flaminio had held suspect theological positions, and they sought to convince others of this opinion. Vida heard that they had succeeded: the prefects of the tribunal intended to have Flaminio's remains exhumed, burned, and scattered to the wind. He expressed amazement at the entire situation. "I don't know where this opinion came from," he said, since Flaminio was not a theologian and wrote little. He was further amazed, he explained, since he had been acquainted with Flaminio and had always considered him a very good and honest person.[37] Why should such a letter be addressed to Cervini? It indicates that, as late as 1553, he was considered a person on the directing board of the tribunal whose opinions differed from those of many other members. If Vida's information was correct and the inquisitors were ready to order such an action, he must have considered the other members to be of a more violent and repressive outlook than Cervini. The letter also indicates that Vida believed Cervini would listen to a reasonable argument and was persuasive enough to influence those of an opposing opinion. This confirms in 1553 the qualities in Cervini that were identified by others earlier in his career, and upon which he apparently prided himself.[38]

Cervini also took part in the inquisitorial initiatives against Reginald Pole and Giovanni Morone. The investigation of Morone proceeded along two lines, at different times. The initiative at first was conducted only *per via denunzia:* gathering information against him that was later used *per via inquisizione* in the actual trial, after Carafa had assumed the papal throne. Action against Pole proceeded *per via denunzia* only, since he died before he could be recalled to Rome for trial (apparently much to the chagrin of Carafa). Cervini participated in the information-gathering stage in each case, and, though his connection with those who completed the inquisitorial action against Morone is well noted, Cervini died before formal charges were filed and the trial began. He did, however, personally inform Pole in the spring of 1553 of the suspicions held by the Holy Office regarding the English prelate's views on justification.[39] At that time Pole received visits from Cervini, Carpi, and Carafa in rapid sequence. The action of this triumvirate was apparently designed to intimidate Pole, as each of them came armed with written notes, inquired into the difference between his view on the doctrine and the position defined at Trent, and then left after indicating continued confidence in his "goodness" and "virtue." But, whatever the motivation behind these almost ritualistic encounters, Carafa undoubtedly constituted the real force behind the investigation. This fact is reinforced by Pole's own reaction to the two papal elections of 1555.[40]

Whether Cervini would have participated in, or approved of, the trial of Morone or the attempt to try Pole is subject for speculation. Carafa conceived of both doctrinal and theocratic reasons for the procedures against these prelates, and some members of the tribunal, like Toledo and Carpi, sided with Carafa against Pole and Morone out of essentially anti-imperial sentiment. Cervini certainly expressed attitudes which would suggest to historians that his motivation for participation in these actions was in part political. Yet it seems equally certain that, unlike Carafa, Cervini did not consider Morone much of a threat. Carafa began the trial of Morone little more than a month after his papal election, with the appointment of Giovan Battista Scotti as inquisitorial commissioner. Cervini on the other hand, although well acquainted both with the character of Morone (through their long association in the curia) and with the suspicions held against him (through Carafa and his own sources), took no such action in the three weeks of his papal administration. In the trial of Morone, he was even cited by witnesses for the defense as one of the many prelates who considered the Milanese cardinal a pious and Catholic person.[41]

Cervini thus obtained a certain independence from the papal curia during this period, which enabled him to focus his efforts and attention on the personal, pastoral, and inquisitorial activities of his choice. This independence should not, however, be overemphasized. He still spent a considerable amount of time in Rome and did not make a habit of denying papal requests for his presence or for his efforts, despite his distaste for Julius III's interest in promoting his relatives rather than instigating effective reform of the church. Cervini was, for instance, one of the cardinals in attendance at a celebration held in honor of

Cardinal Innocenzio del Monte, on December 28, 1550.[42] He also served as one of the *deputati* appointed by Julius III to constitute a general reform commission and, in all probability, was the working head of that body.

GENERAL REFORM COMMISSION

Julius took the first step in this direction in March 1550. He formed a group of cardinals to investigate and recommend initiatives to be taken for a specific portion of the reform—that of the Roman curia. Cervini was not a member of that group, and in the succeeding months Julius indicated he intended more general and comprehensive action. He renewed his predecessor's decree to eliminate the common practice whereby cardinals held multiple metropolitan and cathedral sees. He reinforced this through his insistence that his own new episcopal appointees give up their other sees before acquiring new territories. He expressed a desire to carry out a reform of abuses associated with papal conclaves, and in October of that year he even indicated his intention to reconvene the suspended Council of Trent. He crowned all this with a consistorial act of February 18, 1551, in which he established a commission for general reform. As members, he appointed François de Tournon, cardinal and bishop of Sabinensis, plus Carpi, Toledo, Morone, Verallo, Pisano, and Cervini.[43]

The records of this commission begin with the diaries of Maffei and Cervini, which cover the proceedings in 1552 and 1553. These diaries are fragmentary, at best, but they do indicate the range of topics treated and provide an insight into the creation of Julius's reform bull and into the intentions Cervini later demonstrated during his own pontificate.[44] In his diary, Maffei indicated that the first meeting of the deputies on reform was held on October 26, 1552. The committee met in the Vatican apartments of Cervini, and the list of those in attendance indicates that the constitution of the group had changed since the original appointments. It consisted of six cardinals: Pietro Pacheco, Giacopo Puteo, Sebastiano Pighino, Giovan Battista Cicada, Maffei, and Cervini.

They began the meeting by reading the instructions of Julius III from a consistory on September 16, 1552, which outlined his hopes for the reform of the conclave and included statements suggesting that the work of reform should be extended far beyond that particular institution. He asserted that bishops were to reside in their appointed churches and were not to live in Rome while falsely claiming they remained there at the service of the papacy. He indicated that an exception from this should be made for the judges of the Apostolic Camera and of the Rota, a position with which Cervini later took exception.[45] Julius hoped the commission would "seek out abuses" existing elsewhere in the Datary, Penitentiary, and other offices of the curia, and he insisted that the abuses of the clergy would eventually show forth in bad religious practice among the laity.[46]

After these instructions were read, the commission members composed a more specific list of items they would investigate and treat in their recommendations. This included a host of issues pertaining to the appointment, age, and outward bearing of cardinals and bishops, and to the use and administration of their rights and benefices, which had gone untreated despite heavy and consistent criticism from generations of clerics, most recently in the *Consilium de emendanda ecclesia* and in the statements of Spanish and Portuguese prelates at the early sessions of the Council of Trent. The reform of curial offices that Julius mentioned in the consistory had failed in the years between 1537 and 1552, due to the resistance of many cardinals, and Cervini and Maffei apparently pushed hard for this action in the new commission.[47]

Knowledge of the other meetings of the group, which took place in the winter and spring from 1552 to 1553, comes from Cervini's diary. He chose to record little more than an indication of which members were absent and the general topic of discussion on any particular day. On November 12 they discussed collections made for the issuance of dispensations by the Signatura.[48] That was followed by a meeting on January 28 concerning the duty of residence and a meeting on February 4 treating the validity of various dispensations from that duty. The meetings continued on February 27, March 15, and April 5, with further discussion on the residence issue and on the reform of the office of the Penitentiary.[49] A substantial body of recommendations and treatises on the various topics to be considered were generated over these months, by theologians and canonists at the request of commission members as well as by the members themselves. Maffei, for example, jotted down his ideas regarding the improvement of the Roman curia and the administrative practices it oversaw. He was primarily concerned with the problems associated with the end of a prelate's administration of any particular benefice. Sons of clerics should not be allowed anywhere near their father's churches, he argued—they should be excluded from any prebend or dignity there, apparently because of the possibility they might seek to succeed their fathers in their benefices. He similarly urged that coadjutors in any administration be excluded from succession. He pushed for general legislation excluding incumbents from the resignation of a benefice in favor of (or in order to bestow it upon) another. Neither did he care for the other common practice of resigning a benefice while retaining all or part of the income it generated, in the practice known as reservation.[50]

Other persons provided additional suggestions. Ricciardo Vercello, a canon regular of the Lateran congregation, addressed a text to Cervini in 1553 on the holding of multiple benefices. He had probably met Cervini while serving as a minor theologian during the conciliar discussions at Bologna. Cervini commissioned him to read and synthesize ancient sources on this issue, including Scripture, the decrees of earlier councils, and the writings of the doctors of the church; and Vercello complied. Similarly, suggestions were received on the general problem of benefices and those who held them from Luigi Lippomano and from Ioannes de Melo, the Portuguese bishop of Silves (1549–1564). Julius also had other documents drawn up that detailed his own intentions regarding the Datary, the Penitentiary, and the Signatura.[51]

One other document dating from the period of Cervini's participation in the reform commission had to do with the improvement of established religious orders. The author and the precise date of the document are unknown, but it is important because Cervini edited and corrected it in his capacity as a member of the reform commission. Furthermore, he received reaction and response to it from the general of the conventual Franciscans and from the general of the Dominican order some time later. From the number and location of changes he recommended for the text, it seems Cervini was most concerned with the paragraph regarding election of generals, visitors, and other superiors. Like his colleague Maffei, who also added suggestions, Cervini maintained that such elections should be carried out by secret ballot, rather than by oral voting or by a show of hands. He insisted that the elections be expeditious. He reinforced the wording of the pertinent passage, stating that neither the cardinal protector of any order nor the general or any members who might have been absent from the voting in question would have the power to supplant an election already carried out.[52]

REFORM BULLS OF JULIUS III

All this information reached the attention of the committee and fed into three bulls of Julius III, which were eventually produced as a result of the discussions. One of these covered the reformation of the conclave and was presented to elicit the comments of the other cardinals in March 1553. It appeared in final form on November 12, 1554. This had little to do with the most pressing reform issues, according to the commissioners and their advisers, but it did insist on the resolution of certain practical problems. It placed limitations on the length of the mourning period after the death of a pope, and upon contact between the conclave and members of the laity who might influence the election. This was designed to avoid the sort of conclave that had resulted in the election of Julius, which lasted seventy-two days and was noteworthy for the pressure exerted upon it by a number of secular rulers.[53] In the bull, Julius even revived a rule on food in the assembly from the pontificate of Gregory X (1271–1276), who emerged as pope only after a three-year conclave. Meals were to be simple, and if no pope were elected after fifteen days the college would go on a diet of bread, wine, and water—that would surely encourage a more rapid conclusion.

The second bull covered reform of the Penitentiary. Work on this apparently commenced in 1553 but was never really finished, not even to the point of soliciting a response to the document from the College of Cardinals. One of the problems was the tendency of the Penitentiary, as then constituted, to issue licenses to members of religious orders, which then impinged upon the rights and duties of local ordinaries. The granting of the license to preach constituted a particular danger. One of the commission's preliminary documents on possible changes to the Penitentiary indicated that this license to preach should only be given by the local bishop. Julius's bull repeated the preliminary document and added that the Penitentiary should submit monthly reports on the petitions it received that sought dispensations from "grave and major cases" reserved to the decision of the pope himself. Those cases were then enumerated, and they included voluntary homicide, heresy, simony, and other crimes.[54]

The third bull was one intended to create a general reform, and, although based upon the work of the commission and begun in 1555, it was neither promulgated nor even completed.[55] The document is comprehensive, both in design and in the range of topics discussed, and seems to suggest that Julius had a sincere concern with reform of the church. This impression, however, must be quickly balanced with the fact that the bull (and even the committee charged to create it) took such a long time to assemble. The impression must also be balanced with the fact that the bull was not expedited by Julius. It lay unfinished in 1555 and could in some ways be considered a dead letter. It is important because it was not really a dead letter—it later served as the center of Cervini's own short-lived reform program, and certain ideas expressed in the bull anticipated reform decrees from the later sessions at Trent, specifically those concerning the authority and jurisdiction of bishops, and the examination of candidates for ecclesiastical orders and promotions.

The importance of the reform commission appointed by Julius in formulating the program described in this text is apparent from the beginning. The first seventy-four canons take up systematically the list of problems that, Julius indicated in the instructions the reformers read at the opening meeting, must be resolved by the committee.

In the first group of canons (canon 1 through canon 20), the commission treated the office of cardinal and the administration of cathedral churches with a short passing reference to the papacy as conservator of the temporal possessions of the church. With these, the commission sought to bring under tighter control such things as dispensations allowing the possession of multiple benefices, the practice of reservation, the expansion of the College of Cardinals, and the appointment of titular bishops. But there was an important qualification—this was a promise of *future* policy, not a revision applicable to current officeholders. According to the commission, the appointment of titular bishops *ought* to be very rare, the college was not to be increased above its *current* size, no resignations should be permitted *in the future,* and no *new* dispensations should be granted.[56]

In the next group of canons (canon 21 through canon 41), the commission aimed to answer criticisms leveled at the lower clergy. While certain canons merely repeated the conclusions of the reform discussions at the early sessions of Trent, others anticipated the later work of that council on such topics as examination of candidates for ecclesiastical promotion and the duty of bishops to investigate and, if necessary, improve the moral bearing of clerics under their jurisdiction.[57] The commissioners even gave more power to the canons that were not otherwise likely to generate much fear—they threatened, for example, suspension from clerical office, privileges, and benefices for lack of adherence to the regulations on clerical dress.

Benefices themselves were the subject of the most lengthy set of canons (canon 42 through canon 74). In these, the commission regulated future conferral of the vast variety of benefices, commanded compliance with the residence requirement, and outlawed the union of two or more benefices, unless the union and the justification for it were carefully examined by local ordinaries.[58] The commissioners treated these unions as the moral equivalent of plural cathedral benefices for bishops and cardinals.

Cervini personally exerted crucial influence over the development of the plan elaborated in the bull, and that fact becomes increasingly apparent in later portions of the text. The section on the authority of bishops over their clerics (canon 75 through canon 85) contains substantial similarities with his own criticism of current practices that left him unable to control the choice of benefice holders in his own diocese. These canons also bear similarities with his position regarding the control of public preachers who were members of religious orders, which he identified in his correspondence with Girolamo Seripando. This section asserted the preeminence of the local bishop over all secular clerics and reinforced the clerics' duty of obedience to the bishop. Such an ordinance would have been useful to Cervini during his battle with the cathedral canons of Gubbio. In accord with an earlier reform canon from Trent, any *apostati* (or regulars who lived outside their monasteries after receiving a *licentia extra standi*) were also subject to the authority of the bishop. This squares with Cervini's position concerning episcopal control over all preachers working in any particular diocese.

Cervini may also have influenced the passage in the bull concerning members of religious orders. It is, broadly speaking, far more favorable to the independent interests of individual orders than such reform documents as the *Consilium de emendanda ecclesia*. Cervini did not, however, support such a policy simply in order to enhance papal rule over the church at large through such instruments as the office of cardinal protector. If that had been the case, he might have suggested that cardinal protectors could unilaterally override the completed election of the general of an order. Instead, he supported the idea that such elections, being secret, express the will of the members of the group. He apparently wished to protect, rather than expand or contract, already established lines of ecclesiastical authority.

The passage in the bull concerning religious orders includes a canon urging careful choice of visitors assigned to the correction of convents. This was designed to help ordinaries avoid any suggestion of impropriety, a problem with which Cervini was especially familiar. The final section of the bull, concerning the violation by secular rulers of jurisdictional rights and liberties enjoyed by ecclesiastical persons, also appears to bear the mark of Cervini. The attempt to revive the constitutions of papal predecessors like Innocent II (1130–1143), Innocent III (1198–1216), and Boniface VIII (1294–1303) and to ensure secular non-interference with benefices, marriage regulations, and other spiritual matters would appeal not just to a canon lawyer like Julius, but also to an administrator like Cervini who had encountered his own problems with secular authorities.

The clearest proof of Cervini's leadership of the reform commission comes not from any of these, however, but from the portion of the bull devoted to preaching. A section entitled "that which preachers of the . . . word of God ought to observe" runs from canon 133 through canon 146. This large section is virtually a word-for-word transcription of the instructions Cervini had sent to clerics in the diocese of Gubbio. Each paragraph in the original text constitutes a canon in the bull, and the only real changes are the titles added for each canon and slight variations in wording to make the prescriptions more universal in their application.[59]

Why this lengthy text was taken over wholesale and placed within a bull devoted to general problems of reform is an interesting question. Placing the text in this bull would explain how an individual bishop might put into practice the second reform canon from session five of the Tridentine assembly (June 17, 1546), which affirms that it is a bishop's duty to preach personally and to ensure that only competent persons exercise that office in his territories. It is also the only portion of Julius's bull that contains real suggestions for the practical implementation of reform on the local level. It may simply be a further reflection of Cervini's concern for expeditious implementation of changes designed to improve religious devotion, and of his conviction that his own experience was useful and applicable to the church at large. This conviction is more easily understood in light of the fact that Cervini's ideas about preaching and its control were utilized elsewhere—in the Augustinian order, for example.[60]

Perhaps the most interesting passage in the entire bull is the final paragraph, canon 150. In it, the commission wrote that the power to execute the reform commanded by the bull should be held by those cardinals charged "to extirpate heresy" as the leadership of the Roman Inquisition. Some historians might argue that this reflects a step in the process by which the Roman Inquisition came to impose its own solutions upon the church and to dominate the governance of the institution.[61] Although this canon may have reflected such a step, it is difficult to accept that Cervini sought or intended the completion of the process, which occurred only later during the pontificates of Paul IV and Pius V. According to this provision, the Inquisition would act as executor of the plan generated by the reform commission and not as a body implementing its own program. In addition, Cervini probably viewed the provision made by this canon in terms consistent with the ecclesiology he had developed over his career.

Practically speaking, the canon made good sense. The inquisitorial board was small and could, at least theoretically, reach unanimity of opinion on the implementation of policy and on action against offenders. The members had extensive familiarity and experience with judicial proceedings, while many of the canons specifically (and all of them implicitly) required such proceedings if violated. Cervini probably supported this approach for these practical reasons. He had often expressed his concern that Paul III should quickly undertake just the sort of action described in this bull, and a small group could efficiently oversee the necessary changes. He could also agree to inquisitorial control over the reform program, out of his understanding of ecclesiastical authority. The program was designed to force rapid and effective change in the practices of bishops and cardinals (who had been appointed by the Apostolic See) and in the practices of those whom these subordinates might in turn promote to lesser offices and benefices. It would make sense, from this perspective, for any pope to turn over the administration of such a project to others directly under his control, like the members of the tribunal. And after participating in that directorship for some years, Cervini had every reason to believe it would continue to promote orthodox religiosity throughout the church, by proceeding against clerics who threatened that religiosity with their heterodox preaching or their bad example of moral laxity and financial irregularity. But it was Cervini's papal election in 1555, not the generation of this bull for a man who was notorious for dragging his feet on issues of reform, that really freed Cervini to pursue with consistency the plan he had so incessantly recommended to Paul III.

EPISCOPAL ADMINISTRATOR: THE BISHOP OF ROME

Julius III died on March 23, 1555, and curial officials moved quickly to convene a conclave. Cervini was present for the opening of the assembly on April 5, and there is a fascinating but improbable story concerning his journey to Rome. According to Gaetano Moroni in his *Dizionario di erudizione storico-ecclesiastica*, Cervini was residing in Gubbio that spring and left for Rome when informed of the death of Julius. Moroni related a "sign" of Cervini's impending pontificate that allegedly occurred at the shrine of Loreto, where he said Cervini stopped on his journey to the conclave. The shrine (about twenty-five kilometers south of Ancona on the Adriatic and not far from Cervini's birthplace, Montefano) was one of those pilgrimage centers devoted to the Virgin Mary that were created in the high Middle Ages. By the beginning of the fourteenth century it attracted large numbers of pilgrims.[62]

According to Moroni, Cervini celebrated mass at the shrine on March 25, the feast of Annunciation, and at the beginning of the canon had a vision of the Blessed Virgin, assuring him of his future pontificate. The vision left him trembling. Two letters of Cervini to his brother Alessandro confirm the fact that he did visit Loreto in February 1555, but he makes no mention of a vision. He went for a "change of air," required by the chronic ill health that afflicted him again in Gubbio that winter.[63]

The story of the vision seems dubious because Galieno Benci (who related the events of Marcello's journey to Rome for the conclave in a letter to Alessandro Cervini) did not mention it. He began his account of the trip on Saturday, March 30, when they left Perugia. They arrived that evening at Todi. He indicated that it took the party two more days of travel to reach Rome.[64] If any such vision had taken place at the time, or even on the way back in February, Benci would probably have mentioned it to the obviously pious Alessandro.

The story seems even more dubious after looking at a map. If Julius died, as all the accounts say he did, in the evening of March 23, and the news took only two days to reach Gubbio, a distance of at least 180 kilometers, it would have been virtually impossible for Cervini to go to Loreto (a distance of eighty-five kilometers from Gubbio) and arrive in Rome via Perugia by April 1, since the distance from Perugia to Todi (about thirty-eight kilometers) was considered a day's journey for the party. The suggestion that he could have been in Loreto in time to say mass on the feast of the Annunciation is ridiculous. Julius did fall into his last illness five weeks before his eventual death, and that fact might lend support to the possibility of a visit to Loreto by Cervini, but the story of the vision remains improbable for still another reason. The tradition that has grown up around the shrine and the miracles associated with the *Santa Casa* makes no mention of a vision for Cervini. One source indicates that Cervini visited the shrine, and that he was one of the popes, after Clement VII, who were committed to providing funds and other support for the basilica project.[65]

At any rate, the conclave did open on April 6, and it differed from the one that elected Julius III in two major ways: the number of cardinals in attendance and the length of the meeting. Only thirty-seven cardinals met in the conclave, compared to the fifty-one in attendance in 1549–1550. The length of this conclave was just four days and three hours, in contrast with the previous one, which lasted seventy-two days. There were other interesting complications. The major group not represented at the assembly was the French, who failed to reach Rome before the election had been carried out. Their absence was due to the policy of King Henry II (1547–1559), who would not allow French cardinals to reside in Rome. That left the curia dominated by supporters of Charles V, and, when news of the death of Julius reached France, Henry sent his cardinals to push for a French candidate like Ippolito d'Este or Jean du Bellay. In the event this proved impossible, they were to support Gian Pietro Carafa, but only because of his status as an enemy of the emperor. Henry sent them to block the election of Cervini also, because he considered the prelate a rabid reformer who would seek to reduce the ecclesiastical liberties and powers enjoyed by the monarch and by the French hierarchy.[66] So Cervini faced the opposition of both principal heads of state in Europe: Charles V had blocked his candidacy in the previous conclave and sought to do the same in 1555. The reasons for the opposition of Charles went back to the transferal of the council from Trent to Bologna.

Despite this pressure, Cervini gained election to the papal throne on Tuesday, April 9, at about 11 P.M. An unnamed fortune-teller (according to the papal master of ceremonies, Ludovico Bondoni de Branchis Firmani) predicted the election with considerable accuracy, but most of the diarists agree that Cervini's selection, which met with popular acclaim, was due to the strength of the support given him by Ranuccio Farnese and Guido Ascanio Sforza. One assessor reported that the attitude of Gian Pietro Carafa during the conclave was also instrumental. The Neapolitan, currently the bishop of Ostia (1553–1555), apparently led in the early voting, and when he himself cast a ballot for Cervini, this induced all the others to do the same.[67]

Other interesting details concerning Cervini at the conclave were related by Galieno Benci in a letter to Alessandro Cervini. He reported on the opening of the meeting and indicated that the cardinals chose lots to determine who would first taste the food provided to the closed assembly. Cervini drew that privilege on the morning of the first full day and was cautious—he had his two conclavists test the fare before he ate. Benci also indicated that Cervini became the early favorite for those wagering on the outcome of the election. When they arrived in Rome, the bettors gave him a chance of about one in six of being elected, and by the first day of the conclave his chances were considered a good deal better. Benci expected they would increase that evening to about one in four. If that occurred, he intended to place a wager himself, which he hoped might enable him to repay an unspecified debt.[68]

Thus, the election of Cervini was not unexpected, but when it had taken place and he was asked what he would assume as his papal name, Cervini began to surprise his colleagues (at least according to one of his supporters). Apparently he said, "I was Marcellus, I will be Marcellus: the pontifical office will change neither my name nor my ways."[69] On the next day, Cervini received the episcopal consecration now required for the new office, which he had earlier refused on the grounds that he was unable to reside in his diocese. He was consecrated by Carafa, then the dean of the College of Cardinals, and was crowned Marcellus II by Francesco Pisano, a Venetian cardinal who was prior of the members of the college who were deacons.[70] He also surprised his colleagues by his rejection of a lavish consecration ceremony. He did this because he did not wish to distract attention from the Holy Week devotions, which commenced in earnest on Holy Thursday, two days after his election. His intense desire to avoid distraction from the events celebrated in Holy Week was exemplified in his instructions to vocalists after the Good Friday service. He ordered the pontifical choir to demonstrate due reverence for the events being celebrated. He was irritated because he felt that joy, not sorrow or penitence, was the tone of their work that afternoon. He ordered them to ensure that everything in the liturgy could be understood, suggesting that the music might help teach those in attendance. The penitential focus of Good Friday, he insisted, must not be lost upon the faithful. He also rejected a pompous consecration because of his desire to save money. Half of the considerable savings was retained by the Holy See, while the other half was distributed on behalf of the poor of Rome.[71]

Letters of congratulation poured in, to the Cervini family in Montepulciano as well as to the new pope himself. There is nothing surprising in this, except for the names of some of those who sent the letters. Many were members of the so-called *spirituali*. Reginald Pole, for example, addressed a letter to Cervini on April 28. He began by expressing both his joy at the election and his hope that the new pope would be confirmed with the good health necessary to carry out the reform of the church. God had always given Cervini the desire to undertake reform, Pole maintained, and now God had given him the necessary power as well. He added a personal note, saying that the election had brought him "the greatest joy," because he felt closely joined to Cervini through their common humanistic studies and their common general outlook.[72]

All one needs, to avoid the conclusion that Pole's words were merely a conventional expression of praise addressed to a new pope and empty of any real feeling, is familiarity with the career of Cervini and with the ideas concerning reform and ecclesiastical power he expressed during that career. One could also look at the letter Pole wrote about five weeks later, after the election of Carafa as Paul IV. It is congratulatory, to be sure, but the words of congratulation come at the end of a long paragraph reciting the evils facing the church and extolling the reform work Carafa had previously undertaken. Pole was referring, not to Carafa's recent inquisitorial escapades, but to his much earlier sponsorship and co-inspiration of the Theatine order. He congratulated Carafa's spirit and ability to attend to the reform of the church and expressed the hope that Carafa would do so rapidly, but he suggested that active, effective undertaking of reform work should be the true object of any real praise for the papacy. This letter is devoid of the personal notes and phrases indicating his *summopere gaudeo*, which characterize the letter to Cervini.[73]

Any lingering doubts concerning the sincerity of Pole's joy over the election of Cervini (and his conviction that he was the right man to carry out the kind of reform Pole himself could support) can be dispelled by his letter announcing the election to Queen Mary of England. He wrote on the day after he received the news, and he spoke of the great consolation he felt as a result of the coronation. He described to her his hope for the benefits that might be brought to the church through this man, whom he had always considered worthy of the honor. He knew Cervini, he told Mary, and testified to his goodness, experience, and unusual qualifications. "God," Pole said, "has heard the prayers of his church . . . in giving us such a father."[74] There was little reason for Pole to lavish such praise at such length to Mary if he was not truly convinced it was justified. It is difficult to imagine how Pole could write such letters if he believed Cervini to be a threat to his own safety or if he believed the methods Cervini would employ in reforming the church would be different from those Pole might use himself. Instead, Pole's letters suggest he viewed Carafa alone as a real threat—a view shared by Girolamo Seripando, another frequently linked theologically to the *spirituali*. Seripando, who was also compromised in the investigations of Pole and Morone, had denounced the excesses of Carafa's inquisitorial work since 1545 and, as a result, was in understandable fear at the moment of Carafa's election.[75] He expressed no such fear at the election of Cervini. All this joy on the part of Pole and Seripando was in spite of considerable theological disagreement with Cervini over the Tridentine decree on justification. Still other prelates, as well as secular persons sharing humanist interests and desire for the effective reform of the church, sent congratulatory letters. Among these were Ludovico Beccadelli and the publishing magnate Paolo Manutio.[76]

The new pope immediately set to work on the real reform activity that Pole and the others desired to see. From the moment of his election, according to Massarelli, Marcellus indicated his desire to carry out the long-anticipated reform. He employed Massarelli in much of the work. Two days after the election, he called the secretary in and ordered him to collect materials from all previous popes pertaining to the question of church reform, with particular attention to the documents generated under his immediate predecessor, Julius III. While this was going on, the new pope distinguished himself by his personal attention to the devotional life of Rome, through his attendance at the Holy Week services and through his personal celebration of mass and the distribution of communion in Saint Peter's on Easter Sunday. He distinguished himself by continuing the practice he had begun as legate, instituting spiritual reading and theological disputation during meals with his papal *familia*.[77]

Marcellus took actions in the second week of his pontificate that further underline the practical and pragmatic character he demonstrated throughout his career. On Monday, April 15, he ordered review of the document generated under Julius III designed for the practical reform of the conclave. On the next day, he appointed two family members to the posts directly responsible for insuring his personal safety. He commissioned Giovan Battista Cervini as governor of Castel' Sant'Angelo and Biagio Cervini as captain of the Vatican guard. These appointments effectively render apocryphal the comment attributed to Marcellus that he intended to do away with the Swiss guard, insisting that the vicar of Christ "needs no swords for his protection." His concern for practical considerations was demonstrated also by a meeting he called on Friday, April 19. According to Massarelli's diary, he gathered a congregation of select cardinals associated with the Apostolic Camera and other curial offices that involved the administration of papal income and provisions for the city itself.[78] He probably did so because the revisions he planned in curial practice would put enormous pressure upon those offices and that income.

During the second and third weeks, Marcellus began to attack more systematically the offices and abuses he had so long disdained. He called before him the auditors of the Rota (as Vittore Soranzo reported in a letter, apparently addressed to the pope's family in Montepulciano) and insisted they ignore family connections, patronage ties, and the outward appearance or dress of those who appeared before them and allow themselves to be swayed only by the reasonable pursuit of justice. He added, according to Soranzo, that "he does not think auditors should hold bishoprics." He summoned the head of the Datary and ordered "that no benefices be distributed without his knowledge."[79] On Thursday, April 25, he instructed Massarelli and one member of the College of Cardinals, Giovan Battista Cicada, to resume work on the reform commission's unfinished bull of reformation. On the next day, he ordered Massarelli to collect information concerning the Signatura, and on the following Monday (April 29) to do the same with respect to the Penitentiary. His half-brother and biographer, Alessandro Cervini, even suggested the new pope intended to turn over the Penitentiary to the hands of Gian Pietro Carafa. This suggestion is difficult to accept literally as Angelo Massarelli does not confirm the point in his diary covering the pontificate. In addition, Ranuccio Farnese then held the position of *penitenziere maggiore,* and it was commonly a lifelong appointment. It seems reasonable, however, because prior to his election Cervini had indicated his desire to find means to grant dispensations in certain cases without appeal (or payment) to the office, and Carafa had long hated its employees, whom he had once referred to as "mad dogs."[80]

Jedin, the great historian of the Council of Trent summed up the situation in this way: "There is no possibility of doubt: Marcellus II had decided finally to act." He was largely, but not completely, correct. Marcellus attempted to undertake the real reform of fiscal abuses in the curia, which (as Hallman recently pointed out) never took place in the Tridentine period. He did so because his friends and closest associates, like Seripando, urged the same policy, and also because he understood nepotism and clientage all too well. He had grown up in the system and had seen its degenerative effects at first hand.[81] All this would be strange, if Marcellus was really committed to a war against the *spirituali* in the course of his career and pontificate. If he was pursuing such a war against those prelates, would that not have been the focus of his first days as pope, rather than this program to conduct the sort of revision of curial practices that the *spirituali* themselves had advanced for years?

On the other hand, Jedin's characterization is misleading, because Marcellus was not entirely consistent or comprehensive in applying these reform measures. Among the briefs registered during these days is a number (nineteen in all) through which the new pope granted benefices whose resignation and reconferral had been negotiated during the reign of Julius III.[82] The documents grant small-scale benefices, such as rectorships in parish churches, but they are indicative of Marcellus's basic approach. He envisioned not a retroactive, comprehensive restructuring of benefices—he was a practical man, after all, and probably considered that impossible. He wanted to begin real and efficacious clerical reform, but this did not exclude the temporary continuation and confirmation of decisions made by his predecessor, even when they involved the very areas in which he desired the greatest change. In all probability, he believed such change must begin by his own example within the papal household, and he was known for the frugality and moral vigor he demanded from his familiars. Later, this would filter down to individual holders of minor benefices, when he granted these under his own authority. That seems implicit in his order to curial officers to take no actions concerning conferral of benefices without his personal approval. The remainder of the briefs registered during his pontificate consisted, for the most part, of courtesy letters informing heads of state of his election. Others reconfirm various nuncios and ambassadors who took up posts during the tenure of his predecessor.[83]

The importance Marcellus attributed to this reform is confirmed by other factors and circumstances of those few days. Marcellus was convinced, and for good reason, that his program would have a drastic effect upon the papal financial situation. It is clear he intended to strike at what he considered abusive policies in a number of curial offices, policies that for generations had provided the papacy with vast revenues. He apparently feared the anticipated shortfall, especially in the Apostolic Camera, and the only bull drafted during his short pontificate proves this.[84]

In the bull, Cervini ordered the extension of the direct tax known as the triennial subsidies, for three years, commencing with the completion of the preceding one, which was due to expire in 1556. The tax consisted of three parts: a *Vigesima,* or "twentieth" levied from the Jewish population of the papal states, a "tenth" collected from the secular clergy, and a "fourth" of the fruits and revenues of the regular clergy. The first two were combined income and capital taxes, and all three were designed to reflect accurate, current, and reliable assessments. In his extension of the tax, which became a fixture of policy in the papal secular administration of this period, Marcellus specifically mentioned the poverty of the Apostolic Camera and his desire to reverse the situation.[85]

Another attitude motivating Cervini's policy was the one popes in this period maintained concerning the Jews who lived in the papal states. Current experts on the relationship between Jews and the papacy in this period indicate that the overall policy of the popes was to promote conversion of the Jews, but that the means to gain that end changed dramatically in 1555. Marcellus continued the tradition under which Jews were to be prohibited from damaging the Christian faith but were allowed, for the most part, to live freely in Christian lands, practicing their faith. That policy, which included annual subsidies to support a "house for catechumens" to provide shelter and transition for recent converts, was reversed by Paul IV, who took action aimed at rapid conversion through constant pressure and a crushing taxation, instituted to create impoverishment of the Jewish population. Paul also enforced rigid segregation on the model of the Venetian ghetto, with which he was well familiar since his residence in Venice between 1527 and 1536. During the spring of 1555, Roman inquisitors burned some twenty-five Jews in the city of Ancona. While his successor Pius IV (1559–1565) maintained a more moderate position, Paul's policy was renewed by Pius V (1566–1572), who apparently hated Jews with even greater vehemence.[86]

The importance that Marcellus attributed to reform activity is boldly underlined by the state of his health in those days. Whatever work he undertook in 1555, he must have rapidly come to the conclusion that it would be his last. Antonio Lorenzini, a conclavist for Cervini and head of his papal household, reported frequently to the family on the rapid deterioration of the pope's physical condition. "I have been so occupied after the creation of the pope that I have scarcely had time to breathe," he wrote on April 13. "The Holy Father similarly," he added, "is so breathless from the conclave and from the visits that it is a pity to see him." This activity wore Marcellus out quickly, and on April 19 and 20, Lorenzini explained, came the first indication of real illness. "Since this morning His Holiness is not feeling too well, and he has had some fever" but, he added, "I believe it is nothing dangerous." This fever and *catharro* continued to worsen, and on April 22 Lorenzini wrote to indicate to the pope's brother that from the very beginning his illness really had caused fear. Marcellus lived long enough to receive his old friend Alessandro Farnese, who had been on legation to Germany during the conclave. Farnese and a number of other recently returned ambassadors, including Giovanni Morone, were received by the pope on April 29. The next day, at the "thirteenth hour," Massarelli reported, Marcellus suffered a stroke. He died during the night between April 30 and May 1. As Massarelli said, the days of his pontificate were "only twenty-one, and out of these, ten were spent in health and eleven in illness."[87]

Massarelli appended to his diary a more general description of the man and his pontificate, after relating the story of his death. He focused on the thrift, modesty, and humility of Marcellus and maintained that the pope had an intense desire to preserve the property of the church, while simultaneously retaining his commitment to the eradication of the abuses criticized by both Catholics and Protestants throughout the period. He indicated that Marcellus's disdain for a lavish consecration ceremony was just a part of his larger rejection of any form of vanity or ostentation.

Massarelli insisted that Marcellus could not be swayed to promote unworthy candidates to ecclesiastical orders or office through attention to family connections or ties of patronage. He reinforced this hatred of a well-established practice with the story of the pope's treatment of his own relatives. Marcellus explicitly forbade his half-brother Alessandro to come to Rome at all. In addition, he became incensed when his two young nephews, Ricciardo and Herennio, expected to benefit from their uncle's new position. The two, aged fifteen and thirteen respectively, were in Rome when the conclave elected Marcellus. When he later learned of their ambitions, he ordered them to go home at once, without so much as granting them an audience. One of the two family members he did appoint to office, Giovan Battista Cervini, soon sought the revenues associated with a vacant parish benefice in Spain. Not only did the pope refuse him, according to Massarelli, but he subjected him to a verbal tongue-lashing and bestowed the benefice on a local Spanish candidate.

The secretary explained that the new pope's household was small and characterized by frugality in expenditure, even to the extent of forbidding the usual displays of public joy and celebration (like fireworks) that were common after pontifical elections. In the process, Marcellus apparently generated a mixture of fear and happiness: happiness from those who hoped for such action, and fear from many curial employees who worried that their careers were in serious danger.[88] Massarelli's description is reminiscent of the qualities many contemporary critics of the papacy hoped to find in those who acquired the office once the institution had undergone real reform, such as Paolo Giustiniani and Pietro Querini in their *Libellus* to Leo X and the authors of the famous *Consilium de emendanda ecclesia*. The description is also not unlike that of the "ideal prelate" in the Italian Renaissance tradition of funeral oratory.[89] Archival sources both from Cervini's career at large and from his brief administration as Marcellus II sustain much of Massarelli's portrait.

Giovanni Pierluigi da Palestrina (1525–1594) provided one more contemporary commentary. He named one of his masses the *Pope Marcellus Mass* when he published it in his *Second Book of Masses* in 1567. The prolific composer put together a huge body of music, including 104 masses, some 250 motets, various other hymns and pieces of ecclesiastical music, as well as more than 140 madrigals. He had worked for Julius III, and his reputation was enormous, although he was dismissed from the pontifical choir by Paul IV in September 1555. Palestrina, like Marcellus (from whom he apparently took some inspiration) and like the Fathers at the later sessions of the Council of Trent, maintained that one of the principal goals of ecclesiastical music ought to be intelligibility. The musical composition he dedicated to the memory of Marcellus is an expression of that goal, and also a magnificent coda to a fascinating career.[90]

Conclusion

The history of Cervini's life and career indicates that a revision of the standard assessments of his person and of his influence is necessary. Revision is necessary, for example, of the position maintained by Pogianus that his election received universal acclaim. Although the College of Cardinals was in complete agreement, knowledge of Cervini's relationship with Emperor Charles V and of the position of the French king, Henry II, indicates that political figures were not overjoyed. Similarly, an understanding of Cervini's attitude toward Roman curialists in every office that generated real income for the papacy suffices to demonstrate that unhappiness must have been the reaction in a number of these important circles. The attorneys of the Rota and the Datary would never have used the standard terms *meek* and *amiable* to describe the pope, as some of his colleagues and many later historians have. Given Cervini's actions to limit their authority and influence, it is probable that most of these were offended and angry, at the very least. In fact, it is surprising there has never been a serious suggestion that Cervini might have been poisoned by one of these who apparently had so much to lose by his accession to the papal office.

The evidence from his life suggests there were noteworthy holes in the personality of this prelate. If the *Carte cerviniane* provide an adequate and complete description, then he was an almost humorless man. There is, apparently, absolutely no humor in the letters he wrote, even during his childhood. Very few jokes seem ever to have been addressed to him, and this suggests it was well known Cervini did not have a sense of humor and did not appreciate such a quality.

The catalogues of books acquired during his administration of the Vatican library show that he obviously read and valued highly not just scriptural and patristic literature but also philosophical and scientific works, in addition to poetry and other literary genres. But he did not write much about the things he read, except insofar as they pertained to his administrative tasks. This is unusual for a humanist. Aside from his boyhood letters describing his studies to his father, he does not mention specific works he read, with two exceptions: *Il beneficio di Cristo*, which he read in the context of his episcopal administration of Reggio, and some sermons of Chrysostom and a few other patristic texts, which he read in the context of the discussions on the episcopal office at Trent. In this regard, he retained a singular, restrictive, and probably unbalanced focus upon his duties.

He maintained few relationships with women and was an unemotional person, if his papers are any indication. Most of the women he corresponded with were those he was related to with ties of patronage—they were not so much friends as acquaintances who maintained interest in him because of his connection with the Farnese family. The one important exception to this is his contact with Vittoria Colonna. He appears in his letters as a cold and analytical person. The letters frequently convey irritation over his correspondents' lack of attention to speedy replies and over various forms of papal foot-dragging. They even express outright contempt, for those who opposed papal policies, and occasional sympathy, but little that could be described as emotional warmth.

Beyond these practical corrections, what about the two basic interpretations to which Cervini has been subjected over the years? Does the evidence found in his papers sustain the image of a holy, zealous, spiritually minded prelate snatched away before he could undertake a true reform of the church, as writers from Ignatius of Loyola to Hubert Jedin have maintained? Or is the recent portrait drawn by Firpo and others more correct, which numbers Cervini among the *intransigenti*, a ruthless group bent upon the annihilation, or at least the incarceration, of anyone who appeared conciliatory toward the Protestant opposition?[1] Can both these views be correct? Far more important is the question of Cervini's importance in relation to the rest of his colleagues at Trent and in the ecclesiastical hierarchy of his time. If that contribution can be more precisely defined, it may assist in the generation of a more comprehensive and nuanced picture of the Catholic or Counter Reformation.

The wide-ranging work Cervini undertook has made possible the dichotomy of assessments to which he has been subject. Those who would advocate his sainthood can readily point to instances of piety found throughout the seventy volumes of his correspondence. Such piety is attested to by the vast majority of his contemporaries. They can relate the very spiritual approach he took to the Holy Week services in 1555. He maintained that approach during a period that most of his immediate predecessors and successors in the papacy spent reveling in their elections, planning lavish consecration ceremonies, and plotting ways in which to enrich members of their family with ecclesiastical monies. One can point to his zeal for reform, especially that reform carried out by the bishops for the improvement of the lower clergy. He demanded episcopal residence of himself, and, if the visitation of Reggio he ordered is any indication, this is something he demanded of everyone who held a benefice with the care of souls attached. He viewed clerical celibacy not as an ideal but as an obligation. Although it had been neglected over the recent history of the church, he called clerical celibacy, "with the help of God, impossible to no one" and insisted that priests who failed to adhere to this prescription ought to lose their spiritual faculties.[2] It is fairly obvious that such practices (which Cervini considered obligations) were viewed instead by the majority of his contemporaries as examples of heroic virtue.

Those who would number Cervini among Counter-Reformation reactionaries, on the other hand, also have much evidence to cite. Cervini undertook inquisitorial work that extended far beyond issues in specific dioceses, as he was a high-ranking member of the Roman Inquisition from a time soon after its reinstitution until his papal election. They can point to his participation in the initiatives against Pole and Morone and to his collaboration in the strange three-headed warning given to Pole of the suspicions held against him. They can also point to his consistent promotion of papal authority, and to his friendship and esteem for the fearsome Gian Pietro Carafa. Indeed, it has been related that when Carafa knelt before the newly elected Marcellus II to promise his obedience, Cervini responded, "Take my place, and I will be ready to adore you with all these others."[3] Thus, there is considerable evidence that can be cited in support of both positions.

But both these views are too easy and one-sided. Those who propose them seek a simple way to characterize Cervini and that large and very diverse group of colleagues. Such characterizations flounder on the myriad details in the life of any individual to which the terms have been applied. They neglect, for example, that the persons most commonly accepted as *spirituali* (such as Pole, Contarini, Morone, and Sadoleto) maintained an "orthodoxy" of reform, which they defended just as vehemently as any of those called *intransigenti*. They promoted this orthodoxy in documents such as the *Libellus* addressed to Pope Leo X, Contarini's *De officio episcopi,* and the *Consilium de emendanda ecclesia.* Although the topics addressed in these texts were varied, and the venues in which they called for reform were different, the *spirituali* were rigorous in urging that the reform ideals contained in these writings should be adopted by all members of the hierarchy. The *spirituali* did not hold any clear set of theological positions in common (a fact that has made it difficult for historians to demonstrate their unity as a group with any precision) and so this reform spirit is perhaps the only thing that actually did bring them together.[4] They shared this commitment with most of their other colleagues, who are characterized as *intransigenti.* The "spiritual" characterization also neglects that many of their number supported a curialist notion of papal supremacy in all ecclesiastical matters, and with considerable strength. Beccadelli was anything but lenient toward Protestants and their literature when he undertook the office of papal nuncio in Venice in 1550. Pietro Querini indicated that his support did not stop at the theoretical level, either—he defended one of the boldest exponents of papal power in practice, Julius II.[5]

Some historians may try to assert that only a difference in doctrinal and theological approaches distinguished the two groups. If the *spirituali* were in fact consistently more concerned about a careful reading of the New Testament than about papal authority as a source of theological truth, then Contarini's actions at the end of the discussions on justification at Regensburg are difficult to comprehend. At that point, he chose to follow the papal assertion of Catholic doctrine sent in his instructions from Rome rather than his own theory of "double righteousness," which was perhaps more likely to encourage compromise with his opponents.[6] Those historians who link the *spirituali* with the ideas embodied in *Il beneficio di Cristo* (and the *intransigenti* to the spirit that effectively rendered that text unknown in sixteenth-century Europe) are forced to ignore Cervini's attitude toward the text in his pastoral work. They must ignore his conviction that the will of a religious community as expressed in election of a superior must be upheld over the preference of some other ecclesiastical authority. They must ignore his actions in the Nacchianti investigation and other inquisitorial proceedings, when he appeared cautious and balanced in weighing the evidence. They are forced to ignore that those, like Pole and Seripando, who disagreed most strongly with Cervini about justification—clearly the most significant doctrinal issue of the day—supported his reform plans, applauded his election as pope, and feared not him but his successor in the papacy. Thus, substantial selection of evidence is required to secure Cervini's inclusion among the *intransigenti.*

The characterization of other sixteenth-century prelates as intransigent raises other problems. The churchman who is never missing from that list is Gian Pietro Carafa. The adjective *intransigent* seems accurate in regard to his later life, as he pursued with fanaticism anyone who failed to live up to his personal definition of orthodoxy. But the characterization fails miserably to give adequate attention to the humanist education he shared with those in the other camp and for which he received the praise of none other than Desiderius Erasmus. It fails similarly to account for the central role Carafa played in defining and promoting the principles behind the Theatine order.[7] The basic picture is also less than satisfactory in portraying just what the *intransigenti* could be intransigent about. Familiarity with the career of Cervini indicates that the positions he held most dear, and about which he was most unwilling to compromise, involved no doctrines at all. He wished to deal harshly with just one group—clerics who illegitimately clung to the Roman curia, or who otherwise refused to faithfully take up the ecclesiastical responsibilities for which they were being paid.

Indeed, Cervini constitutes proof that these categories have broken down altogether. Acceptance of either category requires neglect of substantial elements of his background and career. In order to view Cervini as part of a group that had the intention of squashing the *spirituali*, one must accept the suggestion that he wanted to destroy those members of the hierarchy with whom he had the most in common. They shared the culture of Renaissance humanism and attempted to apply it to their understanding of the church and its doctrine. They shared the common goal of reviving the ideal of the apostolic church, as described in the New Testament. Cervini and those of his colleagues who are called the *spirituali* applied this ideal to the pope and the curia, as well as to the average clergy. All were expected to be educated, all were expected to be pastors. Cervini was a churchman who attempted, in his own episcopal see and later during his few days as pope, to create the changes that many argue had to be instituted if the *spirituali* were to be consistent in the pursuit of this goal.

Similarly, one must ignore the affection and mutual respect that existed between Cervini and such prelates as Contarini, Pole, Seripando, Sadoleto, and Bembo. This respect extended from Cervini to those who came under suspicion and active prosecution from the Inquisition, like Chiari, Morone, and Soranzo. His sympathy, for example, toward the Cassinese congregation in general, and toward Chiari in particular, spanned the years from 1545 to 1550. This is difficult to comprehend if Cervini, as one of the *intransigenti*, was supposed to have been at war with any and all prelates suspected of heresy in the 1540s and 1550s.

The correspondence of all these persons indicates that they consistently supported, encouraged, and exhorted one another. Sometimes they even credited one another for bringing out the best in themselves. Seripando, one of Cervini's theological advisers at Trent, made precisely this point seven years after the pope's death. "I wish to tell you," he wrote to Guglielmo Sirleto in 1562, "that I have never found anyone who had the kind of relationship to me that I had with that blessed man, so that I can say that I served him without seeking any glory for myself, unless it be with God."[8]

On the other hand, there are considerable difficulties with adopting Cervini as a member of the *spirituali*. Historians frequently suggest that this group, had it fully controlled the church hierarchy during the early sixteenth century, could have worked out a compromise with the Protestants and avoided schism. But, to place Cervini in such a group, one would have to ignore his view that doctrinal disputes ought to be settled under papal leadership alone, and his view that direct papal action was the necessary and proper cure for virtually all clerical and curial abuses. Similarly, one would have to ignore his conviction that the Protestants had excluded themselves from the church and ought to be left outside, unless they chose to return to obedience. His suggestion in the autumn of 1546, urging the suspension of the synod at Trent and the simultaneous convocation of a reform assembly in Rome, at least sounds like Paul IV's policy to avoid reconvocation of the council and to handle all the questions associated with doctrinal and reform issues himself. Cervini discussed the offices of religious superiors and the powers they held in a manner that has an *intransigent* ring to it, and he certainly attempted to institute a more monarchical form of ecclesiastical organization in Reggio. This confirms his essential belief in the necessity of a rigidly curialist understanding of government in the church. He took actions that can be described as controlling or manipulative, in his relationship with the religious orders under his protection, although he would probably have maintained that his policy was designed to avoid undue secular influence over the organizations and to enhance the ability of legitimate superiors to reform those under their control. When he became pope, he seemed to envision certain practical limits to the comprehensive application of his reform program. To assert that he was one of the *spirituali*, one would have to ignore much of this, as well as his realistic and pragmatic style of work. That style characterized his assessments of his colleagues. "Look if you can," he recommended to Bernardino Maffei, "at the hands of men rather than at their mouth(s)."[9]

The evidence of his life suggests that Cervini was neither *spirituale* nor *intransigente*. He had, for example, ceded benefices to his half-brother Romolo, who he hoped would follow him in an ecclesiastical career, quite in keeping with the contemporary practice that was attacked by reformers both inside and outside the church. Upon his papal election, however, he eschewed contemporary practice and would not permit his nephews so much as an audience in his palace. As legate at Trent, he made comments and suggested actions that make him sound shallow, manipulative, and perhaps even guilty of bribery. He may have been unable to assume a critical outlook in assessing factors that compromised papal leadership on doctrinal and reform issues. But who among his colleagues in papal, imperial, monarchical, or ducal administration was able to assume such a position, when the questions asked concerned a patron to whom the administrator literally owed everything? And who would not admit there was, in the sixteenth century, an exceptionally fine line between bribery and patronage? Patrons and clients in secular and ecclesiastical government during this period frequently crossed that line.

There are more examples that suggest Cervini stood, in a sense, outside both groups. He appealed to papal authority in the adjudication of a pastoral issue in Gubbio that more properly belonged before the Roman Rota, thus circumventing the appeal process in order to insure that his desires were carried out. But when faced with a poor man in Trent who had "contracted and consummated" a consanguinous marriage out of ignorance and who could not afford to pay the Penitentiary the customary offering for the dispensation, Cervini urged the dispensation be given anyway, for the good of the man's soul.[10] At the council, he criticized his opponents whom he thought proud and ambitious, but those for whom he recommended favors and additional benefices might just as easily have been called ambitious, for it was they who came to Cervini asking for revenues.

Similarly, he shut down the appeal of a canon in Chiari's diocese, not with the intention of allowing Chiari or any other bishop to rule arbitrarily, but to halt continued appeals, so that the bishop could effectively exercise the authority implied in his office. His view of ecclesiastical authority could easily be used to support the policies of future popes like Paul IV and Pius V, but the records of Cervini's own pontificate suggest he had no intention of doing so. He stood in continuity not only with defenders of the papacy as the only source of legitimate ecclesiastical authority, but also with episcopal theorists like Contarini, whose ideal for the bishop as an active, resident pastor is echoed in many of Cervini's letters. He saved money at his coronation that many would argue he put to better purpose on behalf of the people of Rome, but he used money at his disposal earlier in his career to build a villa at Vivo d'Orcia on Monte Amiata near Montepulciano. The latter action was quite in keeping with the un-reformed ideal of the cardinal as prince, and with the common practice of other successful curialists in the Renaissance. In building his villa, Cervini did not skimp on construction costs, either—the preliminary sketches for the job were done by none other than Antonio da Sangallo. Even the author of one of Cervini's most glowing assessments indicated that he was a man of contradictions, because, despite his love of literature and his vast library, he experienced no hesitation in purchasing books he considered obscene for the express purpose of burning them.[11]

But when considering Cervini, the challenge is to look beyond these apparent contradictions and inconsistencies, and beyond the earlier, unuseful characterizations of him, in order to see just what motivated his work in the church. The list of those motivations includes his humanist education, the sponsorship he received from the Farnese family, his concern for productive and efficacious administration exercised through existing lines of ecclesiastical authority, and his conviction in the necessity of improved and renewed popular religiosity.

This revised conception of Cervini and his career suggests a number of things about historical understanding of the period as a whole. Inability to place Cervini consistently and unquestionably into either the intransigent or spiritual camp is evidence of a considerable problem with the historical categories themselves. Sustaining the existence of coherent parties along these lines is impossible when examining any of the individuals in detail. Many assert now that it is not status as a humanist or as a reformer that helps distinguish *intransigenti* from *spirituali*, but rather an investigation into which model of the church each would adopt in reform efforts, and what tactics each considered appropriate for that work. But this is also unsatisfactory, if by that means one intends to maintain the standard distinction. Cervini became defensive, at times, when questioned about the legitimacy of inquisitorial procedures, yet he could cooperate and actively work with persons under suspicion, like Chiari and Soranzo. He could also work with Carafa and even hold him in high esteem. Yet Pole believed he could support procedures Cervini would use in papal administration, and Cervini's real, though brief, papal administration suggests he intended to follow a program quite opposed to that which Carafa inaugurated. As pope, Cervini attacked the nepotism of the curia and failed to pursue inquisitorial processes against persons like Morone. Carafa took action in the early days of his pontificate to reinstitutionalize the nepotism Cervini attacked and to initiate the trial of Morone, which Cervini ignored. The fact that Cervini and the others who drafted the reform bull of Julius III gave the power of implementation to the Roman Inquisition suggests that they viewed the reform process as a consistent, one-piece whole. It was Carafa who opposed the elimination of nepotism in the curia and then, seeing the power inherent in the Roman tribunal, manipulated it to proceed against his own personal enemies.

The failure of this methodological criteria may suggest something further: that those like Carafa and Ghislieri who undertook the most active repression of heretics were extremist exceptions to the proper interpretation of the Tridentine movement, rather than examples of a pervasive culture of religious repression.[12] No one pursued inquisitorial initiatives with the vehemence of Paul IV prior to his reign, and no one (with the exception of Ghislieri, Carafa's hand-picked successor in the Holy Office) did so afterward. Even Ghislieri could not do so with the single-minded, fanatical, even crazed consistency of Paul IV. When Ghislieri gained the papal throne as Pius V, his inquisitorial zeal, intransigence, and hot-headedness were indeed the outcome of his collaboration with and esteem for Paul IV. But his work of reforming the hierarchy and implementing the decrees of Trent, in which he employed enemies of Carafa like Giovanni Morone, was the logical conclusion of the long tradition of demands for reform that produced those decrees.

Indeed, the categories probably reflect the ideals and ecclesio-political commitments of twentieth-century historians, and those of their literary progenitors from the Risorgimento, more than they reflect personages in the sixteenth century. Sixteenth-century prelates as a whole, including those considered lenient and those considered repressive, were churchmen whose interests and policies varied according to their background, training, and experience. One must investigate this context to understand each individual, and all of them as a group. This investigation will allow even those who deserve credit for repressive Counter-Reformation initiatives—Carafa and Ghislieri—to be understood with greater sophistication.[13] Much of the work of Pius V, for example, was basically in continuity with the desire for realistic clerical reform and with the application of humanist learning to the understanding of the church, its clergy, and its worship. His political and religious intransigence constitutes an aberration from the outlook of those responsible for the shape of Tridentine Catholicism and is primarily reducible to the inspiration and reinforcement he received in such qualities from Paul IV.

Similarly, the view of the Counter Reformation that states it was born at Trent, where humanistic methodology and learning were used for rigidly apologetic and controversial reasons, must be revised in light of the career of Cervini. He participated, no doubt, in a definition of papal control over the church that was justified by humanistic methodology, but he did not seek to institutionalize such control in an unbending, intransigent papal monarchy that could not take seriously its own need for reform. He was not interested in simply defending and exculpating the church as it existed. He believed the sixteenth-century papacy to be a corrupt institution. Similarly, he believed contemporary clerical practices—including the personal behavior of clerics, their not infrequent illiteracy, and their habit of non-residence, as well as other abuses surrounding the granting of benefices—to be corrupt. He believed that the state of disrepair into which many individual churches had fallen was a symbol of that same corruption. But what he was ready to defend and apologize for was a reformed institution that mirrored the apostolic church. Such an institution, if it be recreated, could validly, from a controversial point of view, demand the obedience of anyone wishing to remain a Catholic. But that institution did not exist in Cervini's world, and he knew it. Because of his awareness that it did not, he dedicated his efforts to creating such an institution by reforming the corrupt one that did. He took as his starting point the commission of Christ to Peter, believing that to be the basis of the apostolic church, and hence the only basis for an adequately reformed church. He chose this method of reform not out of a desire to wage war with those who disagreed, but for two very different reasons. First, his understanding of the past convinced him this was the most authentic method and that it promised to achieve the clearest correlation with a model of the church he considered normative. Second, his pastoral experience convinced him this was also the most practicable method and promised the fastest results. He stood as a curious blend of the idealist and the realist.

Cervini happily participated in the Council of Trent as a defender of the papacy as long as he believed that reform, beginning with the curia and the pope, remained possible. But Paul III dragged his feet in commencing such work, against the incessant recommendations of his legate, so Cervini then pleaded simply for release from his duties, in order to attend to the area in which he could begin a genuine reform: his own diocese. He maintained his conviction that sufficient reform must begin with the pope and curia, especially concerning financial practices, and this is proved through the work Cervini commenced immediately upon his papal election. Those who have, on whatever basis, been identified as *spirituali* did not fear Cervini's full control over the future course of the church. Indeed, by looking at their own words, one might argue they viewed Cervini as the one man who might begin the kind of reform they had desired for some twenty-five years, using the same methodology they had recommended in the *Consilium de emendanda ecclesia.*

A new, radically different political and religious climate existed in the church from the very beginning of the pontificate of Paul IV. This has been demonstrated conclusively by the edition of the documents of the trial of Morone and of others who suffered similar investigations, like Domenico Morando. But the suggestion that the new climate constituted the logical conclusion of a direction into which the papacy and curia was already moving, or that it represented what the Counter Reformation continued to be, is not so conclusively proved. The career of Cervini helps demonstrate that the curia was not systematically moving in that direction, and similar studies, designed to render persons like Pius IV and Pius V as human beings rather than historiographical abstractions, may assist in determining to what extent the new climate survived the demise of its creator, Paul IV.[14]

Above all, Cervini must be evaluated in the context of his entire life and career. His early education under his father was broadly based and helped him begin the administrative career he followed for the rest of his life. His humanist education convinced him that study of the past, and especially of the apostolic church, would present the most authentic and legitimate model for the present. His first administrative duties gave him familiarity and personal acquaintance with problems both inside the church and its curial hierarchy and outside in the Protestant world. His episcopal duties, at times laden with enormous complications, demonstrated to him both the need for diocesan reform and his own competence in ameliorating these situations. The importance of pastoral work in the careers of churchmen like Cervini has been played down in recent historical analysis of these persons and this period.[15] Reconsideration of this pastoral work is needed, and, in the case of Cervini, it establishes him in continuity with the great Italian bishop-reformers like Gian Matteo Giberti and Carlo Borromeo. Such works also demonstrated to him the difficulty of solving curial and episcopal problems.

Cervini never seriously considered giving up, despite these complications. The goal he always sought was an idealistic one—to reshape the papacy and the sixteenth-century church into conformity with the model of the church of the apostolic age. The means he always employed were practical—to encourage immediate action in all his associates, from Paul III to Vittore Soranzo, and to take action on his own when in possession of the necessary authority. His administrative skills became tools that he believed could help to achieve that idealist conformity in the most efficient manner possible. These two considerations came together in the latter part of his administrative career. The apostolic church was founded on Peter, and while its foundation had been upheld by patristic theologians and by the history of the councils, its most directly identifiable image was the pope. He was the one commissioned by Christ who had the proper authority to lead the church back into correspondence with the apostolic age. Cervini also maintained that the leadership of one man would be simpler and more efficient than that of many.

He urged the pope to undertake the reform in two separate ways. First, he recommended that the Council of Trent, operating theoretically under papal authority and in practice under the strict control of papal representatives, ought to settle doctrinal issues. The council fathers were to follow patristic exemplars and the example of earlier councils, leave competing theological schools behind, and thereby arrive at an authentic restatement of Catholic dogma. Second, he urged the pope to institute disciplinary reform, including reform of the curia, by means of a reform bull. He should not, Cervini believed, leave this task to the council. In accordance with the ecclesiological model he had adopted, since all the clergy, however indirectly, received their ordination and jurisdiction through the tradition beginning with Peter, the pope legitimately had the power to do this himself. Cervini considered reform to be a matter of jurisdiction, to be undertaken in any given area by one person: the ecclesiastical superior. If the clergy in a diocese needed reform on whatever level, be it education, preaching, or outward bearing, the bishop or vicar should undertake the work. If a convent needed reform, this was the duty of the bishop as well, except in the case of an exempt order, when a delegate of the papacy should see to the work. If an individual bishop needed correction, it was the responsibility of his superior, the pope, to insure this. If the Roman curia at large, in fiscal procedures or questions of exemption from residence, had overstepped their bounds, revision of their policies should be accomplished by the pope and not by a council. All this, he believed, was specifically provided in the commission of Christ to Peter, and in the interpretation of that commission by patristic theologians.

So, Cervini failed to do any ground-breaking or original work as a theologian. He relied upon his colleagues who were expert in those areas and upon patristic opinions in leading discussions on doctrinal questions at the council. He also relied on a conventional, even curialist, understanding of the hierarchical nature of the church. He is important because he backed his understanding with evidence derived through the humanist methodology he learned as a student: a careful reading of the most ancient Christian sources, Scripture and the church fathers. He is important because this was the process employed by the Tridentine fathers much later, after the aberration of Paul IV's pontificate. The Tridentine fathers buttressed conventional understandings with sources recovered through humanist methodology. They avoided, thereby, both the creation of new doctrinal formulations (for this was precisely their criticism of Protestants) as well as adherence to any one of the theological schools (for this was a source of contention even in their own assemblies). In so doing, they undertook the more precise and normative prescription of doctrines already in existence, relative to the ancient church and to the demands of contemporary experience. Cervini acted to find practical ways and means to solve the problems of the sixteenth-century church in matters of both doctrine and reform, which then reverberated through the later sessions at Trent.

Cervini is best understood as an administrator, a humanistic and pragmatic prelate who was committed to the promotion of a particular kind of change in the sixteenth-century church. In his desire for an improved church, based on models found in the New Testament and in early patristic sources, he was just as spiritual as any of the *spirituali*. In his defense and promotion of papal power and authority, he was just as intransigent as any of the *intransigenti*. Above all, Cervini maintained consistency in both those positions. He criticized inconsistency in others, especially in those prelates who supported the emperor more often than the person Cervini considered their real superior, the pope. He also criticized those who sought to hide their real intentions, as he said, "under the pretext of piety."[16] And perhaps that quality of consistency is what endeared him to such a wide variety of people in a turbulent period in the history of the church—because they knew what to expect from him. The sort of advice he gave remained the same over the years, and that advice was reflected in the methods he followed as episcopal administrator and as pope. He committed himself passionately to the elimination of the myriad ecclesiastical abuses of the sixteenth century. Passionate too was his belief that the elimination of those abuses had to be carried out through the established hierarchy of the church. When frustrated in his hope that the general reform would be carried out in such a manner, his pragmatism took over, and he worked to reform specific areas under his jurisdiction as episcopal administrator. When he attained the position from which he could personally see to a general reform, there too his pragmatism shone through, although death quickly intervened. In fact, he had more in common with practical episcopal administrators and reformers like Gian Matteo Giberti, Domenico Bollani, and Gregorio Cortese than he had with ideologues like Gian Pietro Carafa.

The concept of reform, and all the other ideas Cervini developed, were more than anything else results of the work he did, the manner in which he saw authority exercised, and the set of changes he hoped to see occur in the church. In part, he owed that concept and those ideas to the Farnese family, just as much as he owed to them the beginnings of his dual career as curial and episcopal administrator. Once launched on that career, Cervini combined the diplomatic and political training he received from the Farnese with his own conception of the doctrinal and reform issues then dividing Europe, and he adopted a program that had broad effect upon the Tridentine assembly and upon the manner in which episcopal and curial problems were considered. His concerns and approaches were inherited by the next generation of Catholic Tridentine churchmen like François de la Rochefoucauld, Roberto Bellarmino, and Carlo Borromeo.

NOTES

ABBREVIATIONS

AHC	*Annuarium historiae conciliorum*
AHR	*American Historical Review*
ASF	Archivio di Stato, Florence
ASV	Archivio Segreto Vaticano, Città del Vaticano
AHP	*Archivum historiae pontificae*
BHR	*Bibliothèque d'humanisme et renaissance*
BAV	Biblioteca Apostolica Vaticana, Città del Vaticano
C. Cerv.	*Carte cerviniane* (Collection of seventy manuscript codices, Archivio di Stato, Florence)
CH	*Church History*
CHR	*Catholic Historical Review*
CNS	*Cristianesimo nella storia*
CT	*Concilium tridentinum*, 13 vols. (Freiburg: Herder, 1901–1938)
DBI	*Dizionario biografico degli italiani* (Rome: Istituto della enciclopedia italiana, 1958–)
DIP	*Dizionario degli istituti di perfezione* (Rome: Paoline, 1974–)
JMH	*Journal of Modern History*
MHSI	*Monumenta historica Societatis Iesu* (Madrid and Rome, 1894–)
RQ	*Renaissance Quarterly*
RSCI	*Rivista di storia della chiesa in italia*
RSI	*Rivista storica italiana*
RSLR	*Rivista di storia e letteratura religiosa*
SCJ	*Sixteenth Century Journal*

CHAPTER 1. CERVINI IN HISTORY

1. The major sources on Cervini's life are the biographies by Pietro Polidori, *De vita gestis et moribus Marcelli II* (Rome, 1744), and by Alessandro Cervini, *Vita di Marcello II*. The latter work, a manuscript found in the Biblioteca Pubblica of Ferrara, was published in part in *Archivio storico italiano*, app. 7 (1848):248–51. Another copy of this *Vita* can be found in ASF, *C. Cerv.*, 52/124r–131v. (In all references to the *C. Cerv.*, the first number refers to the filza or volume number, the second to the page number, recto [r] or verso [v].) Gaetano Moroni wrote a biographical sketch of Cervini in his *Dizionario di erudizione storico ecclesiastica*, 153 vols. (Venice: Tipografia emiliana, 1840–1879), 42:238–46. Although *DBI* contains articles in vol. 24 (Rome, 1980) on Marcello's father and half-brother, Ricciardo (1454–1534) and Romolo (1520–1551) Cervini, the editors have chosen to treat Marcello in a later volume, under his papal name. A mass entitled *Missa papae Marcelli*, commemorating the life of Cervini, was composed by Palestrina in 1567—see Giovanni Pierluigi da Palestrina, *Pope Marcellus Mass*, edited by Lewis Lockwood (New York: Norton, 1975).

2. Gilbertus Genebrardus in his *Chronographiae libri quatuor* (Paris, 1590) included a brief note on Marcello's pontificate, and he is the only author who treated with anything other than ridicule the suggestion that Cervini may have been poisoned. Giuseppe Piatti in his *Storia-critico cronologica de' romani pontefici*, 13 vols. (Naples: Raimondi, 1765–1768) said no poisoning was verifiable, since Onofrio Panvinio (d. 1568), a biographer of the popes and author of the official Counter-Reformation history of the papacy, was a familiar of Cervini and did not mention it (10:318–22).

3. The development of such hagiographical traditions around those who took ecclesiastical duties seriously in sixteenth-century Italy was not uncommon. It also occurred in the case of Gian Matteo Giberti (1495–1543), bishop of Verona. See Adriano Prosperi, *Tra evangelismo e controriforma: G. M. Giberti* (Rome: Edizioni di storia e letteratura, 1969), pp. xviii-xxiii, 3–4.

4. Bartolomeo Platina, Onofrio Panvinio, and Antonio Cicarelli, *Historia delle vite de i sommi pontefici* (Venice, 1594), pp. 283–86.

5. Alessandro Cervini in his *Vita di Marcello II* said that the astrologer predicted, "this child would be great in the church of God," a prediction that Marcello's father confirmed with mathematical calculations. *C. Cerv.*, 52/126v.

6. Such characterizations and descriptions are typical in the tradition of the expectation of a *pastor angelicus*, or "angel pope," which began with Celestine V in 1294. Although no pope ever proclaimed himself such, the tradition was expressed in the writings of reformers and apocalyptic publicists through the sixteenth and into the seventeenth century. In the sixteenth century, it was typical to emphasize this coming "holy pope" in contrast to the Protestant characterization of the pope as Antichrist. See Marjorie Reeves, *The Influence of Prophecy in the Later Middle Ages* (Oxford: Clarendon Press, 1969); Bernard McGinn, "Angel Pope and Papal Antichrist," *Church History* 47

(1978):155–73; and my "Marcellus II, Girolamo Seripando and the Image of the Angelic Pope," in Marjorie Reeves, ed., *Prophetic Rome in the High Renaissance Period*, Oxford-Warburg Studies (Oxford: Clarendon, 1992), pp. 373–87.

7. Peter J. Chandlery, *Fasti Breviores: A Daily Record of Memorable Events in the History of the Society of Jesus* (London: Manresa Press, 1910), p. 96. *Fontes narrativi de Santo Ignatio, MHSI* 66 (Rome, Institutem historicum Societatis Iesu, 1943), pp. 581–82.

8. "Neque vero statim cognita non est singularis illa doctrinae vis, probitatis, atque prudentiae: quin etiam, cum talis inde existeret oratio, quae verborum numero, sententiarum, vel oraculorum potius, numerum assequeretur, erupit illico ad hominum existimationem et admirationem neque ullis ipsius modestiae quasi cancellis coerceri potuit Marcelli incredibilis fama virtutum." Julius Pogianus, *Epistolae et orationes*, 4 vols. (Rome, 1762), 1:105–6.

9. "Si non optat, certe, homo non est, sed Angelus carne indutus." Cesare Baronio, *Annales ecclesiastici*, ed., O. Raynaldo, 38 vols. (Lucca: Venturini, 1738–1757), 33:551. The most recent book on Baronio is Cyriac K. Pullapilly, *Caesar Baronius, Counter-Reformation Historian* (Notre Dame, IN: University of Notre Dame Press, 1975). Cf. also Eric W. Cochrane, *Historians and Historiography in the Italian Renaissance* (Chicago: University of Chicago Press, 1981), pp. 457–63; and *DBI*, s.v. "Baronio, Cesare," by Alberto Pincerle. For Seripando, the standard biography is Hubert Jedin, *Papal Legate at the Council of Trent: Cardinal Seripando*, trans. F. C. Eckhoff (St. Louis: Herder, 1947).

10. Paolo Sarpi, *Istoria del Concilio Tridentino*, 2 vols. (Florence: Sansoni, 1966). For some recent evaluations of Sarpi and his work, see Cochrane, *Historians*, pp. 472–78; Corrado Vivanti, "Una fonte dell' *Istoria del Concilio Tridentino* di Paolo Sarpi," *RSI* 83 (1971):630; and A. G. Dickens and John Tonkin, *The Reformation in Historical Perspective* (Cambridge: Harvard University Press, 1985), pp. 98–100.

11. Sforza Pallavicino, *Storia del Concilio di Trento*, in *Opere del cardinal Sforza Pallavicino*, 2 vols. (Milan: Bettoni, 1834), 1:580–84; see also Cochrane, *Historians*, p. 477. Spinello Benci, *Storia di Montepulciano* (Florence, 1646), p. 102.

12. Ludovico Antonio Muratori, *Annali d'Italia*, 12 vols. (Naples: Raimondi, 1751–1755), 10:333. Maurus Sartius, *De episcopis eugubinis* (Pisa, 1755), pp. 222–25. Piatti, *Storia-critico*, 10:321.

13. Giovan Battista Brilli, *Intorno alla vita e alle azioni di Marcello, pontefice ottimo massimo; orazione* (Montepulciano: Angiolo Fumi, 1846), p. 21. Moroni, *Dizionario*, 42:238. For one example of the shift in focus, see Generoso Calenzio, *Saggio di storia del concilio generale di Trento sotto Paolo III* (Rome, 1869), p. 51. Leopold von Ranke, *History of the Popes*, 3 vols. (New York: Ungar, 1966), 1:192. Ludwig von Pastor, *History of the Popes*, ed. R. F. Kerr et al., 40 vols. (London: Keegan Paul, 1938–1953), 14:14–15, 33.

14. Pio Paschini and Vincenzo Monachino, *I papi nella storia* (Rome: Coletti, 1961), p. 628. Giovanni Saccani, *I vescovi di Reggio Emilia* (Reggio Emilia: Artigianelli, 1902), pp. 118–20, and Umberto Pesci, *I vescovi di Gubbio*

(Perugia: Unione tipografica cooperativa, 1919), pp. 108–18. On Cervini's administration of Reggio Emilia, see also Andrea Balletti, *Storia di Reggio nell'Emilia* (Bonvicini: Reggio Emilia, 1925), pp. 384–86.

15. Xavier-Marie Le Bachelet, "Bellarmin et les exercices spirituels de S. Ignace," *Collection de la bibliothèque des exercices de saint Ignace* 37–38 (1912):1–152, and "La prédication ecclésiastique d'après le cardinal Marcel Cervin et d'après les exercices spirituels de saint Ignace," *Collection de la bibliothèque des exercices de saint Ignace* 61–62 (1920):160–65. For another such assessment, see William V. Bangert, *Claude Jay and Alfonso Salmerón: Two Early Jesuits* (Chicago: Loyola University Press, 1985), pp. 180–83, 190, 223.

16. Giovan Battista Mannucci, "Il conclave di papa Marcello," *Bollettino senese di storia di patria* 27 (1920):94–103; Pio Pecchiai, *Roma nel Cinquecento*, vol. 13, *Storia di Roma* (Bologna: Cappelli, 1948), pp. 84–86; Agostino Saba and Carlo Castiglioni, *Storia dei papi* (Turin: Tipografia sociale, 1965), pp. 306–8; Edoardo Del Vecchio, *I Farnese* (Rome: Istituto di studi romani, 1972), pp. 49–60, 86–87; Gregorio Penco, *Storia della chiesa in Italia*, 2 vols. (Milan: Jaca Book, 1977), 1:586; Giovanni Costi, "L'episcopato a Reggio Emilia (1540–1544) del cardinale Marcello Cervini, poi papa Marcello II," in *In memoria di Leone Tondelli*, edited by N. Artioli (Reggio Emilia: Studio teologico interdiocesano, 1980), pp. 203–29; and J. N. D. Kelly, *Oxford Dictionary of Popes* (Oxford: Oxford University Press, 1986), pp. 264–65.

17. Stanley Morison, "Marcello Cervini, Pope Marcellus II: Bibliography's Patron Saint," *Italia medioevale e umanistica* 5 (1962):301–18.

18. Hubert Jedin, *Geschichte des Konzils von Trient*, 5 vols. (Freiburg: Herder, 1950–1975). The work was translated into Italian by G. Basso, *Storia del Concilio di Trento* (Brescia: Morcelliana, 1962; 2d ed., 1974). The first two volumes are available in English, translated by E. Graf, *History of the Council of Trent* (St. Louis: Herder, 1957, 1961). Cervini and his work, especially at the council, are examined in detail throughout the first four volumes of Jedin's history.

19. For two expressions of this conception by contemporary historians, see Hans J. Hillerbrand, *Men and Ideas in the Sixteenth Century* (Boston: Houghton Mifflin, 1969), pp. 89–96, and Nicholas S. Davidson, *The Counter Reformation* (Oxford: Basil Blackwell, 1987), pp. 1–3.

20. Jedin spelled this out most clearly in his essay *Katholische Reformation oder Gegenreformation?* (Lucerne: J. Stocker, 1946). A review of the use of the terms *Reformation* and *Counter Reformation*, especially in German historiography, and some further reflections on this issue were recently published: Wolfgang Reinhard, "Reformation, Counter-Reformation and the Early-Modern State: A Reassessment," *CHR* 75 (1989):383–404. See also John W. O'Malley's introduction to *Catholicism in Early-Modern History: A Guide to Research* (St. Louis: Center for Reformation Research, 1988), pp. 1–9.

21. Jedin, *Storia*, 2:59–60. Giuseppe Alberigo, *I vescovi italiani al Concilio di Trento* (Florence: Sansoni, 1959), pp. 150–52. The rhetoric of a "tide of

immorality" is high-flown. No such tide would have been perceived by most people in the sixteenth century. But that is no reason to believe it is purely imaginary. The reform decree of Session 6 (January 1547) put it this way: "Eadem sacrosancta synodus, eisdem praesidentibus Apostolicae Sedis legatis, ad restituendam collapsam admodum ecclesiasticam disciplinam, depravatosque in clero et populo Christiano mores emendandos." *The Canons and Decrees of the Council of Trent*, edited by H. J. Schroeder (St. Louis: Herder, 1941), p. 324. It is difficult to extricate the facts from such language, and to ascertain their moral quality. But, there can be no doubt, this is precisely the sort of conduct that Cervini's own actions were designed to eliminate, especially when he found it in other clerics. This is abundantly demonstrated by his correspondence. Other recent historiography maintains that clerical immorality was viewed askance by average Christians. See Philip Hoffman, *Church and Community in the Diocese of Lyon* (New Haven: Yale University Press, 1984), pp. 19–21.

22. Delio Cantimori, *Eretici italiani del Cinquecento* (Florence: Sansoni, 1939), p. 24; He elaborated his theses in subsequent articles too numerous to list. "Italy and the Papacy," p. 251.

23. Carlo Ginzburg, *Il nicodemismo: Simulazione e dissimulazione religiosa nell'Europa del '500* (Turin: Einaudi, 1970). Antonio Rotondò, *Studi e ricerche di storia ereticale italiane* (Turin: Istituto di scienze politiche dell'Università di Torino, 1974). Massimo Firpo and Dario Marcatto, *Il processo inquisitoriale del cardinal Giovanni Morone*, 5 vols. (Rome: Istituto storico italiano per l'età moderna e contemporanea, 1981–1989).

24. Paolo Simoncelli, *Evangelismo italiano del Cinquecento* (Rome: Istituto storico italiano per l'età moderna e contemporanea, 1979). See *DBI*, s.v. "Colonna, Vittoria," by G. Patrizi.

25. Dermot Fenlon, *Heresy and Obedience in Tridentine Italy: Cardinal Pole and the Counter Reformation* (Cambridge: Cambridge University Press, 1972), pp. ix-xii, 18–23, 47–49, 137–60. Anne Jacobson Schutte, "The *Lettere volgare* and the Crisis of Evangelism in Italy, *RQ* 28 (1975):639–88. Elisabeth Gleason, "On the Nature of Sixteenth-Century Italian Evangelism: Scholarship, 1953–1978," *SCJ* 9 (1978):3–25, and *Reform Thought in Sixteenth-Century Italy*, Texts and Translations Series, American Academy of Religion (Ann Arbor: Scholar's Press, 1981), pp. 3–5. British and American authors of more general histories also frequently adopt this characterization. See, for example, Bangert, *Claude Jay and Alfonso Salmerón*, p. 79, and Charles Stinger, *The Renaissance in Rome* (Bloomington: Indiana University Press, 1985), pp. 328–30.

26. Paolo Simoncelli, "Inquisizione romana e riforma in Italia," *RSI* 100 (1988):1–125. For a recent work on the topic, see Giuseppe Alberigo, "Dinamiche religiose del Cinquecento italiano tra riforma, riforma cattolica, controriforma," *CNS* 6 (1985):543–60.

27. Barbara McClung Hallman, *Italian Cardinals, Reform and the Church as Property* (Berkeley: University of California Press, 1985). She provided the

archival evidence for the theses expressed by another historian: A. V. Antonovics, "Counter-Reformation Cardinals: 1534–1590," *European Studies Review* 2 (1972):301–28.

28. Marcantonio Flaminio, *Lettere*, edited by A. Pastore (Rome: Edizioni dell'Ateneo e Bizzarri, 1978). Massimo Firpo's review "L'epistolario di Marcantonio Flaminio" appears in *RSI* 91 (1979):653–62. An edition of the *Beneficio* appeared recently: Benedetto da Mantova, *Il beneficio di Cristo*, edited by Salvatore Caponetto (DeKalb, IL: Northern Illinois University Press, 1972). Flaminio, *Lettere*, pp. 40–41. Firpo, "L'epistolario," p. 656.

29. Paul Grendler, *The Roman Inquisition and the Venetian Press, 1540–1605* (Princeton: Princeton University Press, 1977), pp. xxi-xxii, 286–93. Arnaldo D'Addario, *Aspetti della controriforma a Firenze* (Rome: Archivio di Stato, 1972), p. ix. Edward Peters, *Inquisition* (New York: Free Press, 1988), pp. 105–21.

30. Giuseppe Olmi and Paolo Prodi, "Art Science and Nature in Bologna circa 1600," in *Age of Correggio and the Carracci: Emilian Painting of the Sixteenth and Seventeenth Centuries* (Washington: National Gallery of Art, 1986), pp. 213–35; Eric W. Cochrane, "Counter Reformation or Tridentine Reformation? Italy in the Age of Carlo Borromeo," in John M. Headley and John B. Tomaro, eds., *San Carlo Borromeo, Catholic Reform and Ecclesiastical Politics in the Second Half of the Sixteenth Century* (Washington: Folger Books, 1988), pp. 31–46; Eric W. Cochrane, *Italy, 1530–1630*, Longman History of Italy Series (New York: Longman, 1988), pp. 1–5, 106–64; Franco Battistelli, ed., *Arte e cultura nella provincia di Pesaro e Urbino* (Venice: Marsilio, 1986), pp. 281–424; and Brendan Dooley, "Social Control and the Italian Universities: From Renaissance to Illuminismo," *JMH* 61 (1989):205–39. In an older work, Alessandro Visconti went to considerable length to indicate that views of the Counter Reformation as a triumph of papal reaction against "free thought" are compromised by their generation during the political upheaval known as the Risorgimento. See his *L'Italia nell'epoca della controriforma dal 1516 al 1713*, vol. 6, *Storia d'Italia* (Verona: Mondadori, 1958), pp. 79–109.

31. Adriano Prosperi, "L'inquisizione: Verso una nuova immagine?" *Critica storica* 25 (1988):119–45. Anne Jacobson Schutte, "Periodization of Sixteenth-Century Italian Religious History: The Post-Cantimori Paradigm Shift," *JMH* 61 (1989):269–84. Gigliola Fragnito, "Evangelismo e intransigenti nei difficili equilibri del pontificato farnesiano," *RSLR* 25 (1989):20–47. Silvana Seidel-Menchi, "Inquisizione come repressione o inquisizione come mediazione? Una proposta di periodizzazione," *Annuario dell'istituto storico italiano per l'età moderna e contemporanea* 35–36 (1983–1984):53–77.

32. An investigation similar to this one has been pursued on a French prelate from the same period: Joseph Bergin, *Cardinal de la Rochefoucauld: Leadership and Reform in the French Church* (New Haven: Yale University Press, 1987), pp. 4–5. Papal government in the early-modern period is the subject of two other recent works: Paolo Prodi, *Il sovrano pontefice. Un corpo e due anime: La monarchia papale nella prima età moderna* (Bologna: Mulino, 1982), and Peter

Partner, *The Pope's Men: The Papal Civil Service in the Renaissance* (Oxford: Clarendon Press, 1990).

33. The largest published portion is contained in *Concilium tridentinum*, 13 vols. (Freiburg: Herder, 1901–1938). A number of other collections include correspondence of Cervini in far lesser quantities: Gottfried Buschbell, ed., *Reformation und Inquisition in Italien um die Mitte des XVI Jahrhunderts*, Quellen und Forschungen, XIII Band (Paderborn: Schöningh, 1910); Ludwig Cardauns, ed., *Nuntiaturberichte aus Deutschland. I Abteilung 1533–1539, 5–6 Bd. Legationem Farnesus und Cervinis 1539–1541* (Berlin: A. Bath, 1909); Franco Gaeta, ed., *Nunziature di Venezia* (Rome: Istituto storico italiano per l'età moderna e contemporanea, 1976); Ludovico Beccadelli, *Monumenta di varia letteratura*, 3 vols. (Bologna, 1797–1804; reprinted, Farnborough, England: Gregg Press Limited, 1967); and *Monumenta historica Societatis Iesu*, especially vol. 24, *Epistolae PP. Paschasii Broëti, Claudii Jaji* (Madrid: López del Horno, 1971).

34. Christopher Cairns, *Domenico Bollani, Bishop of Brescia: Devotion to Church and State in the Republic of Venice in the Sixteenth Century*, Bibliotheca humanistica et reformatorica, no. 15 (Nieukoop: B. De Graaf, 1976), pp. 139–40; and Bergin, *Cardinal*, pp. 39–91. Cf. James M. Kittelson, "Renaissance and Reformation in Germany: An Agenda for Research," *JMH* 58 (1986):124–40.

35. For a study on the concept of reform as the recovery of primitive purity, see John W. O'Malley, "Reform, Historical Consciousness and Vatican II's Aggiornamento," *Theological Studies* 32 (1971):573–601. Constancy and modulation in the overall papal ecclesiastical program in the sixteenth century has recently been suggested, based on papal policy toward the Jews. See Kenneth R. Stow, *Taxation, Community and the State: The Jews and the Fiscal Foundations of the Early Modern Papal State*, Päpste und Papsttum, no. 19 (Stuttgart: Anton Hiersemann, 1982), p. 70.

36. Here I adopt the terminology delineated by the late Eric Cochrane in his "Counter Reformation" and in his *Italy*, pp. 106–64.

37. On Ochino (1487–1563), a general of the Capuchin branch of the Franciscans before his flight to Geneva to escape inquisitorial proceedings, see Edmondo Solmi, "La fuga di Bernardino Ochino secondo i documenti dell'Archivio Gonzaga di Mantova," *Bollettino senese di storia patria* 15 (1908):23–98; Roland Bainton, *Bernardino Ochino: Esule e riformatore senese del Cinquecento, 1487–1563*, translated by Elio Gianturco (Florence: Sansoni, 1941); and Gigliola Fragnito, "Gli *spirituali* e la fuga di Bernardino Ochino," *RSI* 84 (1972):777–813.

CHAPTER 2. PREPARATION AS HUMANIST AND CURIALIST

1. Vittorio Spreti, *Enciclopedia storico-nobiliare italiana*, 9 vols. (Milan: Edizione enciclopedia storico-nobiliare italiana, 1929–1936), 2:32. Xavier-Marie

Le Bachelet, *Bellarmin avant son cardinalat, 1542–1598* (Paris: Beauchesue, 1911), p. 478. *DBI,* s.v. "Cervini, Ricciardo," by Marco Palma.

2. *DBI,* s.v. "Cervini, Ricciardo," and *C. Cerv.*, 52/125v. Federico Ubaldini, *Vita di Mons. Angelo Colocci. Edizione del testo originale italiano. A cura di Vittorio Fanelli,* Studi e testi, no. 256 (Città del Vaticano: Biblioteca Apostolica Vaticana, 1969), p. 84; see also Armando Verde, *Lo studio fiorentino, 1473–1503. Ricerche e documenti,* 4 vols. (Pistoia: Istituto nazionale di studi sul rinascimento, 1977), 3:854.

3. *DBI,* s.v. "Cervini, Ricciardo." Surprisingly, there is no modern study on the Spannocchi family. Some information is available in Giuseppe Alberigo, "Un informatore senese al Concilio di Trento (1551–1552)," *RSCI* 12 (1958):173–201.

4. Spreti, *Enciclopedia,* 2:32. *C. Cerv.*, 52/126r.

5. *DBI,* s.v. "Cervini, Ricciardo."

6. "Et Mercurio in decima: et ♀ (Venus) et ♄ (Saturn) et il sole in Nona." *C. Cerv.*, 52/126v. "Con esso Messer Ricciardo in quel tempo un grande astrologo . . . fece giuditio che tal figliuolo sarebbe grande nella chiesa di Dio. Il che fu anco confirmato dal padrone il quale essa gratia matematico anchorche poco attendesse alle cose pertinenti alla divinatione." Ibid. Such a suggestion that an individual's character was set at birth was typically found in humanist biographies of this period: cf. Cochrane, *Historians*, p. 415. "Ma vegliando non voleva gustarne, ne vedere ne la Zinna ne la donna in modo nissuno così perseverando per gratia Dio, et vivendo si condusse in età habile che nutristi di più solido cibo." *C. Cerv.*, 52/127r.

7. "Comincerò dalla patria quale di ragione alle altre cose si deve anteposse dico che Marcello hebbe due patrie l'una per natura dove nacque che fû Montefano, della Marca d'Ancona, et l'altra Montepulciano della quale per ragione di origine e domandato; città nobile et ricca." *C. Cerv.,* 52/125r. The town was one of the many in Tuscany with proud and independent communal traditions. See R. Burr Litchfield, *Emergence of a Bureaucracy: The Florentine Patricians 1530–1790* (Princeton: Princeton University Press, 1986), pp. 110–14. *De legibus*, 2.2.3. See Cicero, *Opera omnia*, 4 vols. (London: Dove, 1819), 4/2:702–7.

8. "La madre detta Madonna Cassandra come ho detto fû dei Benci . . . et lei così diligentissima et industriosa governatrice della sua famiglia, et tanto amatrice, et curiosa del marito che potere molto bene aguagliassi a quelle più celebrate donne del secolo antico." *C. Cerv.,* 52/126r.

9. *DBI*, s.v. "Cervini, Ricciardo."

10. On Cintia Cervini and the marriages between the Cervini and Bellarmino families, see Mario Scaduto, *Storia della Compagnia di Gesù in Italia*. Vol. 3, *L'epoca di Giacomo Lainez: Il governo 1556–1565* (Rome: Edizioni "La civiltà cattolica," 1964), pp. 272–78. *DBI,* s.v. "Cervini, Romolo," by Marco Palma.

11. Cf. Litchfield, *Emergence of a Bureaucracy*, pp. 158–62. *DBI,* s.v. "Cervini, Romolo."

12. *DBI,* s.v. "Cervini, Ricciardo." The name of the farm is given as Castiglione di Val d'Orcia, in the manuscript sources: *C. Cerv.,* 52/127v; also 49/6v, 7v, 8v, 9v, 12v. On education in this period, see Giuseppe Saitta, *L'educazione dell'umanesimo in Italia* (Venice, 1928), as well as Eugenio Garin's classic treatment, *L'educazione in Europa 1400–1600* (Rome-Bari: Laterza, 1957), and his *Il pensiero pedagogico dell'umanesimo* (Florence: Sansoni, 1958). The latter work is in a series of selected readings that includes Felice Battaglia, *Il pensiero pedagogico del rinascimento* (Florence: Sansoni, 1960), and Luigi Volpicelli, *Il pensiero pedagogico della controriforma* (Florence: Sansoni, 1960). Paul Grendler published a series of articles on education in the Italian Renaissance and Counter Reformation. See his "What Zuane Read in School: Vernacular Texts in Sixteenth-Century Venetian Schools," *SCJ* 13 (1982):41–53; "The Schools of Christian Doctrine in Sixteenth-Century Italy," *CH* 53 (1984):319–31; and "The Organization of Primary and Secondary Education in the Italian Renaissance," *CHR* 71 (1985):185–205. Grendler recently completed a major work on this topic: *Schooling in Renaissance Italy: Literacy and Learning, 1300–1600* (Baltimore: Johns Hopkins University Press, 1989). See also Anthony Grafton, "Teacher, Text and Pupil in the Renaissance Classroom: A Case Study from a Parisian College," *History of Universities* 1 (1981): 31–70, and his collection of studies on these topics, Anthony Grafton and Lisa Jardine, *From Humanism to the Humanities* (Cambridge: Harvard University Press, 1986).

13. "In quel paese dove era allhora, che fu Castiglione di Valdorcia . . . sotto la disciplina del Padre imparò le prime lettere, il quale a usanza di Giulio Cesare volse insegnarli quelle et anco a notar nell'acqua seimando tal arte per molto necessaria agl'huomini che hanno a praticar il mondo. . . . et per dargli ogni perfettione volse che ancora imparasse la maggior parte dell'arti meccaniche." *C. Cerv.,* 52/127v-128r.

14. Guido de Ruggiero, *Rinascimento, riforma e controriforma,* 2 vols. (Rome-Bari: Laterza, 1930), 1:146–54.

15. William Roscoe, *The Life and Pontificate of Leo X,* 3d ed., 4 vols. (London: T. Cadell, 1827), 4:93–95, 439; see also Verde, *Lo studio fiorentino,* 3:854. Charles-Joseph Hefele et al., *Histoire des conciles,* 8 vols. (Paris: Librairie Letouzey et Ané, 1917), 8:445–51.

16. *C. Cerv.,* 49/6r–6v; see also *DBI,* s.v. "Cervini, Ricciardo." Piccolomini was the archbishop of Siena from 1503 until 1529, when he, in accord with standard Renaissance practice, resigned the see to his nephew, reserving some of the income of the see as a pension. Pastor, *History of the Popes,* 14:12.

17. *C. Cerv.,* 49/6r-v. "Nel architettura, et cognition delle cose antiche non fù a nessuno de suoi tempi secondo. . . . Ma nelli studii di humanità fù veramente eccellente . . . in prosa et in versi con somma facilità, et elegantia da lui formate." *C. Cerv.,* 52/129r.

18. These letters constitute the first forty-eight pages of filza 49 in the *Carte cerviniane.* "Io duro fatiche in nesolidi di Euchlide, che son una materia da le precedenti molto abstracta, perché bisogna quelle figure facte in piano

immaginarsele solide, pure tuttavia, ci duro cum fatiga." Marcello to Ricciardo Cervini, May 19, 1520. *C. Cerv.*, 49/13r.

19. Pio Paschini, "Un cardinale editore: Marcello Cervini," in his *Cinquecento romano e riforma cattolica* (Rome: Facultas theologica pontificii athenaei lateranensis, 1958), p. 185. "Del greco, so gia declinare i nomi, adiectivi et substantivi di tutte le declinatione et li pronomi . . . al principio di maggio cominciaro a udire, bisognerà ancora ingrero comprare parechi libri." Marcello to Ricciardo Cervini, April 21, 1520. *C. Cerv.*, 49/31r. "Ma mi pare una vergogna che lui [?] adisagio di tanti denari per noi, et maxime che haviamo mandato a Venetia per certi libri greci, benché lui, mostra di farlo volentieri pure io non vorrei, et se lui non mi forzara non voglio che lo compri, perché se noi non haremo commodità di farlo staro con questo et per ho vi ho voluto advisare di quello e, successo di questa cosa." Marcello to Ricciardo Cervini, June 2, 1520. *C. Cerv.*, 49/16r.

20. "Io di poi vi scripsi, non ho havuto più doglia di testa, ma non molta bona dispositione di stomaco et son mi sentito non come solevo, ma molto debile, in modo che se non fusse stato per lassare li studi." Marcello to Ricciardo Cervini, March 25, 1520. *C. Cerv.*, 49/19r. "Io sto cioè sano, et vedro attendare più ferventemente posso ali studi." Marcello to Ricciardo Cervini, December 28, 1520. *C. Cerv.*, 49/35r.

21. *C. Cerv.*, 49/21r (May 9, 1520); 49/14r–15r (June 5, 1520); 49/23r (June 10, 1520); 49/24r (June 18, 1520). "Dipoi non ho havuto mai nove di voi . . . desidero intendere che quella calidita del urina se ne sia andata." Marcello to Ricciardo Cervini, June 10, 1520. *C. Cerv.*, 49/23r.

22. Scaduto, *Storia*, 3:273. "Dol mi grandemente, non intendere che voi siate quarito tante ho speranza in lo eterno et omnipotente creatore che vi restituira la pristina sanità vostra, ma in questo interim habbiate bona patientia, perché é sua volonta vi sia venuta questa sorte di male." Marcello to Ricciardo Cervini, December 28, 1520. *C. Cerv.*, 49/35r. A recent book surveys the general context of medicine in Tuscany during the Renaissance: Katherine Park, *Doctors and Medicine in Early Renaissance Florence* (Princeton: Princeton University Press, 1985). See also William L. Eamon, "Science and Popular Culture in Sixteenth-Century Italy: The 'Professors of Secrets' and Their Books," *SCJ* 16 (1985):471–85.

23. *C. Cerv.*, 49/47r, 48r.

24. This may also explain why, after the death of his first wife, Ricciardo moved so quickly to remarry, with the aim of ensuring that the patrimony might be passed on. As Alessandro Cervini put it, "Accade che la madre per lunga infirmità passò di questa à miglior vita, et il padre havendo deputato questo figliuolo (Marcello) per la chiesa perché non restasse la casa sua senza herede prese per nuova moglie Madonna Leonora donna egregia di Montepulciano." *C. Cerv.*, 52/127r.

25. Costi, "L'episcopato," p. 205. *C. Cerv.*, 49/32r.

26. "Il quale [the father] secondo il suo primo disegno desiderava mandarlo à Roma però non molto doppo tempo dippoi già creato Papa Clemente settimo per sommo Pontefice volse che andasse a basiare i piedi a Sua Santità, e farsi conovere per servo suo e di sua casa." *C. Cerv.*, 52/129r.

27. See for example Lynn Thorndike, *A History of Magic and Experimental Science*, 8 vols. (New York: Columbia University Press, 1951) 5:178–233. More recently this planetary conjunction became the subject of a group of articles that were delivered at a conference in Berlin in 1984 and were subsequently published as a book. See Paola Zambelli, ed., *'Astrologi hallucinati': Stars and the End of the World in Luther's Time* (New York: Walter de Gruyter, 1986), pp. 1–28, 239–63.

28. André Chastel, *The Sack of Rome, 1527,* translated by Beth Archer (Princeton: Princeton University Press, 1983), pp. 79–82; Ottavia Niccoli, "Il diluvio del 1524 fra panico collettivo e irrisione carnevalesca," in Paola Zambelli, ed., *Scienze, credenze occulte livelli di cultura* (Florence: Istituto nazionale di studi sul rinascimento, 1982) pp. 369–92; and Alberto Asor Rosa, Vincenzo De Caprio, and Massimo Miglio, "Il sacco di Roma del 1527 e l'immaginario collettivo," *Rivista di studi italiani* 4 (1986):18–63.

29. "Fu aiutato questo disegno perché in quel tempo era universal fama, che nel 1524 dovesse essere inondatione di acque incredibile, e poco minor diluvio che quello universale al tempo di Noè. Fu questa opinione confirmata da molti astrologi, e già il papa si prepareva di fuggire a Tivoli, o in altri luoghi più montuosi. . . . Marcello in compagnia di molti nobili gentil huomini fiorentini e senesi et in trovò a piedi di Sua Santità dalla quale fu grandissimamente riecuto, e in pochi ragionamenti si venne à meriti del diluvio sopra che egli si posso con tanta dottrina e prudentia che il papa resto satisfatto." *C. Cerv.*, 52/129r. Cf. also Chastel, *The Sack of Rome,* pp. 115–16, who also referred to this erroneous prediction.

30. Thorndike, *History of Magic,* 5:233. "E perché per mostrare l'errore . . . il papa lo prego che ritornare al padre et operassa insieme con esso di far le tavoli perfette in emendatione dell'anno e del calendario, e mettere in practica tutta questa teorica, a che Marcello ubbidi volentieri è ritornato al padre si satisfere con gran diligenza a quanto il papa haveva ordinato. . . . E così fatta con ogni perfettione ritornò a Roma Marcello dove se bene fu gratissimo al papa, et che egli [?] accomoda [rsi?] col vescovo Felice fatto dattario di poi nondimeno le guerre, le peste e le carestie impedirno ogni disegno però fu forzato a tornasene cacciato dalla peste e perché ancora non era venuto il suo tempo. Nondimeno non manco per questo di farsi conoscere a tutti quei Signori e pigliare domestichezza con tutti i letterati più eccellenti. Era fra questi il Lamparadio, il Macero, il Tibaldeo, il Bembo e molt'altri di quell'età." *C. Cerv.*, 52/129v.

31. "Si esercito nelle buone lettere latine, e grece onde et in versi et in prosa pote' mostrare a gli amici suoi ingegno raro, et profonda dottrina. Trovanti ancora suoi epigrammi, Inductione di Nerone . . . et di Euclide . . . et

. . . altri authori greghi . . . traduttione in lingua latina." *C. Cerv.*, 52/130r. Vittorio Fanelli, *Ricerche su Angelo Colocci e sulla Roma cinquecentesca* (Città del Vaticano: Biblioteca Apostolica Vaticana, 1979), p. 70.

32. *DBI,* s.v. "Bembo, Pietro," by Carlo Dionisotti. For more on Bembo, cf. Cochrane, *Historians,* pp. 228–32, and William J. Bouwsma, *Venice and the Defense of Republican Liberty: Renaissance Values in the Age of the Counter Reformation* (Berkeley: University of California Press, 1968), pp. 135–40. All of this is related in a letter from Bembo to Cola Bruno on October 31, 1540, in Pietro Bembo, *Opere in volgare,* edited by M. Marti (Florence: Olschki, 1961), p. 828.

33. Ornella Moroni, *Carlo Gualteruzzi (1500–1577) e i corrispondenti.* Studi e testi, no. 307 (Città del Vaticano: Biblioteca Apostolica Vaticana, 1984), pp. 54, 73.

34. See *DBI,* s.v. "Colocci, Angelo," by Sergio Anselmi; also cf. Fanelli, *Ricerche su Angelo Colocci,* pp. 48–53, 70–73, 86–90; and Ubaldini, *Vita di Mons. Angelo Colocci,* pp. 55, 78, 83–85, 90. Colocci has, in fact, been called the "patron of Greek printing" in Rome. See Nicolas Barker, *Aldus Manutius and the Development of Greek Script and Type in the Fifteenth Century* (Sandy Hook, CT: Chiswick Book Shop, 1985), p. 20. Pastor, *History of the Popes,* 14:17; Moroni, *Dizionario,* 42:239.

35. "Ma ritornando a Marcello dirò che essendo (come s'è detto) allevato hebbe fra l'altre discipline et virtuosi ammaestramenti un obsequio verso il padre incredibili: egli non mai gli disse parola se non con gran reverenza si guardo . . . non uscita mai di casa et di poi che fra huomo adulto e di più di 30 anni senza domandargli licentia, e con sua buona gratia." *C. Cerv.*, 52/127v; cf. also Pastor, *History of the Popes,* 14:14. "Obediens figlio." *C. Cerv.*, 49/6r, 19r, 21r, 31r, 35r, 48r, for example.

36. *C. Cerv.*, 52/130r. "Et quando gli occoreva di tornare a casa esercitavasi nel officio di economo. . . . governava il tutto con grande prudentia ampliando il patrimonio. . . . Veggonsi ancora vigne, et oliveti et arboreti di diverse sorti per suo ordine et diligentia." Ibid.

37. Moroni, *Dizionario,* 42:239. Such activities did not disappear from the family either. A cousin, Marcello's namesake, translated Roberto Bellarmino's *Dell'uffitio del principe christiano* (Siena, 1620).

38. *DBI,* s.v. "Cervini, Ricciardo." Moroni, *Dizionario,* 42:239. Marcello's allowance amounted to 1,000 ducats per year. *DBI,* s.v. "Cervini, Ricciardo."

39. Cesare Vasoli, *Profezia e ragione: Studi sulla cultura del Cinquecento e del Seicento* (Naples: Morana, 1974), p. 460. Cf. also Thorndike, *History of Magic,* 5:252–74, and Zambelli, *'Astrologi hallucinati,'* pp. 239–63.

40. Pastor, *History of the Popes,* 14:18; Costi, "L'episcopato," p. 205. On Amaseo, who was secretary to the Bolognese senate and a friend of Pietro Bembo and Gian Matteo Giberti, see *DBI,* s.v. "Amaseo, Romolo," by R. Avesani.

41. "Il quale così giovanetto si mostrò d'acutella di ingegno, et inuncità d'animo non indegno di un tanto principe et fra le prime cose regolo la sua corte, et famiglia con ogni moralità prohibendo la bastemmia et ogni altra sorte di vitio." *C. Cerv.*, 52/131r; Del Vecchio, *I Farnese,* p. 51. Alessandro Farnese (1520–1589) was the son of Pierluigi Farnese (1503–1547) and Gerolama Orsini. Guido Ascanio Sforza (+1564) was the son of Costanza Farnese and Bosio II Sforza. "Papa, il quale dette ordine al giovanne che dispenzando il tempo in opere honorate, et in lettere esercitasse . . . sempre havendo in torno huomini scelti . . . di ogni virtù." *C. Cerv.*, 52/131r.

42. Delio was bishop of Bitonto from January 1538 until his death. Maffei became a cardinal on April 8, 1549. He served for a time as the personal secretary of Paul III, and as the bishop of Massa from 1547 until 1549.

43. "Hora trovandosi in quella corte Marcello cominciò a mostrare evidenti segni della sua prudentia." *C. Cerv.*, 52/131r.

44. Ottavio Farnese to Marcello Cervini, January 4, 1540. *C. Cerv.*, 37/50r. An interesting set of essays on education and the political rule established in Parma and Piacenza by the Farnese family was recently published: Gian Paolo Brizzi et al., *Università, principe, gesuiti: La politica farnesiana dell'istruzione a Parma e Piacenza (1545–1622)* (Rome: Bulzoni, 1980).

45. "Li molti contrari che Vostra Signoria Reverendissima ha havuti, fanno segnalato argomento de la inclination grande che Sua Santità le tiene meritamente et senza altro dir per hora, poi che il corrier' non da tempo, me lo raccomando." Pierluigi Farnese to Marcello Cervini, December 19, 1539. *C. Cerv.*, 37/1r.

46. Gerolama Orsini del Farnese to Marcello Cervini, January 24, 1540. *C. Cerv.*, 37/9r. There are letters from Pierluigi in 1545, from Gerolama in 1546, and from Ottavio in 1552, which all address this concern. *C. Cerv.*, 37/18r, 29r, 92r.

47. "Mi è stato molto caro l'haver cio conosciuto per la sua de 14 et sicome io la ringratio di cose degli amorevoli uffitii ch'ella si degna far ogn'hora verso di me, cosi la prego quanto più efficacemente io posso che voglia perseverare in persuadere à Nostro Signor che io faro conoscer ogni di più quanto io sia fidel vassallo della Santissima Sede, et divoto servitore di Sua Beatitudine." Ottavio Farnese to Marcello Cervini, May 22, 1552. *C. Cerv.*, 37/92r. "Mando à la Signoria Vostra Reverendissima un cinghiale, il quale ella si degnerà per amor mio di goderselo queste Feste, et tenermi ne la buona gratia sua." Gerolama Orsini del Farnese to Cervini, December 23, 1553. *C. Cerv.*, 37/116r. The letter to Pierluigi Farnese is in *C. Cerv.*, 37/31r–v. "Vostra Eccellentissima sa, che può disporre di tutte le cose mie, come dele sue proprie. . . . Onde scrissi allora alli miei agenti in Napoli, che ogni volta che la detta Signora Camilla si volesse valere di quelle stanze, ne l'accomodassero." Marcello Cervini to Gerolama Orsini del Farnese, December 3, 1546. *C. Cerv.*, 37/73r.

48. The term *protonotarii apostolici* was first used in the fourteenth century.

These notaries, added to the seven regional notaries, formed a college whose job it was to register all acts emanating from the Roman curia, and specifically to compile official accounts of the consistories and bulls granting benefices that were issued in consistory. The duties of this office remained essentially the same until Sixtus V instituted changes in 1588. Benci, *Storia di Montepulciano,* p. 101.

49. "Gli fu dato per camera propria luogo da pochi scalini separato da quella dove dormiva Sua Santità di ordine della quale ogni mattina andava mentre Sua Beatitudine era in letto à tratenerla ragionando di varie cose per certo spatio di tempo." *C. Cerv.,* 52/131v. See also Pastor, *History of the Popes,* 14:20.

50. These recommendations on the topic of financial and disciplinary reform in the papal court were drafted by a prominent group of curial officials and presented to Paul III in March 1537. Cf. John Olin, *The Catholic Reformation: Savonarola to Ignatius Loyola* (Westminster, MD: Christian Classics, 1978), pp. 182–97, and Gleason, *Reform Thought,* pp. 81–100. The original Latin text is in *CT,* 12:134–45.

51. That view, expressed by (among others) Pastor, *History of the Popes,* 11:153–72; Jedin, *History,* 1:423–28; Olin, *Catholic Reformation,* pp. 182–85; and Richard M. Douglas, *Jacopo Sadoleto, 1477–1547: Humanist and Reformer* (Cambridge: Harvard University Press, 1959), pp. 100–112, is now being revised by the theses expressed in Hallman, *Italian Cardinals;* Firpo and Marcatto, *Il processo*; and Simoncelli, *Evangelismo italiano.*

52. On Aleander, see *DBI,* s.v. "Aleandro, Girolamo," by Giuseppe Alberigo. On Badia, see *DBI,* s.v. "Badia, Tommaso," by Giuseppe Alberigo. On Carafa, see G.M. Monti, *Ricerche su papa Paolo IV Carafa* (Benevento, 1925), and Firpo and Marcatto, *Il processo.* On Sadoleto, see Douglas, *Sadoleto.* On Pole, see Fenlon, *Heresy and Obedience.* On Fregoso, see Luigi Grillo, *Elogi di Liguri illustri,* 2d ed., vol. 1 (Genoa: Ponthenier, 1846), pp. 390–98, and R. M. Abbondanza, "Federico Fregoso nella storia della diocesi di Salerno e la visita pastorale del 1510–1511," *Quaderni contemporanei* 4 (1971):7–19. On Giberti, see Prosperi, *Tra evangelismo.* On Cortese, see Gigliola Fragnito, "Il cardinale Gregorio Cortese (1483?–1548) nella crisi religiosa del Cinquecento," *Benedictina* 30 (1983):129–69, 417–56, and 31 (1984):45–66; *DBI,* s.v. "Cortese, Gregorio," by Gigliola Fragnito; and Francesco C. Cesareo, *Humanism and Catholic Reform: The Life and Work of Gregorio Cortese, 1483–1548* (New York: Peter Lang, 1990).

53. Olin, *Catholic Reformation,* p. 197; Monti, *Ricerche,* pp. 41–47.

54. On Cervini's friendships and humanistic interests in this period, see Paschini, "Un cardinale editore," pp. 186–89.

55. A. Lynn Martin, "Papal Policy and the European Conflict, 1559–1572," *SCJ* 11 (1980):35–48. Such documentation can also provide information about the actual extent of patronage administered by the curia and its modes of administration. See for example Vincent Ilardi, "Crosses and Carets: Renaissance Patronage and Coded Letters of Recommendation," *AHR* 92 (1987):

1111–26. Another manuscript important for Cervini's particular approach in such correspondence is a register of letters and letter forms of Cervini from about 1548. It includes forms for various patent letters, grants of ecclesiastical faculties, letters of recommendation, and receipts. I am grateful to the staff of H. P. Kraus at 16 East 46th Street in New York, and especially to Ms. Susan Wade, for the chance to consult that manuscript.

56. Moroni, *Dizionario,* 42:239; see also Pastor, *History of the Popes,* 14:20. Jedin, *History,* 1:289–375.

57. Jedin, *History,* 1: 289–375. See also J. Lestocquoy, ed., *Correspondance des nonces en France Carpi et Ferrerio 1535–1540,* Acta nuntiaturae gallicae, 1 (Rome: Gregorian University Press, 1961), pp. xix-xxviii; Pastor, *History of the Popes,* 12:482–84; and James K. Farge, *Orthodoxy and Reform in Early Reformation France: The Faculty of Theology of Paris, 1500–1543,* Studies in Medieval and Reformation Thought, no. 32 (Leiden: Brill, 1985), pp. 155–57.

58. Two recent studies are important for this context: Ingeborg Berlin Vogelstein, *Johann Sleidan's "Commentaries": Vantage Point of a Second Generation Lutheran* (New York: University Press of America, 1986), pp. 1–22, and Maria Rodríguez-Salgado, *The Changing Face of Empire: Charles V, Philip II and Hapsburg Authority, 1551–1559* (New York: Cambridge University Press, 1988).

59. Cardauns, *Nuntiaturberichte,* pp. 40–46; and for another assessment of the position of Paul III at this time, see Joyceline G. Russell, *Peacemaking in the Renaissance* (London: Duckworth, 1986), pp. 39–43.

60. Letter of Cardinal Santa Fiora to Filiberto Ferrerio, May 15, 1540. Lestocquoy, *Correspondance . . . Carpi et Ferrerio,* p. 559.

61. "Mi pareria fare grandissimo torto al nostro vecchio amore, se in questa promotione di Vostra Signoria Reverendissima al cardinalato, io non comunicassi con lei in parte il piacere che ne sento. Et tanto più mi pare di doverlo fare con quella, quanto che con la Santità di Nostro Signore et molti delli nostri Reverendissimi signori cardinali ho prima fatto il medesimo, onde è ben ragione che con Vostra Signoria Reverendissima la quale e causa di questo mi allegri, et congratuli efficacissimamente si come io fo. . . . Et li ricordo anchora che sia soverchio, che non si dimentichi di se stessa, cioè, della sua solita integritade, et virtute, perché così ad un tempo medemo satisfarà et al grado al quale Dio l'ha chiamata, et all'honorato giudito di lei di Nostro Signore, ancho al testimonio ch'io di quella publicamente ho fatto, al quale sono certissimo che Vostra Signoria Reverendissima risponderà molto più largamente con l'opere, ch'io non ho dimostro con parole. Così la bontà di Dio li doni gratia di crescere et operarsi al ben suo." Gasparo Contarini to Marcello Cervini, December 27, 1539. *C. Cerv.,* 3/2r.

62. "La opinion, che io ho delle virtù di Vostra Signoria Reverendissima quando altra causa, ne altro particolare obligo havessi di amarla a sufficientia mi moveriano a rallegrarmi hora di cuore, di vederla exaltata a grado, nel quale a beneficio della Chiesia et di questa Santa sede." Reginald Pole to Marcello Cervini, December 27, 1539. Ibid., 70r.

63. "Facilmente Vostra Signoria Reverendissima hara da se stessa considerato quanto gaudio et allegreza habbi preso dela sua meritevole essaltatione, sapendo lei medesma quanto io li sia debitore per li meriti sui et per diversi offitii fatti in benefitio mio, et anco per servitio del Illustrissima casa Farnese ch'habbi tanti più fidelissimi." Cristoforo Jacobatio to Marcello Cervini, December 19, 1539. Ibid., 41/21r.

64. Pierluigi himself wrote a congratulatory note to Cervini at this time, dated December 19, 1539. Ibid., 37/1r.

65. Ibid., 41/5r. Guidiccione served as bishop of Teramo (1539–1542), of Chuisi (1544–1545), and of Lucca (1546–1549).

66. "Il favore et presidio del Reverendissimo et Illustrissimo Monsignor nostro commune patron et dell' Illustrissimo Signor Duca suo padre ha causato che Sua Beatitudine ne ha fatti degni insieme con lei et aggregatoci in questo sacro collegio." Ubertus de Gambara and Ascanio Parisano to Marcello Cervini, December 19, 1539. Ibid., 41/3r. Ubertus was bishop of Tortona from 1528 until 1548 and also served for a time as papal nuncio to France and England. Parisano held the see of Rimini from 1529 until 1549 and was, for the last six years of his life, protector of the Servite order.

67. "Però se bene a me se aggiunto peso molto disproportionato alle debole spalle mie ne rendo tuttavia gratia a Vostra Signoria Reverendissima la quale per la constantia sua, et per la imperfetione mia sara hora obligato tanto più addiutarmi di conseglio, et admonitioni si come io la prego che sia contenta di fare." Cervini to Pole, February 4, 1540. Ibid., 3/71r. "Et io prometto al incontro a Vostra Signoria Reverendissima et con fare quel poco di bene ch'io potro: essendo molto debole in ogni cosa: et con guardarmi dal male, percioché questo sta tutto in mia potesta: di non l'havere ingannata: non lassate mentire. A che tuttavia mi potra essere non piccolo aiuto: se Vostra Signoria Reverendissima degnara di continuare in avertirmi di quelche o errasse: o, non conoscesse, si come non la prego quanto posso." Cervini to Contarini, February 4, 1540. Ibid., 3/33r-v.

68. "Humilissimo, Il Cardinale di Nicastro." Cervini to Sforza, January 8, 1540. Ibid., 1/110r.

69. "Quanto alli particulari della intrata mia in Parigi Vostra Signoria Reverendissima sapera, che quinto so la sera delli 30 del passato nei borghi della città, mi fu mai in un palazzo preparatomi prima honestamente dove subito mi vennero a visitar li Reverendissimi de Bellay . . . dicendomi esser deputati loro particular et haver ordine da Sua Magistà quale era a Fontanableo per far compagnia al Imperatore di recervermi insieme con gl'altri cardinali che si trovavano qui. Et farmi tutti li honori et cerimonie, che si richiedono farsi a un legato da un Principe devotissimo della sede apostolica . . . la mattina di compagnia delli 3 Reverendissimi sopradetti et di più il Cardinal de Gaddi . . . dove prima ch'io uscissi di casa, quattro presidenti del parlamento et poi quattro similmente del studio intorno a salutarmi, et offerirmi obsequio con molto cortesia in nome della città et dell' università de collegii." Cervini to Sforza,

January 7, 1540. Ibid., 1/105r–v. On this episode cf. also Pastor, *History of the Popes,* 11:365–70.

70. Farge, *Orthodoxy and Reform,* pp. 47–54, 197, 242–43. Dickens and Tonkin, *Reformation,* pp. 10–20. Cf. also Donald R. Kelley, "Johann Sleidan and the Origins of History as a Profession," *JMH* 52 (1980):573–98. There is also a recent study of Sleidan's historical text: Vogelstein, *Sleidan's "Commentaries."*

71. "Et certo che si conosci in questo populi la pura devotion et fede . . . in la chiesa pigliata l'acqua santa . . . orando mentre i preti cantavano un salmo." Cervini to Sforza, January 7, 1540. *C. Cerv.,* 1/106r. On the situation in another French diocese Cervini visited, Lyon, see Hoffman, *Church and Community,* pp. 30–31, 45–69, 167–70.

72. "Fui invitato all'cena di quella sera . . . al palazzo dove era preparata la cena, in una sala . . . grande. . . . A questa cena dunque fu lo Imperatore, Il Re, li serenissimi figli, . . . il Re di Navara, il figlio del Duca di Loreno, il Cardinal di Loreno, il Cardinal Borbon, et io. . . . La quella cena duro un pezzo grandissimo et fu servita . . . con tanto delicatura et tanta richezza de oro et argenta che non si potria imaginar più." *C. Cerv.,* 1/107v–108r. A recent study describes political ceremonies of the French monarchy in this period: Lawrence M. Bryant, *The King and the City in the Parisian Royal Entry Ceremony: Politics, Ritual and Art in the Renaissance,* Travaux d'humanisme et renaissance, no. 216 (Geneva: Droz, 1986).

73. William S. Maltby, *Alba: A Biography of Fernando Alvarez de Toledo, Third Duke of Alba, 1507–1582* (Berkeley: University of California Press, 1983), pp. 38–44. Jedin, *History,* 1:456. Ferrerio (born 1500) was bishop of Ivres, a diocese ceded to him by his uncle in 1518. He held the see until his death in 1549. Lestocquoy, *Correspondance . . . Carpi et Ferrerio,* pp. 570–71.

74. "Pero piaccia a Vostra Signoria Reverendissima comandarmi: et vedra quanto desideri et habbia caro di servirla, et di andar pagando lo infinito debito mio." Cervini to Sforza, January 8, 1540. *C. Cerv.,* 1/110r. Sanguine served as bishop of Orleans from 1533 until 1550 and was appointed cardinal in the same consistory as Cervini.

75. Dittrich, *Nuntiaturberichte,* pp. 74–77.

76. Giovanni Morone to Marcello Cervini, January 4, 1540. Dittrich, *Nuntiaturberichte,* p. 79. Cf. also Pastor, *History of the Popes,* 11:122, 359–64.

77. Karl Brandi, *The Emperor Charles V,* translated by C. V. Wedgwood (New York: Knopf, 1939), pp. 435–38.

78. He complained that the undertaking was beyond the powers of his intellect and physical constitution in a letter of May 26, 1540. Beccadelli, *Monumenta* I/2, pp. 84–85. Peter Matheson wrote a book on the Regensburg episode in Contarini's life. See his *Cardinal Contarini at Regensburg* (Oxford: Clarendon Press, 1972).

79. Morone to Cervini, July 2, 1540. Dittrich, *Nuntiaturberichte,* p. 143.

80. The diet produced, in May 1541, the famous *Book of Regensburg,* a religious compromise that came to be rejected by all sides concerned, over the

months of June and July of the same year. It was a particularly bitter disappointment to Charles V and his chief minister, Nicholas Perronet of Granvelle. Cf. also Pastor, *History of the Popes,* 11:359–480, and Matheson, *Cardinal Contarini,* pp. 119–37.

81. Morone apologized that due to illness he had been able to provide only a summary of recent events in an earlier letter, and Cervini told Farnese that, despite the lack of information gained from Morone, he had been able to procure and was forwarding a complete transcription of the proceedings. Dittrich, *Nuntiaturberichte,* p. 194.

82. Marcello Cervini to Alessandro Farnese, August 10, 1540. Ibid.

83. Ibid., pp. 196, 197.

84. For example, Brandi, *Charles V,* pp. 443–44. Cervini to Farnese, August 10, 1540. Dittrich, *Nuntiaturberichte,* p. 197.

85. Pastor, *History of the Popes,* 11:387–88.

86. On Aleandro, see *DBI,* s.v. "Aleandro, Girolamo," by Giuseppe Alberigo. In addition to the works of Fragnito and Cesareo, information on Cortese is available in Barry Collett, *Italian Benedictine Scholars and the Reformation: The Congregation of Santa Giustina of Padua* (Oxford: Clarendon Press, 1985), pp. 73–81, 148–52, 184–94. On Badia see *DBI,* s.v. "Badia, Tommaso," by Giuseppe Alberigo.

87. Cervini to Farnese, August 10, 1540. Dittrich, *Nuntiaturberichte,* p. 198.

88. "Piacemi che Sua Santità resta satisfatta del mio servire . . . si come la vedra per le lettere che ho scritto et scrivio a Sua Beatitudine ch'io non manco in sollecitar la perfectione della pace, quanto in haver l'occhio all cose di fede et al beni della Christianità." Cervini to Sforza, March 22, 1540. *C. Cerv.*, 1/254v. Also cf. Marcello Cervini to Bernardino Maffei, July 4, 1540. Ibid., 19/5r-v.

89. "In Hollanda ho visto alcune antiquita et tra le altre in Aga comitis [?] due marmori scritti, l'uno a tempo di Severo, et l'altro a tempo di Pertinace. Come alla mia tornata, piacendo a Dio vi mostraro più a longo. Hora mi anco fornito de libri de historio de paesi di qua et della sacra scrittura, gli fo disegno mandare per mare, dovendo altrimente la vettura superare il costo. Voi da altra parte fornitemi costi de libri che venisseno di mano in mano di che si potesse perder la occasione." Cervini to Maffei, August 26, 1540. Ibid., 19/10v–11r.

90. Cochrane, *Historians,* pp. 423–44. "Io di qua non ho trovato se non pochissimi libri dell'humanità." Cervini to Maffei, September 12, 1540. *C. Cerv.*, 19/13v.

91. Jeanne Bignami Odier, *La bibliothèque vaticane de Sixte IV à Pie XI: Recherches sur l'histoire des collections de manuscrits,* Studi e testi, no. 272 (Città del Vaticano: Biblioteca Apostolica Vaticana, 1973), p. 44. On Cervini's literary activities from 1540 through his tenure as Vatican librarian, see also: Pierre Batiffol, *Le Vaticane de Paul III à Paul V* (Paris, 1890), pp. 1–24; Eugene J. Crook, "Manuscripts Surviving from the Austin Friars at Cambridge," *Manus-*

cripta 27 (1983):82–90; Robert Devresse, "Les manuscrits grecs de Cervini," *Scriptorium* 22 (1968):250–70; Léon Dorez, "Le cardinal Marcello Cervini et l'imprimerie à Rome," *Mélange d'archéologie et d'histoire* 12 (1982):289–313; Fanelli, *Ricerche su Angelo Colocci,* pp. 87–90, 108–10; Giovanni Mercati, *Per la storia dei manoscritti grèci,* Studi e testi, no. 68 (Città del Vaticano: Biblioteca Apostolica Vaticana, 1935), pp. 1–5, 15–16; Morison, "Marcello Cervini," pp. 304–12; Paschini, "Un cardinale editore," pp. 187–217; Roberto Ridolfi, "Nuovi contributi sulle 'stamperie papali' di Paolo III," *La bibliofilia* 50 (1948):183–97; and Ubaldini, *Vita di Mons. Angelo Colocci,* pp. 36, 83, 90.

92. The most recent work on Steuco is Mariano Crociato, *Umanesimo e teologia in Agostino Steuco* (Rome: Città nuova, 1988). Ronald Delph also completed a dissertation on him: "Italian Humanism in the Early Reformation: Agostino Steuco (1497–1548)" Ph.D. diss., University of Michigan, Ann Arbor, 1987.

93. Paschini, "Un cardinale editore," pp. 188–89. Martin Lowry, *The World of Aldus Manutius: Business and Scholarship in Renaissance Venice* (Ithaca: Cornell University Press, 1979)

94. D. Redig de Campos, "Francesco Priscianese stampatore e umanista fiorentino del secolo XVI," *La bibliofilia* 40 (1938):161–83.

95. For a modern analysis of Marsilio's platonic commentaries, see Michael J. B. Allen, *The Platonism of Marsilio Ficino: A Study of his Phaedrus Commentary* (Berkeley: University of California Press, 1984). On all these projects, see Paschini, "Un cardinale editore," pp. 192–200, and Dorez, "Le cardinal Marcello," pp. 290–97. Batiffol, *Le Vaticane,* p. 23; Crook, "Manuscripts," pp. 82–83.

96. Giovanni Chrysostom, *Opera,* edited by Genziano Herveto (Venice, 1574). A dedication of the project to Cervini appears on pp. 233r–234v. Herveto was employed early in his career as a tutor to Reginald Pole and lived in the cardinal households of both Pole and Cervini. After Cervini's death, he worked for Jean de Morvillier, bishop of Orleans, and Jean de Hangest, bishop of Noyon. See *Dictionnaire de théologie catholique,* s.v. "Hervet, Gentian," by A. Humbert (Paris: Letouzey et Ané, 1920), 6:2315–20.

97. Cochrane, *Italy,* p. 136. Two historians, Concetta Bianca and Paola Scarcia Piacentini, are currently studying Cervini's library collection. It eventually became incorporated into the Vatican library as a result of a gift of some volumes to Guglielmo Sirleto, custodian of the library while Cervini was on legation, and of a substantial sale of manuscripts to the library by Cervini's family in 1574.

98. For example, Peter Burke, "How to Be a Counter-Reformation Saint," in *Religion and Society in Early Modern Europe 1500–1800,* edited by Kaspar von Greyerz (London: Allen and Unwin, 1984), p. 46.

99. He referred to the work in several letters to Cervini. For example, "Ad aviso di Vostra Signoria Reverendissima ho messo all'ordine et fatti già 4 libri de vitis Sanctorum et sono numero 163 con alcuni scolii contra tutte le

moderne heresie. Et preparo anchoa un'altro libro di esse vite, li probati et buoni autori." Luigi Lippomano to Marcello Cervini, May 5, 1550. *C. Cerv.*, 20/39v–40r. "Ad aviso di Vostra Signoria Illustrissima ho mandato alla stampa il quarto tomo de vite de santi, perché il terzo è già finito, il quale in breve manderò à quella et con il Metaphraste et altre cose, spero riusciranno in tutto sette tomi. Et credo quella conoscerà che non havro perdonato né à tempo né à fatica né à spesa. Et che la chiesa di Dio harrà che leggere synciero et autentico nelle vite de santi." Lippomano to Cervini, December 20, 1550. Ibid., 22/70v–71r. Luigi Lippomano, *Sanctorum priscorum patrum vitae,* 8 vols. (Venice: Spei, 1551–1560); Luigi Lippomano, *Historiae Aloysii Lipomani, de vitis sanctorum,* 2 vols. (Louvain: M. Verhasselt, 1564).

100. On Sirleto, see Pio Paschini, "Guglielmo Sirleto prima del cardinalato," in his *Tre ricerche sulla storia della chiesa nel Cinquecento* (Rome: Edizioni liturgiche, 1945), pp. 155–281, and "Il cardinale Guglielmo Sirleto in Calabria," *RSCI* 1 (1947):22–37; Irena Backus and Benoît Gain, "Le cardinal Guglielmo Sirleto (1514–1585), sa bibliothèque et ses traductions de saint Basile," *Mélanges de l'école française de Rome, moyen age-temps modernes* 98 (1986):889–955; and Odier, *La bibliothèque,* pp. 44–48. He was also assistant of sorts to Caesare Baronius in his historical enterprises—see Pullapilly, *Caesar Baronius,* pp. 33–41. A variety of interpretations have been advanced to explain Sirleto's later arguments with the historian Carlo Sigonio (1523–1584). In a recent work on Sigonio, William McCuaig argued that Sirleto sought, through censorship of Sigonio, "to obscure the reality of medieval Italian history." Eric Cochrane maintained that Sirleto's arguments with Sigonio were linguistic and philological rather than historical or theological and that the "timid" Sirleto had no power of censorship anyway. See William McCuaig, *Carlo Sigonio: The Changing World of the Late Renaissance* (Princeton: Princeton University Press, 1989), pp. 251–90, and Cochrane, *Historians,* pp. 309–14, 423–30, 456–65, 480–81.

101. Cervini commissioned Sirleto to translate the works of Saint Basil into Latin, and to assist in the correction of the letters of Innocent III. He later assigned Sirleto to compose a set of corrections to the Vulgate, which he composed between 1550 and 1555, and which filled thirteen volumes. See Silvana Seidel-Menchi, *Erasmo in Italia, 1520–1580* (Turin: Boringhieri, 1987), pp. 229–32, 427. Sirleto also assisted Lippomano by translating the Greek lives of the saints of Métaphraste, which Lippomano continued in volume 7 of his work. See Backus and Gain, "Le cardinal Guglielmo Sirleto," pp. 91–92.

102. BAV, *Vaticano latino* 6177, 6178, 6186, 6189. (This collection will henceforth be cited as *Vat. lat.*) Appendix 31 of *CT,* no. 10, provides a selected edition of ninety-one of the letters between the two.

103. Odier, *La bibliothèque,* pp. 44–45. Batiffol, *Le Vaticane,* p. 18. *DBI,* s.v. "Amaseo, Romolo," by R. Avesani. The text of Julius's confirmation, dated February 24, 1550, is printed in Pastor, *History of the Popes,* 13:433–34.

104. For the catalogues of his acquisitions, see BAV, *Vat. lat.* 3963, 3965, and *Vaticano greco* 281. For the quotation, see Marcello Cervini to Alessandro

Farnese, September 17, 1554, cited in Miguel Batllori, *Cultura e finanze: Studi sulla storia dei gesuiti da S. Ignazio al Vaticano II* (Rome: Edizioni di storia e letteratura, 1983), p. 379.

CHAPTER 3. AT THE COUNCIL OF TRENT

1. The best account of the efforts and delays that ultimately resulted in the convocation of the Council of Trent in December 1545 is contained in volume 1 of Hubert Jedin's *Geschichte des Konzils von Trient*.

2. Contarini's "Catholicism" and the failure of the attempted dialogue at this diet are examined in numerous sources, among them Matheson, *Cardinal Contarini*, pp. 120–37, 171–81; *DBI*, s.v. "Contarini, Gasparo," by Gigliola Fragnito; and Pastor, *History of the Popes*, 11:432–80.

3. *CT,* 4:329.

4. Jedin, *History*, 1:501–2.

5. With this considerable sum, Cervini maintained a household of thirty-seven persons. Edvige A. Barletta, ed., *La depositeria di Concilio di Trento*, vol. 1, *Il registro di Antonio Manelli, 1545–1549* (Rome: Archivio di Stato di Roma, 1970), p. 68.

6. *CT,* 4:385–88.

7. Nelson Minnich, "Concepts of Reform Proposed at the Fifth Lateran Council," *AHP* 7 (1969):163–251.

8. Cf. for example Hajo Holborn, *A History of Modern Germany*, 3 vols. (Princeton: Princeton University Press, 1959), 1:224–25; or Paul Schmitt, *La réforme catholique: Le combat de Maldonat (1534–1583)*, Théologie historique, no. 74 (Paris: Beauchesne, 1985), pp. 105, 141–52.

9. This was decreed in the separate bull *Decet Nos*, April 17, 1545.

10. Pedro Leturia, "Il papa Paolo III, promotore e organizzatore del Concilio di Trento," *Gregorianum* 26 (1945):22–64. See also Igino Rogger, *Le nazioni al Concilio di Trento durante la sua epoca imperiale 1545–1552* (Rome: Herder, 1952), p. 7.

11. *CT,* 4:393–96.

12. The war itself actually took place later—between June 1546 and the end of April 1547. Paul III envisioned it as another sort of crusade, and in fact Charles succeeded in capturing and sentencing to death John Frederick, the elector of Saxony. The sentence was commuted after John gave up his electoral title. Cf. Holborn, *A History* 1:227–31.

13. *CT,* 10:100–101.

14. "Havendoci Dio donata gratia di stare quest'anno in pace, ove non l'usassemo bene, se potria sdegnare con noi. Et darci tante tribulationi, che quando poi volessemo fare il concilio, non potessemo. . . . Sua Santità con il concilio congregato potria dare maggior aiuto contra infideli et heretici, che hora non può dar solo." Cervini to Farnese, May 27, 1545. *C. Cerv*. 66v–67r.

15. Jedin, *History*, 1:527. Rogger, *Le nazioni*, p. 75.

16. The best overviews of the conciliarist period are John H. Mundy's introduction to Louise Loomis's *The Council of Constance* (New York: Columbia University Press, 1961), pp. 3–51; and the first six chapters of Jedin, *History*, 1:5–138.

17. "Essendoci molti di ogni natione fatti intendere, che non ci saran colti, come quelli di Pisa et di Constanza, quali stabiliti li dogmi, lassorono a far la reformatione ad Alessandro V et Martino et non ne fu fatto altro." Cervini to Farnese, January 27, 1546. *C. Cerv.*, 7/23r. Cf. also Farge, *Orthodoxy and Reform*, p. 234.

18. Jedin said it clearly: "There was to be no repetition of Constance or Basel." Jedin, *History*, 1:506. The accuracy of the papal assessment of some of the Fathers gathered at Trent was confirmed by the actions of some of them after the council, when they opposed implementation of the decrees, still arguing fundamentally over the issue of papal authority. See Thomas I. Crimando, "Two French Views of the Council of Trent," *SCJ* 19 (1988):169–86.

19. The "two-source" doctrine that was so important in Counter-Reformation theology had roots in the fourteenth century. See Paul de Vooght, *Les sources de la doctrine chrétienne* (Bruges: Desclee, 1954), pp. 167–263; Michael Hurley, " 'Scriptura Sola': Wyclif and His Critics," *Traditio* 16 (1960):275–352; Heiko Oberman, *The Harvest of Medieval Theology* (Cambridge: Harvard University Press, 1963), pp. 361–419; and Brian Tierney, " 'Sola Scriptura' and the Canonists," *Studia gratiana* 11 (1967):347–66.

20. Mendoza, who became cardinal in 1544, served as bishop of Coria from 1533 to 1540 and later held the bishopric of Burgos until his death. Pacheco was appointed cardinal in 1545 and held Jaen from 1545 until 1555, when he became bishop of Sigüenza. Francisco de Navarra held the see of Badajoz from 1545 until 1556, when he was transferred to Valencia where he served until his death. Diego de Alaba was bishop of Astorga from 1543 until 1548 and subsequently held the sees of Avila (1548–1558) and Cordova (1558–1562) before he died. The bishop of Huesca was Pedro Augustinus, and he held the see between 1545 and his death in 1572. Ferdinand Loaces served as bishop of Lerida from 1543 until 1553, and then as bishop of Tortosa (1553–1560), of Tarragon (1560–1567), and of Valencia (1567–1568).

21. Giovanni da Fonseca held the see of Castellammare from 1537 until his death; Martiranno served in San Marco from 1530 until his death; and Loffredi was bishop of Capaccio from 1531 until his death. An important source on the ecclesiastical careers of these Italian prelates, as well as those in the papal party is Alberigo, *I vescovi*, pp. 191–240.

22. Croy held the see from 1519 until his death. Madruzzo became cardinal in 1542 and served in the see of Trent from the age of twenty-six in 1539 until his death. For a brief sketch of his life, see Firpo and Marcatto, *Il processo*, 1:341–42; cf. also Alberigo, *I vescovi*, pp. 284–87.

23. Jedin considered Madruzzo something less than a serious churchman. See his *History*, 1:568–73. A considerable number of people worked for Mad-

ruzzo in this effort. Cf. Giuseppe Alberigo, "Un informatore senese al Concilio di Trento (1551–1552)," *RSCI* 12 (1958):173–201; and Paolo Prodi, "Operazioni finanziarie presso la corte romana di un uomo d'affari milanese nel 1562–1563," *RSI* 73 (1961):641–59.

24. Rogger, *Le nazioni*, pp. 150–51.

25. Magno held this metropolitan see from 1544 until 1557. Rogger, *Le nazioni*, p. 110; see also Alberigo, *I vescovi*, pp. 241–70.

26. For the text of the memo, see *CT*, 12:155–58. Campeggio himself was displeased with the nepotism and inquisitorial zeal that characterized the papacy of Carafa (Paul IV). Apparently, in Campeggio's mind as well, that sort of action was an improper approach to the problem of reform. The most recent work on him is in *DBI*, s.v. "Campeggio, Tommaso," by H. Jedin. Cf. also Jedin's *Tommaso Campeggio (1483–1564): Tridentinische Reform und kuriale Tradition* (Münster: Aschendorff, 1958). On his brother and predecessor in the see of Feltre, Lorenzo (1474–1539), see *DBI*, s.v. "Campeggio, Lorenzo," by S. Skalweit.

27. Alberigo, *I vescovi*, pp. 266–67.

28. Scaduto, *Storia*, 3:134–36.

29. On Manelli, see Barletta, *La depositeria*, pp. 80–82, 100–102. "Onde tanto più ringratio Vostra Signoria di quel che sopra ciò ha scritto, quale ho communicato solo con li Reverendissimi di Monte e Morone essendomi S.S.R. venuta questa mattina a vedere mezzo desperata per non li venire in tanto tempo alcuna provisione de danari da pagar questi fanti, non solo della prima paga, che s'è accattata, me dela siconda, che comincia alli due di marzo et per ristoro aspetta domani 250 Svizzari che vengano alla guardia di Sua Santità a quali bisognerà dar la paga senza retardargli, certo è dura cosa questa pecuniaria a esser tratta così et fa disperar ogniuno. Vostra Signoria sia contento di dirlo al Reverendissimo padrone et far che si parli con fatti et non con le parole, altrimenti nasceranno de disordini." Cervini to Maffei, February 29, 1548. *C. Cerv.*, 12/122v–23r. Requests for money and complaints over delay in its arrival are common in the correspondence of secular governments at the time. See Rodríguez-Salgado, *The Changing Face*, pp. 22–25.

30. "Non vorremo esser molesti a Vostra Reverendissima et Illustrissima Signoria, tuttavia importando al servitio et all'honore di Nostro Signore quanto importa, semo sforzati a replicare con ogni instantia, che non si tardi a mandare li danari per la sovventione delli poveri prelati li quali se ancora aiutati stanno mal volentieri qui, Vostra Signoria et Ilustrissima può ben considerare, come si potranno ritenere mancandoseli della loro sovvention." Cardinals Legate to Cardinal Santa Fiore, October 22, 1546. *C. Cerv.*, 7/249v. Rogger, *Le nazioni*, p. 111. Barletta, *La depositeria*, pp. 6–7. Alberigo, *I vescovi*, pp. 268–70.

31. "Et quanto alla precedentia de' vescovi di Germania, i quali sono principi. . . . Aspettaremo a disputarne, quando verrà il caso et tenemo certo, che se durerà fatica ad aquietarla." Cardinals Legate to Santa Fiore, May 16, 1545. *C. Cerv.*, 5/56r. For a detailed description of the arrangement, see *CT*,

10:307–8. Cervini related the new problem in the common letter of the legates to Alessandro Farnese, January 14, 1546. *CT*, 311–14.

32. Ferrerio held Ivrea from 1518 until his death. Sanfelice held Cava from 1520 until 1550. He was arrested with Giovanni Morone in May 1557 on suspicion of heresy and spent twenty-five months in prison, although the charges against him were never proved. He was exonerated in 1560 and later held the obscure and poor diocese of Venosa (1584–1585). Cf. Alberigo, *I vescovi*, pp. 224–25, 365–67; Pastor, *History of the Popes*, 14:312; and Firpo and Marcatto, *Il processo*, 1:317–18.

33. Jedin, *History*, 2:21.

34. "Si questo punto è dubito, cioè che non se sia venuto con Sua Magistà a conclusione o ragionamento alcuno de trasferire . . . et nondimeno se pensi che l'Imperatore non s'habbia da oppore alla traslatione, tutte le volti ch'ella se possa fare con ragioni evidenti o apparenti, pensiamo che similmente se possi allegare l'angustia del luogo, la querela di prelati, la penuria qui et prezzi alti di tutte le vittuaglie, . . . l'aere rigorosissimo d'iverno, la chiesa fredissima, non sol difficultà, ma impossibilità di far congregationi et sessioni, innanzi che venghi la primavera; in super l'indecentia et inconvenientia di far il concilio in li confini di Germania a concorrentia, come altre volti s'è scritto, di colloquii et conventi, il che abhorrimo non solamente noi legati, ma tutt' i prelati; l'ostinazione di Lutherani, la negligentia et freddezza de Catholici, la difficultà di poter espedir bene l'articolo della reformatione in luogo tanto distante da Sua Beatitudine; il disordine che poterebbe partorire un concilio sfrenato, dove non s'estenda l'ombra della presentia o della vicinità della persona de Sua Santità né Sua Magistà." *Instructio* of the Cardinals Legate to Ludovico Beccadelli, August 13, 1545. *C. Cerv.*, 5/164r. On Beccadelli, see *DBI*, s.v. "Beccadelli, Ludovico," by Giuseppe Alberigo. Letter of Giovanni del Monte to Ludovico Beccadelli, August 26, 1545, in Beccadelli, *Monumenta,* 2:277–78.

35. "Il povero Marcello è tartassato terribilmente et lapidato del bene fare." Cervini to Maffei, January 30, 1546. *C. Cerv.*, 19/21r. "Da principio molti vescovi, quali come cavalli stallii s'erano imaginati d'essere gagliardi et bravi . . . combatterono gagliardamente con noi, et al fine perseno. Et non solo perseno, quanto alla cosa in sè, ma odirno incidentemente parole, che forse non si pensavano potersi dire in concilio circa l'autorità de la sede apostolica." Cervini to Farnese, January 27, 1546. *C. Cerv.*, 7/22r.

36. *CT*, 1:368–69, 374.

37. "Appresso di qua non si è restato molto satisfatto delli avvisi de voi altri Signori presidenti, essendo parsi molto secchi, et massime che qua sonno venuti avvisi infiniti di quelli prelati che hanno usato quelle liegerezze, et nominatoli, come Capaccio, Fiesoli, San Marco, et Fratello Cornelio et Mottula. A Sua Santità pare strano, che queste cose le habbia a intendere dalle piazze, essendo là Vostra Signoria, che sa molto bene la natura di Sua Santità, come vole essere avvisata minutamente, si che, in quel meglior modo che li parerà, o

per via del Maffeo o per altri, sia cura sua di avisar minutamente il tutto." Farnese to Cervini, January 22, 1546. *C. Cerv.*, 5/124r.

38. *CT*, 1:28, 5:47–50.

39. Ibid., 1:16.

40. Martelli served in Fiesole from 1530 until 1552, when he became bishop of Lecce. He held Lecce until his death and, during his time at Trent, consistently opposed the legates, provoking the wrath of Cervini on a number of occasions. Martelli's successor at Fiesole was Pietro Camaiani (1519–1579), a close friend of Monte and a prelate who played an important role in the third phase of the council. He served both Pius IV and Pius V in diplomatic work and was active in the implementation of the Tridentine decrees on the diocesan level.

41. *CT*, 10:300–301, 362–64.

42. For example Jedin, *Storia*, 2:61–63. Massarelli filled his diary from the early days at Trent, prior to the opening of the council, with references to Cervini's long walks with various prelates and his frequent dinner guests. It was at such informal meetings that Cervini probably did a good deal of that listening. To cite a few examples, *CT*, 1:177, 178, 185, 191–93, 213, 227, 229.

43. For just a few of examples of his mentioning this debt, see *C. Cerv.*, 1/110r, 254r, 3/33r–v; *CT*, 10:443. "Noi in questo concilio dal primo di fino ad hoggi havemo sempre non solo mantenuta l'autorità de Nostro Signore senza alcuna diminutione, ma ce l'havemo illustrata ogni di più, parte con parole et actioni libere et vive, parte con dolcezza, liberalità et buon modo, sicondo che è occorso mostrarsi con un viso o con altro." Cervini to Farnese, January 27, 1546. *C. Cerv.*, 7/22r.

44. For the letter to Maffei, see *CT*, 10:362–63; for that to Farnese, see ibid., 10:359–62.

45. Fenlon, *Heresy and Obedience*, p. 121. Nacchianti, a Dominican, held Chioggia from 1544 until his death. A brief sketch of his life is available in Firpo and Marcatto, *Il processo*, 1:269–71. Nacchianti later reinforced the essential tenet behind his opposition to the list in a set of remarks during a conciliar assembly on April 5, 1546. He indicated a belief that Scripture ought to be held as more important than apostolic tradition in resolving religious issues. This statement triggered an angry response from the rest of the prelates, because he made the statement during a vote on a decree that placed the two sources on an equal footing. It was understood that general agreement had been reached on the point. These remarks of Nacchianti later triggered an investigation of his views by the Inquisition. For Cervini's characterization of the event, see *CT*, 10:443–44. See also Luigi Carcereri, "Fra Giacomo Nacchianti vescovo di Chioggia e Fra Girolamo da Siena inquisiti per eresia (1548–1549)," *Nuovo archivio veneto* 21 (1911):468–89; Seidel-Menchi, *Erasmo*, pp. 68–72.

46. Walter Brandmüller, "Traditio Scripturae Interpres: The Teaching of the Council on the Right Interpretation of Scripture up to the Council of Trent," *CHR*

73 (1987):523–40. The letters were dated February 27, 1546, to Farnese and February 28, 1546, to Maffei and are printed in *CT*, 10:398–400, 402. For the minutes of the debate on this issue, see *CT*, 1:28–35. Jedin, *History*, 2:66.

47. Angelo Walz, *I domenicani al Concilio di Trento* (Rome: Herder, 1961), p. 126.

48. *CT*, 10:260–61.

49. On Sirleto, see Pio Paschini, *Tre ricerche,* pp. 155–281, and "Il cardinale Guglielmo Sirleto," pp. 22–37; and Georg Denzler, *Kardinal Guglielmo Sirleto (1514–1585)* (Munich: Max Hueber, 1964). Undertaken between 1550 and 1555, the *Annotationes* fill thirteen manuscript volumes: BAV, *Vat. lat.* 6132–43, 6151.

50. See BAV, *Vat. lat.* 6178/7r, 12r, 14r, 20r, 21r, 42r–v, 56r, 85r, 146r, for some examples.

51.Cortese was a Benedictine theologian and abbot who was appointed cardinal in 1542 by Paul III, served on the commission that drafted the *Concilium de emendanda ecclesia,* and was one of the superintendents of the Roman Inquisition during the final three years of his life. The Fourth Council of Constantinople ended the Photian schism and rehabilitated Patriarch Ignatius of Constantinople. *CT*, 1:210.

52. Massarelli received assistance in his work as secretary primarily from Cervini's nephew Trifone Benci (fl. 1571). Benci helped to draft final copies of the correspondence of the legates, and to record the proceedings of the general congregations; on him, see *DBI*, s.v. "Benci, Trifone," by Adriano Prosperi. *CT*, 1:226–30.

53. For an introduction to the fascinating history of that council in Constantinople, see Leone Allacci, *De octava synodo photiana* (Rome: Typis sacra congregatio propoganda fidei, 1662); Joseph Hergenröther, *Photius, Patriarch von Constantinopel, sein Leben, seine Schriften und das griechische Schisma,* 3 vols. (Regensburg: Manz, 1867–1869); Francis Dvornik, *The Photian Schism: History and Legend* (Cambridge: Cambridge University Press, 1948); and Daniel Stiernon, *Constantinople IV* (Paris: L'Orante, 1967). The copy of the documents provided to Cervini by Mendoza was probably the collection allegedly discovered by Caesare Baronius, which he used to shape the legend regarding Photius's supposed denial of Roman primacy; see Dvornik, *Photian Schism*, pp. 129–236, 352–82. *CT*, 1:226, 10:67–68.

54. Louis B. Pascoe, "The Council of Trent and Bible Study: Humanism and Scripture," *CHR* 52 (1966):18–38. Cf. also my "Two Instructions to Preachers from the Tridentine Reformation," *SCJ* 20 (1989): 457–70.

55. Jedin, *Storia*, 2:427–30. Lainez was one of the founding members of the Society of Jesus and an extremely influential theologian at Trent. He served as the second superior general of the Jesuits, from 1556 until 1565. The list is published in *CT*, 5:835–39.

56. Ottaviano Rovere to Marcello Cervini, January 4, 1547. *C. Cerv.*, 42/61r; also published in Buschbell, *Reformation und Inquisition,* pp. 244–45.

57. Jedin, *Papal Legate*, pp. 158–61.

58. "Et cercarne costì in Roma (dove l'uso d'esse indulgentie s'è più continuato che in altro luogo, per esserne il principale dispensatore quella sede)." Cervini to Seripando, July 5, 1547. *C. Cerv.*, 42/105v.

59. "Se ne potesse trovare, o in libri, o in marmori scritte qualche cosa non così nota a tutti, dico marmori perché, si mal non mi ricordo in Santa Praxede, in Santo Sebastiano et in molte altre chiese antiche di Roma si trovano memorie per li muri delle indulgentie che in son state lassate da Pontifici. . . . Appresso si potria forse trovare qualche cosa delle indulgentie de li stazioni, le quali come ella sa, San Thomaso dice essere state poste da San Gregorio et io credo che siano più antiche, percioche li stazioni sonno antichissime come si crede in Tertulliano ne libri che egli scrive alla moglie che restando vedova non si vogli più maritare et in somma, si Vostra Signoria Reverendissima hara tempo che attendare un poco a questa materia." Ibid.

60. Cervini to Seripando, July 24, 1547. Published in *CT*, 11:227; and cf. also Jedin, *Papal Legate*, pp. 405–6.

61. Two lists are published: *CT*, 1:4, and a list including respective nationalities, *CT*, 4:529–30.

62. See *C. Cerv.*, 42/14r, 16r, 21r, 24r, 27r, for examples.

63. "La terza chiave è, che ancora per tutto questo mese et non più potremo ritener qui molti prelati. Nè a ritenere quelli che voglian partire, ci sarà remedio se Sua Santità non mette mano molto in grosso ala borsa, et faccia le spese grasse a tutti, dando non dico 25 scudi in mese, ma 50 et 100 sicondo la qualità dele persone. Perché in vero non possano tollerare la spesa si lungo tempo, et dicano apertamente non essere obligati di ragione a star' in un concilio." Cervini to Maffei, October 10, 1546. *C. Cerv.*, 19/59r–v.

64. "Hanno cercato di guadagnare il cardinal di Trento per far testa." Cervini to Farnese, January 27, 1546. *C. Cerv.*, 7/22r. For Cervini's characterizations of the opposition bishops, see Cervini to Farnese, January 26, 1546. *CT*, 10:332. "Il cardinal di Trento è venuto hoggi a visitarci uno per uno et scusandosi dele cose passate con molta maniera et ce ha fa promesso di far tanto quanto da noi le sarà accennato." Cervini to Farnese, January 27, 1546. *C. Cerv.*, 7/25r–v.

65. In a letter to Contarini, Gregorio Cortese praised the work of Gropper (who became cardinal on December 20, 1555) and asserted his hope that similar learning and pious instruction would assist Christians to avoid the weapons wielded by heretics. "A' giorni passati mi è capitato nelle mani un' opera fatta per lo episcopo di Colonia intitolata *Concilia Coloniensia*, della quale pare a me non avere visto più sincera, più modesta, pia, e vera opera, poiche suscitarono queste eresie abbominande; è pare a me, che con grande ingegno, dottrina, e pieta instruisca tutti li Cristiani, ed everta le munizioni delli eretici." Cortese to Contarini, July 4, 1540. ASV, *Concilium tridentinum*, no. 37/46.

66. "La insolentia del Arcivescovo di Colonia è bene di non tolerare più lungamente, perché la Sede Apostolica ne viene biasimata." Cervini to Maffei, April 4, 1546. *C. Cerv.*, 19/30r. The excommunication was dated April 16,

1546. The pope deposed Wied from his see, but the successor, Adolf von Schaumburg, took possession of the archdiocese only in 1547. He held the see until 1556.

67. Caselli was bishop of San Leone from 1543 to 1544 and later served in the sees of Oppido (1548–1550) and Cava (1550–1572); on him, see *DBI*, s.v. "Caselli, Tommaso," by A. Lauro. Saraceno was appointed cardinal by Julius III in 1551 and held Matera from 1531 until 1556. He later served as bishop of Lecce (1560) and of Sabina (1566–1568). Bertano held the see of Fano from 1537 until his death and also became cardinal under the administration of Julius III. He was considered a candidate for the papal throne in 1555. A friend of Madruzzo, he may have been of assistance in gaining Madruzzo's cooperation in 1546. On him, see *DBI*, s.v. "Bertano, Pietro," by G. Rill. A brief sketch of him is also available in Firpo and Marcatto, *Il processo*, 1:280–81.

68. "Il vescovo di Brittinoro quale similmente fin da principio s'è sempre portato bene et tra l'altre cose e la tiriaca del vescovo di Fiesole." Cardinals Legate to Alessandro Farnese, May 28, 1546. *C. Cerv.*, 7/147r.

69. "Havemo da fare due offitii per dui prelati, che meritano ogni bene. Il primo è l'arcivescovo di Matera, il secondo il vescovo di Brittinoro, a quali se Sua Santità farà qualche dimostratione di gratitudine (come ne la supplichiamo humilmente) darà animo non solo a loro di continuare, ma ancora a molti altri d'andar per le vie, che sono andati essi, et il beneficarli tornerà servitio a Sua Beatitudine. L'arcivescovo di Matera ha havuto hoggi nuova da Roma da suoi, che l'auditor della camera lo torna a molestare per quella pensione, della quale Sua Santità et Vostra Signoria Reverendissima gl'hanno tante volte data intentione di liberarlo. Egl'è da bene, gentilhomo et honorato, et per consequente spende assai, et non può pagare questa pensione, oltre che se la reputaria ad affronto per le cause, che lei sa; è necessario adunque a volerlo tenere contento, come importa grandemente, per esser dotto et dir la sententia tra primi, che Sua Santità, piacendole, lo faccia essonerare una volta per sempre di questo peso, in modo che non ne stia più in timore, et noi facemo fede, che egli il merità." Ibid.

70. "Il vescovo di Brittinoro . . . ha inteso hoggi esser vacato in Calabria, 24 miglie vicino a Rossano, sua patria, il vescovato d'Umbriatico, della diocese del quale è signore (come dice) un suo parente. Desiderà esser permutato dalla chiesa di Bertinoro a questa, non tanto per la differentia dell'entrata, non essendo più che cento ducati in circa, quanto per la comodità et vicinità di sua casa. . . . Ci pare, che la domanda sia molto honesta et da potersi facilmente concedere, et però ne supplichiamo Sua Santità con quella medesima efficacia, che faremo per un nostro fratello, conoscendo maxime che, quando egli doppo tante speranze dateli non potesse conseguire una cosa minima, come saria questa, si dispereria delle maggiori. Consideri Vostra Signoria Reverendissima, che questo concilio importa, et che si fa con vescovi, et per consequente, che bisogna farne stima a voler far bene." Ibid., 7/147v.

71. Cervini to Farnese, May 28/29, 1546. *CT*, 10:505. Cardinals Legate to Farnese, September 7, 1546. *CT*, 10:640.

72. "So sforzato a far quelche è al tutto contrario alla mia natura, cioè di dimandar et far instantia per haver benefici, de quali non ne so mai stato . . . ma per questo priorato (che si tratta dell'honore mio et di casa mia) mi par d'esser muto, se ben tutto il giorno ne scrivesse et ne fusse importuno a Vostra Signoria Reverendissima. . . . M'avvisa ultimamente un mio parente da Roma, amico del nostro Messer Gabriello, che quel Messer Virgilio ne vol far partito, et che si va informando della valuta." Massarelli to Cervini, September 8, 1548. *C. Cerv.*, 23/101r–v.

73. Jedin, *Papal Legate*, p. 455. Cervini to Farnese, May 28/29, 1546. *CT*, 10:505. It is interesting to note that, although much of the correspondence from this legation is encoded, there are no letters of recommendation with codes or signals to indicate when such letters were to be taken seriously. Such signals seemed to be so commonplace to one scholar recently that he surmised "persons of rank everywhere" adopted similar methods. See Ilardi, "Crosses and Carets."

74. Zannettini held Mylopotamos from 1538 until 1555 and had Chironissa added by Paul III in 1543; see Firpo and Marcatto, *Il processo*, 1:315–17. Barletta, *La depositeria*, pp. 55–56. For a letter reporting on this activity, see Grechetto to Cervini, November 10, 1545. *C. Cerv.*, 41/212r–213r. Also published in Buschbell, *Reformation und Inquisition*, p. 246.

75. Carcereri, "Fra Giacomo Nacchianti," p. 470. Sanfelice became suspect of heresy due to remarks like these, although he was exonerated eventually. Cf. Firpo and Marcatto, *Il processo*, 2:30, 836, 840; 3:77–79, 384. He was closely linked to these prelates by a modern biographer of Pole. See Fenlon, *Heresy and Obedience*, pp. 25, 144.

76. Cervini provided an entertaining account of the event in the letter of the Cardinals Legate to Farnese, July 16/17, 1546. *CT*, 10:564–66.

77. Jedin, *History*, 2:192–93. Zannettini faced other problems later, in 1549 and 1552, over his less-than-satisfactory work for the archbishop of Cyprus. See Buschbell, *Reformation und Inquisition*, pp. 267–68, 270–71.

78. "Onde, attendendo nel medesimo tempo ancora all'reformatione vedo che, volendo noi, il concilio si potria finir più presto ch'altri non crede, ogni volta che non sia impedito dalle guerre et discordie de' principi." Cervini to Farnese, February 11/12, 1546. *C. Cerv.*, 7/51v.

79. Jedin, *History*, 2:52–54. "In la congregatione di hieri si prese partito di far tre classe di tutto il concilio, per digerire in esse le materie, prima che si vada all'congregatione generale come tre colloquii da farsi ciascuno dinanzi a uno di noi, il che pensiamo dover tornar molto bene. Et la divisione la facemo noi." Cervini to Farnese, January 26/27, 1546. *C. Cerv.*, 7/24r. Lists of the prelates in each group are published in *CT*, 4:574–77, 5:38.

80. For Farnese's letter, see *CT*, 10:370–71. Fenlon, *Heresy and Obedience*, p. 162.

81. "Questa sera sono comparse le lettere particulari di Vostra Signoria Reverendissima di 17 insieme con la scrittura delle heresie, et essendosi già presentita la divisione fatta tra lei et Monsignor Reverendissimo di Monte,

hanno acquisitato nome l'uno di Marta et l'altra di Maria, et . . . da Vostra Signoria Reverendissima s'aspetta, che preti possino pigliar moglie per far doppia penitentia de loro peccati." Maffei to Cervini, January 23, 1547. *C. Cerv.*, 20/107r.

82. On the theological issues discussed in this paragraph and the next one, see Jedin, *Papal Legate*, pp. 275–403, and his *Storia*, 2:67–146, 193–366.

83. For the text, see *CT*, 12:613–36.

84. Musso served as bishop of Bertinoro from 1541 until his transfer to Bitonto in 1544, a see he held until his death. On him, see Alberigo, *I vescovi*, p. 202; and Firpo and Marcatto, *Il processo*, 1:271–72, which includes a full bibliography. Cervini later demonstrated his concern for Musso by defending him from accusations of heresy before the Roman Inquisition.

85. Jedin, *Papal Legate*, p. 378; Scaduto, *Storia*, 3:135–38. David Gutiérrez, *The History of the Order of St. Augustine*, vol. 2, translated by John J. Kelly (Villanova, PA: Augustinian Historical Institute, 1979), p. 54.

86. Jaroslav Pelikan, *The Christian Tradition: A History of the Development of Doctrine*, vol. 4, *Reformation of Church and Dogma 1300–1700* (Chicago: University of Chicago Press, 1984), p. 291. Pierre D'Hérouville, "Un apôtre de l'eucharistie au XVIe siècle: Le pape Marcel II," *Etudes* 144 (1915):517–26. Massarelli recorded such pastoral activity as well; for example, *CT* 1:168.

87. Jedin, *History*, 2:47–63.

88. "So stato avvertito di qualche bon loco, che in Germania s'è dato per il tempo passato grande scandalo a conceder la licentia alli vescovi de non consecrarsi per tanto tempo, et che hora Nostro Signore edificaria molto, se avanti che la dieta fornisse, scrivesse a quelli, de quali la licentia ancora dura, un breve amorevole et ben composto per uno, dove si exortassero a far interamente l'officio loro, et sebene Sua Santità ha cercato di satisfarli per le cause, quali hanno allegate, non aspettassero però l'ultimo di del tempo, ma più presto cercassero in le tribulationi presenti della Christianità et in questa celebration del concilio di placare Dio." Cervini to Farnese, April 13, 1545. *C. Cerv.*, 5/30r.

89. Cervini to Maffei, January 23, 1546. *CT*, 10:329. "Le reformatione dela chiesa . . . senza essa il mondo non può quietare et la sede apostolica harà ogni dì manco obedientia." Cervini to Maffei, October 26, 1546. *C. Cerv.*, 19/68r. "A una cosa è hora da pensare per iudicio mio, a la reformatione de la corte Romana, quale io vorria vedere, che Sua Santità facesse lei et non lassasse questa parte a la discretione del concilio, ma poichè fusse compilata, gli la mandasse a mostrare per sapere il parere loro; però mi rimetto a chi l'intendesse meglio. La reformatione de frati et delle altre cose la lassaria fare ad esso concilio." Cervini to Farnese, December 19, 1545. *C. Cerv.*, 5/157r. "Pigliare la parta più secura et più honorevole . . . meglio resistere o alle voglie disordinate dei principi o alla malignità di qualche vescovi." Cervini to Farnese, January 26/27, 1546. *C. Cerv.*, 7/23v.

90. See, for example, Nelson Minnich, "Incipiat iudicium a *domo Domini*: The Fifth Lateran Council and the Reform of Rome," in *Reform and Authority in*

the Medieval and Reformation Church, edited by G. F. Lytle (Washington: Catholic University of America Press, 1981), pp. 127–42.

91. Robert Trisco, "Reforming the Roman Curia: Emperor Ferdinand I and the Council of Trent," in Lytle, *Reform and Authority*, pp. 143–333.

CHAPTER 4. SIXTEENTH-CENTURY ECCLESIASTICAL AUTHORITY

1. Salmerón and Lainez were among the first companions of Ignatius of Loyola. Lainez later served as the second superior general of the order (1556–1565). See Mario Scaduto, *L'epoca di Giacomo Lainez—Il governo (1556–1565)*, vol. 3, *Storia della Compagnia di Gesù in Italia* (Rome: Edizioni "La civiltà cattolica," 1964), pp. 123–61, 327–45. On Salmerón, see Bangert, *Claude Jay and Alfonso Salmerón*.

2. His position was similar to that of Gian Matteo Giberti (1495–1543). See Prosperi, *Tra evangelismo*, p. 126.

3. Marcello Cervini to Alessandro Farnese, August 10, 1540, published in Dittrich, ed., *Nuntiaturberichte*, pp. 196–98. Cervini to Farnese, January 26–27, 1546. *C. Cerv.*, 7/23v, and published in *CT*, 10:335.

4. Adrian made the point in an instruction sent to Francesco Chieregati, the papal representative at the Diet of Worms in 1522. See Robert E. McNally, "The Council of Trent and the German Protestants," *Theological Studies* 25 (1964):1–22. The text of that instruction and of the *Consilium* are both available in English translation in Olin, *Catholic Reformation*, pp. 118–27, 182–97. Other prelates, such as François de la Rochefoucauld (bishop of Clermont, 1584–1645), made the same argument in the latter part of the sixteenth and in the seventeenth centuries. See Bergin, *Cardinal*, p. 95.

5. "Et per star più fermo nel senso catholico, è giudicato da Sua Beatitudine che l'ordine si debba esprimere al contrario, cioè che la autorità intera fusse data da Dio a San Pietro, promessa prima in quelle parole 'Tibi dabo claves regni celorum' ante passionem, et poi data in quelle altre cum ascensurus . . . 'Pasce oves meas' [and] . . . ne pigliare quel principio che fa Vostra Signoria Reverendissima che Dio per statuire la hierarchia della chiesa, ponesse in essa i vescovi, arcivescovi et patriarchi et primati eccetera, et dipoi per servare la unità constituisse il Pontefice Romano, eccetera, perché queste parole pare che possino servire a quelli che han detto ch'el primato de la chiesa sia ben utile a conservarla, ma non già ordinato da Dio immediate, per esser i vescovi tutti equali intra loro." Marcello Cervini (for Farnese) to Gasparo Contarini, May 29, 1541. *C. Cerv.*, 3/42v. The full text of this instruction is presented in A. M. Querini, ed., *Epistolarum Reginaldi Poli*, 3 vols. (Brixia, 1744–1757), reprinted in 5 vols. (Farnborough: Gregg Press, 1967) 3:221–30. Cf. also Matheson, *Cardinal Contarini*, pp. 151–55, and Simoncelli, *Evangelismo italiano*, pp. 243–51.

6. Fenlon, *Heresy and Obedience*, pp. 102–14.

7. "Non si restarà hora dal canto nostro di usare ogni diligentia et desterità, che non ce ne bisognerà poca per tenere questo corpo unito et obediente a Nostro Signore, che è il suo capo et così bisognerà all'incontro, che dal capo se influisca nele membra amore et charità et che si mostri di tenerne quel conto che conviene, perché non s'entri (se possibile sarà) a disputare, di chi la autorità sia maggiore." Cervini to Maffei, December 19, 1545. *C. Cerv.*, 19/16v.

8. "La lettera di Vostra Signoria Reverendissima con la nova della sua legatione per Germania mi ha portato quel maggior piacere et contento . . . prego Dio che gli dia gratia di fare qualche bono frutto, obviara à qualche gran male che mi pareva veder." Cervini to Contarini, June 14, 1540. Ibid., 3/34r–v. "Et però Vostra Signoria Reverendissima sequiti et osservi questa cautela interamente in qualunche sorte di articoli che si havessero à trattare, né sotto speranza di concordia si lasci trasportare non solo ad acconsentire in quanto al senso ad alcuna determinatione che non sia del tutto catholica, ma etiam ne la esplicatione delle parole fugga ogni dubietà et non comporti che si pretermetta di esprimere il tutto, et tanto chiaramente che non vi sia pericolo di esser gabbato dala malitia degli adversarii." Ibid., 3/44r. "Et con tutto che si possa creder, che li Protestanti habbino ad esser duri in questa parte della autorità del Papa . . . perché la concordia di tutto il resto sarebbe vana se in questa parte si restasse in discordia o si havesse a concedere cosa alcuna contro a tante determinationi catholice fatte et osservata in tal materia." Ibid., 3/43r.

9. Gregorio Cortese was recently described in just that way. See Cesareo, *Humanism and Catholic Reform*, pp. 162–63, and Collett, *Italian Benedictine Scholars*, p. 152. The point that Contarini's work at Regensburg came under attack in this letter, essentially because of the criticism of papal primacy inherent in the Protestant position at the meeting, was recently reinforced; see Fragnito, "Evangelismo e intransigenti."

10. Jedin, *History*, 5:273–77. "Ne anche (Sua Santità) vuole, che si dieno li denari in caso che la reduttione et concordia de Protestanti con Catholici sia palliata, o che li Protestanti voglino rimanere in alcuna parte delle lor opinione dannate etiam per via de tollerentia. Perché in questo modo si farebbono dui errori, prima consentire et dar maggior forze alla falsità, il che sempre si ha da fuggire massime nelle cose della fede; di poi perché il pagare li homini perché rimanghino nelli errori non sarebbe altro che invitarli à fare ogni di peggio, poiche in cambio di pena, potessero promettersi il premio." Cervini to Contarini, June 9, 1541. *C. Cerv.*, 3/55v–56r.

11. Cervini to Maffei, October 9/10, 1546. *CT*, 10:683. "Habbia l'occhio à tutto . . . in caso che Dio ci facesse gratia, che li Protestanti volessero tornare sinceramente alla vera strada." Cervini to Contarini, June 9, 1541. *C. Cerv.*, 3/56r. Contarini's chosen companion for this legation, Cortese, similarly hoped that the legate would be able to encourage adherence to "authentic" church teaching; Cesareo, *Humanism and Catholic Reform*, pp. 122–25. Cervini to Farnese, May 27, 1545. *CT*, 10:102.

12. I have elsewhere suggested that the text might be more accurately dated at approximately 1549. See my "Two Instructions." For the text of the instruction, see Xavier-Marie Le Bachelet, "La prédication."

13. Le Bachelet, "La predication," pp. 164–65.

14. On all these developments, see Bernhard Poschmann, *Penance and the Anointing of the Sick*, translated by F. Courtney (New York: Herder, 1964), pp. 210–30.

15. Session Twenty-five, Reform decree. Schroeder, *Canons and Decrees*, pp. 253–54.

16. On this development, see Robert L. Benson, "Plenitudo Potestatis: Evolution of a Formula from Gregory IV to Gratian," *Studia gregoriana* 14 (1967):193–217; Gerhard B. Ladner, "The Concepts of 'Ecclesia' and 'Christianitas' and their Relationship to the Idea of Papal 'Plenitudo Potestatis' from Gregory VII to Boniface VIII," *Miscellanea historiae pontificiae* 18 (1954):49–77; and James A. Watt, *The Theory of Papal Monarchy in the Thirteenth Century* (New York: Fordham University Press, 1965). On the later history of the concept, see Giuseppe Alberigo, *Lo sviluppo della dottrina sui poteri nella chiesa universale* (Rome: Herder, 1964), pp. 3–66; and Gabriel Le Bras, *Histoire du droit et des institutions de l'église en occident*, vol. 7, *L'age classique: 1140–1378* (Paris: Sirey, 1965), pp. 11–45.

17. The literature on the conciliar challenge to papal authority in the fifteenth century and the eventual papal triumph over the challenge is enormous. For an introduction, see Loomis, *Council of Constance*, pp. 3–48; Brian Tierney, *Foundations of the Conciliar Theory* (New York: Cambridge University Press, 1955); C. M. D. Crowder, *Unity, Heresy and Reform 1378–1460: The Conciliar Response to the Great Schism* (London: Edward Arnold, 1977); Joachim Stieber, *Pope Eugenius III, the Council of Basel and the Secular and Ecclesiastical Authorities in the Empire: The Conflict over Supreme Authority and Power in the Church* (Leiden: Brill, 1978); Remigius Bäumer, "Die Erforschung des Konstanzer Konzils," in *Das Konstanzer Konzil*, Wege der Forschung, no. 415 (Darmstadt: Wissenschaftliche, 1977), pp. 3–34; Remigius Bäumer, *Die Entwicklung des Konziliarismus: Werden u. Nachwirken d. konziliaren Idee* (Darmstadt: Wissenschaftliche, 1976); Giuseppe Alberigo, *La chiesa conciliare: Identità e significato del conciliarismo* (Brescia: Paideia, 1982); Herman Josef Sieben, *Traktate und Theorien zum Konzil vom Beginn des grossen Schimas bis zum Vorabend der Reformation (1378–1521)* (Frankfurt am Main: Josef Knecht, 1983), pp. 209–80. For a challenge to some of the prevailing theses, see Constantin Fasolt, *Council and Hierarchy: The Political Thought of William Durant the Younger* (New York: Cambridge University Press, 1991).

18. Stinger, *Renaissance in Rome*, pp. 162, 163–64. There is a recent monograph on Torquemada: Thomas Izbicki, *Protector of the Faith: Cardinal Johannes de Turrecremata and the Defense of the Institutional Church* (Washington: Catholic University Press, 1981).

19. Stinger, *Renaissance in Rome*, pp. 165–201. Tommaso de Vio, *Tractatus*

de comparatione auctoritatis papae et concilii (Cologne: Quentell, 1511); and *De divina institutione pontificatus romani pontificis*, edited by Friedrich Lauchert, Corpus Christianorum, no. 10 (Münster: Aschendorff, 1925).

20. Hudon, "Two Instructions"; Stinger, *Renaissance in Rome*, p. 166. Marcello's text is available in a reprint edition: Ridgewood, NJ: Gregg Press, 1966.

21. Friedrich Hünermann, ed., *Gasparo Contarini, Gegenreformatorische Schriften (1530 c.–1542)*, Corpus catholicorum, no. 7 (Münster: Aschendorff, 1923), pp. 20–22.

22. For the counter-argument that the papacy, through persons like Cervini, did create the prototype for absolutism, see Prodi, *Il sovrano pontefice*. Cervini to Farnese, September 16, 1547. *CT*, 11:275.

23. Jedin, *Storia*, 3:71.

24. Cervini to Farnese, January 26/27, 1546. *CT*, 10:336.

25. "A una cosa è hora da pensare per iudicio mio, a la reformatione de la corte Romana, quale io vorria vedere, che Sua Santità facesse lei et non lassasse questa parte a la discretione del concilio, ma poiché fusse compilata, gli la mandassa a mostrare per il sapere il parere loro; però mi rimetto a chi l'intendesse meglio." Cervini to Farnese, December 19, 1545. *C.Cerv.*, 5/157r. Severolus, *Commentarius*, *CT*, 1:64–65.

26. "Perché quanto al Concilio universale non si esprime, che il convocarlo si appartenga solamente al Pontificato Romano, et che a lui solo si aspetti la approvatione di quello che si determinerà in esso." Cervini (for Farnese) to Contarini, May 29, 1541. *C. Cerv.*, 3/41v. The understanding of this power was further complicated in the event of a vacancy in the Roman see. A book on this issue was recently published by Lorenzo Spinelli, *La vacanza della sede apostolica dalle origini al Concilio Tridentino* (Milano: Giuffre, 1985). "Così intese et interpretate da tutti li dottori della chiesa universale, tanto greci quanto latini. . . . A che poi ne seguita il testimonio di molti Concilii, et l'uso, et possessione et iurisdittione esercitata dalli Pontefici romani sopra la chiesa universale successivamenta." *C. Cerv.*, 3/42v–43r.

27. Cervini to Farnese, April 13, 1545. *CT*, 10:39. Cardinals Legate to Farnese, June 20, 1545. *CT*, 10:124. On Querini's views, see Nelson H. Minnich and Elisabeth G. Gleason, "Vocational Choices: An Unknown Letter of Pietro Querini to Gasparo Contarini and Niccolò Tiepolo (April, 1512)," *CHR* 75 (1989):1–20. For Contarini's text, see Hünermann, *Gegenreformatorische Schriften*, pp. 35–43. See also Franco Gaeta, "Sul 'De potestate pontificis' di Gasparo Contarini," *RSCI* 13 (1959):391–96.

28. Gaddi served as bishop of Fermo from 1521 to 1544, when he ceded the title to a nephew. As cardinal he held the titular church of San Viti in Macello. "Et perché intendo che vi si trovano che molti abusi mi sforzerò per vedere piacendo a Dio. Non ho mancare di advertir' Vostra Signoria Reverendissima ma come tra li altri ho trovato che dui prete di questa dioces' sono stati ordinati in Avignon . . . no hanno leggere." Gaddi to Cervini, May 1, 1541. *C.*

Cerv., 41/30r–v. "Parmi che da noi prelati si preterischi l'obligho in molte cose, ma di due, ne segua più scandolo che del altre, l'una di questi preti ignoranti, l'altro di conferire benefitii a persone non idoneo che non risegghino diche non si potria pensare il disordine che di continuo ne nasca." Gaddi to Cervini, June 4, 1541. *C. Cerv.*, 41/31 bis r.

29. "Non volendo gli huomini tolerar più questo modo di vivere de preti et de frati, né che li vescovadi et benefitii ecclesiastici si dieno a persone, che spendino l'entrate, come si spendano hoggi comunemente. Et però mi protesto, che se questo non si farà, piglisi che partito si vuole del concilio, sarà cadere della padella in la bragia, come si dice." Cervini to Maffei, October 26/28, 1546. *C. Cerv.*, 19/68r.

30. Cervini to Maffei, February 11, 1547. *CT*, 10:815. This quotation is reminiscent of the formulation *papa a nemine judicatur*, used by (among others) Augustinus Triumphus in the context of the 1378 schism and what he viewed as combat in defense of the idea of papal monarchy. See Michael Wilks, *The Problem of Sovereignty in the Later Middle Ages* (Cambridge: Cambridge University Press, 1963), pp. 455–78.

31. Cervini to Maffei, February 11, 1547. *CT*, 10:815. At this alleged council, bishops ruled that Marcellinus had condemned himself by worshiping false gods, since the occupant of the highest see can be judged by no mortal.

32. Jedin, *Storia*, 2:227–326, 457–512.

33. "Lo suspendesse et insieme chiamasse tutti questi prelati, che son qui a far' il modello de una buona et general reformatione in presentia sua per non perder tempo." Cervini to Maffei, October 9/10, 1546. *C. Cerv.*, 19/59v. "Vostra Santità sarà reputata prudentissima (come ella è) et buon dialettico a retorcere l'argumento de prelati imperiali contro di loro et chiamarli fuor di qui, cioè alla sua presentia, a far il modello d'una general reformatione, come essi domandano et desiderano . . . il perder tempo non conviene né all'età di Vostra Beatitudine né al bisogno del mondo, il che è verissimo." Cervini to Pope Paul III, October 9, 1546. *C. Cerv.*, 29/321r; ASV *Carte farnesiana* 1:1/126r-v. (This collection will henceforth be cited as *C. Farn.*)

34. Jedin, *Storia*, 2:310–13.

35. Marco Mantova Benavides, *Dialogo de concilio* (Padua, 1541). On Mantova, the text, and the possible connection with Cervini, see Thomas F. Mayer, "Marco Mantova: A Bronze Age Conciliarist," *AHC* 16 (1984):385–408, and "Marco Mantova and the Paduan Religious Crisis of the Early Sixteenth Century," *CNS* 7 (1986):41–61.

36. Reginald Pole, *De summo pontifice, Christi in terra vicario eiusque officio et potestate* (Louvain: Foulerum, 1569: reprinted, Farnborough: Gregg Press, 1967); Gasparo Contarini, *De usu potestatis clavium* (1537), *CT*, 12:151–53. For another discussion of this point, see Alberto Aubert, "Alle origini della controriforma: Studi e problemi su Paolo IV," *RSLR* 22 (1986):303–55.

37. Even before this, Chiari's ideas were questioned by many. His *Ad eos, qui a communi ecclesiae sententia discessere adhortatio ad concordiam* (Milan, 1540)

contained an approval of Melanchthon's doctrine that works are necessary not for justification but as outward signs of faith. Even Gasparo Contarini, for this reason, warned Chiari against publication of the work. See also Seidel-Menchi, *Erasmo*, pp. 34, 99, 384. On Isidoro Cucchi da Chiari, his congregation, and their theology, see Collett, *Italian Benedictine Scholars*, pp. 186–212; H. Outram Evennett, "Three Benedictine Abbots at the Council of Trent, 1545–1547," *Studia monastica* 1 (1959):343–77; Boris Ulianich, "Scrittura e azione pastorale nelle prime omilie episcopali di Isidoro Chiari," in *Reformata Reformanda: Festgabe für Hubert Jedin*, edited by E. Iserloh and K. Repgen (Münster: Aschendorff, 1965), 1:610–34; and A. Marani, "Il clario e la residenza dei vescovi," *Brixia sacra: Memorie storiche della diocese di Brescia* 7 (1972):114–21.

38. "Perché quand'io venni alla badia a far riverenza a Vostra Signoria Illustrissima, communicai con essa il disordine ch'io trovava nel mio clero, massime circa li divini offici, mi pare al presente scriverli il successo de la cosa. Io feci la sinodo, et nelli constitutioni di essa puosi alquanti capitoli, ch'io piglia da Vostra Signoria Reverendissima, tra li quali quello che fa mentione delli divini offici diurni et notturni." Chiari to Cervini, December 21, 1550. *C. Cerv.*, 45/31r–v. "Io ancho ricordandomi quello che Vostra Signoria Reverendissima di dissi, che s'io non puoteva impetrar tutto pigliassi una parte per adesso." Ibid., 45/31r. "Ricevei la lettera di Vostra Signoria Reverendissima de 21 del passato sopra la quale ho parlato con Nostro Signore et si contenta che le differentie tra Vostra Signoria et il suo clero si levino di Rota et si rimettino in un cardinale il qual habbia à deciderla summariamente senza far lite o dilatione lunga, come ho detto a bocca à Monsignor d'Aquino più minutamente alle lettere del quale mi rimetto et a Vostra Signoria Reverendissima mi offero di continuo." Cervini to Chiari, January 3, 1551. Ibid., 45/94r.

39. Cardinals Legate to Alessandro Farnese, May 22, 1546. *CT*, 10:494. Cervini lamented the absences caused by attendance at the council: "le chiese et l'anime patano per la troppa lunga absenza de suoi vescovi, et appartiene a Sua Santità provederci." Cervini to Maffei, December 20, 1546. *C. Cerv.*, 32/4r.

40. Alberigo, *I vescovi*, 142, 150–53.

41. Soranzo held Bergamo from 1547 until 1558. The most recent general works on Soranzo are Pio Paschini, *Un episodio dell'Inquisizione nell'Italia del 500: Il vescovo Soranzo* (Rome: Editore FIUC, 1926); Francesco Rota, *Vittore Soranzo, vescovo di Bergamo (1547–1558)* (Brembate Sopra: Archivio Storico Brembatese, 1974); and Luigi Chiodi, "Eresia protestante a Bergamo nella prima metà del '500 e il vescovo Vittore Soranzo. Appunti per una riconsiderazione storica," *RSCI* 35 (1981):456–85.

42. Rota, *Vittore Soranzo*, pp. 37–41. A summary of the constitutions is provided in ibid., pp. 73–77. The constitutions were not unlike those put together by Cervini for his diocese of Reggio Emilia. On Ghislieri, see Pietro Antonio Uccelli, "Dell'eresia in Bergamo nel XVI secolo e di frate Michele Ghislieri inquisitore in detta città, indi col nome di Pio V pontefice massimo e

santo. Ricerche storiche," *La scuola cattolica* 5 (1875):222–36, 558–69, and 6 (1876):249–62.

43. "Per sua benignità s'è dignata pigliare questa cura . . . così si contenti usare l'autorità datoli, senza aspettare ogni volta nova mia commissione." Cervini to Soranzo, August 2, 1549. *C. Cerv.*, 45/77r.

44. Fabio Mignanelli to Cardinals Legate and Alessandro Farnese, April 9, 1545. *CT*, 10:29. Alessandro Farnese to Cardinals Legate, July 19, 1545. *CT*, 10:152–53.

45. "La traslatione è honesta et necessaria in conspetto di Dio et di tutto il mondo: se ben qualche principe si storcesse a prestarvi il consenso, tra quali però l'Imperatore, che ha fatto questo loco non securo." Cervini to Maffei, August 9, 1546. *C. Cerv.*, 19/47r. Cervini to Maffei, September 2, 1546. *CT*, 10:637.

46. Cervini to Maffei, October 9/10, 1546. *CT*, 10:682. A number of French bishops were opposed to giving such control over reform to the pope—see H. O. Evennett, *The Cardinal of Lorraine and the Council of Trent: A Study in the Counter-Reformation* (Cambridge: Cambridge University Press, 1930), pp. 24–48.

47. "Dico così, perché questa traslatione non è stata opera humana pensandoci noi quattro di prima tanto, quanto ci pensavate voi che non ne sapevate niente. Il caso è stato subito et il partito necessario, se non volevamo restare in mano de Spagnoli, et mettere Sua Santità et la sede apostolica per il presente et per l'avvenire in lor' discretione." Cervini to Maffei, March 23, 1547. *C. Cerv.*, 19/86r. Cervini and Monte defended the translation in a joint letter to Paul III: ASV, *C. Farn.* 1:1/233r.

48. Jedin, *Storia*, 2:312. On Cattaneo, see Prodi, "Operazioni finanziarie," pp. 641–59, and *DBI*, s.v. "Cattaneo, Aurelio," by F. Petrucci.

49. Cervini to Paul III, August 5, 1546. *CT*, 10:592–93.

50. "Et nondimeno, se ciò non fusse stato, l'acqua del mare non haria lavato il suspetto preso che ci intendessemo insieme." Marcello Cervini to Antonio Helio, February 5, 1546, *C. Cerv.*, 42/59r.

51. "A me pare, che nel celebrare de concilii sia stato solito haversi da Pontificii due considerationi principali, l'una all'causa, per quale si convocano, cioè alla conservatione della chiesa et alla salute de populi, l'altra a principi christiani et perché son principi et perché à loro tocca poi l'executione." Cervini to Farnese, August 8, 1545. *C. Cerv.*, 5/104r.

52. A recent article argues that this by no means indicated any special interest for Catholics or Protestants in expanding the early-modern state. See Reinhard, "Reformation, Counter-Reformation."

53. "Uno studio di logica et philosophia a questo coniuncto come s'intende che in altri luochi ha fatto, dove possono stare comodamente un XII studenti, et otto altri frati Conventuali, delche seguendone molti buoni effetti sarà consomma soddisfattione di questo universale, et non meno con utilità delli secolari anchora, stirpando massime l'ignoranza, qual sempre è stata in

questo convento, per non havere havuta una persone della qualità di Magistro Santi, dal quale ne pare habbia preso modo di reformatione." Priors and *gonfalonieri* of Montepulciano to Cervini, January 26, 1541. *C. Cerv.*, 41/48r.

54. Beccadelli to Cervini, December 30, 1542. Biblioteca Palatina, Parma, *Ms. Palatino* 1009/43r–44r. Action to control sexual behavior was not at all unusual—it has a long history in Italy and elsewhere, in both Catholic and Protestant territories, with the regulations stemming from both civic and ecclesiastical authorities. See, for example; James A. Brundage, *Law, Sex and Christian Society in Medieval Europe* (Chicago: University of Chicago Press, 1987), especially pp. 551–75; Guido Ruggiero, *The Boundaries of Eros: Sex Crime and Sexuality in Renaissance Venice* (New York: Oxford University Press, 1985), pp. 70–88; and Lyndal Roper, *The Holy Household: Women and Morals in Reformation Augsburg* (Oxford: Clarendon Press, 1989), pp. 206–51.

55. "A che dovete principalmente mirare, considerando al carico che con l'honor vi s'accresce de havere a render conto di tutti quelli, de quale havete presa la cura." Cervini to Maffei, April 29, 1547. *C. Cerv.*, 19/97r.

56. Of course, there are other places in which such ideas appear, most notably, in canon law. See Gratian, *Decretum Gratiani*, in Emil Richter and Emil Friedberg, eds., *Corpus iuris canonici* (Lipsiae: Tauchnity, 1879), Part I canon 5, Distinction 40; Part II canon 3, Cause 1, question 3; Part I canon 2, Distinction 13. Even some of these, however, come from patristic sources, such as Distinction 40 from Chrysostom. Cervini was apparently more familiar with these literary texts than with the canon law.

57. For Contarini's text, see Gasparo Contarini, *Opera* (Paris: Sebastianus Nivellius, 1571), pp. 393–431. See also the current authority on Contarini, Gigliola Fragnito, "Cultura umanistica e riforma religiosa: Il *De officio viri boni ac probi episcopi* di Gasparo Contarini," *Studi veneziani* 11 (1969):75–189. On Giberti, the standard work is Prosperi, *Tra evangelismo*, chapters 4–6 (pp. 129–290), which treat Giberti's episcopal administration in detail.

58. "Recuperare l'honore all'sedia apostolica et alla corte Romana in cospetto di un concilio congregato per riformare il mondo et malissime satisfatto di essa corte." Cervini to Maffei, January 30, 1546. *C. Cerv.*, 19/21r.

59. "Facesse lei la reformatione et non aspettasse il concilio." Maffei to Cervini, March 13, 1546. Ibid., 20/78r. "Si faccia bene, et sicondo che il mondo aspetta et desidera, non si guardando tanto, dove il bene si faccia o da chi, quanto se si fa o no." Cervini to Maffei, March 23, 1547. Ibid., 19/86r. "Non si possa mai dire da persona che questo tempo s'è perso alla repubblica christiana non essendosi fatto niente." Cervini to Maffei, May 21, 1547. Ibid., 19/100r.

60. Some argue that there is an ecclesiology behind every expression of church reform. See John W. O'Malley, "Priesthood, Ministry and Religious Life: Some Historical and Historiographical Considerations," *Theological Studies* 49 (1988):223–57. Some might even argue that having been raised in an aristocratic conception of society, Cervini could only have adopted this sort of

notion of authority and law. Cf. Oddone Ortolani, "The Hopes of the Italian Reformers in Roman Action," in John A. Tedeschi, ed., *Italian Reformation Studies in Honor of Laelius Socinus* (Florence: Felice Le Monnier, 1965), pp. 11–20.

61. Morone to Cervini, January 4, 1540. Dittrich, *Nuntiaturberichte*, pp. 79–80. Giuseppe Alberigo, "Carlo Borromeo between Two Models of Bishop," in Headley and Tomaro, *San Carlo Borromeo*, pp. 250–63. For a similar argument, derived from a French context, see Bergin, *Cardinal*, pp. 92–118.

CHAPTER 5. EPISCOPAL AND INQUISITORIAL ACTIVITY TO 1550

1. Bembo became a cardinal in 1539. On him and his enormous literary production, see *DBI*, s.v. "Bembo, Pietro," by Carlo Dionisotti.

2. Alberigo, *I vescovi*, p. 142.

3. "Venne rogato del mandato mio da poter renunciar liberamente in man' di Sua Santità la chiesa mia di Nicastro, desidero che li faccia, sentendomi molto gravato di quella cura a che non posso attender'." Cervini to Maffei, August 26, 1540. *C. Cerv.*, 19/11v. For Cervini in Reggio Emilia, see Saccani, *I vescovi di Reggio Emilia*, pp. 113–20, and Costi, "L'episcopato." On Beccadelli, see *DBI*, s.v. "Beccadelli, Ludovico," by Giuseppe Alberigo; Gigliola Fragnito, *Memoria individuale e costruzione biografica: Beccadelli, Della Casa, Vettori alle origini di un mito*, Publicazioni dell'Università di Urbino, serie di lettere e filosofia, no. 39 (Urbino: Argalia, 1978), and "Per lo studio dell'epistolografia volgare del Cinquecento: Le lettere di Ludovico Beccadelli," *BHR* 43 (1981): 61–87. Interesting correspondence between Cervini and Beccadelli survives regarding the availability in Reggio of the text known as *Il beneficio di Cristo*.

4. Lorenzini's diary is preserved in the Archivio Vescovile of Reggio Emilia, but under Cervini's name, since he was bishop: Cervini, *Visita pastorale*, 1543. The manuscript was transcribed and edited by Giovanni Riva in *La visita pastorale del cardinal Cervini, 1543* (Felina, 1968). For a general history of episcopal administration in Gubbio, see Pesci, *I vescovi di Gubbio*, pp. 108–18, which cover Cervini's work. The instruction to preachers in Gubbio was edited by Xavier-Marie Le Bachelet in "La prédication." See also my "Two Instructions."

5. Pastor, *History of the Popes*, 14:23. Cervini for Alessandro Farnese to the treasurer of the papal court, February 12, 1540. *C. Cerv.*, 1/172r.

6. Cervini to Farnese, March 29, 1548. *C. Cerv.*, 48/26r.

7. Hallman, *Italian Cardinals*, pp. 28, 43. See Frederick J. Baumgartner, *Change and Continuity in the French Episcopate: The Bishops and the Wars of Religion 1547–1610* (Durham: Duke University Press, 1986), pp. 10–28, 105–7; Farge, *Orthodoxy and Reform*, pp. 110–11; and Bergin, *Cardinal*, pp. 95–97.

8. Contarini, *Opera,* pp. 399–431. Selections from the text are available in English translation in Olin, *Catholic Reformation*, pp. 93–106. See also Fragnito, "Cultura umanistica."

9. Contarini, *Opera*, pp. 412–13.

10. Ibid., pp. 416–18, 422, 424.

11. Carolus Bretschneider, ed., *Corpus reformatorum*, vol. 4 (Halis: C. A. Schwetschke, 1837), pp. 506–9.

12. The two texts are published in *CT*, 12:151–55.

13. "A' giorni passati mi è capitato nelle mani un'opera fatta per lo Episcopo di Colonia intitolata *Concilia Coloniensia*, della quale pare a me non avere visto più sincera, più modesta, pia e vera opera, poiché suscitarono queste eresie abbominande; e pare a me, che con grande ingegno, dottrina, e pieta instruisca tutti li Cristiani, ed everta le munizioni delli eretici." Cortese to Contarini, July 4, 1540. ASV, *Concilium Tridentinum* 37/46. (This collection will henceforth be cited as *Conc. Trid.*)

14. The memorandum is published in Josse Le Plat, ed., *Monumentorum ad historiam Concilii Tridentini potissimum illustrandam spectantium amplissima collectio*, 7 vols. (Louvain, 1781–1787), 5:778–79.

15. Fragnito, "Cultura umanistica," pp. 78–80; François Fossier, "Premières recherches sur les manuscrits latins du cardinal Marcello Cervini (1501–1555)," in *Mélanges de l'école française de Rome, moyen age–temps modernes* 91 (1979):381–456.

16. Florimonte's letter is conserved in the Biblioteca Palatina, Parma, *Ms. Palatino* 1020; 2/5r–v. "Il buon vescovo desiderà servire a Dio nella vocatione del predicare." Luigi Lippomano to Marcello Cervini, January 4, 1548. *C. Cerv.*, 22/6v. "Et io voglio far predicare nella mia chiesa tutte le feste dell'anno." Lippomano to Cervini, December 29, 1553. *C. Cerv.*, 22/70v.

17. Lippomano held the see until 1558. Some of the letters between him and Cervini are published in Buschbell, *Reformation und Inquisition*, pp. 229–32. On Giberti's efforts in Verona, see Prosperi, *Tra evangelismo*, pp. 129–288.

18. Adriano Prosperi, "Clerics and Laymen in the Work of Carlo Borromeo," in Headley and Tomaro, *San Carlo Borromeo*, pp. 112–38; Giuseppe Alberigo, "L'episcopato nel cattolicesimo post-Tridentino," *CNS* 6 (1985): 71–91.

19. "Una bona reformatione . . . [è] la quale sola può satisfare al mondo tutto scandalizato et desiderosissimo di nuovo vivere." Cervini to Farnese, August 28, 1545. *C. Cerv.*, 5/111r. Cervini to Maffei, March 20, 1546. ASV, *Carte sciolte*, I/A; also published in *CT* 10:424–25. News that the dispensation was approved reached Cervini about a month later: Maffei to Cervini, April 17, 1546. *C. Cerv.*, 20/81r.

20. The bull appointing him cardinal is printed in Baronio, *Annales ecclesiastici*, 32:516, and the one assigning him to the diocese of Nicastro is in *C. Cerv.*, 38/1r. The brief granting him Reggio Emilia is in ASV *Armaria* 41, no. 18/424r–v. (This collection will henceforth be cited as *Arm.*)

21. "Et però vi prego, che supplichiate di nuovo Nostro Signore, che mi sia lecito horamai uscir da questo prigione et andarmi a riposare in la chiesa, che Sua Santità ha voluto ch'io habbia in cura per far da una parte il debito mio, non l'havendo mai potuto fare né a Nicastro né a Reggio, et dal altra per attendere un poco alla mia sanità, che ne ho grandissimo bisogno, ancorché forse non sia creduto." Cervini to Maffei, October 13, 1546. *C. Cerv.*, 19/61r. "Cioè di darmi horamai licentia di riposare et attendare a quella cura che particularmente m'hanno data della chiesa d'Agubio sentendomi la conscientia gravata di quel'che in questa parte ho mancato, quando ho tenuto Nicastro et Reggio. Delli quali due luochi, l'uno non ho mai visto: et nel altro so stato colo una sera. In modo che almeno mi pare essere obligato ala restitutione de frutti mal percetti. Il che non vorrei che m'avvenisse ancora in Agubio." Cervini to Farnese, June 25, 1547. Ibid., 8/28r.

22. Headley and Tomaro, *San Carlo Borromeo*, pp. 70, 235–36.

23. In his letter to Maffei of September 2, 1546, Cervini deleted from his rough draft a line stating he felt as though at Trent he had "aged in these past 19 months as [he] would in 10 years." *C. Cerv.*, 19/51r; *CT,* 10:637–38. Incidentally, Cervini treated Maffei and Farnese in much the same way as Giovanni Morone had earlier treated him. In 1541 Morone addressed many letters to Cervini, defending his reputation against possible rumors, requesting more money for expenses incurred, and pleading for a chance to return from the legation. ASV, *Conc. Trid.* 38/3r–v, and 39/35r–v, 78r–v, 253r, for a few examples.

24. Reinhard, "Reformation, Counter-Reformation," p. 403, and Fragnito, "Gli *spirituali.*"

25. Galeazzo Florimonte to Galasso Ariosto, August 12, 1537, published in Guiseppe G. Ferrero, ed., *Lettere del Cinquecento* (Turin: UTET, 1967), pp. 165–69. Florimonte is also famous for serving as the model for *Galateo,* the treatise of Giovanni della Casa. On Florimonte, see also Carol Maddison, *Marcantonio Flaminio: Poet, Humanist and Reformer* (Chapel Hill: University of North Carolina Press, 1965), pp. 73–74, and Alberigo, *I vescovi,* pp. 210–13, 225–37.

26. On Beccadelli's legation to Venice, see Pio Paschini, *Venezia e l'inquisizione romana da Giulio III a Pio IV,* Italia sacra, no. 1 (Padua: Antenore, 1959), pp. 31–114. The quotation is from Beccadelli to Cervini, March 31, 1554, published in Beccadelli, *Monumenta,"* pp. 107–8.

27. The suspensive effect of such appeals continued throughout the sixteenth century. See, for example, Bergin, *Cardinal*, pp. 188–89.

28. Parisanio faced a problem that is described in the *Carte cerviniane.* A candidate for a vacant cathedral position presented himself in 1542 and even appeared with a letter of reservation to support his claim. Parisanio described him as a vile and ignorant person who was completely unacceptable, and he asked Cervini to recommend the approval of his own candidate. Ascanio Parisanio to Marcello Cervini, May 21, 1542. *C. Cerv.*, 41/70r. On Bollani's

problems, see Daniele Montanari, *Disciplinamento in terra veneta: La diocesi di Brescia nella seconda metà del XVI secolo,* Annali dell'istituto storico italo-germanico, no. 8 (Bologna: Mulino, 1987), and Cairns, *Domenico Bollani*, pp. 169–71. The work of Cairns is not without significant detractors. Gaetano Cozzi published a lengthy critique: "Domenico Bollani: Un vescovo veneziano tra stato e chiesa," *RSI* 89 (1977):562–89. For the situation in Verona, see Prosperi, *Tra evangelismo*, pp. 152, 168–69.

29. Jedin, *Papal Legate*, pp. 474–80. This situation was different from the one found in Germany in the same period, when the Reformation apparently had the effect of forcing bishops and chapters closer together, against their common enemies the princes. See Lawrence G. Duggan, *Bishop and Chapter: The Governance of the Bishopric of Speyer to 1552* (New Brunswick, NJ: Rutgers University Press, 1978), pp. 156–57.

30. Cesi was a canon lawyer and avid collector of benefices. He served as bishop of Todi from 1523 to 1545 and was made a cardinal on December 19, 1544. See *DBI*, s.v. "Cesi, Federico," by Agostino Borromeo. "Per essersi intruso per forza in quella dignità. . . . s'è ingegnato poi con tutte le sue arti et con li suoi fautori et amici di tessere et intrigare una lite in modo, che duri longamente in Rota, dove l'ha messa dinanza a uno auditore suo amicissimo." Cervini to Paul III, October 6, 1541. *C. Cervi,* 5/131r. "Et qui li dissi, che non bastandoli far garbugli in Roma intendeva, che ancho hora s'impediva la elettione d'Augubio con ricorrer al duca, dicendo, che la terra si conturbava udendo, che un forastiero s'haveva da elegger et che il duca proponeva non so chi altro." Beccadelli to Cervini, November 28, 1545. *C. Cerv.*, 5/174r.

31. For example, Guidobaldo della Rovere to Marcello Cervini, October 13, 1549. ASV, *Conc. Trid.* 139/291r. Also published in Buschbell, *Reformation und Inquisition*, p. 315. A. Pelegrini, "Gubbio sotto i conti e duchi d'Urbino," *Regia deputazione di storia patria per l'Umbria* 11–12 (1905–1906), 11:135–246, 483–535; 12:1–50.

32. Beccadelli spent part of the summer and the fall of 1545 in Rome. In August, the legates sent him to report on the number and character of the prelates who were then gathered for the council.

33. "Le supplico, che o per se stessa con un breve, il che saria iustissimo et per corto, o con far ordinare alla Rota, che fra un mese spedisca per iustitia." Cervini to Paul III, October 6, 1545. *C. Cerv.*, 5/131r. "Non esser bene informata de le insolentie et poco rispetto che egli ha portato in questa causa a Dio, a la chiesa de la sua patria et a me." Cervini to Beccadelli, November 8, 1545. Ibid., 5/183v. "Liberi me da questo travaglio di mente, et la mia chiesa dal pericolo grande, ove si trova." Cervini to Paul III, October 6, 1545. Ibid., 5/131r.

34. "Et entrò a dirme di questa causa, dicendo che era certissimo della bona et iusta mente di Vostra Signoria Reverendissima, ma che dubitava, che non le fussero state date male informationi, le quali havessero non solo Magister Galasso, ma lui anchora messo in mala opinione di Vostra Signoria Reverendis-

sima et che per ogni modo voleva ch'io la intendessi acciò potessi far capace quella, et questo diceva, pensando che havessi in breve a tornar a Trento. . . . Io voglio, che ancho che Magister Galasso havesse ragione, che sia rimessa in voler di Sua Signoria Reverendissima." Beccadelli to Cervini, October 31, 1545. Ibid., 5/173v–174r.

35. The older view was expressed in the writings of historians like Ludwig von Pastor and H. Outram Evennett. For the counter-argument, see Antonovics, "Counter-Reformation Cardinals," and Hallman, *Italian Cardinals*, pp. 46, 66, 77, 154.

36. This information comes from a manuscript biographical sketch of Cervini by Antonio Cicarelli. *C. Cerv.*, 5/113v. It was used and cited by numerous historians, including Pastor, *History of the Popes*, 14:43.

37. "Parendomi, che alla dignità ecclesiastiche s'habbia ad intrare per porta dela virtù et non dela forza et modi sinistri, come ha fatto Galasso." Cervini to Beccadelli, November 8, 1545. *C. Cerv.*, 5/183r. Although there is no evidence in these letters to suggest that the consideration was operating in this case, control over cathedral chapters was one of the ways in which Renaissance bishops frequently promoted family members in ecclesiastical careers. See Partner, *The Pope's Men*, p. 166.

38. "Piacemi bene et accetto la offerta fattavi da Galasso in presentia del Reverendissimo cardinal de Cesis, che questa ragione si veda sommariamente et come si suol dire de plano et aequo. Et così per questa vi do commissione di consentire quanto a me in un iudice non sospetto a niuna dele parti, che di ragione, non de fatto, con quanta brevità di tempo si può, termini et decida questa causa." Cervini to Beccadelli, November 8, 1545. *C. Cerv.*, 5/183r.

39. In addition to the manuscript of the diary already cited, excerpts are printed in Pastor, *History of the Popes*, 11:587–89. See also Costi, "L'episcopato."

40. Riva, *La visita*, Introduction, pp. 47–50. The figure is not unusual, when one considers the long history of clerics suspected of sexual incontinence during the Middle Ages. Figures around 10 percent were common since the twelfth century. See Brundage, *Law*, p. 403. To cite one example of scandal: "Capellanus gerit negotium Angellae olim uxori Gobi de Sedrio quo manet Vezani et propter eam multotiens manet absens a cura et fama est quod ex ea habuit filios et est negligens ad visitandos infirmos maxime pauperes." Cervini, *Visita pastorale,* "Liber visitationis collismontis," f. 16. The policy in which ecclesiastical superiors looked the other way as long as clerical fornication and concubinage were not notorious was also common throughout the Middle Ages. See Brundage, *Law*, p. 475.

41. One he did: see Cervini, *Visita pastorale,* "Liber visitationis collismontis," f. 21.

42. Pastor, *History of the Popes*, 11:588.

43. For the text of the bull, see ASV, *Arm.* 32, no. 34/23r–48r. A portion of these are published: Angelo Mercati, *Prescrizioni per il culto divino nella diocesi*

di Reggio Emilia del vescovo cardinale Marcello Cervini (Reggio Emilia: Unione tipografia reggiana, 1933). "Cogitantes nihil acceptius esse dio et fructuosius animarum episcopi fidelium saluti [?] ut per bonos mores personarum ecclesiasticarum et divini cultus augumentum per que devotio populi augent et salus sequuntur animarum in omnibus ecclesiis." For examples of regularizing prayer: "De ordine eundi et standi in choro et de modo dicendi officiam. . . . Omnes interesse debeant nocturno officio dicendo in quibusdam festis. . . . De non ambulando per ecclesias durante divino officio." For examples of the bishop's power: "De ostendendis titulis beneficiorum. . . . De ordinationibus clericorem et de dimissoriis petendis. . . . Contra obtinentes dispensationem, et facientes se ordinari extra diocesis. . . . Religiosi non celebrant extra ecclesias suas." ASV, *Arm.* 32, no. 34/23v–24r, 24r–26r, 27r–29r, 29r–48r.

44. "Attendo ad essaminar tutti li curati della città, sacerdoti e altri chierichi, . . . volendoli conoscer tutti in chiesa et saper, . . . come conversano et come sono atti a fare gli essercitii loro. Et acciò in questo negocio la sappi il tutto: a ciascuno otto giorni innanzi ho fatto intimare le cose, super quibus interrogabuntur, acciò non si lamentino della mia scortesia, che gli voglia coglier all' improviso per farli parer ignoranti per cacciarli delli luochi loro et certo trovo, che la cosa riescie bene, perché ogniuno sene contenta et mi ringratia, quod excitaverim torpentes et rispondeno ad interrogata da valent' homini." Lippomano to Cervini, August 5, 1548. *C. Cerv.*, 43/69r.

45. "Et perché nel breve . . . Sua Santità ha concesso di poter assolvere quelli, che per curiosità havessero letti libri lutherani . . . vi sono alcuni, che sono preti et frati et torriano o potriano ritornare, ma non c'è la facultà dispensandi super irregularitate contracta; si prega Vostra Signoria Illustrissima interceda appresso Sua Santità si degni darla . . . non si dimanda pro accusatis vel inquisitis, sed in foro conscientie tantum et pro peccatoribus occultis." Lippomano to Cervini, July 24, 1548. Ibid., 22/12. "Et quando Vostra Signoria Reverendissima un giorno, piacendo a Dio, passerà di qui via, spero la vedrà delli curati et altri sacerdoti, che non li spiaceranno, attenti li tempi ne' quali siamo et l'apertura di farne in abondantia per via di Roma et di Vinetia, oltra quelli, che ha fatti quel buon suffraganeo, che è stato qui, che ha posti una colluvie di ignoranti nel sacerdoti et per un puzzo ordinava un prete." Lippomano to Cervini, August 5, 1548. Ibid., 43/69r.

46. "Tra molte cose, che erano in mal stato c'era la scola delli clerici, alla quale vi vanno li 24 accoluti et forsi 40 altri clerici, che era macchiata per voce et fama publica di sodomia. Mi sono posto al forte per sradicare questa peste, ma più destramente, che ho potuto, et perché la giurisditione della mensa di questi è commune tra il vescovo et li canonici, hanno deputati quattro a formare meco processo. . . . Et tanto li favoreggiano, che per fugire la tela, vogliono si proceda ordinarie, . . . bisognarebbe prima porli tutti prigioni, dar loro 10 tratti di corda per uno et poi admetterli a diffese, ove forse si trovariano tali et tante cose, che bisognarebbe poi al tutto abrusciarli. Il che sarebbe di grandissimo

dishonore di tutto il clero, et travaglio di questa città, et disturbo mio non poco." Lippomano to Cervini, August 27, 1548. Ibid., 43/84r.

47. "Vene tre anni fa un prete mio diocesano, homo ignorante, di mala vita, peroch' è concubinario e jucator publico, et impetrò da Nostro Signore d'esser vicario del ditto episcopato, quousque provideretur per episcopum. . . . Signore Illustrissimo, se quella si arecorde, ch'io in Trento sopra questa materia me lamentai cum quella, essendo questo episcopato solamente in spiritualibus sotto la cura mia et la intrata la pigliava il capellano del nostro duca, al quale era deputato per suo salario, et questo per la absentia del episcopo, quale da poi fu eleto, che sonno da quindici o vinti anni in circa, . . . mai non è conparsso a prender il posseso, ni meno scriver una littera a quel populo." Sebastianus Lecavela to Marcello Cervini, December 12, 1548. Ibid., 43/126r.

48. "In Frosinon trovai dui preti gioveni di meno età che di 24 anni. Taccio il nome del lor vescovo, che li havea ordinati tanto ignoranti, che non sapeano pur una regola de gramatica, perché non giovarebbe adesso il saperlo. Et dissero, che ciascadun di quei, che furono ordinati al sacerdotio, pagarono nove carlini di regno, all'evangelio mezzo et mezzo alla pistola, ma niuno meno di cinque carlini et furon, diceano, li ordinati intorno a 80. Maravigliamoci poi, se la vigna di Christo sia così malamente coltivata. La dispensa, diceano, esser loro costata in Roma da quattro scudi. . . . Un' altro ne trovai che dimandato: 'Terentia, cuius casus?' rispose: 'Tertie.' 'Et cuius persone?' rispose: 'Passive.' Et perché era della mia diocese, dimandai, dove era ordinato, rispose: 'In San Germano.' 'Chi gli havea fatto la dimissoria?' rispose: 'In Roma.' " Galeazzo Florimonte to Marcello Cervini, October 22, 1548. Ibid., 43/113r.

49. Prosperi, *Tra evangelismo*, pp. 95, 137–44, 181–82, 291; Cairns, *Domenico Bollani*, p. 176; Baumgartner, *Change and Continuity*, pp. 100–101, 117; Umberto Mazzone and Angelo Turchini, eds., *Le visite pastorale: analisi di una fonte*, Annali dell'istituto storico italo-germanico, no. 18 (Bologna: Mulino, 1985), pp. 1–150.

50. Riva, *La visita*, Introduction, pp. 54–56. Hoffman, *Church and Community*, pp. 19–21. Louis Châtellier even argued that European society was fundamentally transformed by the popularity of the Marian sodalities, although his study is limited to evaluation of predominantly French sources. See his *L'Europe des dévots* (Paris: Flammarion, 1987). It is now available in English translation: *The Europe of the Devout: The Catholic Reformation and the Formation of a New Society*, translated by Jean Birrell (Cambridge: Cambridge University Press, 1989). For another recent study, see Christopher F. Black, *Italian Confraternities in the Sixteenth Century* (Cambridge: Cambridge University Press, 1989). See also R. Po-chia Hsia, *Society and Religion in Münster, 1535–1618* (New Haven: Yale University Press, 1984), p. 55.

51. Lots of recent research has been done on popular Italian preaching in this period, the results of which are best exemplified in Roberto Rusconi, "Predicatori e predicazione (secoli ix–xviii)," in *Storia d'Italia, annali IX,*

intellettuali e potere, pp. 951–1035 (Turin: Einaudi, 1981), and in Vittorio Coletti, *Parole dal pulpito. Chiesa e movimenti religiosi tra latino e volgare* (Marietti: Monferrato, 1983).

52. The document is dated June 23, 1534, and can be found in B. Fontana, ed., "Documenti vaticani contro l'eresia luterana in Italia," *Archivio della reale società romana di storia patria* 15 (1892):71–165.

53. Seripando to Cervini, April 15, 1546. Published in Generoso Calenzio, ed., *Documenti inediti e nuovi lavori letterari sul Concilio di Trento* (Rome, 1874), pp. 257–59.

54. "Nela parte che si tratta hora de la reformatione, il più importante punto è quel de predicatore, rispetto a previlegii de regulari, alli quali previlegii qualche uno di questi prelati non haria voluto haver rispetto, ma ordinare, che per l'avvenire nessun regulare possa predicare senza licentia del vescovo. Il che noi non havemo partito, et così fra li deputati questo punto è stato recetto et non si proponerà da loro in congregatione. Ma in qual di cambio si va pensando al modo di tenere essi predicatori in timore et di castigarli, quando erraranno nel luogo proprio, dove haranno errato." Cervini to Farnese, March 30, 1546. ASV, *C. Farn.* 1. "Consideriamo ancora, se pigliando l'altra strada (principale di entrare insieme con qualche dogma a riformare la chiesa, comminciassimo non da sacramenti, ma dalla residentia de vescovi, come ciò saria molto connesso alla parte che si tratta hora) de predicatore (essendo il predicare offitio proprio de vescovi, il che non possono fare non residendo, et il procedere pareria ordinato et il mondo ne resteria satisfatto, consistendo in questo la principale parte della reformatione) cosi ancora, all'incontro, porta con sè quelle difficultà, che nella lettera si contengono." Cardinals Legate to Farnese. April 15, 1546. *C. Cerv.*, 7/110r.

55. Schroeder, *Canons and Decrees*, pp. 26–29; see also Jedin, *Papal Legate*, p. 301–13.

56. See my "Two Instructions," pp. 457–62. The text of Cervini's instructions was found among the personal papers of Roberto Bellarmino. It is published in Le Bachelet, "La prédication."

57. Firpo and Marcatto, *Il processo,* 2:119, 437–38. See also Cesare Bianco, "Bartolomeo della Pergola e la sua predicazione eterodossa a Modena nel 1544," *Bollettino della società di studi valdesi* 151 (1982):3–49. Ghislieri's given name was Antonio. He chose "Michele" as a member of the Dominican order.

58. ASV, *Conc. Trid.*, 139/300r. Buschbell, *Reformation und Inquisition*, pp. 315, 316.

59. For this point and the quotations contained in this and the following four paragraphs, see Le Bachelet, "La prédication," pp. 161–65.

60. "A me pare, che l'heresie sanza freno ogni hor via più si dilatano che quasi dubito, che non si potrà farle riparo. Li predicatori sono li authori et se generalmente non si prohibisse la predicatione, come mi raccordo più anni son' haver dett' a Vostra Signoria Reverendissima Illustrissima costì in Roma, per certo non mi posso figurar' altro rimedio et che si dia licentia a quei, che sanz'

alchun sospett' hanno sempre dispensato l'evangilo, che se l'opre de principi et la malignità de predicatori perseverano da questo modo, actum est, se di sopra altro non si rileva." Tommaso Stella to Marcello Cervini, June 16, 1548. *C. Cerv.*, 43/44r. He made the same point in another letter to Cervini on September 17, 1548. Ibid., 43/97r.

61. Vice-legate of Romagna to Marcello Cervini, March 19 and April 7, 1548. Buschbell, *Reformation und Inquisition*, pp. 300–302.

62. Contarini's text was addressed to preachers in the diocese of Belluno and has been variously dated 1538 or 1540. The text is published in Franz Dittrich, *Regesten und Briefe des Cardinals Gasparo Contarini* (Braunsburg: Von Huye, 1881), pp. 305–9. For more on the text and its similarity with that of Cervini, see my "Two Instructions."

63. Prosperi, "Clerics and Laymen." Session 24, November 11, 1563, chapter 7 in Schroeder, *Canons and Decrees*, pp. 197–98.

64. A recent article even goes so far as to describe Contarini's attitude as "paternalistic": John Martin, "Salvation and Society in Sixteenth-Century Venice: Popular Evangelism in a Renaissance City," *JMH* 60 (1988):205–33. Dittrich, *Regesten*, pp. 305–6.

65. On these two points, see Pole, *De summo pontifice,* and Fenlon, *Heresy and Obedience,* pp. 68, 102–4.

66. Prosperi, *Tra evangelismo*, pp. 236–51. Fragnito, "Il cardinale," pp. 440–42. Davidson, *Counter Reformation*, pp. 32–38. See also *DBI,* s.v. "Bascapè, Carlo," and Thomas B. Deutscher, "Carlo Bascapè and Tridentine Reform in the Diocese of Novara, 1593–1615," Ph.D. diss., University of Toronto, 1978.

67. A manuscript copy of Cervini's text is in *C. Cerv.*, 29/90r–94v. For Morone's text, see Firpo and Marcatto, *Il processo,* 3:302–10; for their assessment of it, see ibid., 3:76–77. The differences between the two texts are tiny and frequently occur where Le Bachelet indicated lacunae in the copy he located in the Bellarmine papers.

68. "Bisogna hora et senza dilatione di tempo far provisione di uno predicatore per questa quadragesima . . . è di grandissima importanza un bon predicatore, et però Vostra Signoria Reverendissima sia contenta mettervi ogni cura, perché questa terra ne sià servita." Beccadelli to Cervini, December 19, 1542. Biblioteca Palatina, Parma, *Ms. Palatino* 1009/39v. "Il Reverendo predicatore di San Francisco va seguitando et si porta bene et satissa molto." Beccadelli to Cervini, February 14, 1543. Ibid., 56v; and "Il predicatore continua à laude di Dio di bene in meglio con satissfattion della città." Beccadelli to Cervini, March 2, 1543. Ibid., 59v. "Reingratiai quella per altra mia della buona opera fatta circa a Don Hercole da Mantova sopra del suo predicare; resta al presente più ringratiarla del frutto ha operato, havendo lui predicato non solo cattolicamente, ma dove è suto di bisogna impugnato le moderne heresie e ripreso le vicii et fatto frutto et ne ho voluto significare a quella, sapiendo certo, che per la sua cattolica et santa mente ne harà consolatione." Pietro Galliano to Marcello Cervini, May 11, 1549. *C. Cerv.*, 44/45r.

69. Scaduto, *Storia*, 3:131. "Reverendo Magistro Jacomo: In risposta dela vostra lettera di XXI del passato, non sarò molto lungo, ma solo vi ringratiarò del esservi transferito per amor mio insino a Reggio, et del haver visitate tanto amorevolmente le monache del nostro monasterio di Santo Thoma, intendendo con mio gran piacere, che le prediche vostre (mediante la gratia di Dio) habbino fatto buon frutto, et che loro si siano mutate, et disposte di tener quella bona vita che conviene alla professione loro, et a vere religiose. . . . Prega hora di Dio, che le faccia perseverare in questo santo proposito, percioché io dal'altra banda non mancarò con mie lettere, finché lo possa fare in presentia, di exhortale." Marcello Cervini to Diego Lainez, February 5, 1541. *Monumenta lainii*, 8 vols. (Madrid: López del Horno, 1912–1917), 1:18–19.

70. The early Jesuits made their decision to seek status as an order at the service of the papacy only after their original goal of evangelization in the Holy Land became impossible. See John Olin, "The Idea of Pilgrimage in the Experience of Ignatius Loyola," *CH* 48 (1979):387–97.

71. Ignatius of Loyola, *Letters to Women*, edited by Hugo Rahner (New York: Herder, 1960), p. 253. Araoz also conducted monastic visitations on three separate trips to Barcelona. Other Jesuits active in this sort of work in the same period were Simon Rodríguez (1510–1579) in Siena, Peter Faber (1506–1546) in Parma, and Claude Jay (ca. 1500–1552) in Faenza.

72. Le Bachelet, *Bellarmin avant son cardinalat*, p. 30. See also his article "Bellarmin et les exercices," pp. 10–11, and Scaduto, *Storia*, 3:273. The *Spiritual Exercises* are a thirty-day retreat, which is the central element in Jesuit spirituality. This retreat aims at helping an individual make the choice of a way of life and to dedicate that life to God. Ignatius wrote a guide for this retreat (which has the same title) based upon his experience of solitude, meditation, and spiritual enlightenment at Manresa, in Spain. See *The Spiritual Exercises of St. Ignatius Loyola,* translated by Louis J. Puhl (Chicago: Loyola University Press, 1959); Joseph de Guibert, *The Jesuits: Their Spiritual Doctrine and Practice* (St. Louis: Institute of Jesuit Sources, 1972); and Paul Begheyn, "A Bibliography on St. Ignatius' *Spiritual Exercises*," *Studies in the Spirituality of Jesuits* 13 (1981):1–42.

73. D'Hérouville, "Un apôtre de l'eucharistie"; Scaduto, *Storia*, 3:405–7; Grendler, *Schooling,* pp. 235–71, 363–81. Jesuit colleges in Italy were frequently short-lived, and Ignatius sought to avoid this by laying down strict rules for more proper, long-term endowment. See A. Lynn Martin, *The Jesuit Mind: The Mentality of an Elite in Early Modern France* (Ithaca: Cornell University Press, 1988), pp. 48–50.

74. Beccadelli, *Monumenta*, pp. 84–86; Jedin, *Papal Legate*, pp. 158–61.

75. For some very recent descriptions, see Henry Kamen, *Inquisition and Society in Spain in the Sixteenth and Seventeenth Centuries* (Bloomington: Indiana University Press, 1985); Gustav Henningsen and John Tedeschi, eds., *The Inquisition in Early Modern Europe: Studies on Sources and Methods* (DeKalb, IL:

Northern Illinois University Press, 1986); Edward Peters, *Inquisition* (New York: Free Press, 1988); Prosperi, "L'inquisizione"; and Paolo Simoncelli, "Inquisizione romana e riforma in Italia," *RSI* 100 (1988): 1–125.

76. Fragnito, "Il cardinale," pp. 454–56. *CT*, 2:405. On Cortese's role, see *DBI*, s.v. "Cortese, Gregorio"; Fragnito, "Il cardinale," pp. 61–62; Cesareo, *Humanism and Catholic Reform*, p. 139. For two examples of this assessment of the tribunal under Paul III, see Peters, *Inquisition*, pp. 105–21, and Jedin, *Papal Legate*, pp. 226–30.

77. Aubert, "Alle origini," p. 338. Simoncelli, "Inquisizione romana," p. 70.

78. He used the terms in a non-pastoral context as well, describing the Protestant position relative to the opening of the council: "Li discursi et resposte a lei fatte sopra l'aperitione del concilio ci hanno dato non piccola ammiratione in quella parte, che concerne il rispetto, qual pare, che s'habbi alla perversa ostinatione di Lutherani, il che secondo il iudicio nostro non si deverebbe proporre per consideratione nuova, et come impedimento non antiveduto dal giorno che s'incominciò a ragionare del concilio. Chi poteva dubitare, che essendosi da loro scosso il giogo della obedientia, fundamento precipuo della religione christiana et proceduto di fatto a tant'impie e scelerate innovationi contra il rito osservato centonara d'anni dalla chiesa, con l'approvatione di tanti celebratissimi concilii, haverebbeno recalcitrato contra il concilio nostro, quanto se sia legitimo, generale et christiano, mettendosi a intrata certa d'haver a esser condennati da quello?" Cardinals Legate to Farnese, May 26, 1545. *C. Cerv.*, 5/64r.

79. "Tre remedie si posson considerare per estinguere il fuoco dell' heresie, che non habbi d'abbrusciare quel poco, che horamai resta di fede et religione. Primo di qualche accordo tolerabile con gl' heretici. Secondo d'indurgli a sottomettersi alla determinatione del concilio. Terzo di adoperare le forze." Cardinals Legate to Farnese, June 7, 1545. Ibid., 5/74v.

80. The *Beneficio*, Catarino's *Compendio*, and the letters between Cervini and Beccadelli cited below are published in Benedetto, *Il beneficio*. The volume also contains edited versions of the English, French, and Croatian translations of the *Beneficio* published in the sixteenth century. See also *DBI*, s.v. "Benedetto da Mantova," by S. Caponetto. Cervini to Beccadelli, January 10, 1544. Benedetto, *Il beneficio*, p. 432. Debate concerning the orthodoxy of the book continued, and it was not fully condemned until the Fathers convened at Trent did so on July 26, 1546.

81. Cervini to Beccadelli, January 19, 1544. Benedetto, *Il beneficio*, pp. 432–34. Cervini stole the "clothed and shoed" characterization from Catarino's criticism of the text. See Seidel-Menchi, *Erasmo*, pp. 149–50.

82. Beccadelli to Cervini, January 29, 1544. Benedetto, *Il beneficio*, pp. 434–36. Beccadelli maintained a different policy later, when he faced a larger problem regarding dispersion of heretical literature in Venice. He was nuncio

there between 1550 and 1554, and very soon after his arrival he suggested that an index of prohibited books be composed in Rome and sent for him to enforce in Venice. See Paschini, *Venezia*, pp. 31–114.

83. Cervini to Beccadelli, February 5, 1544. Benedetto, *Il beneficio*, p. 436.

84. Colonna's letter to Cervini is published in Vittoria Colonna, *Carteggio*, edited by E. Ferrero and G. Müller (Turin: Loescher, 1892), pp. 256–57. For what is known of the relationship between Colonna and Cervini, I am indebted to Concetta Bianca, who kindly permitted me to read her article entitled "Marcello Cervini e Vittoria Colonna" in manuscript. For more on the situation, see Alfredo Reumont, *Vittoria Colonna, Marchesa di Pescara: vita, fede e poesia* (Turin: Loescher, 1892), pp. 151–84; *DBI*, s.v. "Colonna, Vittoria," by G. Patrizi; and Gigliola Fragnito, "Vittoria Colonna e l'inquisizione," *Benedictina* 37 (1990): 157–72.

85. Guidobaldo della Rovere to Marcello Cervini, October 13, 1549. Buschbell, *Reformation und Inquisition*, p. 315.

86. Carlo Vannetti to Marcello Cervini, October 24, 1549. Ibid., pp. 315–16.

87. Vannetti to Cervini, November 16, 1549. Ibid., pp. 317–18.

88. Pastor, *History of the Popes*, 12:505, 13:210–17.

89. "Fui avertito da Venetia che in una carcere v'erà un frate conventuale di San Francesco preso già quattro anni, il più gran lutherano del mondo; il quale tra le altre belle cose che ha fatte, molti che erano, seco priggioni che sono morti gli ha indotti a non si confessare né communicar etiandio nel ponto della morte. . . . Prego Vostra Signoria Illustrissima si degni come da se, pregar Sua Santità si degni fare un caldo officio con quel Signore Oratore Veneto che è costì, che scriva a quel Serenissimo Dominio, che et nel caso costui, et di tutti gli altri di simile . . . si presti et dimostri veramente Christiano et severo . . . contra tali impieta, non essendo cosa che più getti a terra un regno o imperio, che lasciare multiplicare le heresie, et non le voler castigare." Luigi Lippomano to Marcello Cervini, November 16, 1547. C. Cerv., 22/67r–v.

90. "Perché in tutte le terre della chiesa non si pone una severissima inquisitione contra questi tristi Lutherani et non se castigano secondo li loro demeriti? . . . questa heresia comincia dal pater nostra et finisce . . . nel archibuso. Dicono che l'inquisitione di Spagna et Portogallo sono troppo severe, et io rispondo, che sono molto utile, che almeno in quelle parti hanno fatto questo frutto, che questa pestilentissima somenza non è pervenuta sino a lì, né ivi si nomina mai pur' il nome di Martino." Lippomano to Cervini, November 16, 1547. Ibid., 22/67v. Luigi Lippomano, *Confirmatione et stabilmento di tutti i dogmi catholici* (Venice: Domenico Zio, 1553), which, to be precise, runs to 1304 pages. "Piaccià a Vostra Signoria Reverendissima perdonarmi se per la prima volta io gli ho rotto il capo con tante parole. La causa che è di Dio mi ha transportato, ne credo haver errato, perché forse per mezzo suo la maestà di

Dio in questa fatta sarà honorata." Lippomano to Cervini, November 16, 1547. *C. Cerv.*, 22/68r.

91. For more on this case, see Carcereri, "Fra Giacomo Nacchianti"; Benedetto, *Il beneficio*, pp. 441–43, 493–94; and Jedin, *Storia*, 2:573. Angelo Massarelli to Marcello Cervini, January 26 and February 6, 1549, *C. Cerv.*, 23/134r, 136r. Both letters are published in Buschbell, *Reformation und Inquisition*, pp. 297–300. Morone indicated in a letter that Nacchianti was so stubborn a muledriver was required to change his opinions. See Giovanni Morone to Marcello Cervini, December 15, 1548. *C. Cerv.*, 21/158r; also published in Buschbell, *Reformation und Inquisition*, pp. 296–97.

92. Benedetto, *Il beneficio*, pp. 493–94. Collett, *Italian Benedictine Scholars*, pp. 77–118, 157–212.

93. Massarelli to Cervini, August 17, 1548. Buschbell, *Reformation und Inquisition*, pp. 303–4. Giovan Antonio Delphino to Marcello Cervini, October 23, 1548. Ibid., pp. 306–7. It seems unlikely that Cervini received this letter before he responded to Massarelli, since that response is dated October 27, and Cervini answered Delphino on November 2.

94. Cervini to Massarelli, October 27, 1548. Ibid., pp. 307–8. Delphino to Cervini, February 27, 1549. Ibid., p. 309.

95. Massarelli to Cervini, September 11, 1549. Ibid., p. 313. "Da sè non può et io non ho tempo d'attender a simil cause che hanno l'esamine longo et voglian tutto l'huomo, et non posso far altro che dargli il braccio et il favor." Giovan Maria del Monte to Marcello Cervini, February 21, 1549. *C. Cerv.*, 21/170r. "Quello che Vostra Signoria Reverendissima scrive circa il nuovo inquisitore di Bologna, non l'ho conferito ancora con gli Reverendissimi deputati, per dir prima a Vostra Signoria Reverendissima come a me pareria, che potesse elegger lei uno o due di cotesti prelati per commissarii, che aggiutassero l'inquisitione, stimando che così la cosa si risolverebbe più presto et con più authorità sua." Giovan Maria del Monte to Marcello Cervini, March 2, 1549. *C. Cerv.*, 21/228r.

96. Massarelli to Cervini, September 8 and December 3, 1548. Buschbell, *Reformation und Inquisition*, pp. 305, 308–9. On Scotti and his collaboration with Cervini, see Firpo and Marcatto, *Il processo*, 1:291–94, 2:247–48, 4:468.

97. Paschase Broët to Ignatius of Loyola, n.d., 1548. *MHSI*, *Epistolae PP. Paschasii Broëti, Claudii Jaji*, vol. 24 (Madrid: López del Horno, 1971), pp. 43–44.

98. "Ho anco ricevuta un altra lettera di 4 sopra li carcerati costì per heresie. . . . Fin qui mi pareva di vederli inclinati che si facessero abiurare in Bologna, et poi si mandassero qui per ricever la penitentia." Cervini to Monte, August 10, 1549. *C. Cerv.*, 21/232r. Monte to Cervini, August 17, 1549. Buschbell, *Reformation und Inquisition*, pp. 312–13.

99. Antonio Maria Thita to Marcello Cervini, August 18, 1548. Buschbell, *Reformation und Inquisition*, pp. 304–5.

100. Massarelli to Cervini, October 2, 1549. Ibid., p. 314.

101. For an example of Morone's attitude, see Massimo Firpo, "'Gli spirituali,' l'accademia di Modena e il formulario di fede del 1542: Controllo del dissenso religioso e nicodemismo," *RSLR* 20 (1984):40–111.

102. Archival sources do not permit precise dating of Cervini's stay in Gubbio. He left Rome around September 11, and the first letter I have found written by him from Gubbio is dated September 18. He left Gubbio on October 5 and arrived in Rome October 9. The text of Grossi's *Costituzione* was published in 1558. See Balletti, *Storia di Reggio*, p. 386. "Io feci la sinodo et nelli constitutioni di essa puo si alquanti capitoli, ch'io piglia da Vostra Signoria Reverendissima, tra li quali quello che fa mentione delli divini offici diurni et notturni. . . . Et perché in questa causa non solo li va l'honor della dignità episcopale, ma l'honor del culto divino et la salute del clero." Isidoro Chiari to Marcello Cervini, December 21, 1550. *C. Cerv.*, 45/31r–v.

103. Prosperi, *Tra evangelismo*, pp. 95, 291. Monte to Cervini, October 13, 1549. *CT*, 11:519.

104. "Presupponendosi che già Vostra Signoria Reverendissima habbia in bona parte satisfatto al desiderio che la teneva di visitar le cose della sua chiesa . . . a Nostro Signore pare che Vostra Signoria Reverendissima se ne debba ritornare a Roma senza più tardare et trovarvisi alli 8 o alli 9 dell'altro mese." Farnese to Cervini, September 30, 1549. *C. Cerv.*, 8/48r.

CHAPTER 6. EPISCOPAL AND INQUISITORIAL ACTIVITY AFTER 1550

1. *C. Cerv.*, 42/140r. Cf. Jedin, *Papal Legate*, pp. 417–18. On the conclave, which nearly elected Reginald Pole, see *CT* 2:1–145. A number of manuscript diaries cover the assembly and are spuriously attributed to Giovanni Bini, secretary of the conclave. One of these is held in the University of Chicago Library, Department of Special Collections: MS 1259. See also Frederick Baumgartner, "Henry II and the Papal Conclave of 1549," *SCJ* 16 (1985):301–14; Maltby, *Alba*, pp. 76–77; and Rodríguez-Salgado, *The Changing Face*, pp. 42–44. Cervini was absent from a good deal of the conclave, including the day of the actual election, due to illness.

2. *CT*, 1:827; 2:174, 207, 345. See also Moroni, *Dizionario*, 46:154–56.

3. "Non haveva però egli animi di biasimarle publicamente . . . rare volte e tardi in consistorio andava, e con il ritirarsi da negotii e con il silentio ben mostrava." Antonio Cicarelli, *C. Cerv.*, 52/113r. Prosperi, *Tra evangelismo*, p. 129.

4. *CT*, 2:171–74. "Sotto colore di volere mutare aria per una febbre." Cicarelli, *C. Cerv.*, 52/113r.

5. These estimates are based solely upon the dating of correspondence,

and only approximation is possible. For the other years; 1552, mid-June until early November in Gubbio; 1553, July 2 until mid-November in Gubbio.

6. P. C. Van Lierde and A. Giraud, *Le sénat de l'église* (Paris: Fayard, 1963), pp. 90–94.

7. On the Augustinians, see *DIP*, s.v. "Agostiniani," by Balbino Rano; Gutiérrez, *History*. For this specific period in their history, see Peter Iver Kaufman, *Augustinian Piety and Catholic Reform* (Macon, GA: Mercer University Press, 1982); and Jedin, *Papal Legate*, pp. 124–36. On the Servites, who also followed the rule of Saint Augustine, see *DIP*, s.v. "Serviti"; A. M. Lépicier, *L'ordine dei Servi di Maria* (Montmorency-Louvain, 1929); and A. M. Rossi, "La legenda de origine Servorum Virginis Mariae," in *Ordini e congregationi religiose* (Turin, 1952), pp. 495–520.

8. Gutiérrez, *History*, 2:54, 173. Jedin, *Papal Legate*, pp. 193–98, 216–19. Gutiérrez, *History*, pp. 58–62.

9. "Quando arrivai in questa provincia trovai prigione in Macerata alcuni frati di Santo Agostino che stavano in un monasterio di Santa Maria della Fonte qui vicino meno di mezo miglio, et cio per un caso enormissimo et di pessimo esempio successo a giorni passati a Santo Giusto che tutti questi frati della Fonte accordati con un altro monasterio del medesimo ordine in quel luogo hanno violato tutto un monasterio di monache in modo che non solo il detto luogo è sollevato di un male animo contra questo ordine, ma tutta la provincia . . . et essendo la Signoria Vostra Reverendissima et Illustrissima Protettrice di detto ordine, et io tanto suo divoto servitore non ho voluto deliberare cosa alcuna senza sapere la mente sua, et così m'è parso scriverli questa mia sopra questa materia, pregandola humilmente e volermi respondere il parere suo per l'espeditione della causa. . . . "Et acciò che la Sua Vostra Reverendissima Illustrissima possa comprender la brutezza di questo caso, qui alligata li mando una copia di una lettera, che li frati detti scrivevano alle monache." Bernardo Buongiovanni to Marcello Cervini, April 16, 1550. *C. Cerv.*, 45/12r.

10. "Ali quali diamo ogni nostra auttorità ecclesiastica et civile in ogni miglior modo si possa, di visitarvi in chiesa, in monastero, in refettorio, in cucina, in camera, nel dormitorio, nelle vostre celle, alla Marchigiana, alla Lombarda, alla Spagnuola, alla Todesca, alla Franciosa et alla Italiana et così ve li raccommandiamo, credendoli lassarli tornar contenti con havervi perpetuo obligo." Fathers of the Fonte to the Sisters of Santo Giusto, January 1, 1550. Ibid., 45/12 bis. Investigation and control of sexual activity in early-modern Europe was not restricted to Catholic prelates and the monasteries and convents they oversaw. Lyndal Roper has recently demonstrated that guilds and urban councils in Protestant lands attempted to exert the same sort of control. *The Holy Household: Women and Morals in Reformation Augsburg* (Oxford: Clarendon Press, 1989), pp. 56–131, 228–35.

11. "Onde noi prima ci siamo sforzati mettere al servitio della chiesa et convento una buona et honorata famiglia di homini da bene et suffitienti, et

levamo via alcuni di quali, benché hora siano da bene mi dissero che per altri tempi erano stati scandalosi . . . l'anno passato li frati furno molto maltrattati et patirno gravemente di pane, olio et di legna. . . . Tutte queste cose . . . procedano da alcuni li quali sempre sono stati contrarii alla religione et vorrebbeno al tutto impadronirsi delli beni di Santo Augustino." Paolo Mancini to Marcello Cervini, December 21, 1551. *C. Cerv.*, 45/5r-v. Marcello Cervini to Cristoforo Patavino, July 4, 1551. *CT*, 11:634.

12. Vittore Soranzo to Marcello Cervini, September 19, 1549. Buschbell, *Reformation und Inquisition*, pp. 236–37. "Ma perché da diverse parti havemo molte informationi et tutti conformi, ma secrette, sono persone da bene, ma timide et non vogliono esser nominate, per le quali se è fatto intender tanta dishonestà della vita et conversatione di queste monache con istessi frati di San Gottardo, che me vergogno a pensarvi, non che a scriverlo. Se è resoluto di far da novo un' altra et più rigorosa visita per trovar la verità . . . non restarà di dirle queste anchora che a questi di passati nella chiesa di essi frati fu trovati da mezzo giorno una donna con uno di essi frati insieme molto dishonestamento." Soranzo to Cervini, February 3, 1550. *C. Cerv.*, 45/7r–bis r.

13. For background information on Soranzo, see Paschini, *Tre ricerche*, pp. 91–154, and the monograph by Rota, *Vittore Soranzo*. He is also frequently referred to in sources on the Viterbo group, which centered around Reginald Pole, a fellow student at Padua. The group was influenced by the religious teachings of Juan de Valdés. See, for example, Carlo DeFrede, *La restaurazione cattolica in Inghilterra sotto Maria Tudor nel carteggio di Girolamo Seripando* (Naples: Libreria scientifica, 1971), p. 33; Fenlon, *Heresy and Obedience*, pp. 25, 72; Reumont, *Vittoria Colonna*, pp. 129–50, 218–78; and José C. Nieto, *Juan de Valdés and the Origins of the Spanish and Italian Reformation* (Geneva: Droz, 1970), pp. 142–80. For Soranzo's activity against heresy in Bergamo and his own problems with the Inquisition, cf. Luigi Chiodi, "Eresia protestante." On Soranzo's visitation, see Rota, *Vittore Soranzo*, pp. 30–33.

14. If the latter was his motivation, it met with short-lived success. Ghislieri returned again in 1550, and in 1551 Soranzo was imprisoned. The incarceration was the result of a charge made against him by a friar whom he had prohibited from preaching. The friar found his opening to attack Soranzo through the prelate's zealous (and frequent) visits to a convent already suspected of heresy by civic and ecclesiastical authorities in Venice. The ungrounded nature of the attack is proved by the repeated requests of the city of Bergamo for his return, which was permitted in 1554. Upon the election of Paul IV, questions concerning his orthodoxy surfaced again. His deposition from the see in 1558, which signaled the final demise of a well-respected prelate, was apparently based on no additional evidence. Cf. Chiodi, "Eresia protestante," pp. 478–85.

15. "Per la sua delli XXIX del passato ho veduto tutto il progresso che si era fatto per ordine suo intorno alle cose de Frati de Servi, et la cagione del suo procedere in quel modo, et come Vostra Signoria Reverendissima mi conclude

ch' a lei pareria si usasse ogni diligentia per toccare il fondo della piaga, acciochè dipoi col tempo quella non repullulasse." Girolamo Sauli to Marcello Cervini, October 11, 1550. *C. Cerv.*, 45/27r. "Finalmente hieri si risolse la sententia sopra i Frati del Monastero de Servi inquisiti, per la quale se ne sono penitentiati 28. A tre si è levato l'habito, à uno la Messa, ad altri la confessione, alcuni privati delli lor gradi, et alcuni inhabilitati ad tempus, altri castigati col digiuno in pane et acqua, altri col bando, et altri con danari a beneficio del Monastero." Sauli to Cervini, November 1, 1550. Ibid., 45/25r.

16. "[Padre Giovanni Jacomo Milo] il quale mandato dal suo superiore del 1549 a predicare in Sinigaglia dove tutta la Quaresima et la Pasqua io fui presente et audiente, dico che mai non l'intesi dir cosa che non fusse veramente Cattolica et Christiana, et di tal sorte satisfece quel populo et me che mi mossi a dimandarlo al suo Capitolo . . . facendolo predicare non solo in Sinigaglia, ma in diversi altri luoghi della mia diocesi. . . . Peró supplico Vostra Signoria Reverendissima che se contro di lui non ha cosa più che ben chiara da persone degne di fede, sia contenta persuadersi questa essere una persecution fratesca." Urbano Vigerio to Marcello Cervini, January 3, 1551. Ibid., 45/35r.

17. Gutiérrez, *History*, pp. 67–69.

18. Cristoforo Patavino, *Canones verbi dei concionatoribus ordinis fratrum eremitarum S. Augustini* (Rome, 1555). I am grateful to Frederick McGinness for this reference.

19. "Io come quella sa, fui costretto partire di Verona subito intesa la nova de le morte di Monsignore mio." Lippomano to Cervini, December 30, 1548. *C. Cerv.*, 22/23r. Pietro was bishop of Verona from February 18, 1544, until his death on August 9, 1548.

20. "Pur providdi alla principale che fu che le anime havessero qualche cibo spirituale, poi che io non potea con la presentia mia lì fare il debito mio, et usai ogni diligentia per havere il licentiato Salmerón della compagnia di Magistro Egnatio, il quale vi è andato et con grande honor di Dio et salute delle anime legge in quella città con uno grandissimo concorso di persone, facendo mirabile frutto a quello mi scrivono. Hora intendo che si tratta di toglierlomi per mandarlo qui in Germania per un Colleggio. . . . Parendomi, se questo occorresse, che mi fusse fatto grandissimo torto, perché non reputo il licentiato non dover essere manco utile in Verona che in Germania, anzi di maggior frutto essere lì che qui, per rispetto della lengua, ché chi non ha la lengua Alemana, qui mente può fare. . . . Però prego Vostra Signore Reverendissima degnarsi aiutarmi in questo negotio, et operare non mi sia interrotta questa buona opera cominciata, et che almeno mi sia lassato il licentiato sino al mio ritorno. . . . Ho certo che dicendone Vostra Signoria Illustrissima una parola a Magistro Egnatio, non ne sara più altro." Lippomano to Cervini, December 30, 1548. Ibid., 22/23r–v.

21. Canisius, a theologian, saint, and doctor of the church, joined the Jesuits in 1543. He served as the first superior of the German province of the order. In the fall of 1549 he was sent to Germany, along with Salmerón and

Claude LeJay, to found a college. They stopped along the way to stand for doctoral examinations at Bologna and arrived in Ingolstadt on November 13. The standard English biography of Canisius is James Broderick, *St. Peter Canisius* (New York: Sheed and Ward, 1935). See also Engelbert M. Buxbaum, *Petrus Canisius und die kircheliche Erneurung des herzogtums Bayern* (Rome: Institutum historicum Societatis Iesu, 1973). A March 5, 1550, letter from Lippomano to Cervini describes the Jesuit efforts in Ingolstadt, and again Lippomano laments Salmerón's removal from Verona. *C. Cerv.*, 22/39r–40r.

22. He related the story in his dedication of the work to the clergy and people of Verona. Lippomano, *Confirmatione*, pp. iir-iiiv.

23. Georg Schurhammer, *Francis Xavier: His Life, His Times*, 4 vols., translated by M. J. Costelloe (Rome: Jesuit Historical Institute, 1973–1982), 3:480, 508, 636. For the college in Montepulciano, see Le Bachelet, *Bellarmin avant son cardinalat*, p. 6. For the college in Gubbio, see *Monumenta ignatiana, epistolae et instructiones*, 12 vols. (Madrid: López del Horno, 1903–1911), 6:249.

24. On the history of the Roman College and this plan, see Philip Caraman, *University of the Nations: The Story of the Gregorian University with Its Associated Institutes, the Biblical and the Oriental, 1551–1962* (New York: Paulist Press, 1981), especially pp. 6–13.

25. Edvige Aleandri Barletta, *Aspetti della riforma cattolica e del Concilio di Trento* (Rome: Pubblicazioni degli archivi di stato, 1964), p. 85. See also the letter of Ignatius of Loyola to Girolamo Muzzarelli, January 23, 1554. *Monumenta ignatiana*, 6:230–33. See also *Monumenta ignatiana*, 6:283–84.

26. Pastor, *History of the Popes*, 13:218. Fragnito, "Evangelismo e intransigenti," pp. 31–32.

27. The text of the judgment is published in Pastor, *History of the Popes*, 13:436–37.

28. A copy of the denunciation is in *C. Cerv.*, 46, and the document is published in Buschbell, *Reformation und Inquisition*, pp. 318–19.

29. On this case and Cervini's position in it, see Alberto Aubert, "Note su Giovan Francesco Verdura, vescovo 'regnicolo,' e l'inquisizione romana 1552–1560," *RSCI* 39 (1985):109–17, esp. pp. 112–14.

30. Anonymous to Marcello Cervini, December 4, 1552. Buschbell, *Reformation und Inquisition*, p. 319.

31. His full name was Andrea Ghetti da Volterra. See Mario Battistini, *P. Andrea Ghetti da Volterra O.S.A., teologo oratore pedagogista* (Florence: Libreria editrice fiorentina, 1928). This volume edits treatises by Andrea published in 1544, on two topics: grace and works, and education. The former was based upon his 1543 sermons in the church of Santo Spirito in Florence. See also Firpo and Marcatto, *Il processo*, 1:255–56.

32. Michele Ghislieri to Marcello Cervini, September 19, 1554. Buschbell, *Reformation und Inquisition*, pp. 322–23.

33. Cervini to Ghislieri, September 23, 1554. Ibid., p. 323. The copy of the sentence is in ibid., pp. 323–24.

34. Ghislieri to Cervini, August 4, 1553. Ibid., pp. 320–21.

35. Fragnito, "Evangelismo e intransigenti," p. 31.

36. Adriano Prosperi and Carlo Ginzburg, *Giochi di pazienza: un seminario sul Beneficio di Cristo* (Turin: Einaudi, 1975), pp. 14, 62–63, 183.

37. Jerome Vida to Marcello Cervini, June 27, 1553. Buschbell, *Reformation und Inquisition*, p. 320. Vida held the see of Alba in northern Italy from February 7, 1533, until his death on September 27, 1566.

38. For evidence of his willingness to listen to all opinions, see Massarelli's diary, *CT*, 1:176, 178, 185, 191–92, 210, 213, 229.

39. Firpo and Marcatto, *Il processo*, 2: 15–20 (esp. 15–16), 247, 461. It is interesting to note that Pole did have a reputation for obduracy in a different political context—see Rodríguez-Salgado, *The Changing Face*, pp. 95–97.

40. Paolo Simoncelli, *Il caso di Reginald Pole: Eresia e santità nelle polemiche religiose del Cinquecento* (Rome: Edizioni di storia e letteratura, 1977), pp. 82–85. Cf. also Fenlon, *Heresy and Obedience*, pp. 238–40.

41. Aubert, "Alle origini della controriforma," pp. 338–43. Firpo and Marcatto, *Il processo*, 2:19–20. See, for example, the deposition of Giovanni Boccadiferro, in 1560. Firpo and Marcatto, *Il processo*, 4:238–39.

42. Brilli, *Intorno alla vita*, pp. 19–21. *CT*, 2:207.

43. For all of these actions, see *CT*, 13:167–69.

44. For Maffei's diaries, see ibid., 13:172–77. The original copy of Cervini's diary is in *C. Cerv.*, 32/17r–18r. It is also published in *CT*, 13:177–78.

45. The Apostolic Camera was (and still is) the Roman curial office that administers the temporal property of the Holy See. The *camerlengo* is the chief officer of the body, which dates from the eleventh century. In the thirteenth and fourteenth centuries the office acquired judicial functions in civil and penal cases in the papal states, through an appellate court known as the *tribunal plenae camerae*. The senior assistants of the *camerlengo*, known as the *clerci camerae*, served in that court as judges and were those to whom Julius was referring. The *camerlengo* also has the duty to verify the death of the pope and to oversee a number of specific procedures in the papal conclave.

46. The Datary was established in the fourteenth century to oversee the conferral of benefices reserved to the direct control of the Holy See. In the sixteenth century its competence was even more extensive. Among other things, it adjudicated issues pertaining to ecclesiastical inheritances and controlled dispensations from marital impediments to holy orders and from excommunications. The fees it received for these services constituted a substantial source of income for the Apostolic See. The Penitentiary, also institutionalized in the fourteenth century, was one of the three tribunals of the Holy See and held jurisdiction in the "internal forum" (or regarding matters of conscience) and over the granting of indulgences. In the sixteenth century it also regulated licenses given to secular clergymen, and even to members of religious orders, who sought, for instance, transferal to another order within the church.

It was originally created out of the need to care for pilgrims who came to Rome in pursuit of indulgences, or seeking absolution from sins reserved to the pope's jurisdiction. It too collected fees that were an important source of revenue.

47. For the record of the consistory of September 16, 1552, see *CT*, 13:169–71; for the citations from Maffei's diary, see ibid., pp. 172–74. Cf. Jedin, *History*, pp. 461–83.

48. The Signatura was the highest court of appeal in the Roman curia and, as such, frequently revised decisions made by the other curial tribunal, the Rota. Beginning in the twelfth century, the officials of the Signatura, the *referendarii*, studied and sorted out private petitions received by the pope regarding specific cases. The abuse that the commission under Julius apparently wished to root out was the situation that had developed since the fifteenth century wherein individual *referendarii* made more and more decisions on their own, and the resolution of any particular case depended upon which *referendario* handled it. Julius sought to limit the number of these officials, to make the operation of the body more consistent, and to specify which cases were to be decided not by any *referendario* but exclusively by the pope. Cf. *CT*, 13:244–46, 248–49. On the *referendarii*, see Bruno Katterbach, *Referendarii utriusque Signaturae a Martino V ad Clementem IX et Praelati Signaturae supplicationum a Martino V ad Leonem XIII*, Studi e testi, no. 55 (Città del Vaticano: Biblioteca Apostolica Vaticana, 1931).

49. Marcello Cervini, "Fragmentum diarii super reformatione sub Giulio III," *C. Cerv.*, 32/17r-v; also published in *CT*, 13:177–78.

50. *CT*, 13:174–77.

51. Ricciardo Vercello, "De pluralitate beneficiorum," ibid., 13:183–92. For Lippomano's text, see ibid., 13:192–93; for that of Melo, see ibid., 13:193–98. For the other documents, see ibid., 13:232–48.

52. The document itself is found in ASV, *Conc. Trid.* 78/195r–96v. The document and the responses are published in *C.T.* 13:254–60, esp. 256.

53. Baumgartner, "Henry II."

54. *CT*, 13:246–47. *Etsi ex debito* (Bull of Julius III for the reformation of the Penitentiary) is in ibid., 13:249–53.

55. The text of the proposed bull and the opinions of a number of cardinals regarding the draft are edited in ibid., 13:261–312.

56. Emphasis mine, ibid., 13:263–65.

57. Ibid., 13:266, 268–69.

58. Ibid., 13:269–74.

59. The version that appears in the bull is in ibid., 13:284–87. In addition, the paragraph on invocation and depiction of the saints and the one on the preaching of indulgences, from the original text, are transposed in the bull, but their wording is practically identical.

60. See Cristoforo Patavino, *Canones verbi dei*, pp. 4–5, 9–10. Cristoforo insisted on simplicity in preaching, on reinforcing Tridentine decrees, and on

avoiding disputatious language, all in terms similar to those used in Cervini's instruction.

61. Canon 150 is in *CT*, 13:290. See, for example, Aubert, "Note," pp. 109, 117, as well as his "Alle origini," pp. 342–45.

62. Moroni, *Dizionario*, 42:243. According to tradition, the *Santa Casa* located there is the one in which Mary was born, received the Annunciation, and lived with her husband Joseph and her son Jesus. The house was allegedly flown to that place by angels toward the end of the thirteenth century, because of the upheaval of the Crusades and the desire of God to preserve the edifice. (This airlift is part of the reason the Virgin of Loreto has become, in the Catholic tradition, the patroness of aviators, air travelers, and participants in hazardous sports.) The house itself was enclosed in marble walls during the pontificate of Clement VII, and succeeding popes built a basilica there, which was completed in 1754. For the tradition, see Silvio Serragli, *La vera relatione della Santa Casa di Loreto* (Macerata: Serafino paradiso, 1672), and Pietro Paulo Raffaeli, *Notizie della Santa Casa della gran madre di Dio Maria Vergine adorata in Loreto* (Loreto: F. Satori, 1764). There are two modern studies on the architecture of the basilica and the sculpted marble casing of the *Santa Casa*: Floriano Grimaldi, *Loreto: Basilica, Santa Casa* (Bologna: Calderini, 1975), and Kathleen Weil-Garris, *The Santa Casa di Loreto: Problems in Cinquecento Sculpture*, 2 vols. (New York: Garland, 1977). On the place of Loreto in the history of pilgrimage, see Mary Lee Nolan and Sidney Nolan, *Christian Pilgrimage in Modern Western Europe* (Chapel Hill: University of North Carolina Press, 1989), pp. 20, 95–107, 202–7, 255.

63. Moroni, *Dizionario*, 42:243. Marcello to Alessandro Cervini, January 29 and February 3, 1555. *C. Cerv.*, 51/23r and 51/10r, respectively.

64. "Il viaggio nostro fin li Sabato partimo di Perugia, et la sera venimo a Todi, dove trovamo le medesime accoglienze che nelli altri luoghi, con la continuata publica opinione, correspondente alla mia. . . . Da Todi partimo la domenica mattina doppo la messa et la sera arrivamo al borghetto, che fu una longa giornata, et il Cardinale andò sempre a cavallo. . . . Partimo Lunedi a bonissim' hora, et con tutto che ci fermassemo a Castel nuovo più di dui hore, arrivamo a Roma a 22 hore. Venne Magistro Antonio (Lorenzini) con tutti i gentilhomini di casa incontro fino appresso a prima porta." Galieno Benci to Alessandro Cervini, April 3, 1555. *C. Cerv.*, 52/10r.

65. For the hour of Julius's death, see *CT* 2:248. Serragli, *La vera relatione*, pp. 57, 96. There is even a list of the gifts and offerings made by nobles, princes, and ecclesiastics for the embellishment of the *Santa Casa*. But the name Cervini does not appear. Given the piety and prominence of the Tuscan family, this would be surprising if the alleged vision did take place. For the list, see Raffaeli, *Notizie*, pp. 43–81.

66. See Baumgartner, "Henry II," p. 314, which gives some information about the 1555 conclave; also *CT*, 2:250–53; and G. B. Mannucci, "Il conclave."

There were only two French cardinals in attendance, one of whom, Jean du Bellay, said the opening mass of the Holy Spirit at the conclave. On the French position, see Guillaume Ribier, *Lettres et mémoires d'estat*, 2 vols. (Paris: Frédéric Léonard, 1677), 2:604–9; and Frederick J. Baumgartner, *Henry II, King of France 1547–1559* (Durham, NC: Duke University Press, 1988), pp. 121–22.

67. For the prediction, see Firmano's diary for April 9, 1555. *CT*, 2:507. A large number of manuscript accounts of the conclave are held in BAV: *Vat. lat.* 6422, 8408, 7148, 12180–84, 12188, 12522, 12526, 12528, 13154, 13404; *Urbinate latine* 842, 1661, 1719. For the results, see Manucci, "Il conclave," p. 101. On the first poll, Carafa received twelve votes, with Cervini and Este each receiving six.

68. "Questa mattina, che è sabato, hanno havuto el primo cibo, al quale si attende quanto, e possibile, ma non mi pare che si possa fare tanto quanto bisognarebbe et il periculo che ci noto, e da che escir delle mani di Magistro Federico nostro che, e scalco di fore, fino che entra nelle mani di Magister Jeronimo (Bellarmino) che e scalco di dentro, perche uscendo delle mani di Magistro Federico. . . . La procedentia de cibi de Cardinali: ogni di si cava a sorte, per non fare confusione in chi ha da portare prima, et chi poi. Et questa mattina che, è stata la prima, il primo che è venuta a sorte, è stato il cardinale Santa Croce, et cosi sua Signore Reverendissima ha havuto il primo cibo. . . . Le scomesse di banchi vanno ogni giorno augmentando. Quando arrivamo a Roma tra il nostro Cardinale a 16 ½ percento. Adesso, è a 23 o 24. Come viene a 25 che penso sara questa sera, ne vendaro dui politie, et di poi secondo di portaro, et che dara la sorte fino che faccia 90 scudi per potra uscir di debito quest'anno." Benci to Alessandro Cervini, April 6, 1555. *C. Cerv.*, 52/15r.

69. "Marcellus eram: ero Marcellus, nec mores mutabit nec nomen meum pontificatus." Pogianus, *Epistolae et orationes*, 1:125.

70. Manucci, "Il conclave," p. 102. The closeness between Carafa and Cervini is noted by many of the conclave accounts. One account indicates that when it became clear in the bargaining that Cervini would be elected, Pole was sent to find him. Cervini was found in his room, talking privately with Carafa. BAV, *Vat. lat.* 12180/132r.

71. *CT*, 2:256–57. Ribier, *Lettres*, 2:606–7. Such an attitude would seem to eliminate Cervini from that group of popes in the early-modern period, identified by Prodi, who attempted to embellish their authority by imitation of secular practices, including those concerning coronation. See Prodi, *Il sovrano pontefice*, pp. 99–100.

72. All this is quoted and paraphrased from Reginald Pole to Marcellus II, April 28, 1555, published in Heinrich Lutz, ed., *Nuntiaturberichte aus Deutschland. Erste Abteilung 1533–1559, 15 Band, Friedenslegation des Reginald Pole zu Kaiser Karl V und Konig Heinrich II (1533–1556)* (Tübingen: Max Niemeyer, 1981), pp. 256–58.

73. Reginald Pole to Paul IV, June 6, 1555. Ibid., pp. 266–68. In this letter, Pole may have been using a standard manner, employed in identifying

ecclesiastical ideals, of inverting the object of praise in order to encourage the sort of action he hoped to see. On this technique, see John M. McManamon, *Funeral Oratory and the Cultural Ideals of Italian Humanism* (Chapel Hill: University of North Carolina Press, 1989), pp. 68–71.

74. Reginald Pole to Mary of England, April 28, 1555. Lutz, *Nuntiaturberichte*, p. 256, n. 2.

75. Firpo and Marcatto, *Il processo*, 1:104–5, 121; Jedin, *Papal Legate*, p. 18. Other humanists, like Carlo Gualteruzzi, maintained the same hope upon the election of Cervini and also harbored concerns upon the election of Carafa. See Moroni, *Carlo Gualteruzzi*, p. 77. On Pole's fluctuating relationship with Carafa, see Fenlon, *Heresy and Obedience*, pp. 243–44, 269–70. Two other sources reinforce the notion that Carafa, and he alone, was considered by many in this period to be the real threat. See Grendler, *Roman Inquisition*, pp. 116, 126, and Cairns, *Domenico Bollani*, p. 150

76. Beccadelli to Marcellus II, April 17, 1555, published in Beccadelli, *Monumenta*, p. 111. Paolo Manuzio to Marcellus II, April 14, 1555, published in Porcacchi, *Lettere*, p. 119r–v.

77. For the chronology of the activity over the days of Marcellus's pontificate, see Massarelli's diary from April 10 to April 30, 1555, in *CT*, 2:253–60. On his Eucharistic devotion, see Hérouville, "Un apôtre," pp. 523–25. The demand for a limited papal staff that would conduct itself with moderation, piety, and sobriety, which Marcellus seemed to be trying to satisfy, is usually linked to texts like the 1513 *Libellus* to Pope Leo X, by Paolo Giustiniani and Pietro Querini. See Nelson H. Minnich, "*Incipiat.*"

78. Pastor, *History of the Popes*, 14:46. *CT*, 2:258.

79. "Ha Sua Santità chiamati li auditori di Rotta, et ditoli che avertiscano a la iustitia et non ascoltino né parente né servitor suo, né li habbino un rispetto al mondo et expediscano et che non li par bene li auditori di Rotta habbino vescovati. . . . Ha chiamato il Datario et comesso che non dia benefitio senza sua saputo." Vittore Soranzo to ?, April 20, 1555. *C. Cerv.*, 52/58r–v. Cf. Trisco, "Reforming the Roman Curia," p. 147. The Datary was one of the most significant sources of curial abuses in the period—see Filippo Tamburini, "La riforma della Penitenzieria nella prima metà del sec. XVI e i cardinali Pucci in recenti saggi," *RSCI* 44 (1990):110–40; and Hallman, *Italian Cardinals*, pp. 92–128.

80. Gleason, *Reform Thought*, pp. 64–66.

81. Jedin, *Storia*, 4:25. Cf. also his *History*, 5:483. Hallman, *Italian Cardinals*, pp. 162–68. For Seripando's position, see Jedin, *Papal Legate*, p. 497. For an identical attitude toward nepotism and clientage, but from a secular rather than an ecclesiastical source, see Maltby, *Alba*, p. 76.

82. ASV, *Reg. lat.*, 1836/245r–52v, 277r–85v, 301r–12v, and 349r–59v.

83. ASV, *Arm.* 44, no. 4/47r–59r, and ASV, Index no. 305, pp. 389–94.

84. Beyond this bull, the records of the consistory during the vacancy between the reigns of Julius and Marcellus confirm the revenue problem. In the

meeting on March 28, 1555, there was a protracted debate on the unpopular papal tax on meat. It was decided to suspend the tax and leave the problem of its abolition or continuation to the next pope. ASV, *Acta consistoriale*, Acta miscellanea, 33/186r-v.

85. On this tax, which was begun under Paul III in 1543, see Stow, *Taxation*, pp. 1–36. A copy of the bull is preserved in Cervini's papers. *C. Cerv.*, 51/153r. The text is also edited in Stow, *Taxation*, p. 166.

86. For more on the relationship and the turn of events under Paul IV, see Kenneth R. Stow, *Catholic Thought and Papal Jewry Policy, 1555–1593* (New York: Jewish Theological Seminary of America, 1977), pp. xii–xxvi, 3–59; Stow, *Taxation*, pp. 53–70; Brian Pullan, *The Jews of Europe and the Inquisition of Venice, 1550–1670* (Oxford: Basil Blackwell, 1983), pp. 180–98; Fausto Parente, "Il confronto ideologico tra l'ebraismo e la chiesa in Italia," in *Italia Judaica, gli ebrei in Italia tra rinascimento et età barocca; Atti del II convegno internazionale Genova, 10–15 giugno 1984* (Rome: Ministero per i beni culturali e ambientali, 1986), pp. 303–81; Jonathan I. Israel, *European Jewry in the Age of Mercantilism, 1550–1750* (Oxford: Clarendon Press, 1985), pp. 17–31; and Benjamin C. I. David, "Excursus I: The Venetian Ghetto in Historical Perspective," in *The Autobiography of a Seventeenth-Century Venetian Rabbi: Leon Modena's "Life of Judah,"* translated by Mark R. Cohen (Princeton: Princeton University Press, 1988), pp. 279–83.

87. "So' stato tanto occupato doppo la creatione di Nostro Signore che non hauto pur tempo di respirare. Il papa similmente dalle cappelle, et dalle visite è tanto affannato che è una compassione a vederlo." Antonio Lorenzini to Alessandro Cervini, April 13, 1555. *C. Cerv.*, 52/4r. "Nostro Signore da stamattina in qua non sta bene, et non li manca un poco di febre . . . io credo che non sarà cosa di periculo." Lorenzini to Cervini, April 19, 1555. Ibid., 52/5r. "Io so certo che Vostro Signoria hara hauto dispiacere della mia precedenti nella quale gli davo avviso delle indispositione di Nostro Signore quale indispositione per deve il vero da principio ci fece paura." Lorenzini to Cervini, April 22, 1555. Ibid., 52/7r. Massarelli is quoted in *CT*, 2:260.

88. For all of this, see Massarelli's diary. *CT*, 2:261–62. Pastor made heavy use of the assessment. See his *History of the Popes*, 14:43–47.

89. For an analysis of the *Libellus*, see Minnich, "*Incipiat*," pp. 129–33. McManamon, *Funeral Oratory*, pp. 63–87.

90. The score is available in Palestrina, *Pope Marcellus Mass*, pp. 37–73. Cochrane, *Italy*, pp. 216–28.

CONCLUSION

1. Firpo explicitly numbered Cervini among the *intransigenti* in his review of Hallman, *Italian Cardinals*, published in *SCJ* 18 (1987):117–18.

2. "Et quelli che vogliano esser mariti, non possino più exercitare l'officio, né ministrare li sacramenti . . . perché la continentia con la gratia di Dio

non è impossibile a niuno." Marcello Cervini to Bernardino Maffei, April 21, 1548. *C. Cerv.*, 19/126v.

3. Jedin, *Storia*, 4:25.

4. Sadoleto's position on justification and the Diet of Regensburg is evidence for the lack of theological unity on the part of those often called *spirituali*. See Fragnito, "Evangelismo e intransigenti," pp. 20–23.

5. Minnich and Gleason, "Vocational Choices," pp. 10–11.

6. Heinz Mackensen, "Contarini's Theological Role at Ratisbon in 1541," *Archiv für Reformationsgeschichte* 51 (1960):36–57.

7. He even drafted a short document in 1526 that, according to at least one historian, embodies the spirit and original contribution of the organization. See Olin, *Catholic Reformation*, pp. 128–32.

8. Gutiérrez, *History*, 2:173.

9. "Guardate, se potete, più alle mani degli homini che alla boca." Cervini to Maffei, July 25, 1545. *C. Cerv.*, 19/18r.

10. "Un huomo di queste montagne ha contratto et consumato ignoranter il matrimonio con una che gli era conguinta in terzo grado . . . è venuto a noi per la dispensa, et noi lo rimettiamo a Sua Santità per vostro mezzo. Piacciavi far questo bene per l'anime, perché, quanto a denari, costui non ne può spendere." Cervini to Maffei, March 30, 1546. ASV, *C. Farn.* 1.

11. Partner, *The Pope's Men*, p. 167. Sangallo was Michelangelo's predecessor as architect of Saint Peter's in Rome. See David R. Coffin, "Pope Marcellus II and Architecture," *Architectura* 9 (1979):11–29. Pastor, *History of the Popes*, 14:29.

12. For a few suggestions concerning the variety of ways in which Carafa and Ghislieri differed from their contemporaries, see Bouwsma, *Venice*, pp. 347–50; David R. Coffin, *The Villa in the Life of Renaissance Rome* (Princeton: Princeton University Press, 1979), p. 35; and Robert E. McNally, "The Council of Trent and the German Protestants." Carafa was especially noteworthy in this regard and may even have owed his papal election at the advanced age of seventy-nine to the hope that he would soon die. See Rodríguez-Salgado, *The Changing Face*, pp. 150–51.

13. A recent study goes a long way toward accomplishing this in the case of Carafa. See Aubert, "Alle origini," pp. 310–15, 323, 343–55. Cf. also Seidel-Menchi, "Inquisizione come repressione," pp. 53–54, 76–77; and Fragnito, "Evangelismo e intransigenti," pp. 35–36.

14. Questions along these lines have already been suggested. See Jedin, *History*, 5:485–500. Others have sought to prove, especially in the Italian context, that there was little really repressive about the Counter Reformation when consideration is given to the general population, which accepted and supported the changes. See for example Grendler, *Roman Inquisition*, pp. 182, 286–93, and his more recent *Schooling*, pp. 235–71, 377–81. See also Nando Cecini, "Cultura e letteratura nei centri maggiori e minori tra rinascimento e barocco," in Battistelli, *Arte e cultura*, pp. 333–59; and Sara T. Nalle,

"Inquisitors, Priests and the People during the Catholic Reformation in Spain," *SCJ* 18 (1987):557–87.

15. Some are attempting to revive this concept as an important one in understanding early-modern Catholicism. See, for example, John C. Olin, *Catholic Reform from Cardinal Ximenes to the Council of Trent* (New York: Fordham University Press, 1990), pp. 35–37; Headley and Tomaro, *San Carlo Borromeo*, pp. 112–38, 250–64, 277–99; and two articles by John W. O'Malley, "Priesthood, Ministry and Religious Life" and "Was Ignatius Loyola a Church Reformer? How to Look at Early Modern Catholicism," *CHR* 77 (1991):177–93.

16. "Per mio consiglio Sua Santità deve . . . guardarsi dall' artifitii che si potessero ascondere sotto questo pretesto di pietà per non mettere se et il resto del mondo in manifesto periculo." Cervini to Maffei, April 26, 1548. *C. Cerv.*, 19/126r.

SELECTED BIBLIOGRAPHY

ARCHIVAL SOURCES

Archivio di Stato, Florence, Italy. *Carte cerviniane*. Seventy manuscript codices.

Archivio Segreto Vaticano, Città del Vaticano.

Archivium consistoriale, Acta miscellanea, 33.

Armaria 32, nos. 34.

Armaria 41, nos. 18, 19.

Armaria 44, no. 4.

Carte farnesiana 1, Pt. I.

Concilium tridentinum 37, 38, 39, 139.

Legazioni. Bologna 178.

Registra lateranensia 1601, 1836, 1838.

Archivio Vescovile, Reggio Emilia, Italy.

Cervini, Marcello. *Visita pastorale, 1543.*

Biblioteca Apostolica Vaticana, Città del Vaticano.

Urbinate latine 832, 842, 879, 942, 1640, 1661, 1719.

Vaticano greco 281.

Vaticano latino 3946, 3963, 3965, 3967, 3968, 3969, 4104, 6177, 6178, 6186, 6189, 6327, 6416, 6422, 6429, 6694, 6946, 7148, 7160, 8408, 12180, 12181, 12182, 12183, 12184, 12188, 12522, 12526, 12528, 13154, 13404.

Biblioteca Palatina, Parma.

Ms. Palatino 1009, 1010. Letters of Ludovico Beccadelli.

PUBLISHED PRIMARY SOURCES

Beccadelli, Ludovico. *Monumenta di varia letteratura*. 3 vols. Bologna, 1797–1804; reprint ed., Farnborough, England: Gregg Press Limited, 1967.

Benedetto da Mantova. *Il beneficio di Cristo*. Edited by Salvatore Caponetto. Corpus reformatorum italicorum. DeKalb, IL: Northern Illinois University Press, 1972.

Bretschneider, Carolus G. *Corpus reformatorum*. Vol. 4. Halis: C. A. Schwetschke, 1837.

Buschbell, Gottfried, ed. *Reformation und Inquisition in Italien um die Mitte des XVI Jahrhunderts*. Quellen und Forschungen, XIII Band. Paderborn: Schöningh, 1910.

Calenzio, Generoso, ed. *Documenti inediti e nuovi lavori letterari sul Concilio di Trento*. Rome, 1874.

Cardauns, Ludwig, ed. *Nuntiaturberichte aus Deutschland. I Abteilung 1533–1539, 5–6 Bd. Legationem Farnesus und Cervinis 1539–1541*. Berlin: A. Bath, 1909.

Cardella, L. *Memorie storiche di cardinali della santa romana chiesa*. Rome, 1793.

Concilium tridentinum. 13 vols. Freiburg: Herder, 1901–1938.

Contarini, Gasparo. *Opera*. Paris: Sebastianus Nivellius, 1571.

Dittrich, Franz, ed. *Nuntiaturberichte Giovanni Morones vom Deutschen Königshofe, 1539–1540*. Quellen und Forschungen, 1. Band 1. Teil. Paderborn: Schöningh, 1892.

———. *Regesten and Briefe des Cardinals Gasparo Contarini*. Braunsburg: Van Huye, 1881.

Ferrero, Giuseppe Guido, ed. *Lettere del Cinquecento*. Turin: UTET, 1967.

Firpo, Massimo, and Dario Marcatto. *Il processo inquisitoriale del cardinal Giovanni Morone*. 5 vols. Rome: Istituto storico italiano per l'età moderna e contemporanea, 1981–1989.

Flaminio, Marcantonio. *Lettere*. Edited by Alessandro Pastore. Rome: Edizioni dell'Ateneo e Bizzari, 1978.

Fontana, B., ed. "Documenti vaticani contro l'eresia luterana in Italia." *Archivio della reale società romana di storia patria* 15 (1892):71–165.

Gaeta, Franco, ed. *Nunziature di Venezia*. Rome: Istituto storico italiano per l'età moderna e contemporanea, 1967.

Girón, Pedro. *Crónica del emperador Carlos V*. Edited by Juan Sánchez Montes. Madrid: Consejo superior de investigaciones cientificas, 1964.

Le Plat, Josse, ed. *Monumentorum ad historiam Concilii Tridentini potissimum illustrandam spectantium amplissima collectio*. 7 vols. Louvain, 1781–1787.

Lestocquoy, J., ed. *Correspondance des nonces en France, Capodiferro, Dandino et Guidiccione 1541–1546*. Acta nuntiaturae gallicae, 3. Rome: Gregorian University Press, 1963.

———, ed. *Correspondance des nonces en France Carpi et Ferrerio 1535–1540*. Acta nuntiaturae gallicae, 1. Rome: Gregorian University Press, 1961.

———, ed. *Correspondance des nonces en France Dandino, Della Torre et Trivultio 1546–1551*. Acta nuntiaturae gallicae, 6. Rome: Gregorian University Press, 1966.

Lippomano, Luigi. *Confirmatione et stabilmento di tutti i dogmi catholici*. Venice: Domenico Zio, 1553.

———. *Historiae Aloysii Lipomani, de vitis sanctorum*. 2 vols. Louvain: M. Verhasselt, 1564.

———. *Sanctorum priscorum patrum vitae*. 8 vols. Venice: Spei, 1551–1560.

Loyola, Ignatius of. *The Constitutions of the Society of Jesus*. Translated by George E. Ganss. St. Louis: Institute of Jesuit Sources, 1970.

———. *Letters of St. Ignatius Loyola.* Edited by William J. Young. Chicago: Loyola University Press, 1959.

———. *The Spiritual Exercises of St. Ignatius Loyola.* Translated by Louis J. Puhl. Chicago: Loyola University Press, 1959.

Lutz, Heinrich, ed. *Nuntiaturberichte aus Deutschland. Erste Abteilung 1533–1539, 15 Band, Friedenslegation des Reginald Pole zu Kaiser Karl V and Konig Heinrich II (1533–1556).* Tübingen: Max Niemeyer, 1981.

Monumenta Historica Societatis Iesu. Vol. 24. *Epistolae PP. Paschasii Broëti, Claudii Jaji.* Madrid: López del Horno,1971.

Monumenta historica Societatis Iesu. Vols. 30–32. *Epistolae P. Alphonsi Salmeronis.* Rome: Institutum historicum Societatis Iesu, 1971–1972.

Monumenta historica Societatis Iesu. Vol. 66. *Fontes narrativi de Santo Ignatio. Rome:* Institutum historicum Societatis Iesu, 1943.

Monumenta historica Societatis Iesu. Vol. 46. *Bobadillae monumenta.* Madrid: López del Horno, 1913.

Monumenta ignatiana, epistolae et instructiones. 12 vols. Madrid: López del Horno, 1903–1911.

Monumenta lainii. 8 vols. Madrid: López del Horno, 1912–1917.

Palestrina, Giovanni Pierluigi da. *Pope Marcellus Mass.* Edited by Lewis Lockwood. New York: W. W. Norton, 1975.

Panvinio, Onofrio. *Epitome pontificum.* Venice, 1557.

Piatti, Giuseppe. *Storia-critico cronologica de' romani pontefici.* 13 vols. Naples: Raimondi, 1765–1768.

Platina, Bartolomeo, Onofrio Panvinio, and Antonio Cicarelli. *Historia delle vite de i sommi pontefici.* Venice: Basa, 1594.

———. *Opus de vitis ac gestis summorum pontificum.* Cologne, 1562.

Pogianus, Julius. *Epistolae et orationes.* 4 vols. Rome, 1762.

Porcacchi, Tomaso. *Lettere di XIII huomini illustri. Dalle quali oltra tutte l'altre fin qui stampate, di nuovo ne sono state aggiunte molte.* Venice: Vidali, 1576.

Querini, A. M., ed. *Epistolarum Reginaldi Poli.* 3 vols. Brixia, 1744–1757; Reprint ed. in 5 vols., Farnborough: Gregg Press, 1967.

Ribier, Guillaume. *Lettres et mémoires d'estat.* 2 vols. Paris: F. Léonard, 1677.

Sadoleto, Jacopo. *Epistolae.* 3 vols. Rome: Salomonius, 1760.

Santa Cruz, Alonso de. *Crónica del emperador Carlos V.* 5 vols. Madrid, 1920–1922.

Schroeder, H. J., ed. *The Canons and Decrees of the Council of Trent.* St. Louis: Herder, 1941.

SECONDARY SOURCES

Abbondanza, R. M. *Girolamo Seripando: Tra evangelismo e riforma cattolica.* Naples: Ferraro, 1981.

Alberigo, Giuseppe. "Dinamiche religiose del Cinquecento italiano tra riforma, riforma cattolica, controriforma." *Cristianesimo nella storia* 6 (1985): 543–60.

———. "Un informatore senese al Concilio di Trento (1551–1552)." *Rivista di storia della chiesa in Italia* 12 (1958):173–201.

———. "Le potestà episcopali nei dibattiti tridentini." In *Il Concilio di Trento e la riforma tridentina. Atti del convegno storico internazionale*, pp.471–524. Rome: Herder, 1965.

———. *Lo sviluppo della dottrina sui poteri nella chiesa universale.* Rome: Herder, 1964.

———. *I vescovi italiani al Concilio di Trento.* Florence: Sansoni, 1959.

Antonovics, A. V. "Counter-Reformation Cardinals. 1534–1590." *European Studies Review* 2 (1972):301–28.

Aubert, Alberto. "Alle origini della controriforma: Studi e problemi su Paolo IV." *Rivista di storia e letteratura religiosa* 22 (1986): 303–55.

———. "Note su Giovan Francesco Verdura, vescovo 'regnicolo,' e l'inquisizione romana 1552–1560." *Rivista di storia della chiesa in Italia* 39 (1985):109–17.

Backus, Irena, and Benoît Gain. "Le cardinal Guglielmo Sirleto (1514–1585), sa bibliothèque et ses traductions de saint Basile." *Mélanges de l'école française de Rome, moyen age–temps modernes* 98 (1986):889–955.

Balletti, Andrea. *Storia di Reggio nell'Emilia.* Reggio Emilia: Bonvicini, 1925.

Bangert, William. *Claude Jay and Alfonso Salmerón: Two Early Jesuits.* Chicago: Loyola University Press, 1985.

Barker, Nicolas. *Aldus Manutius and the Development of Greek Script and Type in the Fifteenth Century.* Sandy Hook, CT: Chiswick Book Shop, 1985.

Barletta, Edvige Aleandri. *Aspetti della riforma cattolica e del Concilio di Trento.* Pubblicazioni degli archivi di stato, LV. Rome: Archivio di stato, 1964.

———. *La depositeria di Concilio di Trento.* Vol 1. *Il registro di Antonio Menelli, 1545–1549.* Rome: Archivio di Stato di Roma, 1970.

Baronio, Cesare. *Annales ecclesiastici.* 38 vols. Edited by O. Raynaldo. Lucca: Venturini, 1738–1757.

Batiffol, Pierre. *Le Vaticane de Paul III à Paul V.* Paris, 1890.

Batllori, Miguel. *Cultura e finanze: Studi sulla storia dei gesuiti da S. Ignazio al Vaticano II.* Rome: Edizioni di storia e letteratura, 1983.

Battistelli, Franco, ed. *Arte e cultura nella provincia di Pesaro e Urbino* (Venice: Marsilio, 1986).

Baumgartner, Frederick J. "Henry II and the Papal Conclave of 1549." *Sixteenth Century Journal* 16 (1985):301–14.

Begheyn, Paul. "A Bibliography on St. Ignatius' *Spiritual Exercises.*" *Studies in the Spirituality of Jesuits* 13 (1981):1–42.

Bellarmino, Roberto. *Dell'uffitio del principe christiano.* Siena, 1620.

Benci, Spinello. *Storia di Montepulciano.* Florence, 1641; 2d edition, 1646.

Bertelli, Carlo. "The *Image of Pity* in Santa Croce in Gerusalemme." In *Essays in the History of Art Presented to Rudolf Wittkower*, edited by D. Fraser, H. Hibbard, and M. J. Lewine, pp. 40–55. London: Phaidon, 1967.

Bouwsma, William J. *Venice and the Defense of Republican Liberty: Renaissance Values in the Age of the Counter Reformation.* Berkeley: University of California Press, 1968.

Bozza, Tommaso. *Nuovi studi sulla riforma in Italia*. Rome: Edizioni di storia e letteratura, 1976.

Brandi, Karl. *The Emperor Charles V.* Translated by C. V. Wedgwood. New York: Knopf, 1939.

Brezzi, Paolo. *Il Concilio Tridentino: Prospettive storiografiche e problemi storici*. Milan: Editrice vita e pensiero, 1965.

Brilli, Giovan Battista. *Intorno alla vita e alle azioni di Marcello, pontefice ottimo massimo; orazione*. Montepulciano: Angiolo Fumi, 1846.

Broderick, James. *The Life and Work of Blessed Robert Francis Cardinal Bellarmine 1542–1621*. 2 vols. New York: P. J. Kenedy, 1928.

Brundage, James A. *Law, Sex and Christian Society in Medieval Europe*. Chicago: University of Chicago Press, 1987.

Buonsignori, V. *Storia della repubblica di Siena*. Bologna: Form, 1972.

Burke, Peter. "How to Be a Counter-Reformation Saint." In *Religion and Society in Early Modern Europe, 1500–1800*, edited by Kaspar von Greyerz, pp. 45–55. London: Allen and Unwin, 1984.

Cairns, Christopher. *Domenico Bollani, Bishop of Brescia: Devotion to Church and State in the Republic of Venice in the Sixteenth Century*. Bibliotheca humanistica et reformatorica, no.15. Nieukoop: De Graaf, 1976.

Calenzio, Generoso. *Documenti inediti e nuovi lavori letterari sul Concilio di Trento*. Rome: 1874.

———. *Saggio di storia del concilio generale di Trento sotto Paolo III*. Rome: 1869.

Campos, Deoclecio Redig de. "Francesco Priscianese stampatore e umanista fiorentino del secolo XVI." *La bibliofilia* 40 (1938):161–83.

Cantimori, Delio. *Eretici italiani del Cinquecento*. Florence: Sansoni, 1939.

———. " 'Nicodemismo' e speranze conciliare nel Cinquecento italiano." In *Contributi alla storia del Concilio di Trento e della controriforma*, pp. 14–23. Florence: Vallechia, 1948.

———. "Studi di storia della riforma e dell'eresia in Italia e studi sulla storia della vita religiosa nella prima metà del '500." *Bollettino della società di studi valdesi* 76 (1957):29–38.

———. *Umanesimo e religione nel rinascimento*. Turin: Einaudi, 1975.

Caraman, Philip. *University of the Nations: The Story of the Gregorian University with Its Associated Institutes, the Biblical and the Oriental, 1551–1962*. New York: Paulist Press, 1981.

Caravale, Mario, and Albert Caracciolo. *Lo stato pontificio da Martino V a Pio IX*. Storia d'Italia, no. 14. Turin: UTET, 1978.

Carcereri, Luigi. "Fra Giacomo Nacchianti vescovo di Chioggia e Fra Girolamo da Siena inquisiti per eresia (1548–1549). *Nuovo archivio veneto* 21 (1911):468–89.

Cazzani, Eugenio. *Vescovi e arcivescovi di Milano*. Milan, 1955.

Cerchiari, E. *Capellani papae et apostolicae sedis auditores causarum*. 4 vols. Rome, 1921.

Cesareo, Francesco C. *Humanism and Catholic Reform: The Life and Work of Gregorio Cortese, 1483–1548*. New York: Peter Lang, 1990.

Chandlery, Peter J. *Fasti Breviores: A Daily Record of Memorable Events in the History of the Society of Jesus*. London: Manresa Press, 1910.

Chastel, André. *The Sack of Rome, 1527*. Translated by Beth Archer. Princeton: Princeton University Press, 1983.

Chiodi, Luigi. "Eresia protestante a Bergamo nella prima metà del '500 e il vescovo Vittore Soranzo. Appunti per una riconsiderazione storica." *Rivista di storia della chiesa in Italia* 35 (1981):456–85.

Cochrane, Eric W. "Counter Reformation or Tridentine Reformation? Italy in the Age of Carlo Borromeo." In *San Carlo Borromeo, Catholic Reform and Ecclesiastical Politics in the Second Half of the Sixteenth Century*, edited by J. M. Headley and J. B. Tomaro, pp. 31–46. Washington: Folger Books, 1988.

———. *Historians and Historiography in the Italian Renaissance*. Chicago: University of Chicago Press, 1981.

———. *Italy, 1530–1630*. Longman History of Italy Series. New York: Longman, 1988.

———. "New Light on Post-Tridentine Italy: A Note on Recent Counter-Reformation Scholarship." *Catholic Historical Review* 56 (1970):291–319.

Coffin, David R. "Pope Marcellus II and Architecture." *Architectura* 9 (1979):11–29.

Collett, Barry. *Italian Benedictine Scholars and the Reformation: The Congregation of Santa Giustina of Padua*. Oxford: Clarendon Press, 1985.

Costi, Giovanni. "L'episcopato a Reggio Emilia (1540–1544) del cardinale Marcello Cervini, poi papa Marcello II." In *In memoria di Leone Tondelli*, edited by N. Artioli, pp. 203–29. Reggio Emilia: Studio teologico interdiocesano, 1980.

Cristofori, Francesco. *Storia dei cardinali di santa romana chiesa*. Rome, 1888.

Crook, Eugene J. "Manuscripts Surviving from the Austin Friars at Cambridge." *Manuscripta* 27 (1983):82–90.

D'Amico, John F. *Renaissance Humanism in Papal Rome: Humanists and Churchmen on the Eve of the Reformation*. Baltimore: Johns Hopkins University Press, 1983.

Davidson, Nicholas S. *The Counter Reformation*. Oxford: Basil Blackwell, 1987.

Del Col, Andrea. "Il controllo della stampa a Venezia e i processi di Antonio Brucioli." *Critica storica* 17 (1980):457–510.

———. "Note sull'eterdossia di fra Sisto da Siena." *Collectanea franciscana* 47 (1977):27–64.

Delumeau, Jean. *Le catholicisme entre Luther et Voltaire*. Paris: Presses universitaires de France, 1971.

Del Vecchio, Edoardo. *I Farnese*. Le grande famiglie romane, seconda serie, no. 1. Rome: Istituto di studi romani, 1972.

De Maio, Romeo. *Alfonso Carafa, cardinale di Napoli 1540–1565*. Studi e testi, no. 210. Città del Vaticano: Biblioteca apostolica vaticana, 1961.

———. "Michelangelo e Paolo IV." In *Reformata Reformanda: Festgabe für Hubert Jedin*, edited by E. Iserloh and K. Repgen, pp. 635–56. Münster: Aschendorff, 1965.

———. *Riforme e miti nella chiesa del Cinquecento.* Naples: Guida, 1973.

Denzler, Georg. *Kardinal Guglielmo Sirleto (1514–1585).* Munich: Max Hueber, 1964.

De Rosa, Gabriele. "Il francescano Cornelio Musso dal Concilio di Trento alla diocesi di Bitonto." *Rivista di storia della chiesa in Italia* 40 (1986):55–91.

Deslandres, Paul. *Le Concile de Trente et la réforme du clergé catholique.* Paris, 1905.

Devresse, Robert. "Les manuscrits grecs de Cervini." *Scriptorium* 22 (1968):250–70.

Dickens, A. G., and John Tonkin, *The Reformation in Historical Perspective.* Cambridge: Harvard University Press, 1985.

Dorez, Léon. "Le cardinal Marcello Cervini et l'imprimerie à Rome." *Mélange d'archéologie et d'histoire* 12 (1982):289–313.

Douglas, Richard M. *Jacopo Sadoleto, 1477–1547: Humanist and Reformer.* Cambridge: Harvard University Press, 1959.

Drei, Giovanni. *I Farnese: Grandezza e decadenza di una dinastia italiana.* Rome, 1959.

Dusini, Antonio. "L'episcopato del decreto dogmatico sull'ordine sacro, della XXIII sessione del Concilio di Trento." In *Il Concilio di Trento e la riforma tridentina. Atti del convegno storico internazionale*, pp. 577–614. Rome: Herder, 1965.

Evennett, H. Outram. "Three Benedictine Abbots at the Council of Trent, 1545–1547." *Studia monastica* 1 (1959):343–77.

———. *The Spirit of the Counter Reformation.* Cambridge: Cambridge University Press, 1968.

Fanelli, Vittorio. *Ricerche su Angelo Colocci e sulla Roma cinquecentesca.* Studi e testi, no. 283. Città del Vaticano: Biblioteca apostolica vaticana, 1979.

Farge, James K. *Orthodoxy and Reform in Early Reformation France: The Faculty of Theology of Paris, 1500–1543.* Studies in Medieval and Reformation Thought, no. 32. Leiden: Brill, 1985.

Fenlon, Dermot. *Heresy and Obedience in Tridentine Italy: Cardinal Pole and the Counter Reformation.* Cambridge: Cambridge University Press, 1972.

Firpo, Massimo. " 'Gli spirituali,' l'accademia di Modena e il formulario di fede del 1542: Controllo del dissenso religioso e nicodemismo." *Rivista di storia e letteratura religiosa* 20 (1984):40–111.

Firpo, Massimo, and Paolo Simoncelli. "I processi inquisitoriale contro Savonarola e Carnesecchi, una proposta di interpretazione." *Rivista di storia e letteratura religiosa* 18 (1982):200–52.

Fragnito, Gigliola. "Il cardinale Gregorio Cortese (1483?–1548) nella crisi religiosa del Cinquecento," *Benedictina* 30 (1983):129–69; 417–56; and 31 (1984):45–66.

———. "Cultura umanistica e riforma religiosa: Il *De officio viri boni ac probi episcopi* di Gasparo Contarini." *Studi veneziani* 11 (1969):75–189.

———. 'Evangelismo e intransigenti nei difficili equilibri del pontificato farnesiano." *Rivista di storia e letteratura religiosa* 25 (1989): 20–47.

———. "Gli *spirituali* e la fuga di Bernardino Ochino." *Rivista storica italiana* 84 (1972):777–813.

———. *Memoria individuale e costruzione biografica: Beccadelli, Della Casa, Vettori alle origini di un mito.* Publicazioni dell'Università di Urbino, serie di lettere e filosofia, no. 39. Urbino: Argalia, 1978.

———. "Per lo studio dell'epistolografia volgare del Cinquecento: Le lettere di Ludovico Beccadelli." *Bibliothèque d'humanisme et renaissance* 43 (1981): 61–87.

Genebrardus, Gilbertus. *Chronographiae libri quatuor.* Paris: Gorbinum, 1580.

Ginzburg, Carlo. *Il nicodemismo: Simulazione e dissimulazione religiosa nell'Europa del '500.* Turin: Giulio Einaudi, 1970.

Gleason, Elisabeth G. "On the Nature of Sixteenth-Century Italian Evangelism: Scholarship, 1953–1978." *Sixteenth Century Journal* 9 (1978):3–25.

———. *Reform Thought in Sixteenth-Century Italy.* Texts and Translations Series. American Academy of Religion. Ann Arbor: Scholar's Press, 1987.

Grafton, Anthony, and Lisa Jardine. *From Humanism to the Humanities.* Cambridge: Harvard University Press, 1986.

Grendler, Paul. *The Roman Inquisition and the Venetian Press, 1540–1605.* Princeton: Princeton University Press, 1977.

———. *Schooling in Renaissance Italy: Literacy and Learning, 1300–1600.* Baltimore: Johns Hopkins University Press, 1989.

Gutiérrez, David. *The History of the Order of St. Augustine.* Vol. 2. Translated by John J. Kelly. Villanova, PA: Augustinian Historical Institute, 1979.

Hallman, Barbara McClung. *Italian Cardinals, Reform and the Church as Property.* Berkeley: University of California Press, 1985.

Headley, John M., and John B. Tomaro, eds. *San Carlo Borromeo, Catholic Reform and Ecclesiastical Politics in the Second Half of the Sixteenth Century.* Washington, DC: Folger Books, 1988.

Hérouville, Pierre D'. "Un apôtre de l'eucharistie au XVIe siècle: Le pape Marcel II." *Etudes* 144 (1915):517–26.

Hoffman, Philip. *Church and Community in the Diocese of Lyon.* New Haven: Yale University Press, 1984.

Holborn, Hajo. *A History of Modern Germany.* 3 vols. Princeton: Princeton University Press, 1959.

Hudon, William V. "Marcellus II, Girolamo Seripando and the Image of the Angelic Pope." In *Prophetic Rome in the High Renaissance Period*, edited by Marjorie Reeves, pp. 373–87. Oxford-Warburg Studies. Oxford: Clarendon Press, 1991.

———. "Papal, Episcopal and Secular Authority in the Work of Marcello Cervini."*Cristianesimo nella storia* 9 (1988):493–521.

———. "Two Instructions to Preachers from the Tridentine Reformation." *Sixteenth Century Journal* 20 (1989):457–70.

Hünermann, Friedrich, ed. *Gasparo Contarini, Gegenreformatorische Schriften (1530 c.–1542).* Corpus Catholicorum, no. 7. Münster: Aschendorff, 1923.

Ilardi, Vincent. "Crosses and Carets: Renaissance Patronage and Coded Letters of Recommendation." *American Historical Review* 92 (1987): 1111–26.

Jedin, Hubert. "Contarini und Camaldoli." *Archivio italiano per la storia della pietà* 2 (1953):59–118.

———. *L'évêque dans la tradition pastorale du XVIe siècle.* Translated by P. Brouti. Paris, 1953.

———. *History of the Council of Trent.* Vols. 1 and 2. Translated by E. Graf. St. Louis: Herder, 1957, 1961.

———. *Papal Legate at the Council of Trent: Cardinal Seripando.* Translated by F. C. Eckhoff. St. Louis: Herder, 1947.

———. "Il significato del Concilio di Trento nella storia della chiesa." *Gregorianum* 26 (1945):117–36.

———. *Storia del Concilio di Trento.* Vols. 2–4. Translated by G. Basso. Brescia: Morcelliana, 1962.

———. *Tommaso Campeggio (1483–1564): Tridentinische Reform und kuriale Tradition.* Münster: Aschendorff, 1958.

Jung, Eva-Marie. "On the Nature of Evangelism in Sixteenth-Century Italy." *Journal of the History of Ideas* 14 (1953):511–27.

Kaufman, Peter Iver. *Augustinian Piety and Catholic Reform.* Macon, GA: Mercer University Press, 1982.

Ker, Neil. "Cardinal Cervini's Manuscripts." In *Xenia medii aevi historicum illustrantia oblata Thomas Kaeppeli*, edited by R. Creytens and P. Kunzle, pp. 51–71. Rome: Edizioni di storia e letteratura, 1978.

Le Bachelet, Xavier-Marie. *Bellarmin avant son cardinalat, 1542–1598.* Paris: Beauchesne, 1911.

———. "Bellarmin et les exercices spirituels de S. Ignace." *Collection de la bibliothèque des exercices de saint Ignace* 37–38 (1912):1–152.

———. "La prédication ecclésiastique d'après le cardinal Marcel Cervin et d'après les exercices spirituels de saint Ignace." *Collection de la bibliothèque des exercices de saint Ignace* 61–62 (1920):160–65.

Leturia, Pedro. "Il papa Paolo III, promotore e organizzatore del Concilio di Trento." *Gregorianum* 26 (1945):22–64.

Litchfield, R. Burr. *Emergence of a Bureaucracy: The Florentine Patricians 1530–1790.* Princeton: Princeton University Press, 1986.

Litva, Felice. "L'attività finanziaria della Dataria durante il periodo tridentino." *Archivum historiae pontificiae* 5 (1967):22–64.

Loomis, Louise. *The Council of Constance.* New York: Columbia University Press, 1961.

Lowry, Martin. *The World of Aldus Manutius: Business and Scholarship in Renaissance Venice.* Ithaca: Cornell University Press, 1979.

Mackensen, Heinz. "Contarini's Theological Role at Ratisbon in 1541." *Archiv für Reformationsgeschichte* 51 (1960):36–57.

McManamon, John M. *Funeral Oratory and the Cultural Ideals of Italian Humanism.* Chapel Hill: University of North Carolina Press, 1989.

McNair, Philip M. "The Reformation of the Sixteenth Century in Renaissance

Italy." In *Religion and Humanism*, edited by K. Robbins, pp. 149–66. Oxford: Basil Blackwell, 1981.

McNally, Robert E. "The Council of Trent and the German Protestants." *Theological Studies* 25 (1964): 1–22.

———. "The Council of Trent, the *Spiritual Exercises* and the Catholic Reform." *Church History* 34 (1965):36–49.

Maltby, William S. *Alba: A Biography of Fernando Alvarez de Toledo, Third Duke of Alba, 1507–1582*. Berkeley: University of California Press, 1983.

Mannucci, Giovan Battista. "Il conclave di papa Marcello." *Bollettino senese di storia di patria* 27 (1920):94–103.

Martin, A. Lynn. "Papal Policy and the European Conflict, 1559–1572." *Sixteenth Century Journal* 11 (1980):35–48.

Matheson, Peter. *Cardinal Contarini at Regensburg*. Oxford: Clarendon Press, 1972.

Mayer, Thomas F. "Marco Mantova: A Bronze Age Conciliarist." *Annuarium historiae conciliorum* 16 (1984):385–408.

———. "Marco Mantova and the Paduan Religious Crisis of the Early Sixteenth Century." *Cristianesimo nella storia* 7 (1986):41–61.

Meersseman, G. G. "Il tipo ideale di parroco secondo la riforma tridentina nelle sue fonti letterarie." In *Il Concilio di Trento e la riforma tridentina. Atti del convegno storico internazionale*, pp. 27–44. Rome: Herder, 1965.

Mercati, Angelo. *Prescrizioni per il culto divino nella diocesi di Reggio Emilia del vescovo cardinale Marcello Cervini*. Reggio Emilia: Unione tipografia reggiana, 1933.

Mercati, Giovanni. *Codici latini Pico Grimani Pio*. Studi e testi, no. 75. Città del Vaticano: Biblioteca apostolica vaticana, 1938.

———. *Per la storia dei manoscritti greci*. Studi e testi, no. 68. Città del Vaticano: Biblioteca apostolica vaticana, 1935.

Minnich, Nelson H. "Concepts of Reform Proposed at the Fifth Lateran Council." *Archivum historiae pontificiae* 7 (1969):163–251.

———. "*Incipiat iudicium a domo Domini*: The Fifth Lateran Council and the Reform of Rome." In *Reform and Authority in the Medieval and Reformation Church*, edited by G. F. Lytle, pp. 127–42. Washington: Catholic University of America Press, 1981.

Minnich, Neslon H., and Elisabeth G. Gleason. "Vocational Choices: An Unknown Letter of Pietro Querini to Gasparo Contarini and Niccolò Tiepolo (April, 1512)." *Catholic Historical Review* 75 (1989): 1–20.

Minoretti, Dalmario. "La riforma protestante ed il Concilio di Trento." In *Monografia storia politica*, pp. 33–107. Milan, 1901.

Molinari, Franco. "Visite pastorali del monasteri femminili di Piacenza nel secolo XVI." In *Il Concilio di Trento e la riforma tridentina. Atti del convegno storico internazionale*, pp. 679–734. Rome: Herder, 1965.

Monti, G. M. *Ricerche su papa Paolo IV Carafa*. Benevento, 1925.

Morison, Stanley. "Marcello Cervini, Pope Marcellus II: Bibliography's Patron Saint." *Italia medioevale e umanistica* 5 (1962):301–18.

Moroni, Gaetano. *Dizionario di erudizione storico ecclesiastica*. 153 vols. Venice: Tipografia emiliana, 1840–1879.

Moroni, Ornella. *Carlo Gualteruzzi (1500–1577) e i corrispondenti*. Studi e testi, no. 307. Città del Vaticano: Biblioteca apostolica vaticana, 1984.

Nasalli-Rocca, Emilio. *I Farnese*. Varese: Oglio, 1969.

Niero, Antonio. "L'honestas vitae clericorum nei sinodi di Giovanni Trevisan Patriarca di Venezia." In *Il Concilio di Trento e la riforma tridentina. Atti del convegno storico internazionale*, pp. 745–49. Rome: Herder, 1965.

O'Connell, Marvin R. *The Counter Reformation*. New York: Harper and Row, 1974.

Odier, Jeanne Bignami. *La bibliothèque vaticane de Sixte IV à Pio XI: Recherches sur l'histoire des collections de manuscrits*. Studi e testi, no. 272. Città del Vaticano: Biblioteca apostolica vaticana, 1973.

Olin, John. *The Catholic Reformation: Savonarola to Ignatius Loyola*. Westminster, MD: Christian Classics, 1978.

O'Malley, John. "Lutheranism in Rome, 1542–1543—The Treatise by Alfonso Zorrilla." *Thought* 54 (1979):262–73.

———. *Praise and Blame in Renaissance Rome*. Durham: Duke University Press, 1979.

———. "Priesthood, Ministry and Religious Life: Some Historical and Historiographical Considerations." *Theological Studies* 49 (1988): 223–57.

Overfield, James H. *Humanism and Scholasticism in Late Medieval Germany*. Princeton: Princeton University Press, 1984.

Pallavicino, Sforza. *Storia del Concilio di Trento*. In *Opere del cardinal Sforza Pallavicino*, vol. 1, pp. 580–84. Milan: Bettoni, 1834.

Pardi, Renzo. "Gubbio medievale." In *Topografia urbana et vita cittadina nell'alto medioevo in occidente*, vol. 2, pp. 755–65. Spoleto, 1874.

Partner, Peter. *The Pope's Men: The Papal Civil Service in the Renaissance*. Oxford: Clarendon Press, 1990.

———. *Renaissance Rome*. Berkeley: University of California Press, 1976.

Paschini, Pio. "Il cardinale Guglielmo Sirleto in Calabria." *Rivista di storia della chiesa in Italia* 1 (1947):22–37.

———. "Un cardinale editore: Marcello Cervini." In his *Cinquecento romano e riforma cattolica*, pp. 185–217. Rome: Facultas theologica pontificii athenaei lateranensis, 1958.

———. *Tre ricerche sulla storia della chiesa nel Cinquecento*. Rome: Edizioni liturgiche, 1945.

———. *Venezia e l'inquisizione romana da Giulio III a Pio IV*. Italia sacra, no. 1. Padua: Antenore, 1959.

Pascoe, Louis B. "The Council of Trent and Bible Study: Humanism and Scripture." *Catholic Historical Review* 52 (1966):18–38.

Pastor, Ludwig von. *History of the Popes*. Edited by R. F. Kerr et al. 40 vols. London: Keegan Paul, 1938–1953.

Pasztor, Lajos, et al. "L'Histoire de la curie romaine, problème d'histoire de l'église." *Revue d'histoire ecclésiastique* 64 (1969):353–66.

Pecchiai, Pio. *Roma nel Cinquecento*. Vol. 13, *Storia di Roma*. Bologna: Cappelli, 1948.

Pegon, Joseph. "Episcopat et hiérarchie au Concile de Trente." *Nouvelle revue théologique* 82 (1960):580–88.

Pellegrini, A. "Gubbio sotto i conti e duchi d'Urbino." *Regia deputazione di storia patria per l'Umbria* 11–12 (1905–1906): vol. 11, pp. 135–246, 483–535, and vol. 12, pp. 1–50.

Pescatore, Luigi. "Documenti per la storia del Concilio di Trento tratti dall'Archivio farnesiano di Napoli." In *Archivio di stato di Napoli: Scuola di archivistica e paleografia*, pp. 4–33. Naples, 1966.

Pesci, Umberto. *I vescovi di Gubbio*. Perugia: Unione tipografica cooperativa, 1919.

Peters, Edward. *Inquisition*. New York: Free Press, 1988.

Pilot, Giovanni. *Autorità ed istituzioni ecclesiastiche del Concilio di Firenze al Concilio di Trento*. Milan, 1974.

Pontieri, Ernesto. "Il papato e la sua funzione morale e politica in Italia durante la preponderanza spagnuola." *Archivio storico italiano* 96 (1938):64–87.

Prodi, Paolo. *Il cardinale Gabriele Paleotti*. 2 vols. Rome: Edizioni di storia e letteratura, 1959.

———. *La crisi religiosa del XVI secolo*. Bologna: Casa editrice Patron, 1964.

———. "Operazioni finanziarie presso la corte romana di un uomo d'affari milanese nel 1562–1563." *Rivista storica italiana* 73 (1961): 641–59.

———. *Il sovrano pontefice. Un corpo e due anime: La monarchia papale nella prima età moderna*. Bologna: Mulino, 1982.

Prosperi, Adriano. "Clerics and Laymen in the work of Carlo Borromeo." In *San Carlo Borromeo, Catholic Reform and Ecclesiastical Politics in the Second Half of the Sixteenth Century*, edited by John M. Headley and John B. Tomaro, pp. 112–38. Washington, DC: Folger Books, 1988.

———. "L'inquisizione: Verso una nuova immagine?" *Critica storica* 25 (1988):119–45.

———. "Intellettuali e chiesa all'inizio dell'età moderna." In *Storia d'Italia, annali 4*, pp. 159–252. Turin: Einaudi, 1981.

———. *Tra evangelismo e controriforma: G. M. Giberti*. Rome: Edizioni di storia e letteratura, 1969.

Prosperi, Adriano, and Carlo Ginzburg. *Giochi di pazienza: Un seminario sul 'Beneficio di Cristo.'* Turin: Einaudi, 1975.

Pullapilly, Cyriac K. *Caesar Baronius, Counter-Reformation Historian*. Notre Dame, IN: University of Notre Dame Press, 1975.

Quinn, Peter. "Ignatius Loyola and Gian Pietro Carafa: Catholic Reformers at Odds." *Catholic Historical Review* 67 (1981):386–400.

Raffaeli, Pietro Paulo. *Notizie della Santa Casa della gran madre di Dio Maria Vergine adorata in Loreto*. Loreto: F. Satori, 1764.

Reinhard, Wolfgang. "Reformation, Counter-Reformation and the Early-Modern State: A Reassessment." *Catholic Historical Review* 75 (1989): 383–404.

Ridolfi, Roberto. "Nuovi contributi sulle 'stamperie papali' di Paolo III." *La bibliofilia* 50 (1948):183–97.

Riva, Giovanni. *La visita pastorale del cardinal Cervini, 1543.* Felina, 1968.

Rodríguez-Salgado, Maria. *The Changing Face of Empire: Charles V, Philip II and Hapsburg Authority, 1551–1559.* New York: Cambridge University Press, 1988.

Rogger, Igino. *Il Concilio di Trento: Personaggi.* Trent, 1962.

———. *Le nazioni al Concilio di Trento durante la sua epoca imperiale 1545–1552.* Rome: Herder, 1952.

Rolo, Raul de Almeida. *L'évêque de la réforme tridentine.* Lisbon: Centro de estudos historicos ultramarinos, 1965.

Rosa, Mario. "Per la storia della vita religiosa e della chiesa in Italia." In *Religione e società nel mezzogiorno,* pp. 53–81. Bari: Donato, 1967.

Rota, Francesco. *Vittore Soranzo, vescovo di Bergamo (1547–1558).* Brembate Sopra: Archivio storico brembatese, 1974.

Rotondò, Antonio. "I movimenti ereticali nell'Europa del '500." *Rivista storica italiana* 78 (1966):103–39.

———. *Studi e ricerche di storia ereticale italiane.* Turin: Istituto di scienze politiche dell'Università di Torino, 1974.

Saccani, Giovanni. *I vescovi di Reggio Emilia.* Reggio Emilia: Artigianelli, 1902.

Santosuosso, Antonio. "An Account of the Election of Paul IV to the Pontificate." *Renaissance Quarterly* 31 (1978):486–98.

———. "Religious Orthodoxy, Dissent and Suppression in Venice in the 1540s." *Church History* 42 (1973):476–85.

Sarpi, Paolo. *Istoria del Concilio Tridentino.* 2 vols. Florence: Sansoni, 1966.

Sartius, Maurus. *De episcopis eugubinis.* Pisa, 1755.

Scaduto, Mario. *Storia della Compagnia di Gesù in Italia.* Vol 3. *L'epoca di Giacomo Lainez: Il governo 1556–1565.* Rome: Edizioni "La civiltà cattolica," 1964.

Schurhammer, Georg. *Francis Xavier: His Life, His Times.* 4 vols. Translated by M. J. Costelloe. Rome: Jesuit Historical Institute, 1973–1982.

Seidel-Menchi, Silvana. *Erasmo in Italia, 1520–1580.* Turin: Boringhieri, 1987.

———. "Inquisizione come repressione o inquisizione come mediazione? Una proposta di periodizzazione." *Annuario dell'istituto storico italiano per l'età moderna e contemporanea* 35–36 (1983–1984):53–77.

Serragli, Silvio. *La vera relatione della Santa Casa di Loreto.* Macerata: Serafino paradiso, 1672.

Simoncelli, Paolo. *Il caso di Reginald Pole: Eresia e santità nelle polemiche religiose del Cinquecento.* Rome: Edizioni di storia e letteratura, 1977.

———. *Evangelismo italiano del Cinquecento.* Rome: Istituto storico italiano per l'età moderna e contemporanea, 1979.

———. "Inquisizione romana e riforma in Italia." *Rivista storica italiana* 100 (1988):1–125.

Stinger, Charles. *The Renaissance in Rome.* Bloomington: Indiana University Press, 1985.

Stow, Kenneth. *Catholic Thought and Papal Jewry Policy, 1555–1593*. New York: Jewish Theological Seminary of America, 1977.

———. *Taxation, Community and the State: The Jews and the Fiscal Foundations of the Early Modern Papal State*. Päpste und Papsttum, no. 19. Stuttgart: Anton Hiersemann, 1982.

Tacchi-Venturi, Pietro. *Storia della Compagnia di Gesù in Italia*. 2 vols. Rome: Edizioni "La civiltà cattolica," 1950–1951.

Toffanin, Giuseppe. *L'umanesimo al Concilio di Trento*. Bologna: Zanichelli, 1955.

Trisco, Robert. "Reforming the Roman Curia: Emperor Ferdinand I and the Council of Trent." In *Reform and Authority in the Medieval and Reformation Church*, edited by G. F. Lytle, pp. 143–337. Washington: Catholic University of America Press, 1981.

Ubaldini, Federico. *Vita di Mons. Angelo Colocci. Edizione del testo originale italiano. A cura di Vittorio Fanelli* Studi e testi, no. 256. Città del Vaticano: Biblioteca apostolica vaticana, 1969.

Ulianich, Boris. "Scrittura e azione pastorale nelle prime omilie episcopali di Isidoro Chiari." In *Reformata Reformanda: Festgabe für Hubert Jedin*, edited by E. Iserloh and K. Repgen, pp. 610–34. Münster: Aschendorff, 1965.

Vasoli, Cesare. *Profezia e ragione: Studi sulla cultura del Cinquecento e del Seicento*. Naples: Morana, 1974.

Verde, Armando. *Lo studio fiorentino, 1473–1503. Ricerche e documenti*. 4 vols. Pistoia: Istituto nazionale di studi sul rinascimento, 1977.

Visconti, Alessandro. *L'Italia nell'epoca della controriforma dal 1516 al 1713*. Vol. 6, *Storia d'Italia*. Verona: Mondadori, 1958.

Vivanti, Corrado. "Una fonte dell'*Istoria del Concilio Tridentino* di Paolo Sarpi." *Rivista storica italiana* 83 (1971):608–32.

Vogelstein, Ingeborg Berlin. *Johann Sleidan's "Commentaries": Vantage Point of a Second Generation Lutheran*. New York: University Press of America, 1986.

Walz, Angelo. *I domenicani al Concilio di Trento*. Rome: Herder, 1961.

Wright, A. D. *The Counter Reformation*. New York: St. Martin's Press, 1982.

Zambelli, Paola, ed. *'Astrologi hallucinati': Stars and the End of the World in Luther's Time*. New York: Walter de Gruyter, 1986.

Zorzi, Giangiorgio. "Di alcuni documenti inediti sul Concilio di Trento." *Archivio trentino* 24 (1909):3–18.

INDEX